Lecture Notes in Computer Science 14535

Founding Editors

Gerhard Goos
Juris Hartmanis

Editorial Board Members

Elisa Bertino, *Purdue University, West Lafayette, IN, USA*
Wen Gao, *Peking University, Beijing, China*
Bernhard Steffen ⓘ, *TU Dortmund University, Dortmund, Germany*
Moti Yung ⓘ, *Columbia University, New York, NY, USA*

The series Lecture Notes in Computer Science (LNCS), including its subseries Lecture Notes in Artificial Intelligence (LNAI) and Lecture Notes in Bioinformatics (LNBI), has established itself as a medium for the publication of new developments in computer science and information technology research, teaching, and education.

LNCS enjoys close cooperation with the computer science R & D community, the series counts many renowned academics among its volume editors and paper authors, and collaborates with prestigious societies. Its mission is to serve this international community by providing an invaluable service, mainly focused on the publication of conference and workshop proceedings and postproceedings. LNCS commenced publication in 1973.

Anna Bramwell-Dicks · Abigail Evans ·
Marco Winckler · Helen Petrie ·
José Abdelnour-Nocera
Editors

Design for Equality and Justice

INTERACT 2023 IFIP TC 13 Workshops
York, UK, August 28 – September 1, 2023
Revised Selected Papers, Part I

Springer

Editors

Anna Bramwell-Dicks [iD]
University of York
York, UK

Marco Winckler [iD]
Université Côte d'Azur
Sophia Antipolis, France

José Abdelnour-Nocera [iD]
University of West London
London, UK

Abigail Evans [iD]
University of York
York, UK

Helen Petrie
University of York
York, UK

ISSN 0302-9743   ISSN 1611-3349 (electronic)
Lecture Notes in Computer Science
ISBN 978-3-031-61687-7   ISBN 978-3-031-61688-4 (eBook)
https://doi.org/10.1007/978-3-031-61688-4

This Springer imprint is published by the registered company Springer Nature Switzerland AG
The registered company address is: Gewerbestrasse 11, 6330 Cham, Switzerland

If disposing of this product, please recycle the paper.

Foreword

This volume presents a series of revised papers selected from workshops that took place during the 19th IFIP TC13 International Conference on Human-Computer Interaction, INTERACT 2023, held August 28th to September 1st, 2023 at the University of York, York, UK.

Fifteen workshops were held across two days at the start of the INTERACT 2023 conference, including seven that were organized by IFIP TC13 Working Groups (WGs). Revised selected papers from eleven of the workshops are included across these post-proceedings volumes, as below:

- WG 13.2 – Human-Centered Software Engineering: Rethinking the Interplay of Human–Computer Interaction and Software Engineering in the Age of Digital Transformation.
- WG 13.3 – Designing Technology for Neurodivergent Self-Determination: Challenges and Opportunities.
- WG 13.4/2.7 – HCI-E^2-2023: Second IFIP WG 2.7/13.4 Workshop on HCI Engineering Education.
- WG 13.5 – On Land, at Sea, and in the Air: Human-Computer Interaction in Safety-Critical Spaces of Control.
- WG 13.6 – Sustainable Human-Work Interaction Designs.
- WG 13.8 – HCI for Digital Democracy and Citizen Participation.
- WG 13.10 – Designing for Map-based Interfaces and Interactions.
- Algorithmic affordances in recommender interfaces
- Intelligence Augmentation: Future Directions and Ethical Implications in HCI.
- Interacting with Assistive Technology (IATech) Workshop.
- Re-Contextualizing Built Environments: Critical & Inclusive HCI Approaches for Cultural Heritage.

The chapters across these two post-proceedings volumes are the outcome of a competitive selection process that began with selecting the workshops for INTERACT 2023. The IFIP TC13 WG organisers were encouraged to submit workshops that align with the conference theme and extend their remit, while we also invited submission of workshops from outside the designated working groups. We were open to workshop submissions in diverse formats, depending on how the organisers wanted their sessions to run. These formats included fully in-person, hybrid and fully online, and allowed for full and short paper presentations, posters, discussion groups and other hands-on collaborative activities. The selection process of workshops was juried by workshop co-chairs. The workshops preceded the main conference, running August 28th to August 30th, 2023.

Following the conference, workshop organisers selected papers for inclusion in these post-proceedings volumes and invited the authors to revise their papers in line with the comments and feedback received during the workshop. To ensure the quality of these papers in the post-proceedings volumes, we requested the workshop organisers to thoroughly peer-review the papers before submission. The INTERACT 2023 workshop co-chairs undertook a final light-weight check of the accepted peer-reviewed papers. In addition, workshop organisers were invited to write a summary paper for their workshop, introducing the content and aims and reviewing the workshop outcomes. We received summary chapters from all the workshops, which were reviewed by the INTERACT 2023 workshop co-chairs.

The selected papers show advances in the field of HCI, and they demonstrate the maturity of the work performed by IFIP TC13 WGs and beyond. In total, 67 papers are included across the 2 volumes from 11 workshops.

The INTERACT 2023 workshops were made possible by the persistent efforts across several months by the 15 workshop organizing teams. We thank them all.

December 2023

Anna Bramwell-Dicks
Abigail Evans

IFIP TC13 - http://ifip-tc13.org/

Established in 1989, the International Federation for Information Processing Technical Committee on Human–Computer Interaction (IFIP TC13) is an international committee of 37 IFIP Member national societies and 10 Working Groups, representing specialists of the various disciplines contributing to the field of human-computer interaction (HCI). This field includes, among others, human factors, ergonomics, cognitive science, computer science and design. INTERACT is the flagship conference of IFIP TC13, staged biennially in different countries in the world. The first INTERACT conference was held in 1984, at first running triennially and becoming a biennial event in 1993.

IFIP TC13 aims to develop the science, technology and societal aspects of HCI by encouraging empirical research promoting the use of knowledge and methods from the human sciences in design and evaluation of computing technology systems; promoting better understanding of the relation between formal design methods and system usability and acceptability; developing guidelines, models and methods by which designers may provide better human-oriented computing technology systems; and cooperating with other groups, inside and outside IFIP, to promote user-orientation and humanization in system design. Thus, TC13 seeks to improve interactions between people and computing technology, to encourage the growth of HCI research and its practice in industry and to disseminate these benefits worldwide.

The main orientation is to place the users at the centre of the development process. Areas of study include: the problems people face when interacting with computing technology; the impact of technology deployment on people in individual and organisational contexts; the determinants of utility, usability, acceptability and user experience; the appropriate allocation of tasks between computing technology and users, especially in the case of autonomous and closed-loop systems; modelling the user, their tasks and the interactive system to aid better system design; and harmonizing the computing technology to user characteristics and needs.

While the scope is thus set wide, with a tendency toward general principles rather than particular systems, it is recognised that progress will only be achieved through both general studies to advance theoretical understanding and specific studies on practical issues (e.g., interface design standards, software system resilience, documentation, training material, appropriateness of alternative interaction technologies, guidelines, the problems of integrating multimedia systems to match system needs and organisational practices, etc.).

IFIP TC13 also stimulates working events and activities through its Working Groups (WGs). The WGs consist of HCI experts from around the world who seek to expand knowledge and find solutions to HCI issues and concerns within their domains. The list of current TC13 WGs and their area of interest is given below:

- WG 13.1 (Education in HCI and HCI Curricula) aims to improve HCI education at all levels of higher education, coordinate and unite efforts to develop HCI curricula and promote HCI teaching.

- WG 13.2 (Methodology for User-Centered System Design) aims to foster research, dissemination of information and good practice in the methodical application of HCI to software engineering.
- WG 13.3 (Human Computer Interaction, Disability and Aging) aims to make HCI designers aware of the needs of people with disabilities and older people and encourage development of information systems and tools permitting adaptation of interfaces to specific users.
- WG 13.4/WG 2.7 (User Interface Engineering) investigates the nature, concepts and construction of user interfaces for software systems, using a framework for reasoning about interactive systems and an engineering model for developing user interfaces.
- WG 13.5 (Resilience, Reliability, Safety and Human Error in System Development) seeks a framework for studying human factors relating to systems failure, develops leading-edge techniques in hazard analysis and safety engineering of computer-based systems, and guides international accreditation activities for safety-critical systems.
- WG 13.6 (Human-Work Interaction Design) aims at establishing relationships between extensive empirical work-domain studies and HCI design. It promotes the use of knowledge, concepts, methods and techniques that enable user studies to procure a better apprehension of the complex interplay between individual, social and organisational contexts and thereby a better understanding of how and why people work in the ways that they do.
- WG 13.7 (Human–Computer Interaction and Visualization) aims to establish a study and research program that will combine both scientific work and practical applications in the fields of Human–Computer Interaction and Visualization. It integrates several additional aspects of further research areas, such as scientific visualization, data mining, information design, computer graphics, cognition sciences, perception theory and psychology into this approach.
- WG 13.8 (Interaction Design and International Development) aims to support and develop the research, practice and education capabilities of HCI in institutions and organisations based around the world taking into account their diverse local needs and cultural perspective.
- WG 13.9 (Interaction Design and Children) aims to support practitioners, regulators and researchers to develop the study of interaction design and children across international contexts.
- WG 13.10 (Human-Centred Technology for Sustainability) aims to promote research, design, development, evaluation and deployment of human-centred technology to encourage sustainable use of resources in various domains.

IFIP TC13 recognises contributions to HCI through both its Pioneer in HCI Award and various paper awards associated with each INTERACT conference. Since the processes to decide the various awards take place after papers are sent to the publisher for publication, the recipients of the awards are not identified in the proceedings.

The IFIP TC13 Pioneer in Human-Computer Interaction Award recognises the contributions and achievements of pioneers in HCI. An IFIP TC13 Pioneer is one who, through active participation in IFIP Technical Committees or related IFIP groups, has made outstanding contributions to the educational, theoretical, technical, commercial or professional aspects of analysis, design, construction, evaluation and use of interactive systems. The IFIP TC13 Pioneer Awards are presented during an awards ceremony at each INTERACT conference.

In 1999, TC13 initiated a special IFIP Award, the Brian Shackel Award, for the most outstanding contribution in the form of a refereed paper submitted to and delivered at each INTERACT Conference which draws attention to the need for a comprehensive human-centred approach in the design and use of information technology in which the human and social implications have been considered. The IFIP TC13 Accessibility Award, launched in 2007 by IFIP WG 13.3, recognises the most outstanding contribution with international impact in the field of ageing, disability and inclusive design in the form of a refereed paper submitted to and delivered at the INTERACT Conference. The IFIP TC13 Interaction Design for International Development Award, launched in 2013 by IFIP WG 13.8, recognises the most outstanding contribution to the application of interactive systems for social and economic development of people around the world taking into account their diverse local needs and cultural perspective. The IFIP TC13 Pioneers' Award for Best Doctoral Student Paper at INTERACT, first awarded in 2019, is selected by the past recipients of the IFIP TC13 Pioneer title. The award is made to the best research paper accepted to the INTERACT Conference which is based on the doctoral research of the student and authored and presented by the student.

In 2015, TC13 approved the creation of a steering committee for the INTERACT conference. The Steering Committee (SC) is currently chaired by Marco Winckler and is responsible for:

- Promoting and maintaining the INTERACT conference as the premiere venue for researchers and practitioners interested in the topics of the conference (this requires a refinement of the topics above).
- Ensuring the highest quality for the contents of the event.
- Setting up the bidding process to handle future INTERACT conferences. The decision is made at TC13 level.
- Providing advice to the current and future chairs and organizers of the INTERACT conference.
- Providing data, tools and documents about previous conferences to future conference organizers.
- Selecting the reviewing system to be used throughout the conference (as this impacts the entire set of reviewers).
- Resolving general issues involved with the INTERACT conference.
- Capitalizing on history (good and bad practices).

Further information is available at the IFIP TC13 website: http://ifip-tc13.org/.

IFIP TC13 Members

Officers

Chairperson

Paula Kotzé, University of Pretoria, South Africa

Vice-Chair for Awards

Rita Barricelli, Università degli Studi di Brescia, Italy

Vice-Chair for Conferences

Marco Winckler, Université Côte d'Azur, France

Vice-Chair for Communications

Helen Petrie, University of York, UK

Vice-Chair for Membership and Collaboration

Philippe Palanque, Université Toulouse III – Paul Sabatier, France

Vice-Chair for Working Groups

Simone D. J. Barbosa, PUC Rio, Brazil

Vice-Chair for Finance (Treasurer)

Regina Bernhaupt, Eindhoven University of Technology, The Netherlands

Secretary

Janet Wesson, Nelson Mandela University, South Africa

INTERACT Steering Committee Chair

Marco Winckler, Université Côte d'Azur, France

Country Representatives

Australia
Henry B.L. Duh
Australian Computer Society
Austria
Christopher Frauenberger
Austrian Computer Society
Belgium
Bruno Dumas
IMEC – Interuniversity Micro-Electronics Center
Brazil
André Freire
Simone D. Junqueira Barbosa (section b)
Sociedade Brasileira de Computação (SBC)
Bulgaria
Petia Koprinkova-Hristova
Bulgarian Academy of Sciences
Croatia
Andrina Granić
Croatian Information Technology Association (CITA)
Cyprus
Panayiotis Zaphiris
Cyprus Computer Society
Czech Republic
Zdeněk Míkovec
Czech Society for Cybernetics and Informatics
Denmark
Jan Stage
Danish Federation for Information Processing (DANFIP)
Finland
Virpi Roto
Finnish Information Processing Association
France
Philippe Palanque
Marco Winckler (section b)
Société informatique de France (SIF)
Germany
Tom Gross
Gesellschaft fur Informatik e.V.
Ireland
Liam J. Bannon
Irish Computer Society
Italy
Fabio Paternò
Rita Barricelli, (section b)

Carmelo Ardito (section b)
Associazione Italiana per l' Informatica ed il Calcolo Automatico (AICA)
Japan
Yoshifumi Kitamura
Information Processing Society of Japan
Netherlands
Regina Bernhaupt
Koninklijke Nederlandse Vereniging
van Informatieprofessionals (KNVI)
New Zealand
Mark Apperley
Institute of IT Professionals New Zealand
Norway
Frode Eika Sandnes
Norwegian Computer Society
Poland
Marcin Sikorski
Polish Academy of Sciences (PAS)
Portugal
Pedro Filipe Pereira Campos Associacão Portuguesa para o Desenvolvimento da Sociedade da
Informação (APDSI)
Serbia
Aleksandar Jevremovic
Informatics Association of Serbia (IAS)
Singapore
Shengdong Zhao
Singapore Computer Society
Slovakia
Wanda Benešová
Slovak Society for Computer Science
Slovenia
Matjaž Kljun
Slovenian Computer Society INFORMATIKA
South Africa
Janet L. Wesson
Paula Kotzé (section b)
Institute of Information Technology Professionals South Africa (IITPSA)
Sri Lanka
Thilina Halloluwa
Computer Society of Sri Lanka (CSSL)
Sweden
Jan Gulliksen
Swedish Interdisciplinary Society for Human-Computer Interaction
Dataföreningen i Sverige

Switzerland
Denis Lalanne
Schweizer Informatik Gesellschaft (SI)
United Kingdom
José Luis Abdelnour Nocera
Helen Petrie (section b)
British Computer Society (BCS), Chartered Institute for IT

International Members at Large Representatives

ACM
Gerrit van der Veer
Association for Computing Machinery
CLEI
César Collazos
Centro Latinoamericano de Estudios en Informatica

Expert Members

Anirudha Joshi, India
Antonio Piccinno, Italy
Christos Fidas, Greece
Constantinos Coursaris, Canada
Dan Orwa, Kenya
David Lamas, Estonia
Dorian Gorgan, Romania
Fernando Loizides, UK/Cyprus
Ivan Burmistrov, Russia
Julio Abascal, Spain
Kaveh Bazargan, Iran
Marta Kristin Larusdottir, Iceland
Nikolaos Avouris, Greece
Peter Forbrig, Germany
Torkil Clemmensen, Denmark
Zhengjie Liu, China

Working Group Chairpersons

WG 13.1 (Education in HCI and HCI Curricula)

Lara Piccolo, CODE University of Applied Sciences, Germany

WG 13.2 (Methodologies for User-Centered System Design)

Regina Bernhaupt, Eindhoven University of Technology, The Netherlands

WG 13.3 (HCI, Disability and Aging)

Helen Petrie, University of York, UK

WG 13.4/2.7 (User Interface Engineering)

Davide Spano, University of Cagliari, Italy

WG 13.5 (Human Error, Resilience, Reliability, Safety and System Development)

Tilo Mentler, Trier University of Applied Sciences, Germany

WG 13.6 (Human-Work Interaction Design)

Élodie Bouzekri, McGill University, Canada

WG 13.7 (HCI and Visualization)

Gerrit van der Veer, Vrije Universiteit Amsterdam, The Netherlands

WG 13.8 (Interaction Design and International Development)

José Adbelnour Nocera, University of West London, UK

WG 13.9 (Interaction Design and Children)

Gavin Sim, University of Central Lancashire, UK

WG 13.10 (Human-Centred Technology for Sustainability

Masood Masoodian, Aalto University, Finland

Workshop Organization

Human-Centered Software Engineering: Rethinking the Interplay of Human–Computer Interaction and Software Engineering in the Age of Digital Transformation

WG 13.2 – Methodology for User-Centred System Design
WG 13.2 aims to foster research, dissemination of information and good practice in the methodical application of HCI to software engineering.

Carmelo Ardito	LUM Giuseppe Degennaro University, Italy
Regina Bernhaupt	Eindhoven University of Technology, The Netherlands
Stefan Sauer	Paderborn University, Germany

Designing Technology for Neurodivergent Self-Determination: Challenges and Opportunities

WG 13.3 – HCI, Disability and Aging
WG 13.3 aims to make HCI designers aware of the needs of people with disabilities and older people and encourage development of information systems and tools permitting adaptation of interfaces to specific users.

David Gollasch	TUD Dresden University of Technology, Germany
Meinhardt Branig	TUD Dresden University of Technology, Germany
Kathrin Gerling	Karlsruhe Institute of Technology, Germany
Jan Gulliksen	KTH Royal Institute of Technology, Sweden
Oussama Metatla	University of Bristol, UK
Katta Spiel	TU Wien, Austria
Gerhard Weber	Dresden University of Technology, Germany

HCI-E²-2023: Second IFIP WG 2.7/13.4 Workshop on HCI Engineering Education

WG 13.4/2.7 – User Interface Engineering
WG 13.4/WG 2.7 investigates the nature, concepts and construction of user interfaces for software systems, using a framework for reasoning about interactive systems and an engineering model for developing user interfaces.

José Creissac Campos	University of Minho & HASLab/INESC TEC, Portugal
Laurence Nigay	Université Grenoble Alpes, France
Alan Dix	Swansea University, UK
Anke Dittmar	University of Rostock, Germany
Simone DJ Barbosa	PUC Rio, Brazil
Lucio Davide Spano	University of Cagliari, Italy

On Land, at Sea, and in the Air: Human-Computer Interaction in Safety-Critical Spaces of Control

WG 13.5 – Resilience, Reliability, Safety and Human Error in System Development
WG 13.5 seeks a framework for studying human factors relating to systems failure, develops leading-edge techniques in hazard analysis and safety engineering of computer-based systems, and guides international accreditation activities for safety-critical systems.

Tilo Mentler	Trier University of Applied Sciences, Germany
Philippe Palanque	Université Toulouse III – Paul Sabatier, France
Kristof Van Laerhoven	University of Siegen, Germany
Margareta Holtensdotter Lützhöft	Western Norway University of Applied Sciences, Norway
Nadine Flegel	Trier University of Applied Sciences, Germany

Sustainable Human-Work Interaction Designs

WG 13.6 – Human-Work Interaction Design
WG 13.6 aims at establishing relationships between extensive empirical work-domain studies and HCI design. It promotes the use of knowledge, concepts, methods and techniques that enable user studies to procure a better apprehension of the complex interplay between individual, social and organisational contexts and thereby a better understanding of how and why people work in the ways that they do.

Elodie Bouzekri   University of Bordeaux, France
Barbara Rita Barricelli   Università degli Studi di Brescia, Italy
Torkil Clemmensen   Copenhagen Business School, Denmark
Morten Hertzum   Roskilde University, Denmark
Masood Masoodian   Aalto University, Finland

HCI for Digital Democracy and Citizen Participation

WG 13.8 – Interaction Design and International Development
WG 13.8 aims to support and develop the research, practice and education capabilities of HCI in institutions and organisations based around the world taking into account their diverse local needs and cultural perspective.

Jose Abdelnour Nocera   University of West London, UK and ITI/Larsys,
                                       Portugal
Juan José Gómez Gutiérrez   Universidad de Sevilla, Spain
Maria Estela Peralta Alvarez   Universidad de Sevilla, Spain
Lene Nielsen   IT University of Copenhagen, Denmark

Designing for Map-based Interfaces and Interactions

WG 13.10 – Human-Centred Technology for Sustainability
WG 13.10 aims to promote research, design, development, evaluation, and deployment of human-centred technology to encourage sustainable use of resources in various domains.

Masood Masoodian   Aalto University, Finland
Saturnino Luz   University of Edinburgh, UK

Algorithmic affordances in recommender interfaces

Aletta Smits   HU University of Applied Sciences Utrecht,
                                       The Netherlands
Ester Bartels   HU University of Applied Sciences Utrecht,
                                       The Netherlands
Chris Detweiler   The Hague University of Applied Sciences,
                                       The Netherlands
Koen van Turnhout   HU University of Applied Sciences Utrecht,
                                       The Netherlands

Intelligence Augmentation: Future Directions and Ethical Implications in HCI

Andrew Vargo	Osaka Metropolitan University, Japan
Benjamin Tag	Monash University, Australia
Mathilde Hutin	FNRS, France
Victoria Abou-Khalil	ETH Zurich, Switzerland
Shoya Ishimaru	Osaka Metropolitan University, Japan
Olivier Augereau	ENIB, France
Tilman Dingler	Delft University of Technology, The Netherlands
Motoi Iwata	Osaka Metropolitan University, Japan
Koichi Kise	Osaka Metropolitan University, Japan
Laurence Devillers	LISN/CRNS/ Paris-Sorbonne University, France
Andreas Dengel	RPTU, Germany

Interacting with Assistive Technology (IATech) Workshop

Paul Whittington	Bournemouth University, UK
Huseyin Dogan	Bournemouth University, UK
Nan Jaing	Bournemouth University, UK
Raian Ali	Hamad Bin Khalifa University, Qatar
Dena Al-Thani	Hamad Bin Khalifa University, Qatar
Chris Porter	University of Malta, Malta

Re-Contextualizing Built Environments: Critical & Inclusive HCI Approaches for Cultural Heritage

Linda Hirsch	LMU Munich, Germany
Siiri Paananen	University of Lapland, Finland
Eva Hornecker	Bauhaus University, Germany
Luke Hespanhol	University of Sydney, Australia
Tsvi Kuflik	University of Haifa, Israel
Tatiana Losev	Simon Fraser University, Canada
Jonna Häkkilä	University of Lapland, Finland

INTERACT 2023 Workshop Paper Reviewers

Alan Dix
Aletta Smits
Alistair Sutcliffe
Andreas Dengel
Andrew Vargo
Anke Dittmar
Artemis Skarlatidou
Ashley Colley
Barbara Rita Barricelli
Benjamin Tag
Célia Martinie
Chris Detweiler
Chris Porter
David Gollasch
Dena Al-Thani
Elodie Bouzekri
Ester Bartels
Eva Hornecker
Gerhard Weber
Giuseppe Loseto
Harm van Essen
Huseyin Dogan
Jan Gulliksen
Jan Van den Bergh
Jonna Häkkilä
Jose Abdelnour Nocera
José Creissac Campos
Juan José Gómez Gutiérrez
Kathrin Gerling
Katta Spiel
Koen van Turnhout
Koichi Kise
Kristof Van Laerhoven
Laurence Devillers
Laurence Nigay

Lene Nielsen
Linda Hirsch
Lucio Davide Spano
Luke Hespanhol
Marco Winckler
Margareta Holtensdotter Lützhöft
Maria Estela Peralta Alvarez
Marta Larusdottir
Masood Masoodian
Mathilde Hutin
Meinhardt Branig
Melanie Berger
Morten Hertzum
Motoi Iwata
Nadine Flegel
Nan Jaing
Olivier Augereau
Oussama Metatla
Paul Whittington
Peter Forbrig
Philippe Palanque
Raian Ali
Saturnino Luz
Shane Sheehan
Shoya Ishimaru
Siiri Paananen
Simone D.J. Barbosa
Tatiana Losev
Thomas Rist
Tilman Dingler
Tilo Mentler
Torkil Clemmensen
Tsvi Kuflik
Victoria Abou-Khalil

Sponsors and Partners

Sponsors

Partners

In-cooperation with ACM   *In-cooperation with SIGCHI*

Contents – Part I

Designing Technology for Neurodivergent Self-Determination: Challenges and Opportunities

HCI-E^2-2023: Second IFIP WG 2.7/13.4 Workshop on HCI Engineering Education

**On Land, at Sea, and in the Air: Human-Computer Interaction in
Safety-Critical Spaces of Control**

Contents – Part II

Algorithmic affordances in Recommender Interfaces

**Intelligence Augmentation: Future Directions and Ethical
Implications in HCI**

Interacting with Assistive Techology (IATech)

Human-Centered Software Engineering: Rethinking the Interplay of Human–Computer Interaction and Software Engineering in the Age of Digital Transformation

Workshop Report for IFIP WG 13.2's HCSE@INTERACT 2023
International Workshop on Human-Centered Software Engineering: Rethinking the Interplay of Human–Computer Interaction and Software Engineering in the Age of Digital Transformation

Carmelo Ardito[1]([⊠]) [iD], Regina Bernhaupt[2] [iD], and Stefan Sauer[3] [iD]

[1] LUM Giuseppe Degennaro University, Casamassima, Italy
`ardito@lum.it`
[2] Eindhoven University of Technology, Eindhoven, The Netherlands
`r.bernhaupt@tue.nl`
[3] Paderborn University, Paderborn, Germany
`sauer@uni-paderborn.de`

Abstract. This paper presents the results of the International Workshop on Human-Centered Software Engineering, which was part of the 19th International Conference promoted by the IFIP Technical Committee 13 on Human-Computer Interaction (Interact 2023). The leading topic of this edition of the workshop was "Rethinking the Interplay of Human–Computer Interaction and Software Engineering in the Age of Digital Transformation". The workshop was characterized by an innovative format designed to bolster research efforts across various stages. Ten papers were presented by authors and discussed in the workshop. In terms of topics, there were three key sessions focusing on digitizing manufacturing processes, understanding users, and digitization for smart life Seven of these papers were extended in these proceedings.

Keywords: digital transformation · sustainability · agile development · low-code development · digital twins · ethical considerations · cybersecurity

1 Introduction

Human-Centered Software Engineering (HCSE) has been a central research area in the intersection of human–computer interaction and software engineering for the past decades. With the upcoming Fourth Industrial Revolution, characterized by an enhanced use of technologies in almost every aspect of human life, be it work, leisure, economy or politics, the focus on humans within design and development processes has become crucial. In Europe, this revolution is referred to as digitalization, digital transformation, or digital transition.

© IFIP International Federation for Information Processing 2024
Published by Springer Nature Switzerland AG 2024
A. Bramwell-Dicks et al. (Eds.): INTERACT 2023 Workshops, LNCS 14535, pp. 3–6, 2024.
https://doi.org/10.1007/978-3-031-61688-4_1

The definition of digital transformation involves a fundamental change process driven by innovative digital technology use. Key of digitalization can be, amongst many, to improve and redefine an entity's value proposition, but the long-term impact is not well understood. What seems clear at this stage is that this digitalization revolution will bring significant changes in society, affecting how we shop, interact, and live.

There are various technologies that facilitate this transformation, including IoT, Cloud Computing, Big Data, AI, and concepts like Digital Twins. Many technologies enable users to interact with their environment, but challenges remain in synchronizing physical and virtual resources. The digitalization also introduces cybersecurity concerns. AI has brought remarkable advancements, but poses issues like computing power, trust in results, data privacy, and bias. Digital Twin technology creates virtual replicas of real-world objects, offering benefits like risk assessment and predictive maintenance, but faces obstacles such as understanding how to design for interaction with digital twins and how to ensure equal access for everyone.

In this workshop on Human-Centered Software Engineering: Rethinking the Interplay of Human–Computer Interaction and Software Engineering in the Age of Digital Transformation [1] we invited contributions focusing on methods, processes, and approaches for designing interactive systems, with a particular interest in real-life case studies. The workshop's main goal was to enable knowledge and experience sharing and to foster the development of this research domain by special activities during the workshop.

2   Innovations in Research Support – A New Workshop Format

In December 2022, our working group embraced an innovative format designed to bolster research efforts across various stages. This fresh approach centres around dynamic group work during workshops and the bi-annual HCSE conference [2]. To support the development of currently submitted papers, proposals and concepts, we allowed participation in the workshop with abstract submission only (beyond the traditional paper formats). During the workshop participants were divided into three distinct groups, each tasked with evaluating three research papers over a dedicated 90-min session. Each paper underwent a comprehensive 30-min discussion, providing a platform for in-depth analysis.

One of the key features of this format was the active involvement of paper authors in defining the *key goal* of their work. This collaborative effort allowed the group to offer valuable insights and refine the research agenda. Furthermore, participants engaged in constructive deliberations regarding the subsequent steps in the research process. A crucial aspect of this interactive session was providing constructive feedback on the papers. Participants offered suggestions on how to enhance and extend the research, fostering a culture of continuous improvement. Additionally, discussions extended beyond the immediate paper at hand, delving into potential applications of the findings in different domains and contexts.

After the workshop authors were invited to submit an extended version of their work that was peer-reviewed. Alternatively, papers can be developed further to be submitted to the next edition of the HCSE conference. From the 10 presentations within the workshop, 7 have been submitted for the post-proceedings, while other topics will be further developed for other editions.

Overall, this evolved format for activities within our working group has demonstrated its effectiveness in nurturing research endeavours at various stages, underscoring our commitment to advancing knowledge and collaboration in our field.

In terms of topics, we had three key sessions focusing on digitizing manufacturing processes, understanding users, and digitization for smart life. The following list shows the diversity of topics and different stages of development of the contributions in this workshop including an opening keynote by Inah Omoronyia, University of Bristol, on Software Engineering Practices and Data Protection Challenges.

Session 1: Digitizing Manufacturing Processes

- Digitizing Processes in Manufacturing Companies via Low-Code Software.
  Nils Weidmann, Jonas Kirchhoff and Stefan Sauer.

  Towards a Smart Combination of Human and Artificial Intelligence for Manufacturing.
  Jan Van den Bergh, Jorge Rodriguez-Echeverria and Sidharta Gautama.

Session 2: Understanding Users

- A Roadmap for Digital Twin Design.
  Regina Bernhaupt.

  Contextual Think Aloud: A Method for Understanding Users and Their Digital Work Environment.[1]
  Marta Lárusdóttir and Åsa Cajander.
- On Using the Task Models for Refinement and Validation of Requirements Generated through Co-Creation.
  Bilal Naqvi, Célia Martinie, Stepan Bakhaev and Kari Smolander.

  Supporting a Deeper Understanding of Users in Robot-Assisted Therapies by Two-Level Personas.
  Peter Forbrig, Anke Dittmar and Mathias Kühn.

  Towards User Profile Meta-Ontology.
Ankica Barisic and Marco Winckler.

Session 3: Digitizing for Smart Life

- Digital Twins for Sustainability Cities: A Research Agenda.
  Hung Pham and Regina Bernhaupt.

  Towards a Knowledge-Based Approach for Digitalizing Integrated Care Pathways.
  Giuseppe Loseto, Giuseppe Patella, Carmelo Ardito, Saverio Ieva, Arnaldo Tomasino, Lorenzo E. Malgieri and Michele Ruta.

---

[1] This workshop contribution has been evolved into "Digitalisation and the Work Environment: Insights from Evaluating the Contextual Think-Aloud Method" by Marta Larusdottir, Åsa Cajander and Ruochen Wang, which is included in this volume.

A Cross-Domain Investigation of Social Control Design Using Task Models.

Melanie Berger, Harm van Essen and Regina Bernhaupt.

To summarize, this workshop was a success. It allowed us to test a new format with active participation, combining presentations, focused feedback and community development.

Workshop date: August 29th, 2023.

Workshop organizers: Carmelo Ardito, Regina Bernhaupt and Stefan Sauer.

References

1. Ardito, C., Bernhaupt, R., Sauer, S.: Human-centered software engineering: rethinking the interplay of human–computer interaction and software engineering in the age of digital transformation. In: Nocera, J.A., Lárusdóttir, M.K., Petrie, H., Piccinno, A., Winckler, M. (eds.) Human-Computer Interaction – INTERACT 2023: 19th IFIP TC13 International Conference, York, UK, August 28 – September 1, 2023, Proceedings, Part IV, pp. 638–643. Springer Nature Switzerland, Cham (2023). https://doi.org/10.1007/978-3-031-42293-5_86
2. HCSE: International Conference on Human-Centred Software Engineering - Conference series link(s): https://link.springer.com/conference/hcse

Digitizing Processes in Manufacturing Companies via Low-Code Software

Nils Weidmann⬛, Jonas Kirchhoff⁽✉⁾⬛, and Stefan Sauer⬛

Paderborn University, Zukunftsmeile 2, 33102 Paderborn, Germany
{nils.weidmann,jonas.kirchhoff,stefan.sauer}@upb.de

Abstract. Low-code development platforms (LCDPs) recently sparked interest in both academia and industry, promising to speed up software development and make it accessible to users with little or no programming experience. Thus, the mass-development of software applications that are custom-made to the tasks, skills, and preferences of end users is potentially enabled. Although different LCDPs have been analysed with respect to their functionality and applied to exemplary case studies in recent work, there is a shortage of experience reports in which LCDPs are used to digitize business processes in small and medium manufacturing enterprises. In this paper, we therefore summarize our experience from supporting industry partners to identify business processes that are suitable for being implemented with low-code technologies and to select an LCDP that meets the requirements of the business process while aligning with the overall digitization strategy of the respective company. We also present the opportunities and challenges of the low-code approach as perceived by industry partners. In summary, the low-code approach should be seen as an essential factor for the digitization of business processes in small and medium manufacturing companies.

Keywords: Low-code development · Experience report · Manufacturing industry

1 Introduction

The ongoing digital transformation of business environments increases the demand for software applications. Most companies require software that is custom-made for a specific use case to ensure that company employees can efficiently and effectively work on their tasks. However, the availability of custom-made software is significantly restricted by the shortage of trained software developers. Furthermore, the ability of employees to develop or adapt software applications themselves is severely limited by the complexity of traditional programming languages, which require extensive upfront training to understand and apply.

In recent years, low-code development has emerged as a commercial application of model-driven end-user development with the goal to enable the development of effective, custom-made software by domain experts without (extensive)

A. Bramwell-Dicks et al. (Eds.): INTERACT 2023 Workshops, LNCS 14535, pp. 7–19, 2024.
https://doi.org/10.1007/978-3-031-61688-4_2

software development knowledge. The abstraction and reusability offered by a low-code development platform (LCDP) can even enable trained software developers to develop software more efficiently. Especially small- and medium-sized enterprises (SMEs) could profit from the effective and efficient software development enabled by LCDPs. However, our experience shows that the potential of low-code development are still largely unknown to SMEs. Furthermore, they struggle with questions such as "What are the prerequisites for low-code development and are they met in the company?", "How should an LCDP be selected and established within the company?", "How can an LCDP be integrated into the existing IT landscape?", and "What is a suitable development process for software application development with low-code?" [16,17].

The uncertainty of SMEs and the untapped potential of low-code development motivated us to initiate a research project with the goal to observe and document best practices and guidelines for supporting the digitization of SME business processes using low-code development. In this paper, we discuss three case studies from the research project. The first case study focuses on the selection of an LCDP that fits the company's requirements, whereas the second case study investigates to which extent low-code development enables domain experts with little or no programming knowledge to develop simple business applications on their own. In the third case study, low-code concepts are used to implement a model-driven approach to software development in the automation domain. Researchers and practitioners shall be encouraged to understand the low-code approach as a building block of a company's digitization strategy due to its potential to develop task- and human-centered software applications.

After a brief summary of low-code development's characterizing features and related approaches in Sect. 2, we present insights from case studies with our application partners in Sects. 3, 4 and 5. Section 6 draws a generalized conclusion for using LCDPs in the manufacturing domain, before Sect. 7 summarizes our work and discusses future extensions.

2   Research Background and Related Work

Low-code development aims to (largely) replace manual coding effort during software development with the drag&drop composition of prefabricated building to design user interfaces and workflows within an LCDP. The approach thereby (i) speeds up the development process for experienced developers, and (ii) enables domain experts and other employees outside the IT department – the so-called "citizen developers" – to participate in the software development process. The remainder of this section gives an overview of existing research related to low-code development with a focus on studies and experience reports that investigate the practical applicability of low-code development.

Reviews and Surveys: Prinz et al. conducted a systematic literature review on existing LCDP research [21]. The authors find that most papers solely focus on technical aspects of LCDPs, whereas only three papers focus on aspects of human-computer interaction, which is a research gap identified by the authors.

The systematic literature review of Käss et al. focuses on the adaptability of LCDPs, identifying sets of factors that drive and inhibit their adoption in practice [15]. In an overview paper, Rokis and Kirikova describe the state of the art of low-code development and a provide a research roadmap for open challenges [22]. Sahay et al. motivate their overview paper with the existence of around two hundred LCDPs on the market, with different features that are hard to assess for decision makers in companies [25]. As a main contribution, they provide a conceptional, comparative framework for LCDPs, as well as a feature model that is synthesized based on eight chosen LCDPs. Similarly, Farshidi et al. developed an extensive, feature-based comparison of 30 LCDPs [11]. These overview papers compare several LCDPs of industrial relevance with respect to their technical features, but do not give specific advice which LCDP is beneficial for which use case or application domain.

Low-Code and Related Approaches: The underlying concepts of low-code development have already been used in other lines of software development, including programming languages of the fourth generation, generative programming, rapid application development, end user development, and domain-driven design (cf. [29]). Dedicated publications even focus solely on comparing low-code development and Model-driven engineering (MDE) [5,24]. Bock and Frank created a feature-based comparison of seven LCDPs to investigate the novelty of LCDP features [2,3]. The authors state that the features of the investigated LCDPs appear in other lines of development already, but the combination of these features can indeed be considered as a conceptual novelty.

Case Studies and Experience Reports: Existing research investigates the practical applicability of both low-code and model-driven approaches, and identifies opportunities and threats compared to traditional software development, respectively. Waszkowski reports on the implementation of an error recovery process in the manufacturing domain using the Aurea BPM platform [27]. Farshidi et al. present four industrial case studies supporting their assumption that their decision model indeed helps decision makers in companies to select an LCDP that fits their requirements best [11]. Gürcan and Taentzer compared three market-leading LCDPs, i.e., Microsoft PowerApps, Siemens Mendix and OutSystems, based on two case studies [12], describing the development of a stand-alone application and the connection of a low-code app to an existing back end. While the approach of Waszkowski is tailored to a specific business process, all other reports describe use cases outside the manufacturing domain.

Despite its sound theoretical background and tool support, the industrial relevance of MDE has become a controversial topic. Hutchinson et al. conducted quantitative and qualitative studies on the usage of MDE tools in companies, presenting four case studies at one company each [13]. Their key finding is that besides technical challenges, it is also important that MDE tools are introduced by means of iterative, progressive organizational change management, and that a clear business focus is important to successfully employ model-driven approaches in practice. The authors report on use cases from different application domains, not including the manufacturing domain, though.

3 Case Study 1 – LCDP Selection and Introduction

The first case study was conducted at one of the world's leading manufacturers of innovative seating systems for automotives and commercial vehicles. The company decided to use an LCDP to develop software for the quick digitization and optimization of company-specific business processes. Since a large number of LCDPs are available on the market, selecting a platform that meets the company's specific requirements is a non-trivial task. The process of selecting and introducing the platform was based on the procedure developed throughout our research project. The procedure, which was first described by Nikolenko et al. [19], is depicted in Fig. 1. In the following, we will give an overview of the key findings of each phase.

The first phase deals with the **analysis of the status quo** and the **definition of the project** scope. Organizational requirements for introducing a low-code development approach are analysed, independent of specific business processes. According to the company, the goal of introducing an LCDP is to lower the hurdles for programming company-specific software applications and avoiding personal shortage in IT projects.

The goal of the second phase is to **describe use cases**, i.e., business processes to be digitized, and to **determine requirements** for implementing them. To identify the most urgent use cases for digitization, expert

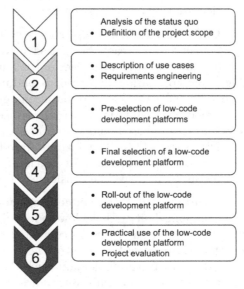

Fig. 1. Procedure model for the selection and roll-out of a low-code platform

interviews were conducted with employees of the company. As a first use case to be implemented, the digitization of shift requests was selected, i.e., shifting machines from one location to another. Besides the physical shift, the process involves some administrative work, which causes long throughput times and a lack of transparency, as the whole process is paper-based. Digitizing the process makes status updates accessible to all stakeholders and reduces the throughput times substantially.

In phase three, a **pre-selection of LCDPs** reduces the pool of available LCDPs to a handful of platforms. This is necessary as analysing the fit of each available platform to the company's requirements is not possible with justifiable efforts. The company associates the choice of a market leader with maturity of the LCDP and reliability with respect to long-term support. Therefore, the pre-selection was based on the latest LCDP reports of Forrester [18] and Gartner [26], who identified the LCDPs *Appian*, *Siemens Mendix*, *Microsoft PowerApps*, *Outsystems*, *Salesforce*, and *ServiceNow* as current market leaders.

After compiling a pre-selection in phase 3, phase 4 deals with the **final selection of an LCDP**. For the company, it is of major importance that the LCDP fits into the existing IT infrastructure, which mostly involves Microsoft application software and SAP products. Furthermore, the overall costs should be minimized. To further restrict the range of suitable LCDPs, a feature-based comparison was set up using research work of Farshidi et al. [11] and Sahay et al. [25]. The final choice was then made between Siemens Mendix and Microsoft PowerApps after an evaluation phase of one month. Due to the seamless integration into the existing IT infrastructure, Microsoft PowerApps was selected as an LCDP to implement the shift request use case.

Phase five deals with the **roll-out of the chosen LCDP**, i.e., Microsoft PowerApps. During the pilot project, the old paper-based and new digitized processes are run in parallel to guarantee stability. Besides the PowerApps application, Microsoft Sharepoint lists are used as data stores to also provide a status overview outside the LCDP. The shift request process was extended with further features in its digitized version, e.g., a login screen with user and password, and textual tool tips that guide users through the application. When status changes occur, email notifications are sent out to all involved stakeholders.

The final phase six deals with the **practical use of the LCDP** and **evaluating the pilot project**. A usability study was conducted with end users using the LCDP, who were asked to fill out a standardized SUS questionnaire [4]. The overall results show that the users are satisfied with the software application, while qualitative feedback was gathered to point out room for improvement. For further details, the interested reader is referred to Adrian et al. [1].

In summary, it can be stated that the LCDP selection process worked out well. Important experiences were gained with respect to process digitization, and the company's expectations with respect to reduced throughput times were met. Subsequent to the shift request use case, further processes shall be digitized using Microsoft PowerApps. To establish the development of low-code applications at the company, one employee is granted half of his working hours to take the responsibility for operating and administrating the LCDP.

4   Case Study 2 – Low-Code Development as an Integral Part of the Digitization Strategy

The second case study was conducted at a manufacturer of products for the storage of hazardous materials and occupational safety. In contrast to the other two industry partners, the company already uses an LCDP for internal software development for multiple years. The LCDP INTREXX [14] was originally used for the implementation of the company's intranet. Later, when the functionality of INTREXX was extended to enable the development of intranet applications via low-code development, the company started to use it for the development of utility applications to support business processes within the company. So far, around 50 applications have been developed using the LCDP.

Motivation: Prior to the case study, applications were mostly developed by experienced software developers. Thus, the LCDP was mainly used to speed up the development process (cf. Sect. 1). It was not attempted, though, to enable the development of applications by citizen developers. Due to the dependency on experienced software developers posing a bottleneck for the digitization of the company, the case study should investigate to which extent citizen developers can be trained to develop simple applications within the existing environment.

Case Study: The implementation of a booking system for electric vehicle charging stations was chosen as a use case for the case study. Before starting the pilot project, there was no booking system for such charging stations on the company site. This leads to an uncoordinated access to the charging stations, which basically works following the "first come, first served" principle. The employees do not have an overview of the availability of charging stations, and cars often block the charging stations longer than necessary. The company expects these problems to become more severe, as more and more electric cars will be used in the future.

Solution Approach: The proposed solution comprises the introduction of a digitized process for booking charging stations by means of an INTREXX application, which is made available to the employees via the company's intranet. With this application, charging stations shall be bookable for time slots that are sufficient to charge a vehicle, but allow for a better utilization of the charging stations. To inform users of events like the end of their booked time slot or the completion of the charging process, email notifications are sent out. Furthermore, it should be possible to prioritise company cars over private cars. An overview of the intended booking process is given in Fig. 2 in form of a business process model and notation (BPMN) diagram.

Implementation: As it is common for low-code applications, the booking system is implemented as a client-server application. The client provides a status overview of existing reservations for charging stations, as well as functionality to book a time slot. On the server, reservations can be administrated, and email notifications can be sent out via a Microsoft exchange server connected to the INTREXX LCDP. The permission management of INTREXX (e.g., existing

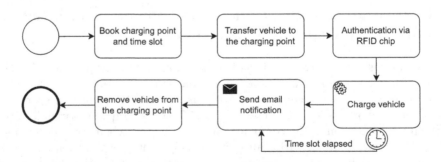

Fig. 2. Digitized process for charging electric vehicles

user groups) can be reused for controlling the access to the booking system. At the charging stations, users can authenticate via an radio-frequency identification (RFID) chip. For further details on the implementation of the use case, the interested reader is referred to Roth and Regtmeier [23].

Lessons Learned: The case study demonstrates that citizen developers can be trained to develop low-code applications in a short time, whereas the administration of the application is still performed by IT experts. For several tasks, programming knowledge is indeed necessary, e.g., for defining the data structures and modelling the event-driven application. Also for the initial configuration of interfaces to third-party systems, IT know-how is required. Another mentionable insight is that citizen developers tend to approach the development task starting at the frontend, professional developers at the backend.

Outlook: Due to the variety of options INTREXX offers for application development and the positive experience gained so far, the company will continue using the LCDP. The company estimates that in the long term, a few citizen developers and a team of experienced software developers will be responsible for developing low-code applications. It seems to be reasonable to assign different tasks to the involved employees: Citizen developers will create draft applications reflecting ideas and requirements that can be subsequently implemented by software developers. In this way, initial versions of applications are quickly available for further elaboration, before the applications are released to be used by all employees of the company.

5 Case Study 3 – Low-Code or Model-Driven Development of Programmable Logic Controllers?

At the interface between MDE and low-code development, a third case study was conducted together with a leading company in the fields of connectivity, automation and digitization, to improve the software development process for programmable logic controllers (PLCs) for plant and series machine construction. For this purpose, a tool chain consisting of different hardware and software components was designed, which enables plant engineers to model large parts of the plant design on the basis of their technical expertise. Executable code for PLCs is generated in several steps from these models and pre-developed code templates. This approach relieves PLC programmers, who are currently a scarce resource on the labour market, and prevents problems in defining plant requirements. The practicability of the approach was evaluated with the help of expert interviews with employees of the company.

Low-Code vs. MDE: As mentioned in Sect. 2, low-code development and MDE are very similar from a conceptual point of view. In this case study, it is necessary to generate code for PLCs, as the application should run on specific hardware components. In contrast to most LCDPs, MDE tools make it possible to access the generated code, and generate code in arbitrary programming languages in principle. Furthermore, no LCDP we are aware of is targeted towards the PLCs in use, such that a model-driven approach is chosen.

Problem Description: In the application domain of plant construction, which this use case falls into, different remote I/O modules are connected via a field bus coupler and controlled by a PLC. PLCs are usually programmed according to the IEC 61131 standard [7], which comprises several textual and graphical languages. The textual language structured text (ST) is used in the current process, which causes multiple difficulties: Experienced ST experts are hard to find, such that companies have to acquire external developers to program their PLCs, which is too expensive for SMEs. Another problem is that ST programmers have to understand requirements given by the plant engineers, which is a time-consuming and error-prone task.

Solution Idea: An idea to overcome these problems with a model-driven approach is that plant engineers as citizen developers should be enabled to write PLC software applications themselves. The approach makes use of reusable libraries, such that ST programming knowledge is not necessary. For distributing the software application to the PLC, the engineering tool CODESYS [6] is in use at the company and shall be kept as part of the tool chain. Therefore, it is necessary to develop (i) a modelling tool for creating a visual model of the plant and (ii) a code generator that converts this model into a format that can be imported into the engineering tool.

Implementation: As a basis for the tool chain, the Eclipse modeling framework (EMF) [9] was chosen, as it offers several plug-ins for visual modelling and code generation. Due to their seamless integration into the EMF, the Eclipse plug-ins Sirius [10] and Acceleo [8] were chosen for visual modelling and code generation, respectively. Furthermore, it turned out to be beneficial to not directly generate ST code – as additional configuration data would have to be added manually – but to generate an XML file that conforms to the PLCopen standard [20]. This file can be imported into CODESYS and other engineering tools, such that a fully functional PLC application can be compiled without further steps. The tool chain is visualized in Fig. 3 in form of a UML component diagram. The green components and interfaces represent the part of the tool chain that was added to employ the model-driven approach, while the black part of the diagram represents the existing setup for PLC code development before the pilot project took place.

Evaluation: To qualitatively evaluate the approach, semi-structured interviews were conducted with three employees of the company. Strengths of the approach and room for improvement were discussed, indicating possibilities for future work. All participants agreed that the practical applicability should be examined with help of further pilot projects. Once the tool-chain is established at a company, code for PLCs can be efficiently generated by reusing existing functionality. In general, employees with a higher affinity towards software development reacted more openly to the proposed approach than the others. Due to the setting, the generalizability of the results is restricted, but still a good indication

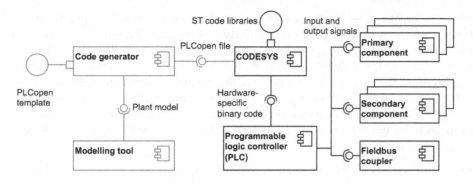

Fig. 3. Tool chain for generating code for a programmable logic controller

of how the model-driven approach is perceived by practitioners. For details, the interested reader is referred to Weidmann et al. [28].

6   Evaluation and Discussion

To draw a generalized conclusion for using LCDPs in manufacturing SMEs, four semi-structured interviews with partner companies were conducted at the end of the research project, in which 2–4 interview partners per company participated. The key findings of the interviews are summarized in the following.

Motivation: The original motivation for using LCDPs was that software development know-how can be gathered by employees of the company outside the IT department, which includes know-how for deploying and monitoring applications. The selection of a particular LCDP is a strategic decision, as the management board must be convinced of the approach, and must grant a time-bugdet for acquiring the necessary know-how. The effort for hosting and administrating an LCDP must not be underestimated.

Platform Selection: For selecting an LCDP, several factors have to be considered: First, the chosen LCDP must fit into the existing IT system landscape, such that not too many different systems and providers are in use. Also, connectors to other systems must exist, e.g., SAP ERP, Microsoft 365 software, manufacturing execution systems, production planning systems, or standard interfaces such as REST and ODATA. Another important factor is the cost of using the LCDP, which often make larger investments necessary. From an organizational point of view, compliance and data security issues, difficulties regarding permission management and concerns of the works council can hinder the introduction of an LCDP. Other points to be considered when introducing an LCDP are the availability of support, tutorials, and an online community, which is especially important for error detection and removal.

Citizen Development: With respect to the targeted user group, it is important to assess the complexity of using a particular LCDP. The group of users who can create apps themselves is often restricted to the IT department, as those employees use the platform regularly. For citizen developers, it takes too much time to acquire the necessary know-how to be able to utilize all LCDP features required for the development of complex business applications. Apart from employees of the IT department, new employees and trainees are predestined for gathering knowledge in this area, as they are not that much involved in the daily business yet. In order to extend the group of target users, the interview partners propose to let employees on different levels of expertise work on a low-code app collaboratively.

Digitization Strategy: In general, low-code development is a good choice for digitizing administrative processes, for which tool support does not yet exist. For business-critical applications which affect production processes, the technology is not (yet) used at the partner companies: This is due to the missing access to the source code, which is harmful in case of critical errors. Risks of introducing an LCDP are vendor lock-ins, which can partly be circumvented if the LCDP is open source or at least extensible in a general purpose language, and the risk of choosing a provider that cannot compete on the market.

Low-Code vs. MDE: In contrast to LCDPs, which have to be adapted to a specific domain via interface configurations, MDE approaches are inherently domain-specific, allowing to exploit domain knowledge, such that software modelling is possible on a high level of abstraction. Furthermore, the respective tools can be hosted locally, whereas the conditions of the platform provider need to be accepted when using LCDPs. In cases where code of a specific language needs to be generated (cf. Sect. 5), the use of MDE approaches is recommendable.

7   Conclusion

This paper presented three case studies from the manufacturing domain that have been implemented by means of low-code development. For the implementation of the first two case studies, state-of-the-art LCDPs were used, whereby the process of selecting an LCDP that best fits the company's requirements was described along with the first case study. The third case study was solved using a model-driven approach, as the specific requirement of generating code for a PLC is not met by any LCDP we are aware of. In semi-structured interviews with different partner companies, criteria for the selection of a particular LCDP as well as opportunities and risks of using it productively were discussed.

We plan to validate our initial results by conducting further case studies with other LCDPs and companies from different branches. The first impressions that practitioners shared with us in semi-structured interviews shall be further underpinned by quantitative experiments, which for example compare the effort of implementing a software application with the low-code approach to traditional software development.

References

1. Adrian, B., Hinrichsen, S., Nikolenko, A., Rohrig, M., Weidmann, N.: Erfolgreiche Auswahl und Einführung einer Low-Code-Plattform bei Isringhausen – eine Fallstudie. In: Hinrichsen, S., Sauer, S., Schroder, K. (eds.) Prozesse in Industriebetrieben mittels Low-Code-Software digitalisieren. Intelligente Technische Systeme – Losungen aus dem Spitzencluster it's OWL. Springer Vieweg, Berlin, Heidelberg (2023). https://doi.org/10.1007/978-3-662-67950-0_6
2. Bock, A.C., Frank, U.: In search of the essence of low-code: an exploratory study of seven development platforms. In: ACM/IEEE International Conference on Model Driven Engineering Languages and Systems Companion, MODELS 2021 Companion, pp. 57–66. IEEE (2021). https://doi.org/10.1109/MODELS-C53483.2021.00016
3. Bock, A.C., Frank, U.: Low-code platform. Bus. Inf. Syst. Eng. **63**(6), 733–740 (2021). https://doi.org/10.1007/s12599-021-00726-8
4. Brooke, J.: SUS: a quick and dirty usability scale. Usability Eval. Ind. **189** (1995)
5. Cabot, J.: Positioning of the low-code movement within the field of model-driven engineering. In: Guerra, E., Iovino, L. (eds.) MODELS '20: ACM/IEEE 23rd International Conference on Model Driven Engineering Languages and Systems, Companion Proceedings, pp. 76:1–76:3. ACM (2020). https://doi.org/10.1145/3417990.3420210
6. CODESYS GmbH (2023). https://www.codesys.com/
7. DIN Deutsches Institut für Normung e. V.: DIN EN IEC 61131-3. Programmable controllers - Part 3: Programming languages (IEC 65B/1229/CDV:2023); German and English version prEN IEC 61131-3:2023 (2023). https://www.din.de/en/getting-involved/standards-committees/dke/drafts/wdc-beuth:din21:370371481
8. Eclipse Foundation: Acceleo. Generate anything from any EMF model (2023). https://www.eclipse.org/acceleo/
9. Eclipse Foundation: Eclipse EMF ™ (2023). https://projects.eclipse.org/projects/modeling.emf.emf
10. Eclipse Foundation: Sirius. The easiest way to get your own modeling tool (2023). https://eclipse.dev/sirius/
11. Farshidi, S., Jansen, S., Fortuin, S.: Model-driven development platform selection: four industry case studies. Softw. Syst. Model. **20**(5), 1525–1551 (2021). https://doi.org/10.1007/s10270-020-00855-w
12. Gürcan, F., Taentzer, G.: Using microsoft powerapps, mendix and outsystems in two development scenarios: an experience report. In: ACM/IEEE International Conference on Model Driven Engineering Languages and Systems Companion, MODELS 2021 Companion, pp. 67–72. IEEE (2021). https://doi.org/10.1109/MODELS-C53483.2021.00017
13. Hutchinson, J.E., Whittle, J., Rouncefield, M.: Model-driven engineering practices in industry: social, organizational and managerial factors that lead to success or failure. Sci. Comput. Program. **89**, 144–161 (2014). https://doi.org/10.1016/j.scico.2013.03.017
14. INTREXX GmbH: INTREXX. Experience Individuality (2023). https://www.intrexx.com/
15. Käss, S., Strahringer, S., Westner, M.: Drivers and inhibitors of low code development platform adoption. In: 24th IEEE Conference on Business Informatics, CBI 2022 - Volume 1, pp. 196–205. IEEE (2022). https://doi.org/10.1109/CBI54897.2022.00028

16. Kirchhoff, J., Weidmann, N., Sauer, S., Engels, G.: Situational development of low-code applications in manufacturing companies. In: Kühn, T., Sousa, V. (eds.) Proceedings of the 25th International Conference on Model Driven Engineering Languages and Systems: Companion Proceedings, MODELS 2022, pp. 816–825. ACM (2022). https://doi.org/10.1145/3550356.3561560

17. Kirchhoff, J., Weidmann, N., Sauer, S., Engels, G.: Strukturierte Entwicklung von Softwareanwendungen mit Low-Code. In: Hinrichsen, S., Sauer, S., Schroder, K. (eds.) Prozesse in Industriebetrieben mittels Low-Code-Software digitalisieren. Intelligente Technische Systeme – Losungen aus dem Spitzencluster it's OWL. Springer Vieweg, Berlin, Heidelberg (2023). https://doi.org/10.1007/978-3-662-67950-0_5

18. Koplowitz, R., Rymer, J.: The Forrester WaveTM: Low-code development platforms for AD&D professionals (2019). https://tinyurl.com/4tce8acc

19. Nikolenko, A., Becker, K.L., Wohlhage, U., Adrian, B., Hinrichsen, S.: Auswahl und Einführung einer Low-Code-Plattform. In: Hinrichsen, S., Sauer, S., Schroder, K. (eds.) Prozesse in Industriebetrieben mittels Low-Code-Software digitalisieren. Intelligente Technische Systeme – Losungen aus dem Spitzencluster it's OWL, pp. 31–51. Springer Vieweg, Berlin, Heidelberg (2023). https://doi.org/10.1007/978-3-662-67950-0_3

20. PLCopen: PLCopen for efficiency in automation (2023). https://www.plcopen.org/

21. Prinz, N., Rentrop, C., Huber, M.: Low-code development platforms - a literature review. In: Chan, Y.E., Boudreau, M., Aubert, B., Paré, G., Chin, W. (eds.) 27th Americas Conference on Information Systems, AMCIS 2021. Association for Information Systems (2021)

22. Rokis, K., Kirikova, M.: Challenges of low-code/no-code software development: a literature review. In: Nazaruka, E., Sandkuhl, K., Seigerroth, U. (eds.) Perspectives in Business Informatics Research. BIR 2022. LNBIP, vol. 462, pp. 3–17. Springer, Cham (2022). https://doi.org/10.1007/978-3-031-16947-2_1

23. Roth, U., Regtmeier, J.: Low-Code-Development als integraler Bestandteil der Digitalisierungsstrategie von DENIOS. In: Hinrichsen, S., Sauer, S., Schroder, K. (eds.) Prozesse in Industriebetrieben mittels Low-Code-Software digitalisieren. Intelligente Technische Systeme – Losungen aus dem Spitzencluster it's OWL, pp. 99–110. Springer Vieweg, Berlin, Heidelberg (2023). https://doi.org/10.1007/978-3-662-67950-0_7

24. Ruscio, D.D., Kolovos, D.S., de Lara, J., Pierantonio, A., Tisi, M., Wimmer, M.: Low-code development and model-driven engineering: two sides of the same coin? Softw. Syst. Model. **21**(2), 437–446 (2022). https://doi.org/10.1007/s10270-021-00970-2

25. Sahay, A., Indamutsa, A., Ruscio, D.D., Pierantonio, A.: Supporting the understanding and comparison of low-code development platforms. In: 46th Euromicro Conference on Software Engineering and Advanced Applications, SEAA 2020, pp. 171–178. IEEE (2020). https://doi.org/10.1109/SEAA51224.2020.00036

26. Vincent, P., et al.: Magic quadrant for enterprise low-code application platforms (2020). https://www.gartner.com/doc/reprints?id=1-26YGZMUG&ct=210727&st=sb

27. Waszkowski, R.: Low-code platform for automating business processes in manufacturing. IFAC-PapersOnLine **52**(10), 376–381 (2019). https://doi.org/10.1016/j.ifacol.2019.10.060, 13th IFACWorkshop on Intelligent Manufacturing Systems, IMS 2019

28. Weidmann, N., Heil, J., Wegener, M.: Software für Speicherprogrammierbare Steuerungen entwickeln: low-Code oder Modellgetrieben? In: Hinrichsen, S., Sauer, S., Schroder, K. (eds.) Prozesse in Industriebetrieben mittels Low-Code-Software digitalisieren. Intelligente Technische Systeme – Losungen aus dem Spitzencluster it's OWL. Springer Vieweg, Berlin, Heidelberg (2023). https://doi.org/10.1007/978-3-662-67950-0_8
29. Weidmann, N., Sauer, S., Kirchhoff, J.: Merkmale und Entwicklungslinien der Low-Code-Programmierung. In: Hinrichsen, S., Sauer, S., Schroder, K. (eds.) Prozesse in Industriebetrieben mittels Low-Code-Software digitalisieren. Intelligente Technische Systeme – Losungen aus dem Spitzencluster it's OWL, pp. 17–29. Springer Vieweg, Berlin, Heidelberg (2023). https://doi.org/10.1007/978-3-662-67950-0_2

Towards a Smart Combination of Human and Artificial Intelligence for Manufacturing

Jan Van den Bergh[1]([⊠])[iD], Jorge Rodríguez-Echeverría[2,3,4][iD],
and Sidharta Gautama[2,3][iD]

[1] UHasselt - tUL - Flanders Make, Diepenbeek, Belgium
jan.vandenbergh@uhasselt.be
[2] FlandersMake@UGent - corelab ISyE, Lommel, Belgium
{Jorge.RodriguezEcheverria,Sidharta.Gautama}@UGent.be
[3] Department of Industrial System Engineering and Product Design,
Ghent University, Gent-Zwijnaarde 9052, Belgium
[4] ESPOL Polytechnic University, Escuela Superior Politécnica del Litoral,
ESPOL, Facultad de Ingeniería en Electricidad y Computación,
Campus Gustavo Galindo Km 30.5 Vía Perimetral, P.O. Box 09-01-5863,
EC090112 Guayaquil, Ecuador
jirodrig@espol.edu.ec

Abstract. The manufacturing industry is evolving toward more automation and digitization. This includes collecting data from sensors, machines, and software used on the shop floor. Human workers and their strengths and needs are still essential, as recognized by the Industry 5.0 vision. This vision is still abstract, and concepts like human-centricity, digital twin, and production intelligence are still semantically ill-defined to be mapped directly, given the complexity of manufacturing environments. In this paper, we center on the quality management process of Failure Mode and Effects Analysis (FMEA) to propose terminology and a framework to reflect on potential solutions in Industry 5.0. We explore the integration of human and artificial intelligence to create a continuous and actioning quality management process that extends the capabilities of the current process FMEA.

Keywords: Industry 5.0 · Internet of Things · Digital Twin · FMEA · Artificial Intelligence

1 Introduction

Industry 4.0 promised companies to be more competitive through the extensive use of data-driven automation. However, Betty and De Boer [3] noticed that while at the start of 2023 Industry 4.0 pilots were still running and expanding,

Supported by Flanders Make and SBO AQUME.

A. Bramwell-Dicks et al. (Eds.): INTERACT 2023 Workshops, LNCS 14535, pp. 20–30, 2024.
https://doi.org/10.1007/978-3-031-61688-4_3

scaling up seems more difficult and few companies are able to transition from pilot to an operational phase. Raptis [11] discusses the role of data and data management in Industry 4.0 as underlying to the cyber-physical convergence in industry. Although data is one of the key enablers in this evolution, Wang [15] states that data is not equal to value and consequently, to create value with data, one needs data processes that transform data to actionable items thus creating value.

At the same time, a shift of focus is appearing in the future of factories. The European commission has recently proposed Industry 5.0 in its policy goals as an improvement over Industry 4.0 and they emphasize the importance and the shift from efficiency to well-being, resilience, and sustainability [5]. This evolution from Industry 4.0 to 5.0 introduces a focus shift from system-centric to human-centric [9]. Leng et al. [8] recently reviewed the state-of-the-art on Industry 5.0. They identified several key enablers as well as three technological challenges and five additional potential challenges. Of the technological challenges, they identify the heterogeneity of systems and the need for human-centric, value-driven technology transformation.

In this paper, we discuss these two challenges in transitioning towards Industry 5.0 in detail, applied to the domain of quality control in production systems. We explore what this transition means for a standardized quality management approach that is current practice in industry domains like automotive and aerospace, namely (process) Failure Mode and Effects Analysis [6]. For companies, pFMEA is a crucial quality instrument to design and improve their manufacturing operations. At the same time, its use is primarily team-driven and involves the human knowledge of different members in the operational chain, ranging from assembly line operators, line engineers to quality managers. This makes it challenging to transform into a pure data-driven system. We discuss the role of Internet-of-Things-enabled systems, digital twin, and cyber-physical systems within this context and how this combines with a human-centered engineering approach. We identify opportunities and challenges offered in an Industry 5.0 context for this process. We further define terms and a conceptual framework that may generalize to other applications and sectors employing quality management systems.

2 From pFMEA to pFMEA2

2.1 pFMEA

Process Failure Mode and Effects Analysis (pFMEA) is an essential tool to detect and address potential failures rooted in the assembly process [6], linked to 4M causes (Man, Machine, Material, environMent). As a team-oriented procedure, it is well established in different industries and even mandatory in sectors like automotive. Current pFMEA however is expensive, subjective, and slow, and the analysis is too narrow to capture propagated effects beyond single-point failures [1,2]. The analysis is difficult to update after mitigation actions and it is hard to capture the learnings for the design of the next generations of the

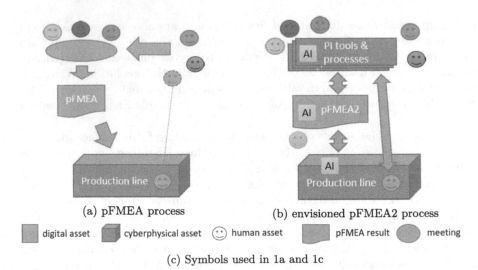

(a) pFMEA process   (b) envisioned pFMEA2 process

digital asset   cyberphysical asset   😊 human asset   pFMEA result   meeting

(c) Symbols used in 1a and 1c

Fig. 1. Envisioned evolution of pFMEA implementation: (a) State of practice; a multi-disciplinary team consults experts and composes a pFMEA document, which is used to create or adapt the production line and (b) the envisioned process; Production Intelligence tools allow all stakeholders to be involved in a continuously running pFMEA2 process, which includes a living pFMEA2 document (digital twin), and production intelligence tools, all tools integrating some form of Artificial Intelligence

assembly system. Figure 1 (a) sketches this process; the team that creates the pFMEA consists of people with different backgrounds. The composition of teams differs between companies, but roles that can be included in the team can be line managers, quality managers, and planning engineers. They consult other experts, including operators who have experience with the production process. For new products, this experience can come from pilot manufacturing. The output of the pFMEA process is a report that documents the process, the identified high-risk failures (including how these were identified) and the taken and planned actions.

2.2   pFMEA2

The increasing digitization of the manufacturing industry offers an opportunity to turn this intermittent process into a continuous improvement process supported by production intelligence (tools and processes) that can exploit a purpose-built digital twin, in this particular case, a live connected pFMEA, that is able to monitor and steer the manufacturing system continuously.

This digital twin pFMEA receives input from human, physical, and digital assets that are part of the manufacturing process and, as such, is always in sync with the physical reality of the assembly system. As a quality management tool, the digital twin aims to detect probable cause-and-effect relationships for quality issues, leading to a root-cause analysis as well as making mitigating decisions. In our view, the step from the current pFMEA process towards a digital twin goes beyond pure connectivity (i.e., linking a pFMEA system to manufacturing data like IoT). Managing quality is a complex process that requires analysis and interpretation beyond pure data analysis.

To ensure the usability and quality of experience of an automated support tool, a human-centered design process is required, and where possible, a participatory design process to create them. For instance, data can come from assembly line operators to gather additional feedback while they are working on a specific process step that might be the cause of an end-of-line quality issue. This involvement of the employees can contribute to a more targeted and reactive pFMEA process. It brings together human knowledge and IoT data in one framework. At the same time, the operator's well-being should be guarded as quality feedback detracts their attention from their main job, and the human-machine interfaces should be designed carefully. The on-demand operator feedback, as well as live mitigation actions that can be triggered by the digital twin pFMEA support a data-supported Process Failure Modes and Effects Analysis and Actioning (pFMEA2) decision support system (Fig. 1 (b)).

3   Artificial and Human Intelligence in pFMEA2

While Fig. 1c does not make a distinction between different types of Artificial Intelligence, the diverse blocks can and do use different types of AI, based on the properties of the data that is available and the specific needs for the tasks that allow them to be combined with human intelligence. This section will discuss these in more detail. The types of AI are highlighted in bold, and named parts of the pFMEA2 process are shown in italics. A summary is given in Table 1 where we identify the potential benefit of human-centric AI in the process.

In the *production line*, **machine learning** (ML) can leverage networked sensors or smart cameras to predict and classify potential anomalies during assembly execution. In case an anomaly happens, it is not always easy to estimate based on data the causality why the anomaly happens (e.g. bad tooling, bad parts, excessive environment noise that distracts the operator). The resulting data can be used by an ML **prediction system** to ask targeted information of data to operators during assembly on potential causes. ML focuses on generating new features (like anomalies). To turn these features into value-adding functions, expert knowledge on what support actions are needed at which time in the process can be added. Data on quality is typically small data, as not all potential occurrences and variations of issues in all production steps can be observed in order to train robust ML systems. Pure data-driven approaches therefore need to be integrated with human expert knowledge in order to come to a robust system with small training data sets. Human-centricity acknowledges both expert knowledge as well as the interface to efficiently capture this operator knowledge on-line during assembly.

Line managers and quality managers use real-time (machine and human) and historical data about system performance to monitor or analyze failures. ML prediction and classification can ease fault and anomaly detection using live system

Table 1. Complementarity of artificial and human intelligence in pFMEA2

Process	Purpose	Target user	Data	AI	Benefit human expert knowledge
Manufacturing	Operator support	Line operators	IoT (e.g. smart camera)	ML prediction/classification AI expert system	what support actions are needed for which type of user
Design, pre-operation	System configuration	Planning, control engineer	Historic order & system performance	Optimization & search methods Recommender methods	assess the company context in which the observed assembly line functions
Flexible Manufacturing	System reconfiguration	Control engineers	Real-time system performance (machine & human execution)	Optimal control (recommender methods)	assess when the system behavior goes out of scope of the initial training data
Quality control	Failure monitoring	Line managers	Real-time order & system performance	ML prediction & classification (e.g. fault detection, anomaly detection)	explainability, link failure modes to mitigation actions, especially across process steps
Quality control	Failure analysis	Quality managers	Historic system performance	Explainable AI root-cause analysis (e.g. data-driven Bayesian Networks)	causal chain definition that can be compared with data-driven analysis

data. Explainable AI, such as data-driven Bayesian Networks (BNs) can help for root-cause analysis and the identification of mitigation actions in *production intelligence* and are a combination of data and human knowledge engineering. For failure analysis, data-driven BNs can be used to challenge or confirm expert-based causal chains as is constructed in the current team-driven pFMEA process as the analysis of the human experts could be biased and dependent on the specific composition of the team. Human-centricity relies on humans being good at causal analysis but integrating this with data for objectivity.

For the (re-)configuration of the system or the *pFMEA2* digital twin, planning or control engineers can use historic or real-time data about order and system performance. This data becomes more manageable through the use of **Optimisation methods**, that can be complemented with recommender methods for real-time performance. Expert knowledge can be used to assess which parts of a complex system need retraining when the context changes (e.g., when transferring it to a new plant) or when system data gets out of the scope of the initial data due to unforeseen disturbances or rush orders. Human-centricity relies both on expert system knowledge as well as efficient interfaces to manage automated control of complex systems.

4   Key Terminology

The discussion of pFMEA [6] and pFMEA2 (Sect. 2.2) used three key terms that deserve a more detailed discussion. These are asset, digital twin, and production intelligence.

Asset has multiple meanings in English. The one we believe is most appropriate 'a person or thing that is very useful or valuable' [4]. This definition fits with the aims of Industry 5.0 about sustainability and resilience as the emphasis, also in other definitions, is on value. Different types of assets are discussed, including human, digital, physical, and cyber-physical assets. Cyber-physical assets (CPA) consist of collaborating assets that exchange data and can be coordinated using computational tools. As is the case with cyber-physical systems [10] understanding the cyber-physical system requires understanding not only the parts, but also their interactions. In pFMEA2, the entire production line can be considered as a single cyber-physical asset consisting of other cyber-physical, digital, physical, and human assets. On a more local level, a CPA can be as small as a smart tool, that sends data during execution and can be automatically configured for a certain operation. The assembly operator is, of course, a human asset. But when operator execution is sensed, e.g., with wearables or AR glasses, data is exchanged on step execution and feedback can be served back, for instance, through light-guided work instructions that trigger differently based on operator experience level. As mentioned in the previous section, even the operator feedback on potential issues in a process step is a form of data exchange. In this sense, the operator also becomes part of the production system CPA. All these CPA's generate streams of information that can be used to assess the overall production and can be fed directly to a digital twin, such as the living pFMEA2 (Fig. 1 (b)).

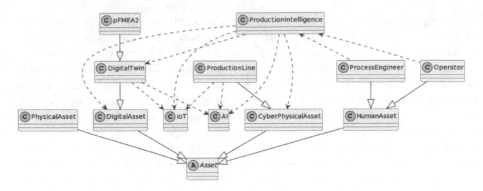

Fig. 2. Relations between asset types, IoT, AI, digital twins, and Production Intelligence.

Digital twins [14] (DT) are a digital representation of an active unique product (real device, object, machine, service, or intangible asset) or unique product-service system (a system consisting of a product and a related service) that comprises its selected characteristics, properties, conditions, and behaviors by means of models, information, and data within a single or even across multiple life cycle phases [13]. In the case of our pFMEA2 digital twin, the active unique product is actually the production line, a cyber-physical asset. The pFMEA2 DT continuously receives data from the production line and its underlying CPAs. These CPAs can be modeled by a digital twin on their own, for instance, an assembly line robot system being modeled and controlled through a robot digital twin. Our pFMEA2 DT would communicate with this robot DT and distill more abstract information from it, which would be difficult if the pFMEA2 DT captured the raw IoT data from the robot directly. The pFMEA2 DT would, however, also capture other data in subsequent steps which might not be directly modeled as a local digital twin, e.g., human assembly steps following the robot assembly step. We note that the pFMEA2 DT is more abstract than the typical model-based examples of digital twin, where a virtual representation of the complete cyber-physical asset is constructed to behave in line with the physical asset, e.g., a 3D model of the robotic system in production. The pFMEA2 DT does not model a detailed virtual representation of the production line and its components. It is a more abstract representation of the production line closer to the current FMEA analysis. It centers on the process flow description of the different assembly steps and the 4M impact (man, machine, material, method) on production quality. To calculate impact, data from IoT or DT in each process step is gathered where available and propagated towards potential effects towards the End-of-Line. In this sense, it is an abstract, virtual representation of a physical process used to understand and predict the physical counterpart's performance characteristics. The focus is, however, much more on decision support and is meant to interact with and support human decision-making.

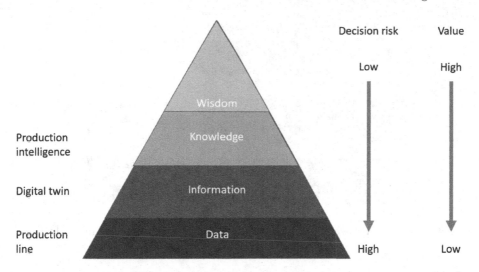

Fig. 3. Data, Information, Knowledge, and Wisdom hierarchy, related risk and value, recreated after [7,12] with the addition of the components of the pFMEA2 process in Fig. 1c

Production Intelligence is a third term that is often used in this context. Engineers and data analysts use various forms of Artificial Intelligence (AI) to analyse and improve various aspects of the manufacturing process. This benefits both the company and the involved employees, who may use the AI processes to generate knowledge and over time maybe wisdom. Figure 3 relates the different parts of pFMEA2 to the DIKW hierarchy [7,12]. The human contribution to this analysis is key in this conversion from data to wisdom, as discussed in Sect. 3. Moving from decisions based on purely data to decisions based on knowledge and wisdom decreases risk [7] and increases value [12]. In our pFMEA2 DT, quality is a complex process with many variables. Data-driven analysis can often find correlation but not necessarily causation. In addition, data is still relatively scarce compared to all the steps and variables present in a full production system. Human experience and expert knowledge are useful to bridge this gap. We define production intelligence as the capability to continuously reason on and improve production through processes and tools that combine human and artificial intelligence.

5   Discussion

In this position paper, we presented a vision of how different concepts and technologies can fit together to create an approach to monitor quality and adapt production processes to quality issues continuously. The core ideas fit into the Industry 5.0 vision and combine Internet-of-Things, Digital Twins, and Artificial Intelligence in a process that is still highly human-centered and uses these

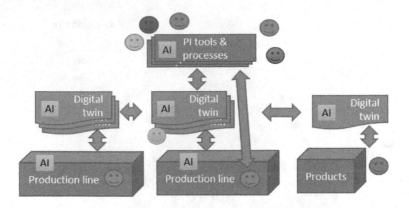

Fig. 4. Generalized schema of the role of digital twins, assets and AI in production

technologies to identify information in the data collected from production processes (and beyond) that can be used to generate knowledge by supporting its combination with contextual human knowledge including operators and process engineers and capturing essential pieces of it in a knowledge base so that it can be reused and built upon.

Our proposed pFMEA2 approach combines human and artificial intelligence in the different aspects of managing the quality of production in production lines; the production line itself, its digital twin for managing (potential) quality issues, the pFMEA2. This would replace the pFMEA2 report in traditional approaches with a living model, connected live to the production line enabling linking with quality-related information coming from the production line, and finally, the production intelligence tools, which support decision-making on quality actions and their follow-up. We will further detail this approach into an integrated research setup that will be validated with an industry-relevant assembly case. However, we believe that the potential application of the core ideas can be much broader within the manufacturing industry and beyond.

The approach is more or less compatible with Lu et al. [9]'s human-centric manufacturing reference model, although they talk about empathic machines. In our case empathy is not a targeted capability of any of the (cyber-)physical assets. These assets should however feature context-adaptive information and control capabilities to there users.

The layers in the visual depiction can be mapped to the generation of data, information, knowledge (and wisdom) pyramid. There is no explicit wisdom level, although wisdom may be the result of a continuous application of this approach through deliberate practice. AI can be involved in all these levels. We believe the combination with human expert knowledge is still necessary at every level. While our analysis was made in the context of the quality management of production lines, similar approaches could be used to create digital twins for other aspects of production and across production lines. The digital twins of these production lines could talk to the digital twins of the products produced on these product lines, resulting in the schema in Fig. 4. In this way, an even richer image of the production quality can be obtained to increase the sustainability of the overall process.

Besides the high-level description of the pFMEA2 approach and the generalized version thereof, this position paper also identifies a set of relevant AI types that can support the human-led process. In doing so, the value of including human knowledge was identified in each step. It also stresses the use of the term assets, which implies the value and usefulness of all the people and systems involved.

We hope that this position paper can contribute to the realization of Industry 5.0, by drawing attention to the diversity of AI techniques that can be used within the approach as well as the importance of human knowledge throughout the process.

Acknowledgements. The research in the paper was funded by Flanders Make, including through the SBO project AQUME (R-13028).

References

1. Albliwi, S., Antony, J., Lim, S.A.H., van der Wiele, T.: Critical failure factors of lean six sigma: a systematic literature review. Int. J. Qual. Reliab. Manag. (2014). https://doi.org/10.1108/IJQRM-09-2013-0147
2. Antony, J., Sony, M.: An empirical study into the limitations and emerging trends of six sigma in manufacturing and service organisations. Int. J. Qual. Reliab. Manag. **37**(3), 470–493 (2020)
3. Betti, F., de Boer, E.: Global lighthouse network: shaping the next chapter of the fourth industrial revolution (2023)
4. Cambridge dictionary: Asset — English meaning (2023). https://dictionary.cambridge.org/dictionary/english/asset. Accessed 28 May 2023
5. European Commission, Directorate-General for Research and Innovation, Renda, A., Schwaag Serger, S., Tataj, D., et al.: Industry 5.0, a transformative vision for Europe – Governing systemic transformations towards a sustainable industry. Publications Office of the European Union (2021). https://data.europa.eu/doi/10.2777/17322
6. AIAG (Automotive Industry Action Group): AIAG & VDA Failure Mode and Effects Analysis - FMEA Handbook, 1st edn. AIAG, 2nd printing Southfild, MI (2022)
7. Hussain, M., et al.: Intelligent knowledge consolidation: from data to wisdom. Knowl.-Based Syst. **234**, 107578 (2021). https://doi.org/10.1016/j.knosys.2021.107578, https://www.sciencedirect.com/science/article/pii/S0950705121008406
8. Leng, J., et al.: Industry 5.0: prospect and retrospect. J. Manuf. Syst. **65**, 279–295 (2022). https://doi.org/10.1016/j.jmsy.2022.09.017
9. Lu, Y., et al.: Outlook on human-centric manufacturing towards industry 5.0. J. Manuf. Syst. **62**, 612–627 (2022). https://doi.org/10.1016/j.jmsy.2022.02.001, https://www.sciencedirect.com/science/article/pii/S0278612522000164
10. Monostori, L.: Cyber-Physical Systems, pp. 1–8. Springer, Berlin, Heidelberg (2018).https://doi.org/10.1007/978-3-642-35950-7_16790-1

11. Raptis, T.P., Passarella, A., Conti, M.: Data management in industry 4.0: state of the art and open challenges. IEEE Access **7**, 97052–97093 (2019)
12. Rowley, J.: The wisdom hierarchy: representations of the DIKW hierarchy. J. Inf. Sci. **33**(2), 163–180 (2007). https://doi.org/10.1177/0165551506070706, https://doi.org/10.1177/0165551506070706
13. Stark, R., Damerau, T.: Digital Twin, pp. 1–8. Springer, Berlin, Heidelberg (2019). https://doi.org/10.1007/978-3-642-35950-7_16870-1
14. Tao, F., Xiao, B., Qi, Q., Cheng, J., Ji, P.: Digital twin modeling. J. Manuf. Syst. **64**, 372–389 (2022). https://doi.org/10.1016/j.jmsy.2022.06.015, https://www.sciencedirect.com/science/article/pii/S0278612522001108
15. Wang, D.: Building value in a world of technological change: data analytics and industry 4.0. IEEE Eng. Manag. Rev. **46**(1), 32–33 (2018). https://doi.org/10.1109/EMR.2018.2809915

Digitalisation and the Work Environment: Insights from Evaluating the Contextual Think-Aloud Method

Marta Larusdottir[1]([✉])[iD], Åsa Cajander[2][iD], and Ruochen Wang[3]

[1] Reykjavik University, Menntavegur 1, 102 Reykjavik, Iceland
marta@ru.is
[2] Uppsala University, Lägerhyddsvägen 1, 752 37 Uppsala, Sweden
[3] Shanghai Nuclear Engineering Research and Design Institute, Shanghai 200233, China

Abstract. The digital transformation of workplaces necessitates understanding the intricate relationship between software systems and their context. In response, this paper introduces an innovative "Contextual Think-Aloud" method, a refinement of the traditional Think-Aloud evaluation method, aimed at providing software developers with deeper insights into the nature of digital work environments. The efficacy of this method was assessed by involving twenty-nine university students in a twelve-week user-centred software development course. The analysis highlighted the method's ability to extend understanding of user-system interactions and specific contexts, proving particularly beneficial in early developmental stages. However, challenges such as its resource-intensive nature, user reluctance to express genuine thoughts, and contrasting user opinions were identified. Suggestions for improvement included creating a conducive evaluation environment and preferring interactive prototypes. Despite its inherent challenges and limitations, the Contextual Think-Aloud method emerged as a valuable tool for understanding user interactions and specific contexts in digital work environments. This study contributes significant insights and enhancements to the field of user-centred design methodologies, addressing the evolving needs of digital workplaces in the contemporary scenario, thus enriching the discourse on optimising user-centred design methodologies in the evolving digital workspace, balancing its multifaceted benefits and challenges.

Keywords: Contextual Think-Aloud method · Think-aloud method · Digital Work Environment · Context of use · User-centred design

1 Introduction

In recent times, the realm of software systems has undergone a notable transformation. Once confined to traditional computing platforms, these systems have permeated various facets of our lives, spanning mobile devices, wearables, and ubiquitous embedded technology. This shift in ubiquity has ushered in dynamic contextual settings for software deployment, distinguishing the contemporary landscape from two or three decades

A. Bramwell-Dicks et al. (Eds.): INTERACT 2023 Workshops, LNCS 14535, pp. 31–46, 2024.
https://doi.org/10.1007/978-3-031-61688-4_4

ago. Consequently, comprehending the contextual nuances of software usage during its development has emerged as a pivotal concern, garnering heightened attention in practical applications and academic inquiry, for example [1, 2]. Today's software encounters a scope of contexts characterised by dynamism, heterogeneity, and unpredictability, unlike 20 years ago, where software predominantly functioned in static, single-context environments with stationary computing systems [3]. A myriad of factors shapes the intricate interplay within this milieu, encompassing the fluidity of business landscapes, organisational cultures, strategic imperatives, project diversity, and the diverse backgrounds of team members [3]. Consequently, in the contemporary epoch, integrating work environment considerations into the software development lifecycle is paramount, spanning user needs analysis and the evaluation of prototype alignment with those needs [4–7].

The rapid pace of digitalisation within work environments has been particularly pronounced. This wave of digital transformation has ushered in an era of automation, streamlined decision-making processes, and facilitated knowledge-sharing within organisations. Termed the "digital work environment," this concept encapsulates using software systems within work-related scenarios [8]. However, alongside its undeniable benefits, the digitalisation of work environments has also brought forth various challenges, ranging from productivity dips to health issues and privacy breaches [9–11]. For instance, the relentless demands imposed by ill-conceived software systems have led to stress among staff, a poignant example of the adverse consequences [11–14]. Addressing these pressing issues necessitates a holistic approach that acknowledges human-centric considerations and contextual factors when crafting software solutions.

In this research endeavour, we embark on a journey that builds upon the foundations of the traditional Think-Aloud method [15]. Our approach involves augmenting this method with elements pertinent to the digital work environment, integrated into the user interviewing and observation process. Within the scope of this study, we delve into the experiences of university students who engaged with the Contextual Think-Aloud method.

Within this paper, we define our research inquiries as follows:

1. What advantages are observed when utilising the Contextual Think-Aloud method?
2. What disadvantages are encountered when utilising the Contextual Think-Aloud method?
3. What suggested improvements emerge for enhancing the future utility of the Contextual Think-Aloud method?

2 Related Work

This section concisely overviews prior research on the digital work environment and the traditional think-aloud method.

2.1 Digital Work Environment

As described by Shravasti and Bhola, the work environment encompasses physical surroundings and social dynamics within the workplace [16]. It pertains to the working conditions at an organisation, which can either encourage or hinder employee performance

[16]. Wright and Davis elaborate on this concept by dividing the work environment into two pivotal components: job characteristics and work context [16]. Job characteristics assess how job responsibilities influence an employee's psychological well-being, encompassing aspects such as the meaningfulness of the work and an employee's sense of growth and development [17]. In contrast, work context delves into organisational aspects, including reward systems and overarching goals. The work environment empowers employees to fulfil their tasks effectively [18].

The term "digital work" denotes tasks carried out by employees using information and communications technology (ICT) [19]. Dittes and Smolnik conceptualise the digital work environment as the online representation of working conditions necessary for employees to perform their duties [20]. Moreover, as defined by Sandblad et al., the digital work environment embodies a multifaceted terrain shaped by the digitalisation of work support systems and tools, encompassing physical, organisational, social, and cognitive aspects [21].

Expanding upon these definitions, an effective digital work environment should address employees' physical, social, organisational, and psychological aspects, enhancing their ability to execute digital work tasks proficiently.

Digital work offers numerous advantages. Digital technologies facilitate collaboration among geographically dispersed colleagues, allowing work activities to transpire in unconventional locations like trains, restaurants, or hotel lobbies [22]. This flexibility grants the ability to engage in digital work anytime and anywhere [8, 23]. Furthermore, digital tools enhance productivity, mitigate human errors, automate processes, assist decision-making, and facilitate knowledge-sharing within organisations [8, 22, 24, 25].

However, the proliferation of digital technologies has introduced challenges. The boundary between work and personal life has blurred, as people tend to address work-related matters via email during leisure time [8]. This integration results in difficulties separating work and personal life, often leading to conflict and compromising recovery time [26, 27].

Digital work can also induce stress, primarily due to asynchronous communication, which pressures recipients to respond promptly [28]. This pressure can manifest as stress-related issues like burnout, sleep disturbances, and health-related absenteeism [28]. For instance, a study reported that nurses experienced stress due to fragmented communication with patients through a digital chat system [12].

Furthermore, the proliferation of information devices in digital workplaces can burden employees, causing cognitive and physical strain by using multiple gadgets and functions to accomplish various tasks [29]. This phenomenon, described as "technology overload," can decrease productivity, heighten work-related stress, and lead to symptoms such as anxiety, fatigue, scepticism, and inefficiency in using technologies [13, 14, 30]. Older individuals, typically less tech-savvy, may be particularly affected, resulting in diminished job engagement [31].

In light of these challenges, employees seek digital technologies that are accessible, user-friendly, and efficient [25]. To achieve this, various initiatives, both in research and practice, have been undertaken, such as developing smart offices and identifying factors to improve the digital work environment.

One promising avenue involves incorporating contextual factors to enhance the digital work environment. This approach involves embedding contextual considerations into digital technologies, making them more adaptable and responsive to specific usage scenarios [32]. Such context-aware technologies have shown greater efficiency, utility, and productivity in digital work environments [33]. By considering contextual factors in the design process, digital systems gain a deeper understanding of users' behaviour, thus improving their usability and effectiveness.

2.2 The Think-Aloud Method

The Think-Aloud method has been rated highly by IT professionals as a useful method during software development for improving the usability and user experiences of the software [44]. The Think-Aloud method offers a unique window into the intricacies of human cognition during problem-solving tasks [15, 34]. As individuals tackle various tasks, their thoughts traverse through working memory, providing a basis for verbalisation [35]. This method has found application in usability testing within the Human-Computer Interaction (HCI) domain, serving research and practical purposes. Typically, participants are asked to articulate their thoughts while performing specific tasks during usability evaluations. This practice grants observers insights into participants' cognitive processes and is particularly valuable in the formative stages of design, where end-users' feedback on early prototypes is essential.

The Think-Aloud method can be categorised into two distinct types: concurrent Think-Aloud and retrospective Think-Aloud [36]. Concurrent Think-Aloud involves data collection during problem-solving tasks, while retrospective Think-Aloud gathers data after task completion, requiring participants to revisit their steps. Research suggests that compared to retrospective Think-Aloud, concurrent Think-Aloud yields richer insights [36].

This method aids designers in obtaining extensive and profound data, even with a small sample size. Typically, participants are presented with a consent form before the Think-Aloud evaluation. Upon signing, they are instructed to verbalise their thoughts as they tackle simulated problem-solving tasks continuously. Moderators must avoid excessive interaction with participants to preserve the flow of their thoughts. Investigators take notes on the verbalised content throughout the evaluation, and video recording is recommended for reference. Practical guidelines have been proposed to ensure the effectiveness and efficiency of the Think-Aloud method. Moderators are advised not to interrupt participants to explain their verbalised thoughts while thinking aloud [15, 34]. Additionally, attention should be paid to participants' speech features, such as moments of silence or verbal fillers like "Emmm" and "Huh," as they can provide insights into the thinking process [37]. Demonstrating the Think-Aloud method and practice sessions before the evaluation can encourage participants to report their thought processes more consistently and comprehensively [34].

The Think-Aloud method is a popular and valuable tool for understanding end-users and enhancing system usability [34, 35, 37]. Research suggests that only 5–9 participants can uncover 80%-90% of severe usability issues [38]. However, criticisms have been raised regarding the validity of self-reported and subjective data gathered through Think-Aloud and the unstructured and incomplete qualitative information often accompanied by gaps of silence [39, 40]. Additionally, the collection and analysis of Think-Aloud data are resource-intensive and time-consuming [41]. Participants may also experience discomfort, as verbalising thoughts during work is unusual and may disrupt their usual workflow [40]. Moreover, a psychological study has indicated that adolescents are less inclined to articulate their thought processes during Think-Aloud sessions [42].

Recent research has explored the automation of Think-Aloud data analysis to alleviate the labour-intensive and time-consuming aspects of the process [37]. By visualising the verbalisation data collected through Think-Aloud, researchers have identified correlations between speech patterns, such as fluctuations in voice pitch, and usability problems [37]. For instance, a higher or lower voice pitch wave may indicate usability issues with the tested systems [37].

Still, The Think-Aloud method has garnered high praise from IT professionals for its effectiveness in enhancing the usability and user experience of software during the development process [44]. Hence, we aimed to propose and assess an enhancement to the method by incorporating contextual aspects of the digital work environment when evaluating software prototypes.

3 The Contextual Think-Aloud Method

This section describes the development of the Contextual Think-Aloud method. The Contextual Think-Aloud method is a variation of traditional think-aloud evaluations with users, focusing more on including the digital work environment. It is recommended to use the method when a prototype has been made for an IT system to be used in a work-related context. The two main objectives for using the Contextual Think-Aloud method are A) To gather feedback from users on how a particular prototype fits into the work context of a given group of workers and B) To interpret the feedback to extend the IT professionals' understanding of users and their broad needs.

The Contextual Think-Aloud method emphasises a structured approach, focusing on evaluating usability in specific work contexts while maintaining the foundational principles of the standard think-aloud method. This method begins by extending a friendly welcome to the participants and providing a brief introduction outlining the evaluation process's objectives and details, establishing a clear framework for the upcoming activities. Following the introduction, participants are immersed in contextual inquiries, where they are prompted to answer questions tailored to understand their unique work environments and roles, such as the nature of their work and the level of support they receive from their leaders. This phase is pivotal as it aims to gather insightful data on the varied work contexts of the participants.

Subsequently, the evaluator introduces the prototype to the participants, allowing them adequate time to familiarise themselves with its features and functionalities before solving the tasks. In the task execution phase, participants are assigned work-related tasks, preferably including aspects from the whole work environment. The users are encouraged to vocalise their thoughts and opinions, providing valuable feedback that allows evaluators to discern whether the prototypes are facilitating users in completing their tasks efficiently and effectively.

Participants engage in reflective discussions, pondering the prototype's alignment with their work situations and drawing comparisons between the prototype and other systems they regularly use after the task-solving session. This post-task reflection is crucial for evaluators to understand the practical applicability and relevance of the prototype in real-world work scenarios.

The main difference between using the traditional think-aloud method and using the Contextual Think-Aloud method is that:

- The background questions include questions related to the work environment
- The user's tasks cover the whole work situation
- The debriefing questions include questions related to the work environment, especially asking how the new system would fit the user in their work situation.

The differences are illustrated in Fig. 1.

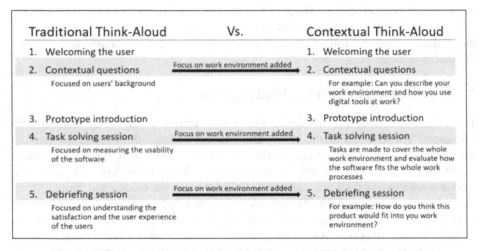

Fig. 1. Differences between traditional and Contextual Think-Aloud methods.

We have made instructions on conducting the Contexual Think-Aloud method available on a website, with this link: https://ucdsprint.com/additional-methods/.

In this book chapter, we describe the method's application, analysing positive and negative experiences through a user-centred software development course involving twenty-nine students. It provides a comprehensive overview, detailing possible improvements for the method and advocating for a more context-aware, human-centric approach to software development.

4   Method

The focal discoveries detailed in this paper originate from a cohort of 29 students enrolled in a user-centric software development course during the Spring semester of 2020 at Reykjavik University. Within the framework of this course, students were tasked with applying the Contextual Think-Aloud method throughout their design projects. Upon the culmination of the course, each student was required to draft an individual report, reflecting upon their encounters with the Contextual Think-Aloud method. In these reports, students compared their experiences utilising the Contextual Think-Aloud approach with their previous encounters involving the Heuristic Evaluation method. We conducted a comprehensive analysis using the thematic analysis approach to distil meaningful insights from these reflective reports.

4.1 Data Collection

Within a user-centred software development course, university students were introduced to the Contextual Think-Aloud method as part of their curriculum. There were 29 students taking part in the study, with 24% being female and 76% male. Their ages ranged from 22 to 39 (with one student not providing the data), with an average age of 25.8 and a median age of 25.

Over 12 weeks, these students engaged in designing a novel system, integrating the Contextual Think-Aloud method during the eighth week of their software development process. Eager to provide valuable insights, the students offered feedback encompassing both positive and negative aspects of their experiences with the Contextual Think-Aloud method and constructive suggestions for refinement and improvement.

To glean a comprehensive understanding of the utility and effectiveness of the Contextual Think-Aloud method, we meticulously analysed 29 student reports originating from Reykjavik University. These reports featured responses to a series of reflective inquiries, including 1) The positive experiences of the Contextual Think-Aloud method, 2) The negative experiences, and 3) Potential improvements to the method. Although most reports were diligently crafted, it is noteworthy that one student submitted an unfinished report.

The responses provided by the students exhibited a remarkable diversity, allowing us to capture a spectrum of perspectives in their reflections. Some students delved into lengthy and intricate discussions, while others opted for brief and concise responses. We must emphasise that our research does not involve identifying idiosyncratic and individualistic meanings and experiences. Instead, our analytical focus centres on discerning common themes prevalent in their responses. Consequently, we adopted the thematic analysis method delineated by Braun and Clarke in 2006 [48], enabling us to unravel these overarching themes within the student reports.

4.2 Data Analysis

Our approach to data analysis adhered to the guidelines outlined by Braun and Clarke [48], which involved a meticulous and systematic process. The initial step in this endeavour was to acquaint ourselves with the reports. Subsequently, responses to each question were methodically extracted from the reports, creating a structured foundation for our analysis.

To establish a structured framework for analysis, we embarked on the journey of initial coding. This phase entailed identifying succinct segments within the responses that could unequivocally address each question. The codes thus generated were the building blocks for our subsequent analysis.

Following the initial coding phase, patterns and potential themes began to emerge. In many instances, multiple relevant codes were amalgamated to form overarching themes, encapsulating the essence of the data. In some instances, codes stood out as distinct themes in their own right. However, some codes were deemed too vague or irrelevant to the specified question and were subsequently discarded. Also, codes that did not neatly align with existing themes were grouped under "miscellaneous." Drawing from the potential themes identified, we constructed a thematic map. All candidate themes were revisited to ensure their accuracy in representing the data. This is a meticulous review of all extracted codes for each theme, assessing whether they cohesively contributed to the theme's essence. Codes that did not harmonise with the existing themes were redefined and reallocated. Any codes that proved irrelevant or overly vague were excluded from the analysis. The congruence between candidate themes and the dataset was affirmed through a comprehensive comparison, ensuring these themes authentically mirrored the dataset.

The categorisation into themes reached its culmination when no significant gaps or substantial additions could be identified within the candidate themes. Once all candidate themes received validation, we created thematic maps for each question, grouping pertinent themes.

These thematic maps adopt a hierarchical structure, comprising central overarching themes and sub-themes for each of the three questions under scrutiny. Each central overarching theme may encompass one or several related sub-themes, effectively illustrating the interrelationships between all the themes within our analysis.

4.3 Limitations of the Study

This study is accompanied by several limitations that warrant acknowledgement. Initially, the scope of the study was bound to a distinct educational setting, utilising a comparatively confined sample size. Furthermore, the dependence on self-reported feedback brings forth potential biases and limitations characteristic of self-report methods. The study also neglected to incorporate viewpoints from other significant stakeholders, such as end-users and industry experts, the inclusion of which might have offered a richer, more holistic comprehension of the method under consideration.

Moreover, the study needed to include more encapsulation of the full spectrum of real-world software development contexts and restrictions, subsequently influencing the relevance and applicability of the findings. Exploration into potential adverse impacts or unintended ramifications was similarly restricted. Additionally, the course's specific timeframe and structural confines may limit the capability to observe enduring effects and impacts.

Considering these limitations, it is crucial to undertake further explorative studies to corroborate and expand upon the preliminary insights gained from this research, addressing the mentioned constraints and broadening the understanding of the subject matter.

5   Results

This section presents our findings identified from the 29 reports. In this section, we first describe the positive aspects of the Contextual Think-Aloud Method. We describe the negative aspects, and finally, we describe the suggested improvements of the method.

5.1 Positive Aspects of the Contextual Think-Aloud Method

The positive aspects of the Contextual Think-Aloud method extracted from the student reports were grouped into three themes.

1. **Extend the understanding**: Using the method helps designers and developers understand how users will interact with the system and why users interact in this way. First, respondents reported that the Contextual Think-Aloud method could help to visualise users' interaction paths. Just as one respondent mentioned:

    "Probably my favourite aspect and the most important one [...] is that [...] you see the path that he/she takes while operating your software. [...] you catch things and ideas that you might have otherwise missed [...] if you hadn't conducted the method."

Additionally, most respondents reported that the contextual think-aloud method enables them to gain a deeper understanding of their users by hearing their thoughts. Besides, the tone of the users' voice and speech patterns also help them better understand their feelings. As one respondent reflected in her report:

"Listening to what users say is very crucial since then we can locate the problems. [...] and [...] prevent harmful mistakes. If the users are frustrated [...], it indicates we did something wrong, and we'd better reverse it before too late."

2. **Better understanding of the specific context.** Respondents mentioned that considering Contextual factors while designing the system helps designers and developers better understand the specific context and state that it is essential to the end users. The Contextual Think-Aloud method allows them to investigate the contextual aspects with the actual users and helps them gain many insightful ideas on contextual factors.
3. **Help the team gain valuable feedback about the prototype.** Most respondents reported that such feedback could help them understand the prototype's good and bad sides before they start their coding work.

    "[I]t is good to get people to test your prototypes before making them because you might be creating something that will not be used or even confuses a user."

In summary, the results indicate a prevailing preference for using this method, primarily in the early stages of development, with some suggesting its application throughout the design process. The study reveals that the method aids in extending the understanding of user interaction with the system. It provides insights into user interaction paths and enables developers to comprehend user thoughts, speech patterns, and emotions. It also offers an understanding of the specific context and valuable feedback about prototypes before coding begins.

The positive aspects indicate the method's role in enhancing user-centred design by providing deep insights into user interactions and specific contexts and offering prototype feedback. However, the need for meticulous planning, execution, and managing contrasting opinions is evident, given the resource-intensive nature and potential compromise in the authenticity of user feedback.

5.2   Negative Aspects of the Contextual Think-Aloud Method

The negative aspects of the Contextual Think-Aloud method extracted from the student reports were grouped into three themes.

1. **The Contextual Think-Aloud method requires much time, resources, and effort.** Respondents reflected that conducting the Contextual Think-Aloud method required more time and involved more working staff to take notes, and the collected data could be significant and complicated. One respondent described this as follows:

   "The negatives are that setting up the environment is time-consuming and often requires 3 to 4 people to get all information from the user that could become quite expensive (2 observers/ notetakers, interviewer and prototype operator)."

2. **Users may need to speak their genuine opinion.** Almost every respondent (28 out of 29) reported that users did not express their true thoughts because they did not want to hurt the developers who designed the prototype or were too shy and felt uncomfortable expressing their opinions being observed by others.

   "People may be too polite to say what they are thinking and might not give much useful feedback."

3. **Collusion of opinions.** Some respondents reported that they could receive contrasting opinions from different users, making it difficult for the design team to decide how to improve the prototype.

   "[I]t is natural that different opinions and ideas pop up from different users. It is very likely to get contrasting opinions that go against each other during the evaluation phase. When that happens, it can be both time-consuming and difficult for the development team to decide how to improve the product to please everyone's needs."

Respondents highlighted some negative aspects of this method, including its extensive time and resource consumption and the need for a significant amount of personnel, making the process perceived as resource-intensive. The validity of user feedback is also challenged, with a common observation being a reluctance among users to express genuine and contrasting opinions, leading to difficulties in reaching a consensus for improvements.

5.3   Suggested Improvements of the Contextual Think-Aloud Method

The respondents also provided their ideas on improving the Contextual Think-Aloud method.

1. **Create a better experience during evaluation.** The respondents suggested creating a better experience to make the evaluation environment comfortable for users. For example, they wanted to reduce the number of interviewers in the room so that the

users would not feel stressed. Additionally, they wanted to let users explore the prototype by themselves before the test. The respondents think a "warm-up" could be helpful for users to get familiar with the prototype and perform a better think-aloud evaluation.

"I think that users do not know the context of the system before the evaluation and if they would get some exploration time before the evaluation to look at the prototypes that could improve the results because then they don't have to figure out what's in front of them when switching prototype pages."

Furthermore, they suggested to make the opening concise. Some respondents think the introduction to the users during the Contextual Think-Aloud should be cut because a long introduction would distract the users at the beginning of the evaluation.

2. **Avoid noting down unimportant problems.** Some respondents reflected that the note taker should be notified not to note very trivial and unimportant details because that could result in gaining invaluable data.

"I would try to make the conductors and note takers try to focus on what is really important, and not note out everything that they see the users stumble on."

3. **Interactive prototypes are better for evaluation.** Half of the respondents reported that a running and interactive prototype is better than a paper prototype.

"Digital prototypes are easier to imagine as real software: Paper prototypes require a lot of imagination from the evaluators, it might be easier for them to navigate through and review the product if it is prepared digitally."

The respondents suggested several improvements to optimise the process, such as making the evaluation environment more comfortable, reducing the number of interviewers, making the introduction more concise, focusing on significant problems only, and preferring interactive prototypes over paper ones.

6 Discussion

The Contextual Think-Aloud method offers advantages over the traditional Think-Aloud method. It provides a broader scope by considering the work environment and context, resulting in a more comprehensive understanding of how the system fits users' needs in a particular work environment. The method promotes user engagement and a user-centred approach, involving users directly in the evaluation process of a work-related system. However, challenges include users' difficulty thinking aloud about contextual aspects and the need for nuanced facilitation. Developers should consider these differences when selecting the most suitable method for their software development projects.

The findings indicate that careful application and execution of the method are crucial, with room for optimisation to foster genuine user feedback and effectively develop user-centric designs. While the suggested improvements and the preference for inter-active prototypes contribute to addressing some challenges, there is a need for further refinement.

Addressing the stated drawbacks and integrating the proposed improvements can optimise the method's application, enabling more precise and user-friendly applica-tions, fostering genuine user feedback, and contributing to developing intuitive and user-accommodating designs. The preference for interactive prototypes underlines the importance of a realistic and user-friendly approach, allowing for more accurate and relatable user feedback.

The Contextual Think-Aloud method, akin to holistic evaluation approaches like the Digital Work Environment Rounds [43], can face challenges related to the diversity and complexity of the systems evaluated, including standard, small, and large systems. Imple-menting changes in such varied systems is intricate due to their unique requirements and interactions. The complexity necessitates meticulous planning and a nuanced approach to ensure effective modifications do not disrupt the work environment, addressing the multifaceted nature and dependencies inherent in diverse systems. Also, the change and improvement processes take time to understand.

The Think-Aloud evaluation method received high acclaim among IT professionals, as demonstrated by a survey conducted in Sweden 2012 [44]. However, intriguingly, the same study revealed that, despite its high ranking, the method is seldom employed by IT professionals. This paradox raises questions regarding the practical applicability and execution of the method in real-world scenarios. The Contextual Think-Aloud method, viewed as a more complex version of the Think-aloud method, may need more utilisation due to its perceived complexity. This complexity may drive IT professionals to opt for simpler, more straightforward methods, possibly compromising the depth and breadth of insights obtained during evaluations.

Moreover, time pressure is a critical factor influencing the selection of evaluation methods, and professionals with tight schedules might prefer less time-consuming meth-ods that are easier to implement [45]. This prioritisation could compromise the depth and breadth of insights obtained during evaluations, as professionals may lean towards simpler, more straightforward methods.

In the pursuit of integrating the digital work environment into software develop-ment, various methodologies have been proposed, one of which is the Contextual Per-sonas method. A critical distinction between the Contextual Think-Aloud method and Contextual Personas arises in the involvement of users during the implementation of the former and their absence in the latter. This distinction is pivotal, considering the centrality of user involvement in the foundational principles of user-centred design.

User involvement is integral to deriving insights into user preferences, needs, and behaviours, significantly impacting software application design and development [46, 47]. Therefore, the Contextual Think-Aloud method emerges as a viable approach in adhering to user-centered design principles within software development processes.By contrast, the non-participatory nature of Contextual Personas could result in less align-ment with user needs, given the absence of direct user inputs during the development process.

7 Conclusion and Future Work

In conclusion, the research has laid a foundation for understanding and refining the Contextual Think-Aloud method in software development, opening avenues for enhancing user-centred design methodologies and improving user-software interactions. The Contextual Think-Aloud method provides a conduit through which user perspectives can be integrated, ensuring that the resultant software aligns closely with user expectations and requirements, fostering enhanced user satisfaction and experience.

Future research should focus on optimising the application of the method by examining various environments and user dynamics, aiming to create universally applicable improvements. There is also a need to investigate ways to ensure the authenticity of user feedback, manage contrasting opinions effectively, and mitigate the resource-intensiveness of the method. The possibility of integrating the Contextual Think-Aloud method with other user-centred design methodologies and its adaptability across different stages of software development should also be explored.

Acknowledgements. We sincerely thank AFA Insurance for their invaluable financial support, which made this research project, conducted under the banner of AFA in the project System Development Methods for a Digital Work Environment (STRIA, dnr 180250), possible. Additionally, our heartfelt thanks go out to all the participants in this study, whose generous contributions of time and insights were instrumental to the success of this research endeavour.

References

1. Cajander, Å., Grünloh, C.: Electronic health records are more than a work tool: conflicting needs of direct and indirect stakeholders. In: CHI 2019, May 4–9, 2019, Glasgow, Scotland. ACM, New York (2019). https://doi.org/10.1145/3290605.3300865.44
2. Daniels, M., Cajander, Å., Clear, T., McDermott, R.: Collaborative technologies in global engineering: new competencies and challenges. Int. J. Eng. Educ. **31**, 267–281 (2015)
3. Eshet, E., Bouwman, H.: Context of use: the final frontier in the practice of user-centered design? Interact. Comput. **29**, 368–390 (2017)
4. Lárusdóttir, M., Cajander, Å., Gulliksen, J.: The big picture of UX is missing in scrum projects. In: Law, E.L.-C., Abrahão, S., Vermeeren, A.P.O.S., and Hvannberg, E.T. (eds.) Proceedings of the 2nd International Workshop on the Interplay between user Experience Evaluation and Software Development, in Conjunction with the 7th Nordic Conference on Human-Computer Interaction, pp. 42–48. Audio Visual Services, University of Leicester, UK, Copenhagen, Denmark (2012)
5. Wang, R., Larusdottir, M., Cajander, Å.: Describing Digital Work Environment Through Contextual Personas. In: INTERACT 2021 (2021)
6. Cajander, Å., Larusdottir, M., Eriksson, E., Nauwerck, G.: Contextual personas as a method for understanding digital work environments. In: Nocera, J.A., Barricelli, B.R., Lopes, A., Campos, P., Clemmensen, T. (eds.) HWID 2015. IAICT, vol. 468, pp. 141–152. Springer, Cham (2015). https://doi.org/10.1007/978-3-319-27048-7_10
7. Cajander, Å., Lárusdóttir, M.K., Lind, T., Nauwerck, G.: Walking in the jungle with a machete: ICT leaders' perspectives on user-Centred systems design. Behav. Inform. Technol. **41**(6), 1230–1244 (2021). https://doi.org/10.1080/0144929X.2020.1864776

8. Brahma, M., Tripathi, S.S., Sahay, A.: Developing curriculum for industry 4.0: digital workplaces. High. Educ. Ski. Work-Based Learn. **11**, 144–163 (2021)
9. Hicks, M.: Why the urgency of digital transformation is hurting the digital workplace. Strateg. HR Rev. **18**, 34–35 (2019)
10. Cajander, Å., Sandblad, B., Stadin, M., Raviola, E.: Artificial intelligence, robotisation and the work environment. Swedish Agency for Work Environment Expertise
11. Golay, D., Salminen-Karlsson, M., Cajander, Å.: Negative emotions induced by work-related information technology use in hospital nursing. Comput. Inform. Nurs. **40**, 113–120 (2021)
12. Cajander, Å., Larusdottir, M., Hedström, G.: The effects of automation of a patient-centric service in primary care on the work engagement and exhaustion of nurses. Qual. User Exp. **5**, 1–13 (2020)
13. Karr-Wisniewski, P., Lu, Y.: When more is too much: operationalizing technology overload and exploring its impact on knowledge worker productivity. Comput. Hum. Behav. **26**, 1061–1072 (2010). https://doi.org/10.1016/j.chb.2010.03.008
14. Tarafdar, M., Tu, Q., Ragu-Nathan, T.S., Ragu-Nathan, B.S.: Crossing to the dark side: examining creators, outcomes, and inhibitors of technostress. Commun. ACM **54**, 113–120 (2011). https://doi.org/10.1145/1995376.1995403
15. Fonteyn, M.E., Kuipers, B., Grobe, S.J.: A description of think aloud method and protocol analysis. Qual. Health Res. **3**, 430–441 (1993). https://doi.org/10.1177/104973239300300403
16. Shravasti, R., Bhola, S.S.: Study on working environment and job satisfaction of employees in respect to service sector: An analysis. Rev. Res. **4** (2015)
17. Wright, B.E., Davis, B.S.: Job satisfaction in the public sector: the role of the work environment. Am. Rev. Public Adm. **33**, 70–90 (2003). https://doi.org/10.1177/0275074002250254
18. Veitch, J.A.: Workplace design contributions to mental health and well-being. Healthc. Pap. **11**, 38–46 (2011)
19. Davison, R., Ou, C.: Digital work in a pre-digital organizational culture (2014)
20. Dittes, S., Smolnik, S.: Towards a digital work environment: the influence of collaboration and networking on employee performance within an enterprise social media platform. J. Bus. Econ. **89**, 1215–1243 (2019)
21. Sandblad, B., Gulliksen, J., Lantz, A., Walldius, R., Åborg, C.: Digitaliseringen och arbetsmiljön. Studentlitteratur (2018)
22. Byström, K., Ruthven, I., Heinström, J.: Work and information: which workplace models still work in modern digital workplaces? In: 9th International Conference on Conceptions of Library and Information Science (CoLIS 9) (2016)
23. Meske, C., Junglas, I.: Investigating the elicitation of employees' support towards digital workplace transformation. Behav. Inf. Technol. **40**, 1120–1136 (2021). https://doi.org/10.1080/0144929X.2020.1742382
24. Wiggins, M.W., Auton, J., Bayl-Smith, P., Carrigan, A.: Optimising the future of technology in organisations: a human factors perspective. Aust. J. Manag. **45**, 449–467 (2020). https://doi.org/10.1177/0312896220918915
25. Williams, S.P., Schubert, P.: Designs for the digital workplace. Procedia Comput. Sci. **138**, 478–485 (2018)
26. Barber, L.K., Santuzzi, A.M.: Please respond ASAP: Workplace telepressure and employee recovery. J. Occup. Health Psychol. **20**, 172–189 (2015). https://doi.org/10.1037/a0038278
27. Diaz, I., Chiaburu, D.S., Zimmerman, R.D., Boswell, W.R.: Communication technology: pros and cons of constant connection to work. J. Vocat. Behav. **80**, 500–508 (2012). https://doi.org/10.1016/j.jvb.2011.08.007
28. Barley, S.R., Meyerson, D.E., Grodal, S.: E-mail as a source and symbol of stress. Organ. Sci. **22**, 887–906 (2011). https://doi.org/10.1287/orsc.1100.0573

29. Grandhi, S.A., Jones, Q., Hiltz, S.R.: Technology overload: is there a technological panacea? In: AMCIS 2005 Proc. 493 (2005)
30. Salanova, M., Llorens, S., Ventura, M.: Technostress: the dark side of technologies. In: Korunka, C., Hoonakker, P. (eds.) The Impact of ICT on Quality of Working Life, pp. 87–103. Springer Netherlands, Dordrecht (2014). https://doi.org/10.1007/978-94-017-8854-0_6
31. Vehko, T., et al.: Experienced time pressure and stress: electronic health records usability and information technology competence play a role. BMC Med. Inform. Decis. Mak. **19**, 1–9 (2019)
32. Dourish, P.: What we talk about when we talk about context. Pers. Ubiquitous Comput. **8**, 19–30 (2004)
33. Heuwing, B., Mandl, T., Womser-Hacker, C.: Contextual design methods for information interaction in the workplace. J. Libr. Inf. Sci. **42** (2016)
34. Charters, E.: The use of think-aloud methods in qualitative research an introduction to think-aloud methods. Brock Educ. J. **12** (2003)
35. Cowan, J.: The potential of cognitive think-aloud protocols for educational action-research. Act. Learn. High. Educ. **20**, 219–232 (2019). https://doi.org/10.1177/1469787417735614
36. Sela, H.K.U., Ab, P., Pau, I.: A comparison of concurrent and retrospective verbal protocol analysis. Am. J. Psychol. **113**, 387–404 (2000)
37. Fan, M., Lin, J., Chung, C., Truong, K.N.: Concurrent think-aloud verbalizations and usability problems. ACM Trans. Comput.-Hum. Interact. **26**(5), 1–35 (2019). https://doi.org/10.1145/3325281
38. Eccles, D.W., Arsal, G.: The think aloud method: what is it and how do I use it? Qual. Res. Sport Exerc. Health. **9**, 514–531 (2017). https://doi.org/10.1080/2159676X.2017.1331501
39. Abowd, G.D., Dey, A.K., Brown, P.J., Davies, N., Smith, M., Steggles, P.: Towards a better understanding of context and context-awareness. In: Gellersen, H.-W. (ed.) Handheld and Ubiquitous Computing, pp. 304–307. Springer Berlin Heidelberg, Berlin, Heidelberg (1999). https://doi.org/10.1007/3-540-48157-5_29
40. Alhadreti, O.: Comparing two methods of usability testing in saudi arabia: concurrent think-aloud vs co-discovery. Int. J. Hum.-Comput. Interact. **37**, 118–130 (2021). https://doi.org/10.1080/10447318.2020.1809152
41. Perski, O., Blandford, A., Ubhi, H.K., West, R., Michie, S.: Smokers' and drinkers' choice of smartphone applications and expectations of engagement: a think aloud and interview study. BMC Med. Inform. Decis. Mak. **17**, 25 (2017). https://doi.org/10.1186/s12911-017-0422-8
42. Alhadreti, O., Elbabour, F., Mayhew, P.: Eye tracking in retrospective think-aloud usability testing: Is there added value? J. Usability Stud. **12**, 95–110 (2017)
43. Gulliksen, J.: Digital work environment rounds – systematic inspections of usability supported by the legislation. In: Ardito, C., et al. (eds.) Human-Computer Interaction – INTERACT 2021: 18th IFIP TC 13 International Conference, Bari, Italy, August 30 – September 3, 2021, Proceedings, Part II, pp. 197–218. Springer International Publishing, Cham (2021). https://doi.org/10.1007/978-3-030-85616-8_13
44. Jia, Y., Larusdottir, M.K., Cajander, Å.: The usage of usability techniques in scrum projects. In: Winckler, M., Forbrig, P., Bernhaupt, R. (eds.) Human-Centered Software Engineering, pp. 331–341. Springer Berlin Heidelberg, Berlin, Heidelberg (2012). https://doi.org/10.1007/978-3-642-34347-6_25
45. Cajander, Å., Larusdottir, M., Geiser, J.L.: UX professionals' learning and usage of UX methods in agile. Inf. Softw. Technol. **151**, 107005 (2022)
46. Lárusdóttir, M., Wang, R., Cajander, Å.: Contextual personas – a method for capturing the digital work environment of users. In: Ardito, C., et al. (eds.) Sense, Feel, Design: INTERACT 2021 IFIP TC 13 Workshops, Bari, Italy, August 30 – September 3, 2021, Revised Selected Papers, pp. 98–112. Springer International Publishing, Cham (2022). https://doi.org/10.1007/978-3-030-98388-8_10

47. Kujala, S.: User involvement: a review of the benefits and challenges. Behav. Inf. Technol. **22**, 1–16 (2003). https://doi.org/10.1080/01449290301782
48. Braun, V., Clarke, V.: Using thematic analysis in psychology. Qual. Res. Psychol. **3**(2), 77–101 (2006)

On Using the Task Models for Refinement and Validation of Requirements Generated Through Co-creation

Bilal Naqvi[1]([⊠]) [iD], Célia Martinie[2] [iD], Stepan Bakhaev[1] [iD], and Kari Smolander[1] [iD]

[1] Software Engineering, LENS, LUT University, 53850 Lappeenranta, Finland
syed.naqvi@lut.fi
[2] ICS-IRIT, Université Toulouse III Paul Sabatier, Toulouse, France

Abstract. Among the several other approaches for gathering software requirements, co-creation is often used. The co-creation approach based on elements of participatory research is aimed at involving the end users during the requirements elicitation process. While this approach has many merits, certain limitations need to be addressed. Two limitations include (i) limitations induced due to the subjective judgment of requirements analysts during the analysis and translation of user statements, goals, and desires (gathered during co-creation) into software requirements, and (ii) limitations induced due to varying abilities of different users to conceptualize the systems being developed during early phases of the system development lifecycle, specifically during the co-creation workshops conducted for requirements gathering. To address these limitations the paper proposes a three-step task model-based approach for validation and refinement of requirements generated through co-creation. To instantiate the approach, the paper also presents an illustrative case study featuring the development of a novel electronic identity (e-ID) scheme.

Keywords: co-creation · requirements · task models · usability · usable security · validation

1 Introduction

Amid the digital transformation which has arguably revolutionized every sector from finance to health and from education to governance, several challenges have also emerged that need to be addressed. Among these challenges are cyber security threats, several of these cyber security threats can be attributed to human mistakes and negligence. Consequently, there has been a focus on the development of more robust yet usable security technologies and mechanisms that can withstand threats from both internal and external attackers while ensuring user experience. One such technology that enables ease of use (in terms of the less cognitive burden on the user's mind) while ensuring security is a biometric-based electronic identity (e-ID) scheme for authentication.

© IFIP International Federation for Information Processing 2024
Published by Springer Nature Switzerland AG 2024
A. Bramwell-Dicks et al. (Eds.): INTERACT 2023 Workshops, LNCS 14535, pp. 47–58, 2024.
https://doi.org/10.1007/978-3-031-61688-4_5

Biometrics-based e-ID authentication is centered around authenticating an individual based on their anatomical, physiological, and behavioral characteristics [2]. It includes a variety of methods, such as fingerprint scans, finger, hand geometry, iris, or retina scans, etc. As said earlier, besides the well-documented security benefits, biometric-based e-ID schemes are based on the premise of reducing the cognitive burden on the user.

Furthermore, there has been a debate on involving the end-users during the system development lifecycle to ensure a human-centered focus in the development of novel technologies. Co-creation approach attempts to actively involve the people who are being served by a design, in the process of problem-solving [17]. While users may not be able to communicate precisely or technically some requirement or other, they can explain their goals and how they approach their tasks [10]. Therefore, users should not be passive informants as they have different values in relation to a system and its use [11]. Involving the end-users to participate in a design process by means of co-creation practices encourages the elicitation of requirements from a human-centered perspective. However, with the benefits of this approach, there might be additional challenges, such as during the translation of users' goals into software requirements, it is critical to accurately translate the users' goals and statements into software requirements. Moreover, an additional challenge is that the users at the early stages of the software development lifecycle might not be able to conceptualize the system and accurately contribute their desires for the system being built. It is therefore vital to validate these requirements before development.

This paper considers a primary research question i.e., *'how to validate and refine the user requirements gathered by co-creation before development?'*. In line with the research question and to overcome the challenges discussed earlier, the paper proposes a three-step task models-based approach to validate the requirements gathered by co-creation approaches. To instantiate the approach, we present a case study featuring the development of a novel biometric-based e-ID scheme across six public administrations in five European countries. The limitations in the requirements gathered by co-creation were identified using the proposed approach and the requirements were refined.

Structure of the Paper.   Sect. 2 presents the co-creative approach for requirements elicitation, Sect. 3 presents the task model-based approach for validation of the requirements generated from co-creation, Sect. 4 presents the validation case study, Sect. 5 presents the related work, Sect. 6 presents the discussion, and Sect. 7 concludes the paper.

2   Co-creative Approach for Requirements Elicitation

This section presents the co-creation approach adopted for the identification of requirements for the development of an e-ID scheme. The same approach was executed across six public administrations in five European countries. During the co-creation process, workshops at each public administration were conducted to identify the requirements. A common (five-step) template was created for all workshops. The workshops were executed by each public administration locally in both physical and online settings. The participants (prospective users of the technology) were asked to give their consent individually for participation in the workshop. The total number of attendees in each workshop was between 12 and 20 persons. During each workshop, data in the form of audio recordings, screen captures, and other visual recordings as well as the minutes taken during the workshop sessions were recorded and later analysed for identification of the software requirements. The data was garnered in the local languages of the respective workshop venue; however, it was translated into English before being analysed and incorporated into the findings. Each workshop was organized in 5 steps.

- **Step 1 – Introducing the workshop goals and objectives:** At the beginning of each workshop session, participants were introduced to the key objectives and goals. The workshop facilitators communicated these objectives framed in a "What? How? Why?" outline, using short and simplified statements.
- **Step 2 – The positives:** This step involved exploring the positive user expectations from the e-ID technology. This was mainly a warm-up exercise designed to engage the participants and acclimate them to the workshop format.
- **Step 3 – The negatives:** This step involved exploring the user's pain points. It was completed in three parts, i.e., activities aimed at defining and prioritizing the potential problems. Accordingly, in the first part, participants were tasked to write down their concerns and issues. These negative anticipations reflected the potential drawbacks in the technology design from a human-centred perspective. Next, the participants were asked to vote for the concerns they deemed most important using red voting dots. Each of the participants was given three of those dots to vote for any idea placing one, two, or all three dots on one or more sticky notes with a negative statement. Finally, the participants were asked to engage in discussion about the top-voted concerns and explain their priorities.
- **Step 4 – "How might we...?":** This step was done in two rounds where at least five top-voted problems from Step 3 served as inputs. The participant's task was framed to overcome the concerns (from the third step), devise solutions, and think of the benefits they can get from them. For this task, the workshop participants are randomly assigned to five groups. This activity was designed to represent the World Café method.
- **Step 5 – Categories:** The final step of the workshop was essentially an open discussion about the benefits and solutions that the participants had voted for in the previous step. All participants could overview the statements selected in the priorities to find similar ideas and create the categories. These categories were labelled based on their perceptions and feelings evoked with the solution in mind.

After the workshops, the user statements grouped by the context were assigned with unique identifiers that reflected the case study origin, the nature of the requirement (i.e., 01 – user expectation, 02 – user pain point, 03 – user need), and a serial number. Furthermore, a cross-case analysis was performed to identify the similarities and differences across the six different cases. Finally, the resembling features of the user needs and concerns identified in the cross-case analysis allowed for transforming the user statements into formal requirements. For exemplary purposes, a subset of the requirements gathered following the process just discussed are presented in Table 1.

Table 1. List of requirements gathered using the co-creation approach

Requirement statement
1. The system shall be interoperable with the legacy (national) e-ID schemes to ensure user uptake
2. The system shall inform users about the processing of their data
3. The system should provide simple and well-guided user actions when collecting image samples for face recognition
4. The system shall provide users with informed consent in a legal language and accessible with dedicated icons
5. The system shall allow users to control their data in a self-sovereign manner
6. The system shall reduce the cognitive burden (remembering many user accounts and passwords) for users
7. The system shall prevent unauthorized access and processing of user data
8. The system shall issue a challenge to verify that the user who is trying to authenticate is the owner of the VC (e.g., OTP via SMS or email)

3 Task Model-Based Approach for the Refinement and Validation of Requirements

Before discussing the approach, it is vital to discuss the rationale behind it. The software requirements generated from co-creation approaches (such as the one just discussed) can be prone to (i) limitations induced due to by the subjective judgment of requirements analysts during the analysis and translation of user statements, goals, and desires (gathered during co-creation) into software requirements, and (ii) limitations induced due to varying abilities of different users to conceptualize the systems being developed during early phases of the system development lifecycle (specifically during the co-creation workshops conducted for requirements gathering). Therefore, to overcome these limitations, we propose a three-step approach for the validation of software requirements gathered by co-creation (see Fig. 1).

- The *first step* involves modelling the user tasks according to each requirement. The task models depicting the users' tasks are generated and analysed.
- The *second step* involves the assessment of the task models (generated in the first step) and identifying possible limitations. If the task model depicts that the elements of usability have been catered to, the requirements are finalized for development. However, if there are limitations identified, the proposal for refinements is created and the requirements are refined to overcome these limitations.
- The *third step* involves modelling user tasks according to the refined requirements. The task models thus specified are analysed. If the task model depicts that the elements of usability have been catered to, the refined requirements are subjected to validation by the participants of the co-creation workshop and finalized for development. However, if there are limitations identified, another refinement iteration (starting from the second step) is performed.

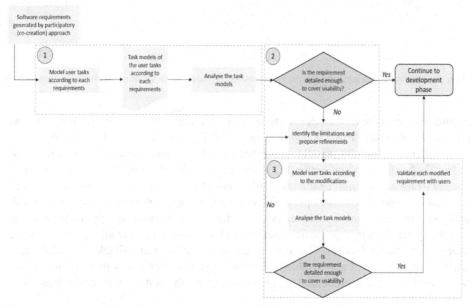

Fig. 1. Three-step task model-based approach for the validation and refinement of requirements gathered from co-creation

The three-step approach just discussed was instantiated by considering the requirements gathered during the case study considered in this paper, the details of which are presented in the following Section.

4 Instantiation of the Approach: An Illustrative Case Study

In this section, we instantiate the proposed approach by generating the task models for two randomly selected requirements from Table 1. The selected requirements are as follows:

- **Requirement 3:** The system should provide simple and well-guided user actions when collecting image samples for face recognition.
- **Requirement 8:** The system shall issue a challenge to verify that the user who is trying to authenticate is the owner of the VC (e.g., OTP via SMS or email).

Both these requirements were subjected to the three-step approach presented earlier and discussed in the relevant subsections.

4.1 Model User Tasks According to Requirements

We selected the HAMSTERS notation [13], it is tool-supported and embeds the common ground elements required to model user tasks [12]. It enables the modelling of refined user task types, as well as of objects required to perform the tasks. In line with the approach, the first step involved modelling the user tasks according to each requirement.

52   B. Naqvi et al.

Provide image samples

Fig. 2. Task model describing the user actions to provide image samples (from requirement 3)

Figure 2 presents the task model produced using requirement 3. As shown in the Figure, it contains one task, *"Provide image sample"*, which is the main goal for the user.

Furthermore, the task model for requirement 8 was also specified, which is presented in Fig. 3. As shown in the figure, the main user goal involved in this requirement is to *"undergo the verification of the verifiable credential"* and is composed of a sequence (sequence temporal ordering operator under the main goal) of an interactive output task and a subtree below the disable temporal operator. The interactive input tasks describe that the system will inform the user that the user has to undergo a challenge to verify the user's verifiable credentials. The subtree describes that the user will take up a challenge, which will be stopped and disabled when the system either issues that the user is the owner of the verifiable credential or not. In both cases, the system informs the user about the issue.

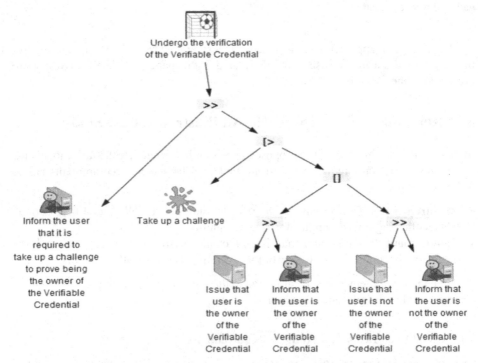

Fig. 3. Task model describing the user actions to undergo the verification of verifiable credentials (from requirement 8)

4.2 Identify the Limitations and Propose Refinements

In line with the second step, the limitations of both requirements were identified. As depicted in the task model specified for requirement 3 (see Fig. 2), the requirement description contains information only about the main user goal. However, it does not provide information about the possible relevant tasks for reaching the goal (i.e., to provide image samples), which may have a huge impact on usability. The requirement is thus not detailed enough to take into account elements of usability. Several alternatives can be proposed for supporting the users to provide image samples. They can use a local repository, a live camera, or a cloud repository. Considering these aspects, the requirement was modified. Table 2 presents a comparison of requirements before and after being subjected to the approach.

Table 2. Comparison of requirements before and after being subjected to the approach

Requirement 3 (before refinement)	Requirement 3 (after refinement)
The system should provide simple and well-guided user actions when collecting image samples for face recognition	The system should provide several simple ways and well-guided user actions when collecting image samples for face recognition and in particular, should propose to upload image samples from a local repository, from a live camera, or from a cloud repository. The system should inform the user when enough valid samples have been provided

Furthermore, the same procedure was performed for requirement 8. From the task model (see Fig. 3), it was identified that the requirement description contains partial information about the user tasks. The system shall issue a challenge to the user but there is no information about the possible relevant tasks to perform the challenge. The tasks may be different depending on the type of challenge and may thus impact usability. This requirement is also not detailed enough to take into account usability. Several alternatives can be proposed for supporting the users to take up a challenge for the verification of the verifiable credentials. The user can enter a one-time password (OTP) received by email or SMS, but the user can also answer a set of personal questions, or scan fingerprints. While considering these aspects, the requirement was modified and presented in Table 3.

4.3 Model User Tasks According to the Refined Requirements

Finally, in line with the third step, task models for the refined requirements were specified. The Fig. 4 presents the task model specified for the refined requirement 3. When compared to the task model of the initial version of the requirements (in Fig. 2), the main goal has been refined. The user can provide image samples iteratively (abstract iterative task "Provide an image sample"), using different sources of images, until (temporal ordering operator "DISABLE") the system issues that the samples are enough and valid.

54   B. Naqvi et al.

Table 3. Comparison of requirements before and after being subjected to the approach

Requirement 8 (before refinement)	Requirement 8 (after refinement)
The system shall issue a challenge to verify that the user who is trying to authenticate is the owner of the VC (e.g., OTP via SMS or email)	The system shall issue a challenge to verify that the user who is trying to authenticate is the owner of the VC. The challenge can be of the following types: to enter an OTP received via SMS or email, to answer a set of personal questions, or to scan fingerprints

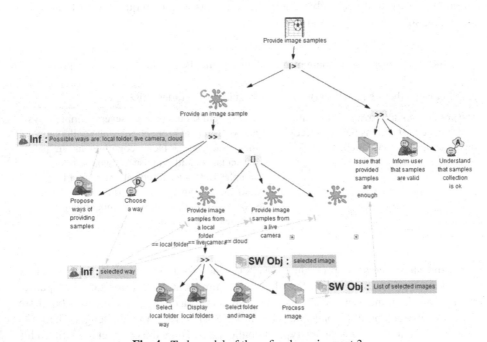

Fig. 4. Task model of the refined requirement 3

Similarly, Fig. 5 presents the task model produced using the modified requirement 8. Compared to the task model of the initial version of the requirements (in Fig. 3), the abstract goal "Take up a challenge" has been refined. The user can either receive an OTP, answer a set of personal questions, or scan fingerprints.

The refined requirements along with their associated task models now contain information about the tasks to be performed by the user and their temporal ordering. They can be used to analyze the effectiveness dimension of usability, as well as to support the discussion with the users. As the tasks get more concrete, the users can indicate whether they match their needs or not. Such feedback may lead to refining the requirements again and going again through the loop composed of steps 2 & 3.

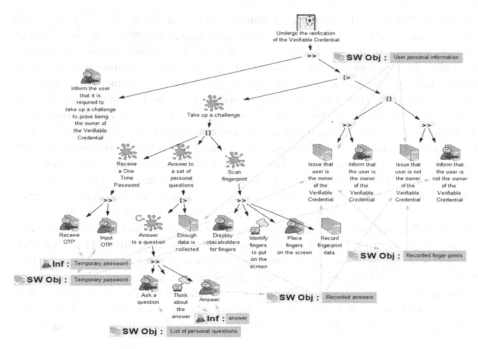

Fig. 5. Task model of the refined requirement 8

5 Related Work

Task models enable the identification and description of the required functions for interactive systems [16]. Furthermore, task models enable [2]: to create an understanding of the user requirements, illustrate and validate them, as well as to communicate these requirements with the different stakeholders. The existing literature recommends the usage of task models but does not provide explicit methods or processes for requirements engineering. Garrido et al. [5] proposed task diagrams (in the COMO-UML format) to specify collaboration requirements. The produced models are then used in a model-driven approach to contribute to the automatic generation of a groupware application that matches collaborative user tasks. The modeling technique is closer to workflows and different from the hierarchical point of view available in task models. It thus only captures the computer-supported collaborative tasks. Task models have also been used to automatically generate prototypes [4, 15] that users can interact with. The provided feedback then helps to elicit the requirements. This type of approach does not directly use task models to communicate with the stakeholders and is constrained by the software platform used to generate prototypes. It frames the point of view of the user on the final user interface and may not apply when designing user interactions with new technologies.

Alternative solutions to task models are storyboards [7], business process models [18], probing techniques [6], and the use of semi-formal scenarios, including Behaviour Driven Development (BDD) [1]. These techniques are complementary to the use of task models. Storyboards [7] aim to support multidisciplinary teams in specifying functional and non-functional requirements. Their main advantage is that they are understandable by members having different backgrounds. This technique mainly focuses on building scenarios. Scenarios are complementary to task models as they contain specific sequences of user tasks, whereas task models provide a systematic and abstract view of all the possible user tasks [12]. Business process models [18] aim to describe the possible workflows between users and interactive systems (i.e. flow of events or scenarios). This technique removes the ambiguities of textual descriptions that are scenarios because it is based on a specified notation. It is also complementary to the use of task models because task models provide a systematic and abstract view of all the possible temporal ordering of user tasks [12] whereas workflows describe sets of sequences. Probing techniques [6] aim to understand how users may engage with a novel device, by observing them interact with a prototype, and by discussing with them their thoughts when interacting with the prototype. This technique is also complementary to the use of task models, which can be used to record the tasks the users engaged with the prototype. BDD [1] is a software development approach that uses executable user stories to capture requirements. This technique removes the ambiguities of textual descriptions that are scenarios because it is based on a specified language. It is also complementary to the use of task models because task models provide a systematic and abstract view of all the possible temporal ordering of user tasks [12] whereas executable user stories describe sets of sequences.

6 Discussion

Task models are an accurate mean to represent the outcomes of task analysis and they consist of a graphical representation of the work the users perform with an interactive application or system. Task models enable ensuring the effectiveness of an interactive system, i.e., to guarantee that users can perform their work and reach their goals. Complete and unambiguous description of the users' tasks is a cornerstone of user-centred design approaches as they provide a unique way of describing precisely and entirely users' actions that have to be performed for them to reach their goals [13].

the potential benefits. Task identification and description are part of the UCD process. Standard ISO 9241-210 on "Human-centred design for interactive systems" [8] indicates that the specification of the context of use requires to identification of user goals, user tasks, and sub-tasks, but also that the production of design solutions requires allocating tasks and sub-tasks to the user and to the system. Moreover, it indicates that the evaluation of the design requires verifying the accuracy and completeness with which the user achieved their tasks. This is why almost all UCD techniques require identifying and describing user tasks. Thus, task models have been proven useful for making a predictive assessment of user performance when interacting with the system [9], and in particular for assessing task complexity and workload (motor, cognitive, perceptive) [14]. Task models have also been proven to increase the coverage of usability issues when performing the heuristic evaluation of the usability of interactive applications [3].

In this paper, we presented how task models can be used by designers and developers for the refinement and validation of requirements. The next step of the work is to investigate if the task models can be used as support for discussions with the end users during the co-creation phases. For that purpose, we need to investigate to what extent the task modelling notation is usable for end users, and if a short tutorial or training could help to use them during co-creation sessions. Then, we also need to investigate alternative representations based on task models or produced from task models.

7 Conclusion

Task models have been proven to be useful for supporting the user-centred design of interactive systems in many ways, from the identification of the required system function-alities to the preparation of usability evaluations. This paper argues for the need for a systematic approach to task models-based refinement and validation of user requirements. Moreover, the paper proposed a three-step approach that integrates with user-centred design practices and in particular with participatory design sessions. The results from the application of the approach to the case study discussed in the paper enabled refinements to the requirements generated using the participatory mechanism. The next steps are to apply several user feedback loops of the process to determine the user-perceived benefits of this approach.

Acknowledgment. This work is supported by the European Union's Horizon 2020 research and innovation program under grant agreement No 101004459, project IMPULSE (Identity Management in Public Services).

References

1. Alhaj, M., Arbez, G., Peyton, L.: Using behaviour-driven development with hardware-software co-design for autonomous load management. In: 2017 8th International Conference on Information and Communication Systems. ICICS, IEEE, pp. 46–51 (2017)
2. Balbo, S., Ozkan, N., Paris, C.: Choosing the right task-modeling notation: a taxonomy. In: Diaper, D., Stanton, N.A. (eds.) The Handbook of Task Analysis for Human-Computer Interaction, pp. 445–466 (2004)
3. Cockton, G., Woolrych, A.: Understanding inspection methods: lessons from an assessment of heuristic evaluation, pp. 171–192. People and Computers, Springer (2001)
4. Fischer, H., Rose, M., Yigitbas, E.: Towards a task driven approach enabling continuous user requirements engineering. In: 2nd Workshop on Continuous Requirements Engineering (CRE) (REFSQ-JP 2016), Gothenburg, Sweden, March 14, 2016.CEUR-WS.org, vol. 1564 (2016)
5. Garrido, J.L., Noguera, M., González, M., Hurtado, M.V., Rodríguez, M.L.: Definition and use of Computation Independent Models in an MDA-based groupware development process. Sci. Comput. Program. **66**(1), 25–43 (2007)
6. Gough, P., et al.: Co-designing a technology probe with experienced designers. In: Proceedings of the 33rd Australian Conference on Human-Computer Interaction (OzCHI'21). Association for Computing Machinery, New York, NY, USA, pp. 1–13 (2022). https://doi.org/10.1145/3520495.3520513
7. Haesen, M., Luyten, K., Coninx, K.: Get your requirements straight: storyboarding revisited. In: Gross, T., et al. (eds.) Human-Computer Interaction – INTERACT 2009, pp. 546–549. Springer Berlin Heidelberg, Berlin, Heidelberg (2009). https://doi.org/10.1007/978-3-642-03658-3_59

8. ISO 9241–210:2019 (en), Ergonomics of human-system interaction — Part 210: Human-centred design for interactive systems, International Standard Organization (2019)

9. John, B., Kieras, D.E.: The GOMS family of user interface analysis techniques: comparison and contrast. ACM Trans. Comput.-Hum. Interact. **3**(4), 320–351 (1996)

10. Kujala, S.: User involvement: a review of the benefits and challenges. Behav. Inform. Technol. **22**(1), 1–16 (2003). https://doi.org/10.1080/01449290301782

11. Kujala, S.: Effective user involvement in product development by improving the analysis of user needs. Behav. Inform. Technol. **27**(6), 457–473 (2008). https://doi.org/10.1080/014492 90601111051

12. Martinie, C., Palanque, P., Barboni, E.: Principles of task analysis and modeling: understanding activity, modeling tasks, and analyzing models. In: Handbook of Human Computer Interaction. Springer, Cham (2022). https://doi.org/10.1007/978-3-319-27648-9_57-1

13. Martinie, C., Palanque, P., Bouzekri, E., Cockburn, A., Canny, A., Barboni, E.: Analysing and demonstrating tool-supported customizable task notations. Proc. ACM Hum.-Comput. Interact. **3**(EICS), 1–26 (2019). https://doi.org/10.1145/3331154

14. O'Donnell, R. D., Eggemeier, F. T. Workload Assessment Methodology; In Handbook of Perception and Human Performance (Vol. II Cognitive Processes and Performance, pp. 42–41 - 42–49). Wiley and Sons, 1986

15. Reichart, D., Forbrig, P., Dittmar, A.: Task models as basis for requirements engineering and software execution. In: Proceedings of the 3rd annual conference on Task models and diagrams (TAMODIA'04), pp. 51–58. ACM, New York, NY, USA (2004)

16. Paternò, F. Task models in interactive software systems. In: Handbook of Software Engineering and Knowledge Engineering, vol. 1, pp. 1–19. World Scientific (2002)

17. Sanders, L.: An evolving map of design practice and design research. Interactions **15**(6), 13–17 (2008). https://doi.org/10.1145/1409040.1409043

18. Sindhgatta, R., Thonse, S.: Functional and non-functional requirements specification for enterprise applications. In: Bomarius, F., Komi-Sirviö, S. (eds.) Product Focused Software Process Improvement, pp. 189–201. Springer Berlin Heidelberg, Berlin, Heidelberg (2005). https://doi.org/10.1007/11497455_16

Towards User Profile Meta-Ontology

Ankica Barišić[(✉)] [iD] and Marco Winckler [iD]

Université Côte d'Azur, CNRS, Inria, I3S, Nice, France
{Ankica.Barisic,Marco.Winckler}@univ-cotedazur.fr

Abstract. With the rapid advancement of digital transformation, a large amount of data related to human activities is being gathered. Whilst knowing and understanding users is an essential activity for designing and evaluating interactive systems, describing users is a daunting task. This paper investigates the challenges for describing users' profile and how using Ontology for creating and representing user profiles might be a suitable solution for ensuring interoperability and facilitating data federation. This paper proposes a solution in the form of a meta-ontology for user profiling and explores its creation, use, and effective federation. As we shall see, Ontology for describing users' profile is not a new idea but it required an update to cope with the advent of new practices for collecting users' data, the variety of attributes used nowadays to describe users, and the huge amount ammassed informaiton about user profiles.

Keywords: User profiling · Persona · Ontology · Modeling

1 Introduction

The ongoing global technological transformation has revolutionised our interactions with software and systems. As the user base becomes increasingly diverse, it is crucial to enhance development support for creating interactive systems that adapt to users' varied characteristics and needs. To achieve this, a deep understanding of user mindset, interaction objectives, preferences and awareness is crucial.

Developers require approaches that enable them to empathise with and address the challenges faced by different end users, incorporating software solutions that cater to a wide range of human characteristics. Design support is also necessary, equipping developers with advanced techniques and tools to effectively address the complexities posed by diverse end users [21].

User-centred design approaches [17], considering factors like knowledge expertise and performance monitoring, have proven essential in understanding end users' profiles. A *user profile* is the main component needed for the evaluation, personalisation and adaptation of interactive systems. It has played an active role in various domains such as healthcare sectors, banking sectors, social media, e-commerce, security, access control, and social networking [18]. Moreover, establishing a strong link between human characteristics and the application domain provides valuable insights into user behaviour and preferences [13].

© IFIP International Federation for Information Processing 2024
Published by Springer Nature Switzerland AG 2024
A. Bramwell-Dicks et al. (Eds.): INTERACT 2023 Workshops, LNCS 14535, pp. 59–79, 2024.
https://doi.org/10.1007/978-3-031-61688-4_6

With the rise of digital transformation, an abundance of data on human activities, and emotional, mental and physical states can be collected. This data, captured through mobile and wearable devices or biosensor cameras, holds immense potential. However, to harness its power, data sharing, reuse, and understanding patterns of unwanted human states are crucial. This data can be used to train AI models, adapt systems to individuals' needs, and create personalised experiences.

To effectively leverage this data and assist developers in modelling, reusing, and sharing user profiles, there is a pressing need for a general ontology for creating user profiles [18,26]. Such an ontology offers a standardised framework for creating and representing user profiles, ensuring interoperability and facilitating data federation. Model-driven engineering is a promising approach to enable developers to design user profiles, generate software models, reuse existing user data, and receive guidance in modelling profiles from scratch.

A standardised user profile is expected to enable the implementation of interoperable adaptive systems sharing modelling information. Ontology-based user profiling is particularly vital for systems reasoning across multiple profiles, so-called social adaptive systems, or benefiting from complex inference on multiple ontologies representing different knowledge [34].

This paper presents the User Profile Meta Ontology (UPMO) as a proposed solution. In Sect. 2, we examine various techniques for acquiring user profiles. In Sect. 3, we present an overview of the existing ontologies in the field of user profile creation. Section 4 explores the effective design, utilization, and federation of UPMO. Additionally, in Sect. 5, we analyze the User Dimension, which serves as a guiding factor for the implementation of UPMO. Finally, in Sect. 6, we conclude the paper and outline our ideas for future research directions.

2   Techniques for Obtaining User Profiles

The concept of a *User profile* refers to the representation of an individual user, real or fictional, or a group of users. This profile is essential for understanding and catering to individual user needs in various applications [18]. User profiles are instantiated as a *User model*, a data structure to capture specific characteristics about an user, which serves as software component/artefact. These models can be static or dynamic, with static models representing unchanging user data and dynamic models evolving based on user interactions and interests.

To meet the demands of human-centered socio-technical systems, *highly adaptive user models*, representing one paticular user, are required. These models focus on personalized solutions allowing high adaptability of the system, rather than relying solely on demographic data, like stereotype based models [34]. Gathering extensive information is crucial for highly adaptive models to reach their full potential.

Thematic analysis and content analysis are common techniques used to extract valuable insights for creating user profiles and models. The research methods to gather relevant information about the user are devided to qualitative and quantitative. *Qualitative* methods involve understanding and interpreting subjective experiences, behaviors, and perceptions of individuals or groups. These methods focus on gathering non-numerical data through techniques such as interviews, observations, focus groups, case studies, and user storytelling. They provide detailed insights into the meanings, contexts, and interpretations of the target user. *Quantitative* research methods, such as surveys, experiments, statistical analysis, machine learning, and data mining, offer ways to analyze large datasets, identify patterns, and make predictions. Combining qualitative and quantitative methods provides a comprehensive understanding of users.

We highlight three common approaches to obtaining user profiles and models: user profiling, persona development, and role-based approach. The *role-based approach* creates user profiles based on the specific roles and tasks of users when interacting with a system. This approach focuses on understanding task sequences, interactions, and user roles in accomplishing those tasks. *User profiling* aims to create detailed representations of real users or user groups, capturing individual characteristics based on actual user data. *Persona development*, on the other hand, involves creating fictional characters that represent target user archetypes, guiding design decisions and representing user groups.

Role-based Approach: In the role-based approach, user profiles are created based on the roles and tasks that users perform within the system, regardless their individuals differences. This approach focuses on capturing the user's responsibilities, goals, and behaviors related to particular tasks or activities. The process typically begins by identifying the key tasks or activities that users engage in during their interactions with the system. To gain insights into the underlying cognitive mechanisms involved, cognitive task analysis methods are often employed [35]. These methods analyze and capture the cognitive aspects of tasks, such as problem-solving, decision-making, and information processing. Understanding how individuals think, reason, and make decisions during task execution can be leveraged to inform the design of various interventions aimed at enhancing task performance and supporting cognitive workload. Once the tasks are identified, the associated roles are defined. A uniform task meta-model is developed to facilitate the transformation of individual task models into their standardized counterparts while minimizing the loss of information [27].

Persona Development: Personas are fictitious, sterotyped representations of target users that resemble real people while telling a meaningful story describing their behaviour and needs. They provide shared mental models, facilitate communication among team members, and help empathize with end-users [30]. Personas are useful for segmenting diverse online audiences and integrating human aspects into the development process. They are commonly used in requirements engineering, often represented as text-based descriptions obtained through qualitative approaches like focus groups and workshops [24]. Personas enhance stakeholder satisfaction, prioritize human-centric design, support developers, and are often combined with scenarios to depict user behaviour. Salminen et al. [31] investigated the application of personas in different domains, highlighting their predominant usage in software development (40% of cases) and other fields such as healthcare, higher education, marketing, and robotics. Personas were found to be valuable in organizing user information, and adapting to both short-term tasks and long-term goals. They also proved useful in expert verification during testing, usability testing, and guiding semi-structured interviews. In a separate study [30], the authors focused on quantitative persona creation, emphasizing the potential of algorithmic methods to generate accurate and up-to-date personas from numerical and textual data. They noted the absence of a unified metric for evaluating persona quality but highlighted clustering as the most commonly employed technique.

User Profiling: User profiling helps organizations better understand their users, anticipate their needs, and make informed decisions during product design and personalization [19]. It focus on differences among individuals in population. The process involves data collection, analysis, and interpretation. Recent studies have focused on authorship attribution, social annotation profile modeling, data acquisition, feature extraction, modeling techniques, and performance metrics. These studies highlight the need for user profiling approaches that support general-purpose user profiles, are language-independent, have ontological representation, and address dynamic, distributed, and secure user profiles with predictive and temporal features [18].

3   Toward Ontology for Creating User Profile

User profiles encompass a wide range of user information, from demographics to personal preferences, and are essential for achieving user-centred design and personalization. However, they also raise concerns about data privacy, ethical considerations, and algorithmic bias. Furthermore, user profiles have economic implications, enabling targeted advertising but also posing risks of data exploitation for financial gain. Responsible and ethical use of user profiles is essential. This includes providing user empowerment and control over their data, continuous adaptation and feedback mechanisms, and addressing issues related to cross-platform and cross-device compatibility. While user profiles offer great potential for enhancing user experiences, their use requires a thoughtful approach that respects individuality and privacy while mitigating the risks associated with data collection and utilization.

To facilitate the exchange and sharing of user profiles, it is imperative to establish standardized domain representations and common vocabularies. Although numerous user-adaptive systems rely on ontologies for semantic representation and knowledge acquisition, these ontologies frequently exhibit a pronounced tethering to particular domains, impeding their reusability. Furthermore, conventional taxonomies in the realm of software engineering often exhibit limitations in adequately encompassing human values, needs, and characteristics. This underscores the necessity for ontological structures capable of describing universal user profiles, disentangled from domain-specific constraints [21].

This section analyse in detail the existing ontologies dedicated to user profiles, offering an exploration of both general and domain-specific user attributes through a comparative alignment with these pre-existing ontological frameworks.

In order to gain a comprehensive understanding of the contemporary landscape concerning methodologies for constructing user profiles and to procure extant ontological frameworks, a systematic review of the existing scholarly literature pertaining to this subject matter was undertaken. The review was conducted through the utilization of the Google Scholar platform, with a deliberate selection of keywords, namely: "User Profile, User Profiling, User Group, User Model, User Modelling, Persona," in conjunction with "Survey, Literature Review, Ontology." A total of 23 papers were analysed within the temporal scope spanning from 2005 to 2022. Among these, 14 papers were identified as secondary studies, presenting a synthesis of existing research, while the remaining 9 publications were identified as primary research contributions that specifically addressed the development of ontologies for the purpose of user profile creation.

3.1   Existing Ontologies for Creating User Profile

The General User Modelling Ontology (GUMO) [23] defines user dimensions and analyses in detail properties such as heartbeat, age, position, birthplace, or swimming ability. This ontology identifies 1000 groups of auxiliaries, predicates and ranges. The User Profile Ontology (UPO) [20] aims to model user profiles at a high level, incorporating relevant concepts and properties. The Ontology-based User Modeling framework (OntobUMf) [28,29] focuses on analyzing user behaviour in knowledge management systems. The Grapple ontology [10] supports the rule-based creation of domain-related statements for users. The Holistic Persona Ontology (HPO) [11] proposes a persona ontology framework with five dimensions, encompassing factual, personality, intelligence, knowledge, and cognitive process aspects. The Persona Ontology (PO) [32] provides a comprehensive set of concepts related to personal characteristics and environment, by having separate ontologies for requirements and behavioural aspects which are connected in a model-driven way. The User Modelling Meta-Ontology [38] offers a top-level classification of the user modelling field, analyzing diverse data collection and interpretation approaches.

As demonstrated in Table 1, we found five ontologies that group various user characteristics into different user profile dimensions. Three ontologies show how to use the proposed dimensions by giving a complete instance model, while two introduce partial instantiation. Finally, four of the ontologies introduce limited implementation details based on OWL syntax. although they provide the links to their implementation, they are not functional at the time of writing this article, and ontologies can not be retrieved. Currently, there is a broadly used ontology for social networks *Friend of a Friend (FOAF)*[1], which serves to represent relations of user with other people. Further, there is a vocabulary class that characterizes generic RDF resources within a Knowledge Graph[2], which focuses

---

[1] http://xmlns.com/foaf/0.1/ (Access date 30, September 2023).
[2] https://schema.org/Person, (Access date 30, September 2023).

Table 1. Overview of analysed ontologies X - exist in the article, O - was partially presented

Ontology	Domain	Dimension	Instance	Implemented
General User Modeling Ontology (**GUMO**) [23]	General	X	O	OWL
User Profile Ontology (**UPO**) [20]	Personal information management	X		
Ontology-based User Modeling Framework (**OntobUMf**) [28,29]	Knowledge-management system	X	O	KAON (OWL)
Holistic Persona Ontology (**HPO**) [11]	User Centered Design	X	X	
Persona Ontology (**PO**) [32,33]	Requirement engineering	X	X	Protege (OWL)
Grapple ontology [10]	User model pipes		X	OWL
User Modeling Meta-Ontology [38]	User modeling field			

on representing the notion of the person with the particular instance for the medical field.

It is important to note that analysed ontologies are predominantly static and do not address how the analysed property can change with time or new data retrieval. There is a lack of support for dynamic and temporal features (for instance the features that can change in a matter of ms, like one captured by IoT devices and often stored in time-series databases. The existing approaches primarily adopt a top-down approach, requiring developers to start from scratch. There is a need for bottom-up approaches that enable the generation of user profiles from existing datasets, particularly ones that are domain-independent and applicable to various applications. Analyzing general user profile characteristics and establishing mappings to domain-specific profiles is the crucial starting point in addressing these requirements.

3.2   Extracting User Profile Dimensions

The core idea of adaptation is based on the assumption that differences in some user characteristics affect the usefulness of the services or information provided to the individuals. Thus if a system's behaviour is tailored according to such individual characteristics, its value to individuals will be increased. We propose fixed user dimensions in Table 2 to guide user profile ontology implementation.

We differentiate between domain-specific and general dimensions. Domain-specific are highly dependent on the application domain, e.g. they are not valid in the other domain. General, or domain-independent, characteristics are ones

Table 2. User Profile Dimensions and Encapsulated Concepts

Dimension	Description
Demographic [18,23,34]	encompass the fundamental information commonly used for segmentation and categorization purposes. This includes basic user details such as name, date of birth, email, and contact information [23], as well as information related to the user's place of residence and type of housing [20]
Characteristic [18,20,23,34]	represent a range of attributes that can be categorized into general physical traits and personality traits. General characteristics include physical features such as eye colour, height, and weight, while Personality traits encompass qualities such as talkativeness, dominance, reservedness, shyness, kindness, warmth, and openness to experience. Commonly used models like the Five-Factor Model define a set of properties that describe personality, including extroversion/introversion, thinking, feeling, and sensing [11].
Role [23]	encompass various aspects such as user Profession [20] and Occupation [32]. Additionally, roles refer to specific positions or responsibilities that users hold within a particular system or context. These roles can include administrator, manager, employee, customer, guest, moderator, contributor, and other relevant roles based on the specific application or domain.
Ability [20,23,32]	represent the user's Proficiency [23] or Expertise [20] in performing various tasks or activities. These abilities can vary widely including user's level of Education [20,32], Qualifications, Certifications, and Licenses [28], user's Knowledge which comprises factual, procedural, conceptual, and metacognitive aspects providing insights into their cognitive abilities, such as learning process (remembering, understanding, applying, analyzing) [11] or their Intelligence [11], technical skills, physical capabilities, and language proficiency.
Relation	represents the connections or associations between users and other entities or users within a system or context. It signifies the relationships to Thing (Ownership), Contact (Other persons) [20] or to certain Organisations.
Human state	encompasses various aspects of the user's well-being, including their nutritional status, emotional state (such as worry, boredom, hope, joy), mental state (including sleep, drowsiness, stress), physiological indicators (such as heartbeat, blood pressure, temperature), and even their motion or facial expressions [23]. These states are observed and captured to gain insights into the user's Experience and overall Condition.
Behaviour [28,32]	include user activity patterns, interaction sequences, frequency of actions, duration of engagement, and other behavioural indicators exhibited by the user while interacting with a system or engaging in specific activities.
Interest [20,28,32]	refer to the topics or subjects that attract the user's attention or curiosity or areas of expertise that they find engaging or enjoyable
Preference [20]	refer to the individual choices, inclinations, or options that a user favours or selects in various contexts. They encompass a wide range of aspects, like preferences for specific features, functionalities, or settings of a system or application. They can also include preferences for certain types of content, styles, layouts, or presentation formats.
Goal/Task [28,32]	represent the specific objectives, aims, or activities that a user intends to accomplish within a system or context. They reflect the user's intended outcomes or desired results while interacting and provide insights into the user's motivations, intentions, and priorities.
Environment [32]	include physical location where the user interacts with a system (e.g., home, office, public space), the social context in which the user operates (e.g., social networks, online communities), and the technological infrastructure and devices available to the user (e.g., IoT devices, internet connectivity)
Requirement [32]	include functional requirements, which describe the specific features, functionalities, or capabilities that the user expects from a system or application and non-functional requirements, which focus on aspects such as performance, reliability, usability, security, or accessibility.

which we can reuse in between domains. They can represent the general user characteristics and abilities, which later we can relate to the context of the study to understand their impact. They can also represent the existing data from which the human state is interfered with for the user. In most cases when the user profile dimensions are measured person has a rough idea about the expected expiry [23]. For instance, human states are highly dynamic, and some of them can change within a few seconds, while user demographics and characteristics, in general, don't change too often.

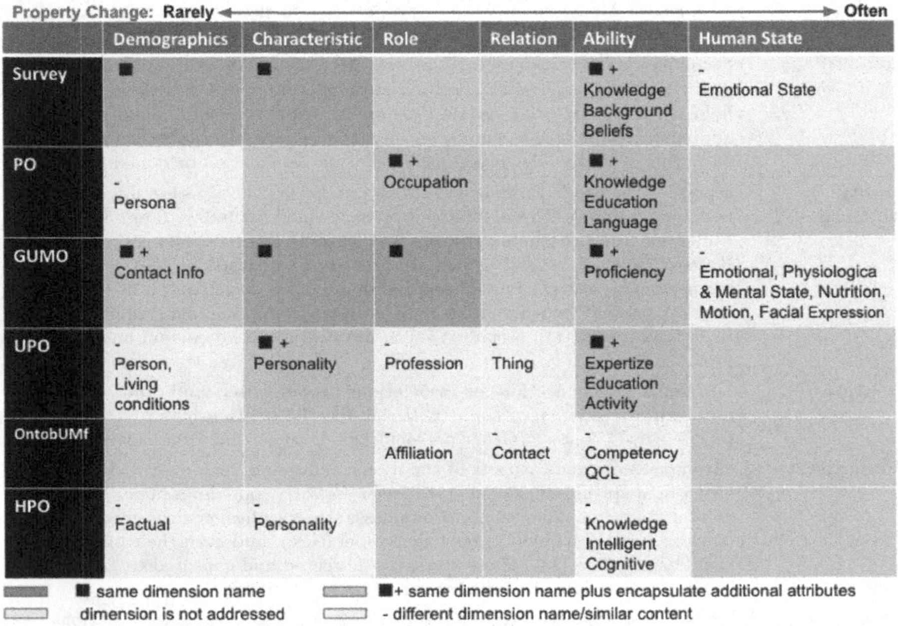

Property Change: Rarely ←————————————————————————————→ Often

	Demographics	Characteristic	Role	Relation	Ability	Human State
Survey	■	■			■ + Knowledge Background Beliefs	- Emotional State
PO	- Persona		■ + Occupation		■ + Knowledge Education Language	
GUMO	■ + Contact Info	■	■		■ + Proficiency	- Emotional, Physiologica & Mental State, Nutrition, Motion, Facial Expression
UPO	- Person, Living conditions	■ + Personality	- Profession	- Thing	■ + Expertize Education Activity	
OntobUMf			- Affiliation	- Contact	- Competency QCL	
HPO	- Factual	- Personality			- Knowledge Intelligent Cognitive	

■ same dimension name   ■+ same dimension name plus encapsulate additional attributes
dimension is not addressed   - different dimension name/similar content

Fig. 1. Linking general dimensions with existing ontologies

We introduce the mapping of the dimensions introducing general properties with one proposed by the existing ontologies and the existing surveys ([18,34]) in Fig. 1. We sort the dimensions by frequency of how likely it is that their inner property will change; on the left *Demographics* being rare to change, while on the right ones that more often change, especially the dimension encapsulating *Human State*. We can note that the user *Ability* dimensions were widely analysed by all proposed ontologies, while the *Relation* and *Human State* were examined only by two proposed ontologies.

We derived the existing mapping table, and proposed dimensions, by linking the dimensions proposed by existing ontologies (Table 1 based on the provided definitions, as well as, the given instance examples. In Fig. 2 we can see an example of linking of existing dimensions proposed by Persona ontology [32]. In this case, in addition to the Ability dimension, dimensions related to Knowledge,

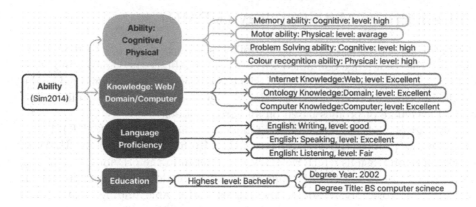

Fig. 2. Mapping Ability dimension to the one proposed by PO [32]

Education and Language are derived. When taking a look at the given model instance, we can see that all of these dimensions actually represent the user's ability or expertise in something. It is possible to reuse the proposed dimensions as subcategorises that guide the developer when creating the ontology and selecting existing properties if needed.

	Behaviour	Interest	Preference	Goal/Task	Environment	Requirement
Survey	■	■	■	■ + Plans Needs		
PO	■	■+ Concern	- Usability Preference	■ + Scenario	≡	≡
GUMO						
UPO		■	■			
OntobUMf	■ + Identification Accessibility Activity	■		■		
HPO						

■ same dimension name   ■+ same dimension name plus encapsulate additional attributes
dimension is not addressed   - different dimension name/similar content

Fig. 3. Linking domain-specific dimensions with existing ontologies

Further, in Fig. 3 we introduce the domain-specific dimensions. These dimensions can't be ordered by the expectations on how often their properties will change (e.g. to differentiate between transitory and long-lasting states), as this is highly domain-dependent. We can see that Sim and Brouse [32] cover this dimension widely in their PO ontology, although focusing only on Usability preferences.

4   User Profile Meta-Ontology (UPMO)

The ontology representation of user profiles serves as a means to define and represent the knowledge contained within them, enabling the sharing and reuse of domain knowledge [18]. It facilitates the analysis and extraction of domain-specific information from operational knowledge and supports the explicit sharing and exchange of profiles based on an agreed model.

Ontology engineering is a subfield of model-driven engineering (MDE) [12]. In this paper, we propose the development of User Profile Meta-Ontology (UPMO), based on the dimensions which we analysed in detail in the previous Sect. 3. The idea is to rely on Knowledge Graphs (RDF) [25] for describing user models as they allow us to apply reasoning techniques and enable finding relationships between data. On the other hand, it is to use the MDE environment to create ontology-based domain-specific modelling language.

In the rest of this section, we draw from the existing surveys on user profiles ([18,26,34]) to establish the current requirements. We also delineate the essential role that UPMO plays in the user model development process, alongside providing an overview of the envisioned modeling environment.

4.1   UPMO Requirements and Role During System Development

According to presented research trends, there are several requirements that contribute to the wide dissemination of user profiles [18,26,34], and which are defined in Table 3. These requirements aim to ensure the versatility, effectiveness, and adaptability of UPMO, promoting their widespread implementation and usability across different contexts and applications.

UPMO is expected to play a significant role in designing, implementing, and testing emerging socio-technical systems. We highlight here how it can contribute to each of these development phases:

Design: UPMO is expected to help in the design phase by providing a standardized vocabulary and a conceptual model that captures the key concepts, relationships, and constraints regarding user linked to a specific domain. It helps designers understand and model the characteristics and needs of the target users, by capturing user preferences, interests, demographics, and other relevant factors, designers can create user personas, profiles and role/task models. Obtained artefacts serve as a foundation for designing tailored interactions, content recommendations, and personalized features while ensuring consistency and interoperability between the user profiling model and other system components.

Implementation: UPMO is expected to guide the implementation of personalized features and adaptive functionalities. Developers can integrate the ontology into the system architecture, allowing user data to be collected, stored, and processed in a structured manner. It serves as a common representation that facilitates communication between different software modules and enables the effective utilization of user profile information. Developers can use UMPO to define rules, algorithms, and mechanisms for personalization and adaptivity.

Table 3. Requirements for User Profile modelling

Requirement	Description
Generality	UPMO should exhibit generality by explicitly representing domain-independent properties of user profiles. They should be designed to be compatible with various applications and domains, enabling their utilization in different contexts
Expressiveness	UPMO should demonstrate a high degree of expressiveness, enabling it to effectively represent a wide array of facts and rules pertaining to the user. This includes accommodating diverse types of information, allowing for the comprehensive and flexible representation of user attributes, characteristics, and behaviours
Import of external data	UPMO should possess the capability to integrate data from multiple heterogeneous sources into a unified data source, regardless of their formats, structures, or locations. This data federation is expected to provide a unified and consistent view of data, enabling querying of integrated data as if it were stored in a single centralized database
Integrating multiple ontologies	UPMO should support combining ontologies from different sources to enhance reuse, knowledge sharing and interoperability. Ontology federation allows for the integration of ontologies that capture different perspectives of user profiles or specialize in specific domains. It involves establishing mappings between the concepts and relationships which enable the knowledge exchange
Extensibility	UPMO should provide the interface for the modelling of new features at the meta-level and APIs that allow for the exchange of user information between user modelling tools, such as data collection methods, analysis algorithms, and modelling approaches. It should be capable of accommodating evolving user modelling techniques and supporting a wide range of user modelling tasks and applications
Privacy	It is essential for the user model to adhere to privacy policies, conventions, and both national and international privacy legislation. To ensure user privacy, the UPMO should incorporate robust tools and services that safeguard sensitive user information
Reasoning abilities	The UPMO should possess capabilities to perform diverse forms of reasoning and effectively handle conflicts that may arise from contradictory facts or rules. Model verification enables the user modeller to effectively handle ambiguity and reconcile conflicting information
Usability	The UPMO should prioritize comprehensibility, efficiency, effectiveness, and learnability. This can be achieved through clear and thorough documentation that explains the ontology's purpose, structure, and how it is used. It's also important to adhere to standard naming conventions and organize the hierarchy of classes logically. Alignment with existing user representations and the availability of user-friendly tools are essential. It should foster collaboration and actively seek feedback from the user community. This feedback loop can result in valuable improvements and a broader perspective on the ontology's usability

Testing: Testers can use the generated user model to simulate different user profiles and interactions, evaluate the data collection, interpretation mechanisms and system's ability to deliver personalized content, adapt to user preferences, and provide relevant recommendations. It helps in defining test cases, expected outcomes, and criteria for assessing the system's performance in terms of user modelling and personalization accuracy.

4.2 Envisioned UPMO Development Environment

To develop the UPMO we propose using the interrelated domain-specific languages (DSLs) provided by openCAESAR platform [37]. This platform represents ontology DSL precisely using the semantics of web ontologies while integrating information in engineering tools based on code generation and model transformation. It supports information authoring, federation, linking change management, and configuration management while making the system engineering process more agile with DevOps (CI/CD) practices.

The core part of this opensource platform is Ontological Modeling Language (OML)[3], which is inspired by the Ontology Web Language 2 (OWL2) [4] and the Semantic Web Rule Language (SWRL) [2]. The abstract syntax is defined with Ecore, and it generates Java API published as a Maven dependency and Eclipse feature. Default serializations are in XMI and it works with all standard Eclipse Modeling Frameworks (EMF) [3] like OCL, ATL, QVT etc.). The textual syntax is defined with Xtext [9], and the graphical syntax with Sirius framework [6].

OML natively support merging and validating of datasets, tools for reporting differences and Descrite Logic (DL) [1] reasoning over OWL datasets, as well as sending query to SPARQL [7] endpoints or rules to SHACL endpoints [5]. There are several adapters which are supported like Ecore to OML, OML to OWL and transformations with UML profile and model [8].

In summary, this framework enables smooth integration of the tools commonly used by data scientists to define the ontology and to work with the data integration and analysis, and ones used by software and system engineers to create system architecture, enable code generation and create different editors empowering all stakeholders to work collaboratively on the same model.

In Fig. 4 we illustrate the envisioned user profile modeling environment, an ontological DSL, interpreted from UPMO, which supports common techniques for creating the user profile, namely Personas, User Profiling and task/role modeling (see Sect. 2. The environment enables linking of the existing user data, which can be retrieved from the web, empirical studies, IoT devices as well as public institutions (e.g. medical, educational etc.). Also, it is to enable linking of the existing domain ontologies, like existing user ontologies and the ontologies describing the part of the system to be related to the domain-specific characteristics. The provided model is to generate data storage and interpret the User Model component which is to be integrated into the runtime environment or to the analysis and simulation platform. The resulting ontological DSL for modeling of User Profiles can also natively be combined with other modeling languages, like for instance with the one for usability evaluation [13], or for the requirements gathering [14].

---

[3] https://www.opencaesar.io/oml/, (Access date 30, September 2023).

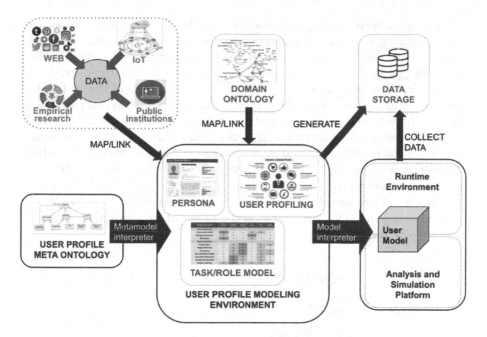

Fig. 4. Envisioned UPMO-based modeling environment

Using a UPMO is expected to provide developers and domain experts with a solid foundation, standardized representation, and guidance throughout the development process. It can help them align their understanding of user profiles with established best practices, facilitating knowledge sharing and collaboration. The interpreted modelling environment is expected to save time, promote consistency and interoperability, facilitate integration with external data sources and domain ontologies, and allow for iterative improvements based on feedback and evolving user modelling needs.

5 Illustration of Modelling Process with UPMO

In this section, we partially illustrate the iterative and incremental modeling process with UPMO-based ontological DSL on the driver model described in [15]. In the given case study the objective was to design the driver model, the so-called Fallback Ready User, which captures the minimum awareness necessary from the driver to detect and react to a Take-Over Request in an autonomous vehicle.

1. **Identify User Profiling Needs** - UPMO is envisioned to provide a comprehensive set of concepts and relationships, guiding developers in identifying user profile requirements specific to their system and determining the types of user information needed for personalization and automation, such as their abilities, characteristics, roles, or system specific preferences, behaviours or objectives.

To design the driver model, the idea is to use the set of proposed dimensions and identify the high-level properties important in their scenario, starting from general ones to domain-specific ones. For instance, the driver's state is important in the given case study as it should be monitored inside the cabin. The biosensor camera is used to capture the state of the driver, and the important system requirement is that this is captured in real-time. However, to have the means to interpret the relevant state of the driver in their scenario, like stress or sleepiness, it is necessary also to think of the means of reusing the existing related data if the same one can be obtained. Further, demographic information, as well as driver abilities are relevant for the driver to react to autonomous transfer requests from the vehicle. As the process is iterative and incremental, the developers are advised not to go too wide, and instead to capture in the first iteration the most critical properties of the user profile to be tested in the given scenario.

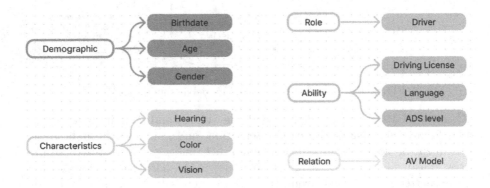

Fig. 5. High level features and long term properties

2. **Create/Extend the User Profile Ontology** - UPMO serves as a starting point for developers to extend and customize the ontology, and to link existing domain ontologies necessary for capturing user profiles in the given context. This saves significant effort and time compared to starting from scratch, as developers can build upon the existing ontology structure and relationships by using the ontology alignment approach [36].

   In the case of the driver model, the developers examine the properties regarding their user which they want to test in the first iteration. For instance to capture high-level features and long-term properties they introduce them in the correlated dimensions (see Fig. 5. Users are encouraged to engage in thoughtful reasoning about the properties within each dimension that align with their specific requirements. For instance, they may seek information regarding substantial, long-term attributes within demographics, such as age, gender, or a person's role as a driver, including their connection to the vehicle they use, any potential auditory or visual impairments, and their driving capabilities. The profile designer should have the flexibility to select property definitions from established ontologies or introduce new ones. If a newly introduced property already exists, the framework should offer suggestions for existing properties. Furthermore, understanding how existing properties are interrelated and characterized can serve as a guide for users when implementing their own properties.

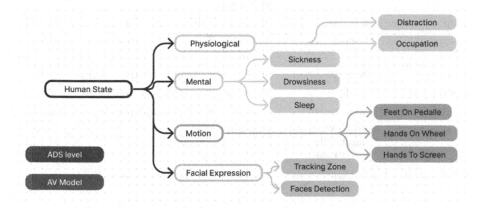

Fig. 6. Real-time properties

Additionally, we encounter scenarios where real-time properties need to be captured, such as time-sensitive data from signals that indicate whether the driver has their foot on the pedal or hands on the wheel, their gaze direction, distractions, engagement in driving, or other activities. This data can also help determine if the driver is fatigued, drowsy, or experiencing stress (see Fig. 6). In such cases, it is beneficial to leverage categorizations and mental state definitions that have been thoroughly analyzed in GUMO [23]. Reusing static property definitions for naming and employing their expiration reasoning can prove particularly useful.

3. **Capture and map User Profile Data** - Identify the data sources available from IoT devices (e.g. cameras, motion sensors, security devices), web (e.g. social networks, e-commerce platforms), public institutions (e.g. education institution, healthcare institutions) or existing empirical studies (e.g. surveys, user logs, usability studies). Having a UPMO helps developers map the ontology's predefined concepts and relationships with collected data to ensure data consistency and interoperability.

In the case of the driver model, the user dynamic properties are gathered by the biosensor camera device inside the vehicle. The raw data which is gathered doesn't have the format, or naming which can be easily interpreted, used or analysed. The tendency of developers when using this data is to keep the raw structure that was found as the output of given devices, which prevents the reuse and often stores a lot of information which is never used by a system. In Table 4 we illustrate the resulting data format and interpreted meaning, which are represented as Triple (variable, timestamp, confidence).

Table 4. Dynamic properties (taken from [15])

variable	value	description
distraction	boolean	indicate if the driver is occupied with non-driving task
occupation	boolean	indicate if the driver is occupied with driving task
sleep	boolean	indicates if driver is in sleep state
sickness	boolean	indicates if a driver is experiencing sudden sickness
drowsiness	boolean	indicates if driver is tired or sleepy
feet_on_pedalle	boolean	Indicates if driver's feet are on the pedals
hands_on _wheel	hand_none hand_left hand_right hand_both	Indicates which hand(s) the driver has on the wheel
hand_to_screen	boolean	indicates if driver's hand is at the touch screen
tracking_zone	string	Indicates where the driver is looking
faces_detection	.front: int .rear: int .occupation: int	N of detected humans in front N of detected humans in rear N of seat occupied

This information is typically stored in a time-series database, and the idea is to incorporate existing approaches like [16] to include this type of data linking to be supported by UPMO.

4. **Implement Data Storage and Retrieval** - UPMO provides guidance on how to organize and store user profile data, enabling developers to create efficient and scalable storage systems that are compatible with the ontology. Based on the previously linked data and the vocabulary definitions the modelling environment generates the data structure for data collection, which we call User Model. To retrieve the data from this artefact, the developer needs to create SPARQL queries over the RDF data to get results, for instance in JSON format, which answers certain questions, like for instance: 'Is driver looking at the road?'; 'Is driver sleepy?', 'Does the driver have hearing problems?', 'Is the driver ready to take over the control of the vehicle (e.g. his hands are on the steering wheel, the feet are on the paddle, he is looking at the road and is mentally ready)?'. In this phase, the developer is also encouraged to think about the methods for deducting user properties, like data mining techniques (e.g. clustering, classification, association rules, sequential patterns, latent variable models).

5. **Test and Integrate User Model** - UPMO is generating a user model component which can be integrated with a simulation environment. It supports the development of test cases and scenarios to validate the user profiling func-

tionality of the system. It helps to verify that the system correctly collects, stores, and retrieves user profile data and that it effectively uses ontology to personalize interactions.

UPMO allows developers to integrate user profiling capabilities with system components. They can design modules that utilize user model components to access and leverage user profile data enabling personalized automation, adaptive interfaces, and decision-making processes based on standardized representations.

In our case study, we want to generate the User Model component in a simulation environment, a cockpit equipped with seat shakers, a biosensor camera and a front screen running the simulation for a driving experience. First, it is to perform *Unit testing* to verify that based on the existing or automatically generated data, SPARQL queries return correct reports (i.e. answers to the questions). Further, it is to perform *Integration testing*, where it is to test that data collection is working properly (e.g. camera captures correctly information in the user model) or that the cabin monitoring system receives the analysis reports in the correct format and is able to use the provided information as expected from system. For instance, it is to test a time delay from data collection, analysis and returning a report to another component. Finally, it is to perform a *System testing*, basically validating the complete takeover scenario, while having a human driver in the cockpit, and focusing on testing the performance, usability and user experience of the system.

6. **Iterate and Refine** - By leveraging the UPMO as a starting point developers benefit from the iterative refinement process when extending the user profiling ontology [22]. It helps them to continuously iterate and refine the ontology and its implementation based on feedback, user evaluations, and system performance.

In our example, in the following interaction, the developers should focus on analysing domain-specific dimensions. For this purpose, they are encouraged to map domain ontologies, like the ones describing the autonomous vehicle, or introduce this domain concept from existing UML models or DSLs. It will be also necessary to analyse the rules and relations between properties and dimensions introduced in the proposed model.

For instance, in the Behaviour dimension, it is to introduce the driver's reaction when the system alert is transmitted. For instance to collect the sequence of the relevant actions. For Intrest, it can be that the driver wants to make customized alerts. Further drivers could have preferences regarding the auditive signal for instance because the person has hearing problems. The task the driver wants to perform is to take over the control of the vehicle when the alert is transmitted. Regarding the Environment, it is to introduce a specific system environment which can be imported from existing UML models. For instance, ones describing the driving condition simulation component, cabin monitoring system or cabin experience manager. Finally, some of the relevant requirements could be the definitions of the response time related to the specific reports, e.g., when the driver is in the fallback ready state, the frequency of checking if the driver is sleepy.

6   Conclusions and Future Work

This paper presents the design of the User Profile Meta Ontology (UPMO) and conducts an analysis of the user dimensions, which serve as high-level concepts guiding the development of UPMO. We explore the anticipated development process for adaptive systems and examine the potential benefits for developers and domain experts through UPMO-supported artefacts. UPMO provide unified standardized terminology for representing User Profiles, enable sharing of User Models and collected data, and support federation and linking of existing user data

As part of our future work, we are planning to achieve several key objectives. First, we aim to align the User Profile Meta-Ontology (UPMO) with existing ontologies for user profiles and propose a systematic alignment process. This alignment will enhance interoperability and data sharing across different ontologies.

Additionally, we intend to introduce user profile-guided semantics to support integrative data analysis of existing data. This will allow for more effective and comprehensive data analysis, driven by user profile information.

Another important aspect of our future work is to validate the feasibility of the proposed dimensions by mapping them to existing user and data models introduced by previous researchers. This will help us ensure that the dimensions are well-defined and compatible with established practices in the field.

We also plan to delve deeper into the detailed structure of the envisioned metamodel and analyze the interrelationships among its components. Understanding these relationships is crucial for the effective utilization of the ontology.

Furthermore, we will enhance the iterative development process of the user profile ontology by introducing collaborative workflows. Collaborative development will involve multiple stakeholders, including users, developers, and domain experts, to ensure that the ontology remains relevant and effective.

In parallel, we will consider various system-related aspects, such as how data is captured, analyzed, and represented in UPMO components. This holistic approach will enable a more comprehensive understanding of how the user model informs the system and, in turn, how the system serves the user.

Overall, our future work is focused on aligning, expanding, and validating UPMO to make it a more powerful and user-centric tool for developing user profiles and supporting user data analysis.

References

1. Handbook, T.D.L.: Theory, Implementation and Applications, 2nd edn. Cambridge University Press, Cambridge (2007)
2. A Semantic Web Rule Language Combining OWL and RuleML (SWRL). https://www.w3.org/Submission/SWRL/
3. Eclipse Modeling Framework (EMF). https://www.eclipse.org/modeling/emf/

 4. OWL2 Computational Properties. https://www.w3.org/TR/owl2-profiles/#Computational_Properties
 5. Shapes Constraint Language (SHACL). https://www.w3.org/TR/shacl/
 6. Sirius UI Framework for Eclipse. https://www.eclipse.org/sirius/overview.html
 7. SPARQL Query Language for RDF. https://www.w3.org/TR/rdf-sparql-query/
 8. Unified Modeling Language (UML). https://www.uml.org/what-is-uml.htm
 9. XText. https://www.eclipse.org/Xtext/. Accessed 12 Feb 2021
10. Abel, F., et al.: A framework for flexible user profile mashups. In: Balint, G., Antala, B., Carty, C., Mabieme, J.M.A., Amar, I.B., Kaplanova, A. (eds.) Proceedings of the International Workshop on Adaptation and Personalization for Web 2.0 (APWEB 2.0 2009) in conjunction with the International Conference on User Modeling, Adaptation, and Personalization (UMAP 2009), vol. 7, pp. 1–10. CEUR-WS.org (2009). https://doi.org/10.2/JQUERY.MIN.JS, https://research.tue.nl/en/publications/a-framework-for-flexible-user-profile-mashups
11. Anvari, F., Tran, H.M.T.: Persona ontology for user centred design professionals. In: Balint, G., Antala, B., Carty, C., Mabieme, J.M.A., Amar, I.B., Kaplanova, A. (eds.) Proceedings of the ICIME 4th International Conference on Information Management and Evaluation, vol. 7, pp. 35–44. Academic Conferences and Publishing International (2013). https://doi.org/10.2/JQUERY.MIN.JS, https://researchers.mq.edu.au/en/publications/persona-ontology-for-user-centred-design-professionals   .
12. Atkinson, C., Kühne, T.: Model driven development: a metamodeling foundation. IEEE Softw. **20**(5), 36–41 (2003). https://doi.org/10.1109/MS.2003.1231149, http://portal.acm.org/citation.cfm?id=942589.942704
13. Barišić, A., Amaral, V., Goulão, M.: Usability driven DSL development with USE-ME. Comput. Lang. Syst. Struct. (ComLan) **51**, 118–157 (2018). https://doi.org/10.1016/j.cl.2017.06.005
14. Barišić, A., Blouin, D., Amaral, V., Goulão, M.: A requirements engineering approach for usability-driven DSL development. In: 10th International Conference on Software Language Engineering (SLE), pp. 115–128. ACM, Vancouver, British Columbia, Canada (2017). https://doi.org/10.1145/3136014.3136027, https://dl.acm.org/citation.cfm?id=3136027
15. Barisic, A., Sigrist, P., Oliver, S., Sciarra, A., Winckler, M.: Driver model for take-over-request in autonomous vehicles. In: UMAP 2023 - Adjunct Proceedings of the 31st ACM Conference on User Modeling, Adaptation and Personalization, pp. 317–324, June 2023. https://doi.org/10.1145/3563359.3596994, https://dl.acm.org/doi/10.1145/3563359.3596994
16. Donkers, A., Yang, D., De Vries, B., Baken, N.: Real-time building performance monitoring using semantic digital twins. In: Proceedings of the 9th Linked Data in Architecture and Construction Workshop [Internet], vol. 12 (2021)
17. Earthy, J., Jones, B.S., Bevan, N.: The improvement of human-centred processes-facing the challenge and reaping the benefit of ISO 13407. Int. J. Hum.-Comput. Stud. **55**(4), 553–585 (2001). https://doi.org/10.1006/IJHC.2001.0493
18. Eke, C.I., Norman, A.A., Shuib, L., Nweke, H.F.: A survey of user profiling: state-of-the-art, challenges, and solutions. IEEE Access **7**, 144907–144924 (2019). https://doi.org/10.1109/ACCESS.2019.2944243
19. Farid, M., Elgohary, R., Moawad, I., Roushdy, M.: User profiling approaches, modeling, and personalization. SSRN Electron. J. (2018). https://doi.org/10.2139/SSRN.3389811, https://papers.ssrn.com/abstract=3389811

20. Golemati, M., Katifori, A., Vassilakis, C., Lepouras, G., Halatsis, C.: Creating an ontology for the user profile: method and applications. In: Proceedings of the AI* AI Workshop RCIS, pp. 407–412 (2007)
21. Grundy, J., et al.: Addressing the influence of end user human aspects on software engineering. Commun. Comput. Inf. Sci. **1556 CCIS**(c), 241–264 (2022). https://doi.org/10.1007/978-3-030-96648-5_11
22. Hannou, F.Z., Charpenay, V., Lefrançois, M., Roussey, C., Zimmermann, A., Gandon, F.: The ACIMOV methodology: agile and continuous integration for modular ontologies and vocabularies. In: MK 2023-2nd Workshop on Modular Knowledge associated with FOIS 2023-the 13th International Conference on Formal Ontology in Information Systems (2023)
23. Heckmann, D., Schwartz, T., Brandherm, B., Schmitz, M., von Wilamowitz-Moellendorff, M.: GUMO – the general user model ontology. In: Ardissono, L., Brna, P., Mitrovic, A. (eds.) UM 2005. LNCS (LNAI), vol. 3538, pp. 428–432. Springer, Heidelberg (2005). https://doi.org/10.1007/11527886_58
24. Karolita, D., Kanij, T., Grundy, J., Mcintosh, J.: Use of Personas in Requirements Engineering : A Systematic Literature Review Use of Personas in Requirements Engineering : A Systematic Literature Review (February) (2023)
25. Klyne, G.: Resource description framework (RDF): concepts and abstract syntax (2014). http://www.w3.org/TR/rdf-concepts/
26. Kobsa, A.: Generic user modeling systems. In: Brusilovsky, P., Kobsa, A., Nejdl, W. (eds.) The Adaptive Web. LNCS, vol. 4321, pp. 136–154. Springer, Heidelberg (2007). https://doi.org/10.1007/978-3-540-72079-9_4
27. Limbourg, Q., Pribeanu, C., Vanderdonckt, J.: Towards uniformed task models in a model-based approach. In: Johnson, C. (ed.) DSV-IS 2001. LNCS, vol. 2220, pp. 164–182. Springer, Heidelberg (2001). https://doi.org/10.1007/3-540-45522-1_10
28. Razmerita, L.: Ontology-based user modeling. In: Sharman, R., Kishore, R., Ramesh, R. (eds.) Ontologies: A Handbook of Principles, Concepts and Applications in Information Systems, LNCS, pp. 635–664. Springer US, Boston, MA (2007).https://doi.org/10.1007/978-0-387-37022-4_23
29. Razmerita, L.: An ontology-based framework for modeling user behavior-a case study in knowledge management. IEEE Trans. Syst. Man Cybern. Part A: Syst. Humans **41**(4), 772–783 (2011). https://doi.org/10.1109/TSMCA.2011.2132712
30. Salminen, J., Guan, K., Jung, S.G., Chowdhury, S.A., Jansen, B.J.: A literature review of quantitative persona creation. In: Conference on Human Factors in Computing Systems - Proceedings, April 2020.https://doi.org/10.1145/3313831.3376502, https://dl.acm.org/doi/10.1145/3313831.3376502
31. Salminen, J., Guan, K., Jung, S.G., Jansen, J.: Use cases for design personas: a systematic review and new frontiers, pp. 1–21 (2022). https://doi.org/10.1145/3491102.3517589
32. Sim, W.W., Brouse, P.: Towards an ontology-based persona-driven requirements and knowledge engineering. Procedia Comput. Sci. **36**(C), 314–321 (2014). https://doi.org/10.1016/J.PROCS.2014.09.099
33. Sim, W.W., Brouse, P.: Developing ontologies and persona to support and enhance requirements engineering activities - a case study. Procedia Comput. Sci. **44**(C), 275–284 (2015). https://doi.org/10.1016/J.PROCS.2015.03.060
34. Sosnovsky, S., Dicheva, D.: Ontological technologies for user modelling. Int. J. Metadata Semant. Ontol. **5**(1), 32–71 (2010). https://doi.org/10.1504/IJMSO.2010.032649

35. Stanton, N.A.: The Handbook of Task Analysis for Human-Computer Interaction THE HANDBOOK OF TASK ANALYSIS FOR HUMAN-COMPUTER INTER-ACTION Edited by Dan Diaper Bournemouth University (September 2003) (2014)

36. Tounsi Dhouib, M., Faron Zucker, C., Tettamanzi, A.G.B.: An ontology alignment approach combining word embedding and the radius measure. In: Acosta, M., Cudré-Mauroux, P., Maleshkova, M., Pellegrini, T., Sack, H., Sure-Vetter, Y. (eds.) SEMANTiCS 2019. LNCS, vol. 11702, pp. 191–197. Springer, Cham (2019). https://doi.org/10.1007/978-3-030-33220-4_14

37. Wagner, D.A., Chodas, M., Elaasar, M., Jenkins, J.S., Rouquette, N.: Ontological metamodeling and analysis using openCAESAR. In: Madni, A.M., Augustine, N., Sievers, M. (eds.) Handbook of Model-Based Systems Engineering, LNCS, pp. 1–30. Springer, Cham (2023). https://doi.org/10.1007/978-3-030-93582-5_78

38. Yudelson, M., Gavrilova, T., Brusilovsky, P.: Towards user modeling meta-ontology. In: Ardissono, L., Brna, P., Mitrovic, A. (eds.) UM 2005. LNCS (LNAI), vol. 3538, pp. 448–452. Springer, Heidelberg (2005). https://doi.org/10.1007/11527886_62

Supporting a Deeper Understanding of Users in Robot-Assisted Therapies by Two-Level Personas

Peter Forbrig[✉] [iD], Anke Dittmar[iD], and Mathias Kühn[iD]

Department of Computer Science, University of Rostock, Rostock, Germany
{peter.forbrig,anke.dittmar,mathias.kuehn}@uni-rostock.de

Abstract. The users of assistive technologies are often insufficiently represented in design processes. As a consequence, designed systems can allow too few adjustments to specific contexts of use. The paper describes insights and challenges from a project on robotic-assisted rehabilitation therapies. It is suggested to use two-level personas to better cover two groups of users in therapeutic sessions. Patients are end-users of the therapeutic robots; they are assisted by therapists who should also be provided with means to act as designer-users. It is argued that proven user-centered design methods and representations need to be adapted or revised to better cope with the specific challenges of new technologies and consequences of their use.

Keywords: Human-centered software engineering · domain-specific languages · end-user development · two-level personas

1 Introduction

The notion of user is a fundamental construct in human-computer interaction (HCI) and related design and development approaches [5]. The user is in need of something and the designer takes into account those needs by working with appropriate techniques and models. Often triggered by new technologies, the understanding of the user, and thus their representation and their participation in design processes, has evolved over time. For instance, task models are dominant design representations within the cognitive paradigm or first wave of HCI [4, 14]. They are used, for instance, in model-based development approaches of user interfaces and in usability evaluation methods. With the emergence of collaborative technologies, the situative perspective (second wave) of HCI developed and, with it, ideas of co-design and end-user development. The focus in the third HCI wave is on digital artefact use in public and private life. Here, techniques such as personas, scenarios and storyboards not only cover the users' goals and tasks but help us to reflect on a broader spectrum of (user) experiences.

This position paper aims at providing a detailed picture of users in robot-assisted therapies. Much of the research in this area is focused on the therapeutic interaction between the robot (often a humanoid one) and the patient. However, Guffroy et al. [13]

A. Bramwell-Dicks et al. (Eds.): INTERACT 2023 Workshops, LNCS 14535, pp. 80–90, 2024.
https://doi.org/10.1007/978-3-031-61688-4_7

point out that in the context of assistive technology, potential users are often insufficiently represented in design processes. Not only the disabled person should be considered but also stakeholders who are "direct or indirect users of the interactive system in different physical and human environments" [13] (e.g., family care givers and therapists).

In this paper, we use insights gained from an interdisciplinary project on robot assistance in neurorehabilitation and explore the potential of two-level personas to better represent users in a therapeutic context. Two-level personas [6] is a persona variant that was developed for supporting the design of end-user design tools. Their use in the domain of robot-assisted therapies can promote an understanding of therapists being end-user designers for their patients. Two-level personas can not only support the professional designers' understanding but also discussion and reflection on therapy sessions in the whole interdisciplinary design team. In conclusion, we argue that proven user-centered design methods and representations (such as personas and scenarios) do not lose their meaning but need to be adapted or revised to better cope with the specific challenges of new emerging technologies and consequences of their use.

2 The Project: Insights and Challenges

In the project E-BRAiN (Evidence-Based Robot Assistance in Neurorehabilitation) [7], collaborators from neurorehabilitation, psychology, sociology, software engineering and smart computing aimed to develop robotic-assisted rehabilitation therapies for stroke patients, based on the medical training programs in [17]. Therapists and patients should be supported by a humanoid robot Pepper in therapies with highly standardized and repetitive training schedules. Considered training tasks can be classified into four categories: arm ability training, arm basis training, mirror therapy and neglect therapy (see [10] for more details). In this paper, we use mirror therapy as an illustrative example. Stroke patients with severe arm paresis sit in 90 degrees next to a mirror placed with their non-affected arm in front of the mirror and the affected arm behind the mirror. The image of the moving non-affected arm gives the illusion of normal movement in the affected arm (see Fig. 1).

Fig. 1. Situation during Mirror Therapy

By this setup, different brain network regions for movement of the affected arm are stimulated promoting the recovery of movement function in the paretic limb.

Within the project, the neurorehabilitation expert developed detailed future scenarios of the patient-robot dialogue for the different training tasks. In a first step, the robot's behavior including spoken dialogues and the presentation of linked texts, pictures and video material on the tablet of Pepper (see Fig. 2) has been implemented in Java and in Python.

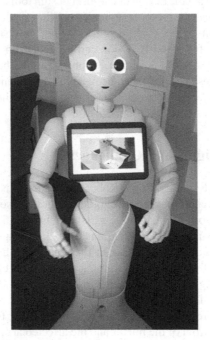

Fig. 2. Pepper displaying a guiding video.

For most therapies, the software engineering experts in the project specified hierarchical cooperative task models in the domain specific language CoTaL [9] to check the correct understanding of the training tasks. These models also informed the design and implementation of the textual domain specific language TaskDSL4Pepper and related tool support to specify patient-robot dialogues and to control the behavior of Pepper. TaskDSL4Pepper comes with a set of basic operations the robot can perform (*say* *<text>, show <picture>, play <video>, wait <time>*) and can be used for prototyping approaches. Figure 3 depicts an example model for a specific mirror therapy consisting of three parts: greeting, repetitive training task, closure.

The interaction with the humanoid robot is intended to guide and motivate a patient and to support the therapist. Created task models stimulated discussion in the project team about useful variations of the fixed set of scenarios that was implemented in the first prototype. Additionally, the domain specific language TaskDSL4Pepper provided opportunities to define and explore alternative training scenarios. However, the emphasis on the interactions between the patient and the robot may have resulted in an insufficient discussion of the role of the therapist in specific therapeutic situations. The dominant view of the therapist's role was that they monitor therapeutic interactions between the humanoid robot and the patient and step in in erroneous situations [18] (Fig. 5).

```
team coop {
  root training = greeting >> train{*} [> end_exercises
    task greeting = pepper.greet |=| patient.greet
    task end_exercises = pepper.end_exercises |=|
                          patient.finishes_exercises
}
role patient {
  root train = greet >> listens >>
                  perfoms_exercises{*} [> finishes_exercises
    task perfoms_exercises = perform_correctly [] perform_wrong
}
robot pepper {
  root armtraining= greet >> training{*} [> end_exercises
    task greet = say greeting
    task training = introduce >> train
      task introduce = say introduction ||| show startEndPict
      task train = play exerVid ||| say ten >> imagine
          task imagine = wait 8 >> say look >> say imagine
      task end_exercises = say bye
}
text greeting = "Good morning.";
text introduction = "Let us start to perform our second exercise"
image startEndPict = "st_pic_10_1.jpg"
video exerVid = "st_10_1.mp4"              // *    Iteration
                                          // >>   Enabling
text imagine = "Imagine it is your arm"    // [>   Disabling
text look    = "Look in the mirror"        // |||  Interleaving
text ten     = "Train ten times"           // []   Choice
text bye     = "Bye, till next time"       // |=|  Order independence
```

Fig. 3. TaskDSL4Pepper model of a specific mirror therapy (from [11]).

Winkle et al. [19] suggest that therapists, based on their knowledge about a patient, can help to personalize assistive robots in rehabilitation therapies (e.g., in terms of exercise explanations, exercise style of the tasks, style to increase the patient's motivation, and use of feedback). Following this idea, therapists must be understood as end-user developers [15]. An ad-hoc evaluation of TaskDSL4Pepper has shown limitations of its suitability as end-user specification language. Therapists were able to modify provided models to a certain extent indicating that TaskDSL4Pepper could be used as basis for an end-user design tool. However, more knowledge about therapeutic situations is needed to allow therapists to adjust training scenarios to a specific situation more easily. In this paper, we suggest to use personas, in particular two-level personas, in the interdisciplinary design process to discuss existing and possible future therapeutic practices.

3   Exploring the Potential of Two-Level Personas

This section briefly introduces the idea of two-level personas and explores their potential to better understand the needs of patients and therapists in robot-assisted therapeutic contexts.

3.1   Two-Level Personas

Generally, a persona is a fictional character "that is given a name and a face, and it is carefully described in terms of needs, goals and tasks" [2]. In interaction design, personas are used to represent user groups. It is assumed that designers engage better with personas than with abstract information about users. Grudin and Pruitt [12] refer to the generative nature of personas which allows designers to make predictions about the persona's behavior based on a precise description of their background and goals. This makes personas an effective tool for communication in (interdisciplinary) design teams [12]. Typically, a small set of personas is created to support discussion and reasoning about the system under design from the perspectives of the different relevant user groups (see the abstract illustration on left-hand side of Fig. 4).

Two-level personas [6] is a persona variant that was introduced in the context of end-user design tools where users act as designers themselves to create applications for their end-users. They are referred to as designer-users. A simple example is a questionnaire design tool that can be used, e.g., by teachers or researchers (the *designer-users*) to design digital questionnaires and provide them to their students and study participants respectively (the *end-users*). Professional designers of end-user design tools have to understand the goals and needs of the designer-users but they also have to consider the end-users' needs and the relationships between designer-users and end-users. In other words, they are faced with *nested design spaces*: their own more generic design space within which they generate and explore design ideas for the end-user design tool, and the more situated design spaces of the designer-users, which are partly created and, at the same time, constrained by this design tool. Design decisions of the professional designer also affect the relationship between designer-users and end-users. If, in the above example, the researcher has no option in the questionnaire design tool to allow their study participants to ignore some questions in the questionnaire it may negatively affect their relationship to the study participants.

A two-level persona takes nested design spaces into consideration and consist of a first-level persona representing a group of end-user designers and a few second-level personas representing groups of their end-users (see right-hand side of Fig. 4). In contrast to 'classical' personas, two-level personas additionally describe shared practices, mutual expectations and attitudes of the first-level and the second-level personas. The professional designers are provided with explicit descriptions of designer-users, end-users and their relationship. This may support them in developing a clearer understanding of the various situations of use. The empirical study in [6] compares the use of 'classical' and two-level personas by novice designers. The results suggest that two-level personas more powerfully support them in generating design ideas and becoming aware of their role as meta-designers in shaping the interaction space between designer-users and end-users.

Fig. 4. Left: three 'classical' personas represent user groups of the tool under design, right: two two-level personas, each consisting of a first-level persona and two second-level personas (from [6]).

3.2 Application to Robot-Assisted Therapies

The two-level persona approach can help to view robot-assisted rehabilitation therapies (as depicted in Fig. 5) as *robot-mediated meetings* between the therapist and the patient. It acknowledges the expertise of the therapist and their ability to appropriately respond to the specific therapeutic context. The therapist is then in need of an end-user design tool to play a more active role in adjusting the humanoid robot's behavior to the specific situation, as for example suggested in [19]. Adaptations include modifications to exercises and the robot's 'social' behavior.

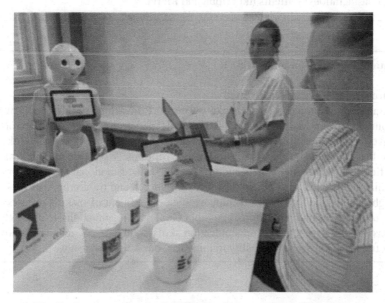

Fig. 5. A robot-assisted rehabilitation therapy session (from [18]).

The identification and creation of the two-level personas (with fictive therapists at the first level and fictive patients at the second level) can be informed by studies on characteristics of patients and therapists. For instance, the study in [3] indicates that attributes therapists use to characterize patients include frequency of reassurance during training, awareness about disease and treatment options, intrinsic motivation and concentration. Therapist's characteristics such as trustworthiness, enthusiasm, interest in the patient, helpfulness and friendliness have an impact on the patient-therapist bond [19]. Of course, the personas also contain descriptions about the training exercises (from the patient's and therapist's perspective), technology-related skills, and attitudes, and other contextual factors (e.g., time constraints).

An example of a two-level persona with therapist Jane as first-level persona and patients John and Maria in the second level is indicated below.

Therapist Persona (first level)

Name: Jane, 45 years old, divorced, one child
Education: Neuro physiotherapist **Occupation:** Senior therapist at Medical Centre York, United Kingdom since 2001 **Experience:** expert for neglect, arm ability and mirror therapy **Values:** Empathy, compassion, and respect for all individuals **Tasks:** Performs and instructs therapies for about 50 patients per week, member of the management group of neurorehabilitation, ventilation and intensive care **Goals:** To help people overcome their challenges and live fulfilling lives **Personal interests:** Yoga, meditation, and hiking **Needs:** Work-life balance, and personal growth **Attitudes:** Positive, non-judgmental, and open-minded **Limitations:** Boundaries with clients, time constraints, and ethical considerations **Patients like:** John and Maria.

Patient Persona1 (second level)

Name: John, 65 years old, married
Occupation: Automotive mechanic (retired) **Education:** High school diploma **Location:** Malton **Medical History:** Hypertension, high cholesterol, and type 2 diabetes **Stroke History:** Experienced an ischemic stroke two weeks ago that affected the right side of his body **Symptoms:** Weakness in right arm, difficulty speaking and understanding speech **Needs:** Emotional support from family and friends, rehabilitation services for speech and right arm **Attitudes:** Highly motivated to perform therapy exercises, confident of making progress in recovering as much function as possible **Goals:** To regain ability to use both arms, improve speech and communication skills, to play chess and cards with his friends **Therapy**: Arm ability training for four weeks twice a week.

Patient Persona2 (second level)

Name: Maria, 47 years old, married, two children
Occupation: Homemaker **Education:** High school diploma **Location:** Leeds **Medical History:** Hypertension, high cholesterol, and type 2 diabetes **Stroke History:** Experienced a hemorrhagic stroke 2 months ago that affected the left side of her body **Symptoms:** Paralysis on the left side of her body, difficulty speaking and understanding speech, vision problems, cannot move the left arm **Needs:** Rehabilitation services to regain mobility and independence, emotional support from family and friends, assistance with managing chronic health conditions **Attitudes:** Frustrated with limitations caused by stroke, concerned about burden on family members, motivated to recover as much function as possible but has doubts about her progress in therapies, not very confident **Goals:** To regain ability to walk independently, improve speech and communication skills, to be able to cook for her family again **Therapies:** Neglect training, mirror training, both every second day 10 weeks long.

Two-level personas also describe the relationship between the first-level and second-level personas. In the example above, Jane observed that John has made rapid progress. He seems to have a strong intrinsic motivation to regain his motoric abilities and she does not need to provide additional praise or encouragement. However, Jane is a little concerned for some time about Maria. Although progress can be seen, Maria seems to be dissatisfied and needs her support and encouragement during the therapy sessions. Therefore, Jane may want to be able in the future to customize the humanoid robot's behavior according to the current situation of a patient. It should provide a lot of positive feedback to Maria while this is not necessary or even detrimental for John. However, Jane would like to change this strategy according to the therapy success and the observed motivation.

The professional developers can use two-level personas to better understand both how patients (described by the second-level personas) can be supported by the robot and how the therapists (described by the first level persona) want to adapt the robot's behavior for a specific therapeutic session with a patient. Additionally, two-level personas can be used in the interdisciplinary team to generate a design space for robot-assisted training scenarios and to discuss what are appropriate design options for the therapists, i.e. what kind of adaptation should be possible for therapies. Two-level personas support both the design and implementation of the humanoid robot's behavior and the development of the end-user design tool for the therapists.

4   Discussion

A differentiated picture of the user is needed in many design contexts. For instance, Faulkner [8] introduces four categories of users: 1) 'direct users', 2) 'indirect users' who ask other people to use the system on their behalf, 3) 'remote users' who do not use the system but depend on the output, and 4) 'support users' who ensure that the system works for others. If social human-robot interactions in therapies are embedded in interactions between the therapist and the patient the paper suggests to distinguish between two 'types' of users: the therapist as designer-user and the patient as end-user.

Generally, end-user robot programming is increasingly important [1]. It frees the developers from premature design decisions about the robot's behavior and "allows the end-users of robots to modify the operation of robots to work within their contexts" [1]. Instead of pre-programming certain training scenarios for robot-assisted therapies, developers should create tools that allow therapists to use their experience and perception of the current situation to specify or customize the robot's behavior and 'personality'. Two-level personas support this change of focus and the design of such tools for designer-users.

Personas in general are representations intended to establish the designer's empathy and understanding of the users of the system to be designed, but typically the emphasis is on the individual user. Persona variants such as two-level personas or collaborative personas [16] take into account more complex relationships between users of a system (e.g., designer-user relationships between users or collaborative relationships), and thus address specific design problems more adequately (e.g., end-user design tools or collaborative tools) [6]. Two-level personas in the domain of robot assisted therapies provide concrete and vivid descriptions of the therapists' attitudes and knowledge about patients, training programs, and humanoids robots (first level) and of the patients' perspectives (second level). Their combined use with scenarios of possible therapy situations helps the design team not only to reason about the humanoid robot's behavior but also to reason about possibilities for the therapist to personalize or adapt the robot (e.g., the way the robot greets the patient or gives feedback). What is an appropriate space for adjustments for the therapists and how should it be presented to them (the user interface of the end-user design tool)?

Winkle et al.'s study [19] on persuasion strategies for socially assistive robots suggest that patients rather assign credibility to a third party than to the robot as an independent social agent. For instance, one participant said: "I felt like it [the robot] was genuine but also I'm very aware that somebody else programmed it to be genuine, but I'm ok with that because I feel like whoever had made the programme in the first place did want the person [exercising] to feel comfortable and to feel cared about…it's the intention behind it" [19]. The statement also reveals that this third party is anonymous. This may change if the patient sees the therapist adjusting the humanoid robot and the robot rather has a mediating or supporting role in the interaction between the therapist and the patient.

5   Conclusions and Future Work

Robot-assisted rehabilitation is often seen as therapeutic interaction by the humanoid robot (instead of the human therapist). The position paper introduces the complementary view of robot-mediated interactions between therapists and patients. As a consequence, therapists must be provided with means to adjust or modify the behavior of the robot for certain therapeutic situations. While user-centered design representations such as personas and scenarios generally foster creativity and discussion in interdisciplinary design teams they need to be adapted or revised to the specific challenges of new technologies and situations of use. It is argued that, in the considered domain, two-level personas support the development of design tools or domain-specific languages for therapists. In future work, we want to gain more experience in applying our ideas in practical settings.

References

1. Ajaykumar, G., Steele, M., Huang, C.M.: A survey on end-user robot programming. ACM Comput. Surv. (CSUR) **54**(8), 1–36 (2021)
2. Blomquist, A., Arvola, M.: Personas in action: ethnography in an interaction design team. In: Proceedings of NordiCHI'02, pp. 197–200, ACM (2002)
3. Bundea, A., Forbrig, P.: Patient and therapist model attributes for social robot stroke therapies based on implicit knowledge from expert interviews. In: Zimmermann, A., Howlett, R.J., Jain, L.C. (eds.) Human Centred Intelligent Systems: Proceedings of KES-HCIS 2022 Conference, pp. 41–51. Springer Nature Singapore, Singapore (2022). https://doi.org/10.1007/978-981-19-3455-1_4
4. Bødker, S.: hen Second Wave HCI Meets Third Wave Challenges. In Proceedings of NordiCHI'06, pp. 1–8. ACM (2006)
5. Cooper, G., Bowers, J.: Representing the User: Notes on the Disciplinary Rhetoric of Human-Computer Interaction. In: Thomas, P.J. (ed.) The Social and Interactional Dimensions of Human–Computer Interfaces, pp. 48–66. Cambridge University Press (1995)
6. Dittmar, A., Hensch M.: Two-level personas for nested design spaces. In: Proceedings of CHI'15, ACM (2015)
7. E-BRAiN Homepage, https://www.ebrain-science.de/en/home/. Last accessed 29 Jan 2023
8. Faulkner, X.: Usability Engineering. Palgrave Macmillan (2000)
9. Forbrig, P., Dittmar, A., Kühn, M. 2018. A Textual Domain Specific Language for Task Models: Generating Code for CoTaL, CTTE, and HAMSTERS. EICS 2018 conferences, , p. 5:1–5:6.
10. Forbrig, P., Bundea, A., Pedersen, A., Platz, T.: Digitalization of training tasks and specification of the behaviour of a social humanoid robot as coach. In: Bernhaupt, R., Ardito, C., Sauer, S. (eds.) HCSE 2020. LNCS, vol. 12481, pp. 45–57. Springer, Cham (2020). https://doi.org/10.1007/978-3-030-64266-2_3
11. Forbrig, P., Umlauft, A., Kühn, M., Dittmar, A.: The role of stories in software development and business-process modeling. In: Elstermann, M., Dittmar, A., Lederer, M. (eds.) Subject-Oriented Business Process Management. Models for Designing Digital Transformations: 14th International Conference, S-BPM ONE 2023, Rostock, Germany, May 31 – June 1, 2023, Proceedings, pp. 83–90. Springer Nature Switzerland, Cham (2023). https://doi.org/10.1007/978-3-031-40213-5_6
12. Grudin, J., Pruitt, J.: Personas, participatory design and product development: An infrastructure for engagement. In: Proceedings of the PDC'02, pp. 144–161 (2002)
13. Guffroy, M., Nadine, V., Kolski, C., Vella, F., Teutsch, P.: From human-centered design to disabled user & ecosystem centered design in case of assistive interactive systems. Int. J. Sociotechnol. Knowl. Dev. (IJSKD) **9**(4), 28–42 (2017)
14. Harrison, S., Tatar, D., Sengers, P.: The Three Paradigms of HCI. In: Proceedings of CHI'07. ACM (2007)
15. Ko, A.J., et al.: The state of the art in end-user software engineering. ACM Comput. Surv. **43**(3), 21:1-21:44 (2011)
16. Matthews, T., Whittaker, S., Moran, T., Yuen, S.: Collaboration Personas: A New Approach to Designing Workplace Collaboration Tools. In: Proceedings of the CHI'11, pp. 2247–2256. ACM (2011)

17. Platz, T.: Impairment-oriented Training (IOT) – scientific concept and evidence-based treatment strategies. Restorative Neurol. Neurosci. **22**(3–5), 301–315 (2004). https://pubmed.ncbi.nlm.nih.gov/15502273/
18. Platz, T., Pedersen, A.L., Deutsch, P., Umlauft, A.N., Bader, S.: Analysis of the therapeutic interaction provided by a humanoid robot serving stroke survivors as a therapeutic assistant for arm rehabilitation. Front, Robot. AI **10**, 1103017 (2023)
19. Winkle, K., Caleb-Solly, P., Turton, A., Bremner, P.: Social robots for engagement in rehabilitative therapies: Design implications from a study with therapists. In: Proceedings of the 2018 ACM/IEEE International Conference on Human-Robot Interaction, pp. 289–297 (2018)

Towards a Knowledge-Based Approach for Digitalizing Integrated Care Pathways

Giuseppe Loseto[1], Giuseppe Patella[1,2], Carmelo Ardito[1]([✉]),
Saverio Ieva[3], Arnaldo Tomasino[3], Lorenzo E. Malgieri[2],
and Michele Ruta[3]

[1] University LUM "Giuseppe Degennaro", 70010 Casamassima, BA, Italy
{loseto,patella.adr,ardito}@lum.it
[2] CLE S.r.l., 70126 Bari, Italy
lorenzo.malgieri@clebari.com
[3] Polytechnic University of Bari, 70125 Bari, Italy
{saverio.ieva,arnaldo.tomasino,michele.ruta}@poliba.it

Abstract. Clinical pathways play a crucial role in guiding the treatment of specific medical conditions or patient populations, but often rely on basic textual documentation, leading to potential inefficiencies and delays in patient care. This paper reports the early stages of a research aiming at exploring the application of knowledge representation techniques in the digitalization of diagnostic and therapeutic care pathways. These techniques are used to annotate contextual data, patient information and medical guidelines with respect to a reference ontology. In this way, a comprehensive knowledge graph can be processed using rule-based approaches to support the patient care management process, providing physicians and medical practitioners with valuable insights about specific diseases.

Keywords: Knowledge representation · Human-centered design · Healthcare

1 Introduction and Motivation

Integrated Care Pathways (ICPs) outline the recommended sequence of activities, interventions, and decisions involved in the diagnosis and treatment of a specific medical condition or patient population. These pathways are designed to standardize care, improve patient outcomes, and enhance the efficiency and coordination of healthcare procedures. The digitalization of ICPs represents a significant advancement in healthcare information management, aiming to streamline and optimize the delivery of diagnostic and treatment processes. Traditionally, care pathways consist of multiple steps involving several healthcare professionals forced to use textual documentation lacking standardized formats and often leading to fragmented care. However, with the advent of digital technologies, there is a growing opportunity to transform ICPs and enable intelligent data analysis and data-driven algorithms aiming to improve the quality of patient care.

© IFIP International Federation for Information Processing 2024
Published by Springer Nature Switzerland AG 2024
A. Bramwell-Dicks et al. (Eds.): INTERACT 2023 Workshops, LNCS 14535, pp. 91–103, 2024.
https://doi.org/10.1007/978-3-031-61688-4_8

By capturing and digitizing relevant health data, such as patients medical history, test results, imaging studies, and treatment plans, novel comprehensive and interconnected frameworks can be defined for managing the entire care process and support all healthcare professionals. Benefits of digitalizing ICPs includes the ability to automate complex tasks and create reference workflows by implementing digital decision support systems able to assist medical practitioners in diagnosis and lead to more personalized treatment planning and monitoring.

Anyway, digitalization procedures must be applied with a focus on user-oriented perspective to create effective healthcare solutions. Recent studies suggest that Human-Centered Software Engineering (HCSE) has a relevant impact in medical scenarios by providing the foundation for designing and developing software systems that are essential for achieving enhanced healthcare professionals experiences and improved patient outcomes (see, for example, [5,24]). One of the key aspects of HCSE is the involvement of end users throughout the whole software development lifecycle [19]. This user-centered approach helps in identifying and addressing usability requirements specific to the healthcare context, ensuring that the software meets the needs of its intended users. The need of interoperability standards to enable a digital representation of information in a standardized and meaningful way is also highlighted.

Health data modeling is a critical aspect for digitalizing health-related information. One of the most important and widely adopted framework is the Health Level Seven (HL7) [26]. HL7 includes a suite of international standards that enable the annotation and sharing of health information, also providing a comprehensive set of guidelines and messaging standards for representing clinical data.

Further clinical terminology standards such as the Systematized Nomenclature of Medicine - Clinical Terms (SNOMED-CT) [8] and Logical Observation Identifiers Names and Codes (LOINC) [22] have been proposed for representing healthcare concepts, observations, and measurements. SNOMED-CT provides a comprehensive clinical terminology system that enables the consistent representation of medical knowledge, whereas LOINC focuses on terms related to laboratory and clinical observations.

According to [6], despite all these standards seek to provide a sufficient degree of data interoperability, a semantic-oriented representation is essential for modeling health data and achieving a seamless exchange of information between different healthcare users and systems. Standards and languages proposed for knowledge representation can be used to capture and provide information in a standardized and meaningful manner, providing a common framework and vocabulary for representing and sharing health-related knowledge, allowing healthcare professionals, researchers, and technology systems to understand, interpret, and utilize the data consistently.

Following this vision, the proposed approach aims to apply knowledge representation techniques for digitalizing ICPs. Clinical data about both patients and diagnostic and therapeutic pathways will be annotated with respect to well-known reference ontologies.

The overall framework has been defined following key aspects of human-centered design for innovating health care described in [23], which articulates in the following steps: (a) engaging physicians from early on and throughout the design process; (b) identifying the needs and behaviors of the people we want to affect with our solution; (c) evaluating concepts at an early stage of development to simulate and test how people will experience a future design. At every step, the focus is on understanding needs, goals, and characteristics of the target users and incorporating their feedback and input throughout the process.

The remaining of the paper is organized as in what follows. Related work is discussed in Sect. 2. Section 3 outlines the framework architecture. Section 4 clarifies benefits of the proposal in an example scenario about Parkinson's disease. Finally, Sect. 5 reports conclusions and future work directions.

2   Related Work

In recent years, several studies and initiatives have explored the exploitation of digital transformation strategies and semantic-based approaches for digitalizing diagnostic-therapeutic care pathways. A general-purpose approach to integrate Electronic Health Records (EHRs) from heterogeneous resources has been detailed in [31]. Data are first mapped to RDF and then further annotated by means of specific healthcare ontologies and terminologies to integrate domain semantics. In accordance with the proposed architectural framework, data transformation is executed in a fully automated manner. This methodology has the main advantage of improving reusability and interoperability among diverse standards to face the growing generation of new and heterogeneous data in the healthcare domain. In [3], Shareable and Reusable Clinical Pathway Ontology (ShaRE-CP) was proposed to specifically model clinical pathways. It takes into account both medical guidelines and contextual information serving as a basis for developing knowledge-enhanced decision support systems. Furthermore, different frameworks have been proposed exploiting ontologies and rule-based engines for modeling clinical guidelines and optimizing healthcare procedures. In [1], disease-specific knowledge, clinical pathways and medical activities are annotated according to SNOMED-CT concepts and properties, whereas strategic hospital decisions were expressed as rules in Semantic Web Rule Language (SWRL) [18]. This framework was conceived with the purpose of tackling the unstructured nature of healthcare data, that still relies on paper-based records for the majority. By presenting this approach as a step forward to the digitalization and automation of CPs, it also addresses the challenge of missing and incomplete information. An explanation framework for rule-based clinical decision support is presented in [36] modeling reference guidelines in N3 and supporting health providers with evidence-informed recommendations.

Despite semantic-based techniques are valuable for modeling and organizing knowledge in healthcare scenarios, all the works reported above solely focus on analyzing the problem from an ontology engineering perspective and overlook important factors such as user experience. Due to this reasons, the field of human-centered design (HCD) in healthcare has gained significant attention in recent years, with numerous studies focusing on improving the user experience and effectiveness of healthcare systems. Main benefits and challenges of HCD in health care ecosystem are described in [33]. Moreover, human-centered techniques have been successfully applied for supporting physicians in several healthcare scenarios about chronic disease prevention [21], pediatric asthma treatment [9] and kidney disease management [13]. These studies have shown how getting input and comments from users at every stage of the design process can be beneficial in enhancing the usability and offering more precise suggestions. This is especially crucial in the healthcare field, where professionals emphasize the importance of thoroughly reviewing clinical data alongside recommendations and considering all the individual patient factors [13].

Furthermore, the proposed methodology shares several aspects with current Healthcare Recommender Systems (HRSs) basically focusing on identifying potential recommendations related to disease diagnosis and treatment plans [32]. In particular, knowledge-based recommendation systems interact with users to capture their needs and preferences, and define constraints to link their requirements to items [11]. In [12], a knowledge-based HRS has been proposed leveraging patient's historical medical records to ascertain the likelihood of future diseases in individuals by utilizing machine learning methodologies, including Markov models, clustering, and association analysis. Nonetheless, a notable limitation of this method arises from the potential for biased results, as the dataset was confined exclusively to a specific subset of patients, namely elderly individuals residing within a limited geographic region in Italy. Unlike HRS, our approach does not depend on data-driven machine learning algorithms, which helps mitigate challenges associated with building extensive user profiles [32]. Appropriate recommendations can be based on more complete clinical annotations that encompass not only medical insights, but also demographic information, current health conditions, and general medical knowledge, which collectively contribute to the outcome of the system.

Summarizing, most semantic-enhanced frameworks in healthcare currently support meaningful data description and interpretation, but offer limited human-centered functionalities [19]. They often lack explicit understanding of user requirements, user experience-driven design, and ongoing user involvement throughout the entire system development process. Conversely, classical HCD approaches can provide innovative and person-oriented solutions, but frequently do not rely on machine-understandable formats and their outcomes lack explainability. This paper proposes an approach aiming to combine the benefits of knowledge representation technologies with state-of-the-art HCD guidelines, particularly for adopting digitalized care pathways and supporting healthcare professionals.

3   Framework Architecture

With specific regard to the Italian National Health Service (NHS), ICPs are predefined, articulated and coordinated sequences of services provided at the outpatient, inpatient and territorial level, which involves the integrated participation of different specialists and professionals in order to achieve the most appropriate diagnosis and treatment for a specific pathological situation. The same sequence can be ensured by different organizational models depending on the demographic, social, and welfare realities in which the interventions are to be applied. Consequently, a different operational protocol is defined for each identified ICP containing several data about prevalent and incident cases, process of care indicators, specific sources of data, clinical complexity indexes and evaluation procedures. The operational protocol is then submitted for evaluation by scientific societies and professional associations and finally published as clinical practice guidelines, *i.e.,* recommendations aiming to enhance clinician's decision-making by translating complex scientific research findings into reference workflows.

In addition, World Health Organization (WHO) has released and continuously updated several evidence-based recommendations; however, it is well known that passive dissemination of recommendations is insufficient for its optimal implementation [16].

An early domain investigation was conducted with a small number of medical specialists to identify user requirements and potential areas of improvement in current procedures related to the analysis and application of textual diagnostic and therapeutic care pathways. The identified issues provided further validation of the findings previously reported in [2]: information overload experienced by physicians; limited expressiveness of current formalisms; challenges associated with the application of clinical guidelines.

According to these findings, the reference architecture reported in Fig. 1 has been defined to improve existing clinical workflows. In particular, the proposed knowledge-enhanced framework aims to support primary care physicians and medical practitioners in the following tasks:

- model ICPs and medical information related to the whole patient care management process exploiting languages for knowledge representation;
- generate a reference Knowledge Graph (KG) to be processed by means of rule-based engines;
- identify most suitable guidelines for a specific disease which will then be validated and confirmed by the human operator.

The knowledge graph represents the core of the framework and contains domain information related to clinical application scenarios annotated with respect to well-known vocabularies proposed for the health sector. In particular, the KG is continuously updated with the latest evidence-based information including: (i) all parameters required to define patient profiles, consisting of user

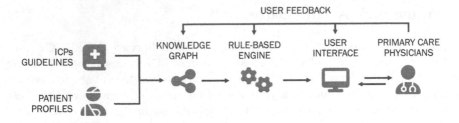

Fig. 1. Reference Architecture

habits and clinical status (*e.g.,* risk factors, previous illnesses, current symptoms); (ii) best practices and protocol therapies for specific diseases described by diagnostic and therapeutic care pathways.

The effective representation and modeling of health data in the KG is of utmost importance for ensuring accurate and effective analysis and decision-support procedures. The Resource Description Framework (RDF) [28] and the Web Ontology Language (OWL) [27] have been used for representing health data. RDF provides a standardized format for expressing data relationships and linking resources, whereas OWL is exploited to create formal ontologies for defining concepts, properties, and constraints in a specific domain of interest. Ontologies also provide a foundation for knowledge-based systems that support personalized healthcare approaches. According to ontology engineering principles and best practices [7], the KG reuses and combines well-known RDF vocabularies and OWL ontologies. In particular, *schema.org* [15] and *Friend Of A Friend* (FOAF) [14] have been adopted as reference vocabularies providing a core set of terms required to annotate basic healthcare entities. Data about human anatomy and medical specialties has been modeled using an OWL-based version on the SNOMED-CT terminology [10], while the Human Disease Ontology (DO) [29] is used for representing human disease concepts. In particular, the knowledge graph has been modeled exploiting the Notation3 (N3) format [34], an RDF-based assertion and logic language widely-used for representing knowledge and data in a human-readable and machine-understandable manner. N3 extends the RDF data model by adding logical implication and functional predicates. ICPs are mapped as N3 rules representing the various components of the pathway, such as clinical activities, decision points, care guidelines, and patient data, expressed using RDF triples. Each rule is modeled in consultation with domain experts and studies available in the literature. By annotating care pathways in N3 format, primary care physicians can benefit from reasoning capabilities of rule-based engines (*e.g.,* Pellet [30] or EYE [37]) to automate decision support, pathway validation, and adherence monitoring. Automated reasoning and inferences can be also performed over the pathway data, facilitating the identification of deviations, optimization of care plans, and generation of alerts or recommendations based on specific rules and guidelines. Finally, results obtained by the processing of N3 rules are reported to the user by means of graphical user interfaces, accommodating the diverse needs of healthcare professionals.

4   Illustrative Usage Scenario

The following example aims to clarify the proposed approach by presenting a decision support workflow in presence of patients affected by Parkinson's disease (PD), a chronic-progressive neurodegenerative disorder that affects the nervous system causing involuntary shaking of particular parts of the body. PD is the second most widespread neurological disease in the world [20] with an extremely relevant impact on patients and their family also in terms of psycho-social and welfare issues. It is characterized by a triad of movement symptoms (rest tremor, rigidity and bradykinesia) associated with non-movement symptoms: depression, anxiety, cognitive impairment, hyposmia, constipation, sleep disorders. In Italy, the annual cost per patient suffering from Parkinson's disease varies between 3,500 and 4,800 euros for the National Health Service, between 1,500 and 2,700 euros for patients and between 10,000 and 17,000 euros for the Society. By relating these data to the number of people with Parkinson's disease in Italy, it has been calculated that the total burden for the NHS, relating to this pathology, is between 1.1 and 1.3 billion euros and that for the Society between 2.2 and 2.9 billion of Euro. Although the considerable resources put in place by the Italian NHS for PD, there is still ample room for maneuver for optimization, which could first of all go through the clear definition of ICPs that improve continuity of care and ensure better patient management. ICPs are regionally defined programs to ensure consistent, quality treatment for specific medical conditions, such as Parkinson's. All of the regional ICPs for Parkinson's disease in Italy are based on a Chronic Care Model. It is a model of medical care for patients suffering from chronic diseases which aims to promote the improvement of the condition of chronic disease patients and suggests greater involvement between healthcare personnel and patients themselves, with the latter becoming an integral part of the care process. ICPs begin with the diagnostic phase and then move on to a therapeutic phase, not only pharmacological but also a rehabilitative one in which specialists in physiotherapy and speech therapy are involved. The selected case study focuses on the integrated care pathway approved in Italy by Marche region, representing a comprehensive guideline about diagnosis and treatment of patients affected by PD. It includes different procedures, reported as textual directions or simple flowcharts, to identify the progression of the disease according to different stages measured through the Hoehn & Yahr (HY) scale [17]. By means of the proposed approach, information provided by the ICP are modeled in RDF according to a standardized and structured data model. An excerpt of the knowledge graph is reported below, showing basic symptoms of PD.

```
@prefix : <http://example.org/parkinson#> .
@prefix rdf: <http://www.w3.org/1999/02/22-rdf-syntax-ns#> .
@prefix rdfs: <http://www.w3.org/2000/01/rdf-schema#> .
@prefix owl: <http://www.w3.org/2002/07/owl#> .
@prefix foaf: <http://xmlns.com/foaf/0.1/> .
@prefix schema <https://schema.org/>
@prefix snomed: <http://purl.bioontology.org/ontology/SNOMEDCT/> .
```

```
@prefix doid: <http://purl.obolibrary.org/obo/>


# Parkinson's disease
:ParkinsonsDisease a schema:MedicalCondition ;
    owl:sameAs snomed:49049000 ;
    rdfs:label "Parkinson's disease" ;
    rdfs:comment "A neurodegenerative disorder characterized by motor
        and non-motor symptoms." .

# Symptoms
:Tremor a schema:MedicalSymptom ;
    owl:sameAs snomed:26079004 ;
    rdfs:label "Tremor" ;
    rdfs:comment "Involuntary shaking or trembling of the body." .

:Bradykinesia a schema:MedicalSymptom ;
    owl:sameAs snomed:399317006 ;
    rdfs:label "Bradykinesia" ;
    rdfs:comment "Slowness of movement and difficulty initiating
        voluntary actions." .

:MuscularRigidity a schema:MedicalSymptom ;
    owl:sameAs snomed:16046003 ;
    rdfs:label "Muscular rigidity" ;
    rdfs:comment "Stiffness and resistance to movement of muscles." .

:PosturalInstability a schema:MedicalSymptom ;
    owl:sameAs doid:SYMP_0000860 ;
    rdfs:label "Postural instability" ;
    rdfs:comment "Impaired balance and coordination, leading to
        difficulty maintaining posture." .
```

For each patient, the physician will further enrich the KG defining a specific personal profile including patient behaviour and medical symptoms. An early version of the proposed DSS user interface is shown in Fig. 2. Moreover, a Personal Health Knowledge Graphs (PHKG) can be also generated exploiting external applications [25] and representing a complete disease activity summary report that can be imported into the DSS. The KG also includes diagnostic guidelines reported as N3 rules. The following example illustrates two rules for the identification of diseases starting from symptoms reported in the patient profile. In the first rule, the presence of bradykinesia and tremor indicates a suspected disease activity and a diagnostic procedure is suggested. Additionally, a specific stage of PD can be detected through the second rule in case of other symptoms.

```
:ParkinsonsDisease schema:stage :ParkinsonsDiseaseStage4 .
:ParkinsonsDiseaseStage4 a schema:MedicalConditionStage ;
    schema:stageAsNumber 4 .
```

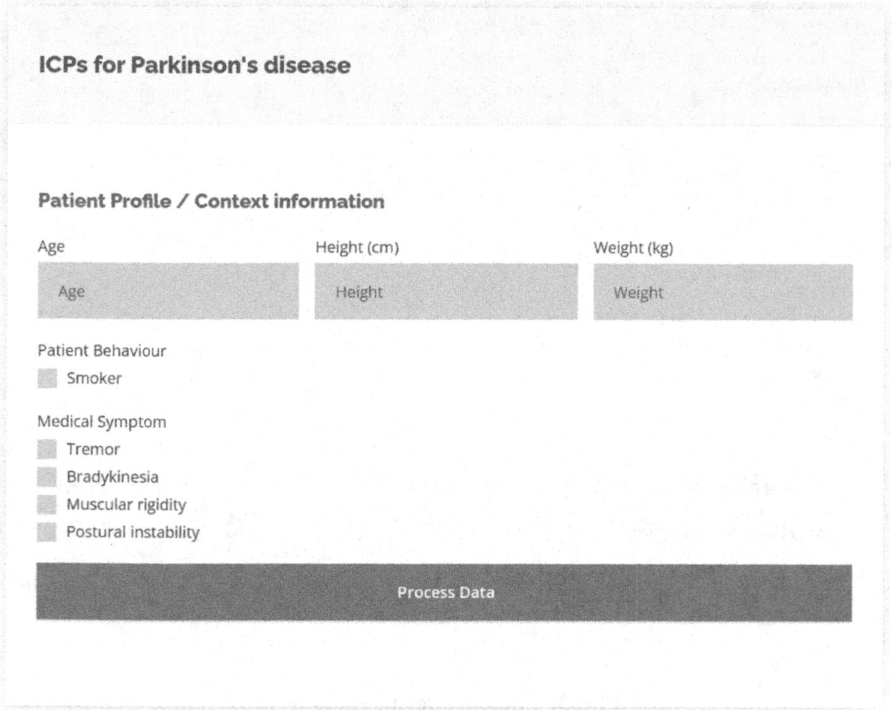

ICPs for Parkinson's disease

Patient Profile / Context information

Age

Height (cm)

Weight (kg)

Age

Height

Weight

Patient Behaviour

☐ Smoker

Medical Symptom

☐ Tremor
☐ Bradykinesia
☐ Muscular rigidity
☐ Postural instability

Process Data

Fig. 2. User interface for patient profile definition

```
{
    ?patient doid:hasSymptom :Bradykinesia , :Tremor .
} => {
    ?patient schema:diagnosis :NervousSystemDisease .
    ?patient :suggestedProcedure :ParkinsonDiagnosticProcedure .
} .

{
    ?patient schema:diagnosis :NervousSystemDisease .
    ?patient doid:hasSymptom :Rigidity , :PosturalInstability .
} => {
    ?patient schema:diagnosis :ParkinsonsDiseaseStage4 .
} .
```

EYE rule-based reasoner [37] is used to draw such inferences automatically, in order to support diagnostic and therapeutic tasks also enriching the reference knowledge graph for further inferences. The system returns to the physician a list of clinical findings and suggested procedures as depicted in Fig. 3. Final outcomes also include textual explanations tailored for end users. These explanations will be progressively revealed through the UI, along with relevant clinical details.

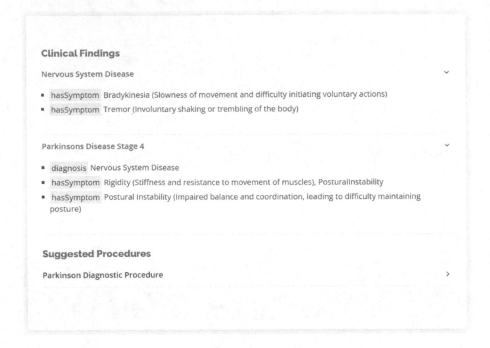

Fig. 3. Inference result section

Since the system validation has been conducted in a single medical branch, the reference KG currently includes a complete model only for Parkinson's disease. This has allowed to control the modeling effort while being able to evaluate the effectiveness of the proposed knowledge-based approach for decision support. By extending the KG using the adopted patterns, it becomes possible to model other diseases and therapies, thus expanding the domain knowledge into additional medical fields without requiring any modifications to the proposed architecture and algorithms.

Finally, an early quality evaluation has been conducted to highlight critical aspects of the proposed solution. These findings, derived from an initial assessment of the system, provide insights into both its potential advantages and limitations. In particular, exploitation of knowledge representation techniques has notable strengths, such as improvements in terms of explainability of results and comprehensive insights for healthcare professionals. Knowledge Graph technologies facilitate the annotation of automatically gathered health data with respect to online data sources related to biomedical ontologies (e.g., SNOMED-CT [8], FHIR [4]). The use of rule-based approaches in managing clinical pathways introduces automation and consistency into the decision-making process. However, the evaluation also reveals several weaknesses, including data integration challenges and potential end user resistance. Medical knowledge and guidelines are constantly evolving. Ensuring the accuracy and consistency of clinical data sources is paramount and can be technically challenging. Moreover, the healthcare industry is often characterized by a certain degree of resistance to change, and the adoption of novel approaches may require training and gradual adjustment. User trust is a critical factor in healthcare, where the accuracy and reliability of information directly impact patient care. These findings highlight the need for careful consideration and planning of future activities also underscoring the importance of end user involvement when considering the implementation of such a system in the healthcare domain.

5   Conclusion and Future Work

This paper presented a reference framework exploiting knowledge representation languages for modeling care pathways. By leveraging ontologies and knowledge graphs, healthcare professionals can benefit from rule-based decision support that assist in diagnosis and monitoring of specific disease. In addition, human-centered design techniques ensured that digitalized clinical guidelines and functionalities provided by the system are aligned with and physicians needs, resulting in improved user experiences. Future work in this area aims to refine the framework architecture. The reference user interface will be also improved considering the different human factors involved in the interaction between healthcare users and the system. Following the guidelines described in [35], the user interface will include a more detailed human-readable explanation and support different types of explanations (*e.g.,* trace-based and counterfactual). Starting from the current implementation, a more extensive evaluation will be also conducted, involving a significant number of users in multiple facilities for a long time span, to assess both effectiveness and usability of the proposal. This will be achieved through user interviews, surveys, observations, and usability testing. By actively engaging end-users, developers will gain insights into their requirements, challenges and expectations, in order to create a complete framework enhancing the overall quality of care.

Acknowledgements. This work has been partially supported by project *T.I.C.P.* (Technology for Integrated Care Pathways) and program *RIPARTI*, both funded by the Apulia Region.

References

1. Alahmar, A.D., Benlamri, R.: SNOMED CT-based standardized e-clinical pathways for enabling big data analytics in healthcare. IEEE Access **8**, 92765–92775 (2020)
2. Ardito, C., Bellifemine, F., Di Noia, T., Lofu, D., Mallardi, G.: A proposal of case-based approach to clinical pathway modeling support. In: 2020 IEEE Conference on Evolving and Adaptive Intelligent Systems (EAIS), pp. 1–6. IEEE (2020)
3. Bediang, G., Falquet, G., Geissbuhler, A.: An ontology-based semantic model for sharing and reusability of clinical pathways across context (ShaRE-CP). In: MED-INFO 2021: One World, One Health–Global Partnership for Digital Innovation, pp. 86–90. IOS Press (2022)

4. Bender, D., Sartipi, K.: HL7 FHIR: an agile and RESTful approach to healthcare information exchange. In: Proceedings of the 26th IEEE International Symposium on Computer-Based Medical Systems, pp. 326–331 (2013)
5. Blandford, A.: HCI for health and wellbeing: challenges and opportunities. Int. J. Hum Comput Stud. **131**, 41–51 (2019)
6. Braunstein, M.L.: Health care in the age of interoperability: the potential and challenges. IEEE Pulse **9**(5), 34–36 (2018)
7. Corcho, O., Fernandez-Lopez, M., Gomez-Perez, A.: Ontological engineering: what are ontologies and how can we build them? In: Semantic Web Services: Theory, Tools and Applications, pp. 44–70. IGI Global (2007)
8. Donnelly, K., et al.: SNOMED-CT: the advanced terminology and coding system for eHealth. Stud.n Health Technol. Inform. **121**, 279 (2006)
9. Eberhart, A., Slogeris, B., Sadreameli, S., Jassal, M.: Using a human-centered design approach for collaborative decision-making in pediatric asthma care. Public Health **170**, 129–132 (2019)
10. El-Sappagh, S., Franda, F., Ali, F., Kwak, K.S.: SNOMED CT standard ontology based on the ontology for general medical science. BMC Med. Inform. Decis. Mak. **18**, 1–19 (2018)
11. Etemadi, M., et al.: A systematic review of healthcare recommender systems: open issues, challenges, and techniques. Expert Syst. Appl. **213**, 118823 (2023)
12. Folino, F., Pizzuti, C.: A recommendation engine for disease prediction. IseB **13**(4), 609–628 (2014)
13. Garabedian, P.M., Gannon, M.P., Aaron, S., Wu, E., Burns, Z., Samal, L.: Human-centered design of clinical decision support for management of hypertension with chronic kidney disease. BMC Med. Inform. Decis. Mak. **22**(1), 1–12 (2022)
14. Graves, M., Constabaris, A., Brickley, D.: FOAF: connecting people on the semantic web. Cat. Classif. Q. **43**(3–4), 191–202 (2007)
15. Guha, R.V., Brickley, D., Macbeth, S.: Schema. org: evolution of structured data on the web. Commun. ACM **59**(2), 44–51 (2016)
16. Haddad, S.M., et al.: Building a digital tool for the adoption of the World Health Organization's antenatal care recommendations: methodological intersection of evidence, clinical logic, and digital technology. J. Med. Internet Res. **22**(10), e16355 (2020)
17. Hoehn, M.M., Yahr, M.D.: Parkinsonism: onset, progression and mortality. Neurology **17**(5), 427–427 (1967)
18. Horrocks, I., Patel-Schneider, P.F., Boley, H., Tabet, S., Grosof, B., Dean, M.: SWRL: a semantic web rule language combining OWL and RuleML. W3C Member Submission, W3C, May 2004. https://www.w3.org/Submission/SWRL/
19. International Organization for Standardization: Ergonomics of human-system interaction – Part 210: Human-centred design for interactive systems. ISO 9241-210:2019 edn. (2019). https://www.iso.org/standard/77520.html
20. Lampropoulos, I.C., Malli, F., Sinani, O., Gourgoulianis, K.I., Xiromerisiou, G.: Worldwide trends in mortality related to Parkinson's disease in the period of 1994–2019: analysis of vital registration data from the WHO mortality database. Front. Neurol. **13** (2022)
21. Matheson, G.O., Pacione, C., Shultz, R.K., Klügl, M.: Leveraging human-centered design in chronic disease prevention. Am. J. Prev. Med. **48**(4), 472–479 (2015)
22. McDonald, C.J., et al.: LOINC, a universal standard for identifying laboratory observations: a 5-year update. Clin. Chem. **49**(4), 624–633 (2003)

23. Melles, M., Albayrak, A., Goossens, R.: Innovating health care: key characteristics of human-centered design. Int. J. Qual. Health Care **33**(Supplement_1), 37–44 (2021)
24. Nazar, M., Alam, M.M., Yafi, E., Su'ud, M.M.: A systematic review of human-computer interaction and explainable artificial intelligence in healthcare with artificial intelligence techniques. IEEE Access **9**, 153316–153348 (2021)
25. Patton, E., Van Woensel, W., Seneviratne, O., Loseto, G., Scioscia, F., Kagal, L.: Development of AI-enabled apps by patients and domain experts using the punya platform: a case study for diabetes. In: Michalowski, M., Abidi, S.S.R., Abidi, S. (eds.) Artificial Intelligence in Medicine. AIME 2022. LNCS, vol. 13263, pp. 431–435. Springer, Cham (2022). https://doi.org/10.1007/978-3-031-09342-5_45
26. Quinn, J.: An HL7 (Health Level Seven) overview. J. AHIMA **70**(7), 32-4; quiz 35-6 (1999)
27. Rudolph, S., Hitzler, P., Patel-Schneider, P., Krötzsch, M., Parsia, B.: OWL 2 Web Ontology Language Primer (Second Edition). W3C Recommendation, W3C, December 2012. https://www.w3.org/TR/owl2-primer/
28. Schreiber, G., Raimond, Y.: RDF 1.1 Primer. W3C Working Group Note, W3C, June 2014. https://www.w3.org/TR/rdf11-primer/
29. Schriml, L.M., et al.: The human disease ontology 2022 update. Nucleic Acids Res. **50**(D1), 255–261 (2021)
30. Sirin, E., Parsia, B., Grau, B.C., Kalyanpur, A., Katz, Y.: Pellet: a practical owl-dl reasoner. J. Web Semant. **5**(2), 51–53 (2007)
31. Sun, H., et al.: Semantic processing of EHR data for clinical research. J. Biomed. Inform. **58**, 247–259 (2015)
32. Tran, T.N.T., Felfernig, A., Trattner, C., Holzinger, A.: Recommender systems in the healthcare domain: state-of-the-art and research issues. J. Intell. Inf. Syst. **57**(1), 171–201 (2020)
33. Vagal, A., et al.: Human-centered design thinking in radiology. J. Am. Coll. Radiol. **17**(5), 662–667 (2020)
34. Van Woensel, W., Arndt, D., Tomaszuk, D., Bialystok, L., Kellogg, G.: Notation3. Draft Community Group Report, W3C, April 2023. https://w3c.github.io/N3/spec/
35. Van Woensel, W., Scioscia, F., Loseto, G., Seneviratne, O., Patton, E., Abidi, S.: Explanations of symbolic reasoning to effect patient persuasion and education. In: Third International Workshop on eXplainable Artificial Intelligence in Healthcare (XAI-Health), co-located with 21st International Conference of Artificial Intelligence in Medicine – AIME 2023 (2023)
36. Woensel, W.V., et al.: Explainable clinical decision support: towards patient-facing explanations for education and long-term behavior change. In: Michalowski, M., Abidi, S.S.R., Abidi, S. (eds.) Artificial Intelligence in Medicine. AIME 2022. LNCS, vol. 13263, pp. 57–62. Springer, Cham (2022). https://doi.org/10.1007/978-3-031-09342-5_6
37. Verborgh, R., De Roo, J.: Drawing conclusions from linked data on the web: the EYE reasoner. IEEE Softw. **32**(3), 23–27 (2015)

**Designing Technology
for Neurodivergent Self-Determination:
Challenges and Opportunities**

Designing Technology for Neurodivergent Self-determination: Challenges and Opportunities – Workshop Results

David Gollasch(✉) [ID] and Meinhardt Branig [ID]

Department of Computer Science, Chair of Human-Computer Interaction, TUD Dresden
University of Technology, 01062 Dresden, Germany
{david.gollasch,meinhardt.branig}@tu-dresden.de

Abstract. This paper presents the results of the workshop on Designing Technology for Neurodivergent Self-Determination: Challenges and Opportunities. The workshop was part of the 19th International Conference promoted by the IFIP Technical Committee 13 on Human-Computer Interaction (INTERACT 2023). Eight position papers and two Lived-Experience Reports were presented and discussed in the workshop. During a creative design thinking session, multiple challenges focussing on typical human-centred design processes with a specific target user group of neurodivergent people were examined and opportunities were derived. Interestingly and worth highlighting, the COVID pandemic revealed insightful experiences regarding the use of technology for neurodivergent people.

Keywords: Assistive Technology · Users with Disabilities · Neurodivergence

1 Introduction and Background

Neurodivergent individuals, encompassing those with atypical neurocognitive functioning such as autism, ADHD, and sensory processing differences, often confront challenges in education, work, and leisure tailored for neurotypical norms [1, 3, 4]. While HCI research has extensively explored technology to support neurodivergence [7], critiques arise from its sometimes prescriptive, normalization-focused approach rather than emphasizing the lived experiences and self-determination of neurodivergent individuals [8]. Moreover, significant concerns surround the limited involvement of the neurodivergent community in research that directly affects them [9].

During the INTERACT 2023 workshop, we delved into three core areas:

1. Neurodivergence in Education [2]: Addressing the disparities in inclusive education, focusing on the challenges and potential solutions for both general and higher education settings. Emphasis was laid on the benefits of digitization for facilitating asynchronous learning and promoting place-independent education [5].

© IFIP International Federation for Information Processing 2024
Published by Springer Nature Switzerland AG 2024
A. Bramwell-Dicks et al. (Eds.): INTERACT 2023 Workshops, LNCS 14535, pp. 107–114, 2024.
https://doi.org/10.1007/978-3-031-61688-4_9

2. Neurodivergence at Work [4]: Discussing the prevalent employment challenges faced by neurodivergent individuals, from verbal communication barriers [6] to sensory overload. We evaluated the potential of Augmentative and Alternative Communication tools, and assistive technologies like noise-cancelling headphones [10], to improve the workspace experience for the neurodivergent community.
3. Neurodivergence and Leisure [11]: Exploring the role of technology in facilitating neurodivergent individuals' engagement in leisure activities, and advocating for a positive, strengths-based perspective on neurodivergence.

The workshop underscored the need for co-designed solutions, grounded in neurodivergent experiences and perspectives, to ensure that technology serves as an enabler of self-determined, meaningful engagement in society.

1.1 Objectives

Building upon our discussions during the INTERACT 2023 workshop, our primary objective is to stimulate critical dialogues in the HCI research community about the nuances of crafting technologies for neurodivergent individuals. We emphasize the significance of facilitating self-determined outcomes, allowing them to thrive and derive fulfilment from their engagements.

Key focal points include:

1. Inclusive Design Approaches: Developing robust design methodologies that cater to the unique needs and aspirations of diverse user demographics, while harmoniously managing varying access requirements.
2. Participatory Research: Prioritizing the active involvement of neurodivergent individuals in the research process. This ensures a balanced power dynamic, creating an authentic partnership between users and research teams.
3. Critical Reflection: Engaging in introspective discussions regarding our research positions, the theoretical frameworks we employ, and their ramifications in the realm of neurodivergence. This objective underscores the importance of ensuring that our technological innovations truly benefit their intended recipients without inadvertently reinforcing negative stereotypes.

Through these objectives, we aim to steer HCI research towards a more empathetic, informed, and holistic direction, ensuring technologies genuinely resonate with and empower the neurodivergent community.

2 Workshop Activities and Participants

2.1 Position Papers

During the workshop, a total of 8 papers and 2 lived-experience reports were presented, each of which sparked intensive discussions among participants. All 10 accepted submissions were showcased through presentations, providing valuable insights and reflections on the subject. Following the workshop, participants were encouraged to submit their papers for publication, leading to the submission of the 8 position papers that follow in this volume.

ADHD and Knowledge Work: Exploring Strategies, Challenges and Opportunities for AI In this study from Northumbria University, researchers explore how individuals with ADHD manage knowledge work. They conducted an online survey with 49 participants and found that while various strategies and tools are employed, challenges in prioritization and task management persist. The study highlights the potential of AI-powered tools, underscoring the need for raising awareness, co-designing inclusive tools, and fostering support to address the complex needs of neurodiverse individuals in knowledge work.

Co-design and Physical Computing with ADHD Learners: Preliminary Investigations. This position paper from the Free University of Bozen-Bolzano and Ca' Foscari University of Venice discusses the potential of engaging children with ADHD in technology co-design and physical computing. It explores how such activities can empower ADHD children, providing them with new expressive outlets and promoting self-agency. The paper highlights the characteristics of ADHD children that are relevant for their involvement in co-design with physical computing and outlines future research challenges in this context.

Diversity-centred Design: Thinking Through Video-Mediated Communication Systems for Disability and Neurodiversity. In this paper from Birkbeck, University of London, the author explores the challenges and nuances of video-mediated communication for neurodiverse individuals and those with disabilities. The article emphasizes the importance of understanding the failures of technology in these contexts and how they can inform more inclusive design, rather than simply seeking automatic fixes.

Co-design A Multisensory Tool To Support Collaborative Play With and For Autistic Children: A Methodological Approach. This paper presents a co-design methodology for creating a multisensory tool to facilitate collaborative play among autistic children, a group often overlooked in co-design processes. The approach involves extensive research, including interviews and observations with 18 autistic children in Qatar, to ensure that the tool meets their needs. The study sets the foundation for further work to validate and adapt this co-design method for different contexts and user requirements.

Coping with Depression. This article from the Czech Technical University in Prague provides an overview of depression, highlighting its common symptoms, risks, and treatment options. The authors propose an application based on cognitive therapy to help individuals cope with depression. The app includes an activity planner and thought reliever to assist users in managing their cognitive processes and potentially reducing the severity of depressive symptoms.

"That's Our Game!": Reflections on Co-designing a robotic Game with Neurodiverse Children. This article discusses the co-design of an inclusive robotic game for neurodiverse classrooms, addressing the issue of social exclusion often faced by neurodivergent children in mainstream schools. The authors conducted interviews with neurodivergent adults and educators to identify barriers and facilitators for inclusion and engaged in a co-design process with 81 children, including 19 neurodivergent individuals. They reflect on the process and the resulting game, considering its impact on the intrinsic motivations of neurodivergent children through the lens of Self-Determination Theory.

Understanding the Concept of Cognitive Disability. This article critically examines the terminology used to describe individuals with cognitive disabilities, intellectual impairments, and other related conditions. It discusses how medical diagnoses inform these terms and proposes "cognitive disability" as a more suitable and inclusive term based on an analysis of policy documents and academic publications.

Applying a User-Centred Design (UCD) Approach to the Increasing Number of Anxiety Disorders in Students and Workers. This article discusses the importance of addressing anxiety disorders in students and workers and highlights the role of user-centred design (UCD) in creating solutions. The focus is on developing apps and design products to reduce stress and enhance mental well-being, emphasizing the need for innovative solutions and user testing to meet the specific needs of the target group.

2.2 Lived Experience Reports

Complementing the eight position papers, our workshop featured two lived experience reports. These poignant presentations provided a deeply personal view of life as a neurodivergent individual, touching on the transformative power of technology in enhancing daily experiences. The emotional depth and insight from these talks stirred the audience, enriching the subsequent creative session with a heightened sense of purpose and empathy, which became a cornerstone for the productive discussions that followed.

First Experience Report by Denise Lengyel and Amy K. Hoover: I Might Change Colours: A Draw-Tell Exploration of Technology Use During Bereavement and Chemo Therapy Brain Fog. This contribution encapsulates a study on how individuals navigate technology use during challenging life events such as bereavement and chemotherapy-induced cognitive impairment. Through a "Draw-Tell" method, the participants—Amy, an AI researcher grappling with cancer treatment during COVID-19, and Denise, an HCI researcher handling bereavement—depict and discuss their reliance on technology for maintaining connections and managing daily tasks. Their narratives reveal contrasting experiences of technological engagement and its impact on self-determination. This introspective dialogue highlights the diverse, nuanced needs for technological interaction during personal crises, underscoring the importance of user-centred design in supportive technologies.

Second Experience Report by Derianna Thomas. The COVID-19 pandemic revealed the potential for technology to significantly improve the work and social lives of neurodivergent and disabled individuals. The shift to online platforms reduced barriers such as overstimulation from open offices and public transport. Personalized private spaces, with technology like noise-cancelling headphones and customizable devices, allow for a tailored environment conducive to productivity and comfort. However, the post-pandemic return to "normal" signalled a regression as accommodations for able-bodied and neurotypical individuals ceased, resulting in a loss of community for those reliant on these technologies. This personal account underscores the broad benefits of accessible technology, which the author's PhD research aims to advance, enhancing the work-from-home experience for all.

2.3   Challenges and Opportunities; Creative Session

Our workshop transcended traditional presentations by incorporating a dynamic design thinking session aimed at tackling the unique challenges encountered when creating technology for neurodivergent users. We divided participants into three groups, each engaging with distinct phases of the participatory and co-design process. The first group delved into the requirements engineering phase (cf. Fig. 1), unravelling the nuances of identifying needs and aspirations. The second group engaged hands-on with the intricacies of the co-design process (cf. Fig. 2), crafting collaborative strategies. Meanwhile, the third group navigated the evaluation phase (cf. Fig. 3), discussing methodologies tailored for and with neurodivergent individuals. Utilizing a Miro board, teams were able to document their findings visually, fostering a collaborative environment. The outcomes, captured in the Miro results, not only reflected the depth of the discussion but also highlighted both the challenges and opportunities this inclusive approach presents.

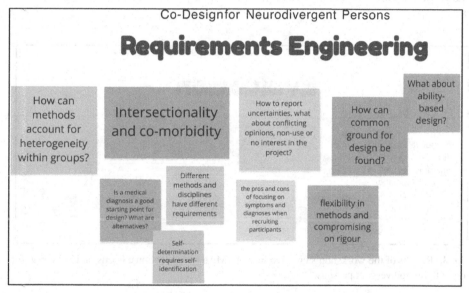

Fig. 1. Results of the workshop's creative session (Miro board section); Focus on Requirements Engineering for neurodivergent persons.

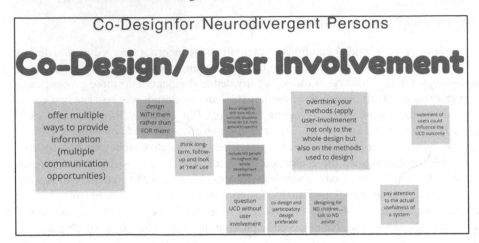

Fig. 2. Results of the workshop's creative session (Miro board section); Focus on the Co-design phase.

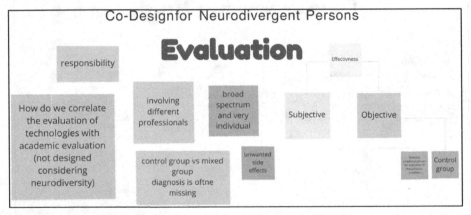

Fig. 3. Results of the workshop's creative session (Miro board section); Focus on Evaluation for and with neurodivergent persons.

3 Final Remarks

In summary, our one-day workshop gathered participants from various countries, facilitating a rich tapestry of perspectives. The event featured presentations of position papers and lived-experience reports, interspersed with dedicated sessions for discussing the intricate challenges of designing for neurodivergent individuals. The fervour for ongoing collaboration was evident, culminating in the establishment of a Discord community aimed at maintaining momentum and raising awareness about the subject matter. A novel aspect of our workshop was the introduction of Lived-Experience Reports, which bridged theoretical research and real-world implications. This format illuminated the practical challenges and opportunities that lie ahead. Such insights not only reinforce the necessity of our collective efforts but also chart the course for future endeavours in this vital area of HCI research.

Acknowledgements. We wish to extend our appreciation to the IFIP Working Group TC 13.3 Human-Computer Interaction, Disability, and Aging for their consistent support and commitment to enhancing HCI accessibility. We acknowledge the significant contributions of our program committee. Notable mentions include Kathrin Gerling (KIT) and Jan Gulliksen (KTH) for their extensive work in HCI accessibility; Katta Spiel from TU Wien, Oussama Metatla from the University of Bristol, and Gerhard Weber from TU Dresden. Their expertise greatly contributed to the workshop's success.

The project is funded by the German Federal Ministry of Labour and Social Affairs (BMAS) under the grant number FT 1 – 58330.

References

1. Bader, M., Labruier, M., Proft, J., Vogeley, K.: Menschen mit Autismus im Arbeitsleben – Informationen und Handlungsempfehlungen (2018). https://publi.lvr.de/publi/PDF/823-18_1040-Arbeitsheft-Autismus-im-Beruf-barrierefrei.pdf (retrieval: 02 November 2021)
2. Booth, T., Ainscow, M., Black-Hawkins, K., Vaughan, M., Shaw, L: Index for inclusion. Developing learning and participation in schools, 2. (2002)
3. Bryen, D.N., Potts, B.B., Carey, A.C.: So you want to work? What employers say about job skills, recruitment and hiring employees who rely on AAC. Augment. Altern. Commun. **23**(2), 126–139 (2007). https://doi.org/10.1080/07434610600991175
4. Das, M., Tang, J., Ringland, K.E., Piper, A.M.: Towards accessible remote work: understanding work-from-home practices of neurodivergent professionals. Proc. ACM on Hum.-Comput. Interact. **5**(CSCW1), 1–30 (2021). https://doi.org/10.1145/3449282
5. Hähne, C., Marquardt, G., Rudolph, E., Schmidt, H.J., Weber, G., Wegner, G.: Inklusion benötigt verschiedene Prozesse: Aktivitäten und Strategien an der TU Dresden. Zeitschrift für Hochschulentwicklung **15**(3), 363–376 (2020)
6. Happ, M.B., et al.: Effect of a multi-level intervention on nurse patient communication in the intensive care unit: results of the SPEACS trial. Heart Lung **43**(2), 89–98 (2014)
7. Johansson, S., Gulliksen, J., Gustavsson, C.: Disability digital divide: the use of the internet, smartphones, computers and tablets among people with disabilities in Sweden. Univ. Access Inf. Soc. **20**(1), 105–120 (2021)
8. Spiel, K., Gerling, K.: The purpose of play: how HCI games research fails neurodivergent populations. ACM Trans. Comput.-Hum. Interact. **28**(2), 1–40 (2021). https://doi.org/10.1145/3432245
9. Stefanidi, E., Schöning, J., Feger, S.S:, Marshall, P., Rogers, Y., Niess., J. (2022). Designing for care ecosystems: a literature review of technologies for children with ADHD. In: Interaction Design and Children (IDC'22), pp. 13–25. ACM, New York, NY, USA. https://doi.org/10.1145/3501712.3529746

10. Wali, L.J., Sanfilippo, F.: A review of the state-of-the-art of assistive technology for people with ASD in the workplace and in everyday life. In: Pappas, I.O., Mikalef, P., Dwivedi, Y.K., Jaccheri, L., Krogstie, J., Mäntymäki, M. (eds.) Digital Transformation for a Sustainable Society in the 21st Century: 18th IFIP WG 6.11 Conference on e-Business, e-Services, and e-Society, I3E 2019, Trondheim, Norway, September 18–20, 2019, Proceedings, pp. 520–532. Springer International Publishing, Cham (2019). https://doi.org/10.1007/978-3-030-29374-1_42
11. Wyeth, P., Summerville, J., Adkins, B.: Stomp: an interactive platform for people with intellectual disabilities. In Proc. of the 8th International Conference on Advances in Computer Entertainment Technology (ACE'11), Article 51, pp. 1–8. Association for Computing Machinery, New York, NY, USA (2011). https://doi.org/10.1145/2071423.2071487

ADHD and Knowledge Work: Exploring Strategies, Challenges and Opportunities for AI

Jennifer Campbell🆔, Sena Çerçi🆔, and Marta E. Cecchinato(✉)🆔

Northumbria University, Newcastle Upon Tyne, UK
{jennifer.c.campbell,sena.cerci,
marta.cecchinato}@northumbria.ac.uk

Abstract. While neurodiversity research in HCI has primarily focused on Autism Spectrum Disorder and children, other conditions (such as ADHD) and demographics remain underexplored. To address this gap, we conducted an online survey with 49 participants to investigate how individuals with ADHD manage their work. Findings reveal that while participants employ a range of strategies and tools, these still leave challenges around prioritisation, time estimation, and task switching. While AI-powered tools could be beneficial and some participants called for them, there was limited awareness and utilisation of them. However, those that did make use of AI tools found them very helpful in progressing with tasks. This study emphasises the need to raise awareness about existing tools for work management among individuals with ADHD. Co-designing inclusive tools and fostering support from managers and colleagues were also found to be crucial. Ultimately, we argue that we need to advance the discourse on inclusive productivity to account for the complex needs of neurodiverse individuals.

Keywords: neurodiversity · ADHD · productivity · knowledge workers

1 Introduction

While the importance of creating diverse and inclusive workplaces is widely acknowledged, existing productivity strategies mainly cater to neurotypical individuals [1]. Limited research exists on how neurodiverse workers manage work [2–4], highlighting the need for further investigation.

Neurodiversity, including ADHD (Attention-Deficit Hyperactivity Disorder), affects around 15–20% of the global population. Individuals with ADHD often struggle with executive function tasks [5], such as focusing, time management, and task completion, impacting both their personal and professional lives. The prevalence of ADHD diagnoses is increasing [6], with a 400% rise in adults seeking diagnosis in the UK since 2020 and a 20% increase in those seeking medication between 2020 and 2022 [7].

Research in HCI looking at neurodiversity has focused primarily on children with autism and their development [8–13]. A similar trend was observed for ADHD, where the focus remained on children and young individuals [14–16] and their support networks

© IFIP International Federation for Information Processing 2024
Published by Springer Nature Switzerland AG 2024
A. Bramwell-Dicks et al. (Eds.): INTERACT 2023 Workshops, LNCS 14535, pp. 115–123, 2024.
https://doi.org/10.1007/978-3-031-61688-4_10

[17, 18]. However, academic research looking into supporting those with ADHD has focused primarily on children, leaving adults and those who receive a diagnosis later in life out of the conversation. There is currently a gap in the literature and a call for more work to be done to create a better understanding of how neurodiverse people manage their work and what tools they use.

Therefore, we conducted an exploratory qualitative study with 49 participants who completed an anonymous online questionnaire, looking into how knowledge workers with ADHD manage their work and the role that technology plays in that. Our findings show that the challenges mentioned by participants could be easily addressed by AI-powered tools. While on one side we found there is still scepticism around the benefits and practicalities of using AI for work, those who make use of it find it incredibly helpful. Our work has implications for rethinking inclusive tools and practices for work and advancing a more inclusive productivity discourse.

2   Related Work

'Neurodiversity' in HCI was introduced by Dalton [19] as a research agenda that differentiated neurodiversity from traditional disabilities for its 'positive aspects', and expands the current accessibility discourse, contributing to the development of diversity computing as an alternative to normative research frameworks [20, 21]. Neurodiversity offers a different standpoint than the medical or social models of disability due to its origin and agenda as a heterogeneously-expanding movement [13].

Despite the growing number of HCI researchers with disabilities [22], as well as the increasing number of tech workers receiving a diagnosis in adult stages of life [3], there is limited work into the wellbeing of neurodiverse adults and how they structure and manage their daily lives. Adult ADHD has received even less attention within technology research [4], and certain demographics, such as ADHD in adult women, received even less so [23, 24]. It has been argued that this is because HCI research tends to either mitigate the disability markers [13, 25] or recognize disability as a category of identity [26], rather than meaningfully engage with the politics of disability and explore neurodiverse subjectivity as a different standpoint that could benefit technology research as a whole.

Despite the plethora of research on computer-supported collaborative work and digital tools to support individuals' productivity, what we know about neurodiversity in the work context is limited and fragmented in regards to technology [2, 3, 27–35]. Furthermore, the often co-occurring nature of the conditions like Autism Spectrum Disorder (ASD) and ADHD poses challenges in delineating the impact of a certain condition [3], calling for more research into understanding neurodiverse productivity for designing technologies that could potentially support individuals in the workplace.

Nonetheless, existing research into neurodiverse productivity outside HCI tackles productivity from a normative perspective. When ADHD is contemplated in an employment context, it is often viewed mainly in terms of the economic and societal burden that individuals with ADHD may create, rather than inquiring into their lived experiences of productivity [36–38]. As our understanding of neurodiversity in the workplace improves, previously marginalised individuals within the workforce, such as female ADHD workers [23], have started receiving more attention, potentially contributing to these individuals' productivity and overall wellbeing. Yet, we need to be wary of not imposing normative understandings of productivity on neurodiverse workers and attributing value to their labour based on their compliance with these implicitly neurotypical expectations.

It is therefore important that we understand how individuals with ADHD understand and manage their productivity on their own terms using the existing technology made available to them in order to support them in their flourishing in the workplace. A neurodiverse framing of productivity is likely to benefit all of us as some argued for accessibility [2, 3, 33, 39], considering how the expectations of productivity in the workplace are often imposed on the individuals and likely to make assumptions about their executive functioning, regardless of their identities.

3 Method

We designed and deployed an anonymous online survey with 49 participants based in the UK, currently working (full-time or part-time), who self-identify as knowledge workers and have ADHD. The study was developed using Qualtrics, with recruitment facilitated via Prolific and participants were remunerated for their time ($\approx$£9/ph). We received ethical approval from Northumbria University (ref: 4022) and all participants provided informed consent.

Open-ended and multiple-choice questions covered how people managed tasks, communications, meetings, their views around AI, their workplace set up, perceptions of what it means to be (un)productive, and experiences around disclosing their status at work. Data was analysed using thematic analysis [40]. In this paper we report on initial findings from task management and perspectives on AI tools for work.

3.1 Participant Information

Our sample consists of 49 participants: 25 men, 22 women, and 2 non-binary. 50% of participants were aged between 35–44 years old, 14% were between 45–64, and 37% were aged between 18–34. Occupations included a range of knowledge work roles, including IT professionals, healthcare professionals, educators, researchers, and professional services staff. 42 were employed full-time, while 7 were part-time, of which 3 were self-employed.

Of our sample, 20 participants received a diagnosis of ADHD (14 of which within the last 4 years), while a further 12 were currently on a waiting list. The remaining 17 self-assessed having ADHD and when asked whether they had considered seeking a formal diagnosis, answers mentioned being put off by the long waiting lists (2–3 years). While five preferred not to say, 23 participants disclosed presenting other neurodiversities, naming ASD (n = 12), Asperger's (n = 3), dyspraxia (n = 1), Tourette's (n = 1) as other conditions. 65% did not disclose their status at work, with reasons being they did not have an official diagnosis or were concerned about judgement and repercussions: "*I don't want to be seen/treated differently*", and "*I feel concerned about potential stigma or discrimination in the workplace*".

4 Findings

4.1 Having (Most of) the Tools, Yet Still not Getting Things Done

The range of daily tasks participants reported was varied and individual to each role, as expected. Despite this, almost every participant used some form of routine to manage the working day, generally including a combination of: to-do lists to be checked off, calendar events for appointments and tasks, and reminders. In addition to some paper based tools (e.g. post-its and scraps of paper), digital tools used included OneNote, Trello, Notion, Monday.com, Azure DevOps and todolist.com. Only one participant highlighted their lack of planning, which was coupled with a sense of anxiety: "*I just get on with it and hope I get it right and don't forget anything*".

The concept of "body doubling" in ADHD work management, involving the presence of another person, is frequently mentioned in online resources as a way to improve focus and reduce distractions, yet limited research exists on its effectiveness. Among our participants, 11 reported using body doubling, with 6 using digital tools (e.g., StudyTogether, Teams, Zoom), while 2 relied on their managers for support in staying on track during the day.

Challenges. Two consistent challenges reported by participants were being able to stay focused on a task, and the ability to effectively prioritise multiple tasks, as one summarised: "*staying motivated when it's slow day, and slowing down when I get hyper and want to do everything*". Many participants also complained about their intrinsic lack of organisation causing issues at work: "*I still manage to forget a lot of tasks*". The impact of this on the individual is hugely detrimental. One participant described themselves as feeling 'overwhelmed' to the extent where they wanted to be "*curled in a corner and not have to face work*". Another one described themselves as 'slower' than their colleagues and another indicated that the tools they used (paper notebook and Excel tabs) were not helpful for them as "*I use it inconsistently*".

Opportunities. It is no surprise that given the issues reported, participants were keen to have better support around task prioritisation, task switching ("if my laptop could buzz me or make a noise when I move from one task to the other"), and time estimation. Given deficits in executive functioning, time management is one of the most challenging aspects of working life for an individual with ADHD and some mentioned having a Personal Assistant or even AI as potential solutions: "*a PA to tell me exactly what I need to be doing and when*". However, besides the instrumental support, many also wished for more emotional support and understanding of ADHD from their employers and colleagues: "*Better instructions from management and an awareness of my needs. I like to have clear, concise instructions with written expectations including deadlines*".

The lack of connectedness between the tools and resources was an issue: "*They aren't always connected and don't 'follow me' or integrate in the way I want or need.*" These challenges could be addressed through technology and automation, combining the strengths of many of the tools currently adopted by ADHD workers into one instinctual system, as participants suggested: "*A system that integrates reminders, schedules and regular tasks*", and a "*more automated reminder system*". However, some participants also noted that the issue is not necessarily with a lack of tools, but their own executive functioning: "*I feel all tools are there I just need to remember to use them*" and "*I don't feel I lack resources, it's a lot more to do with willpower and focus*", and finally "*I've bought planners and organising spreadsheets and set alarms but they don't mean things get done*". This suggests that while an intelligent, integrated system to help with task management might be of support to individuals with ADHD, these need to be (re)designed to counteract an unintentional non-use.

4.2 Leveraging AI Tools

Of our 49 participants, about half (n = 23) had made use of AI-powered tools to help with work, while the other half had not (n = 24) or was not sure (n = 2). Those who did not make use of AI explained that they either did not even think about it ("*I just never thought of it until now*"), or they were concerned it might have too big of a learning curve ("*scared it would be too overwhelming*", "*I am not comfortable with learning this tool yet*"), or more commonly they had not thought how it could benefit them ("*I have not seen the need for them. I was unaware of their benefits*"). Conversely, those who did make use of AI-tools for work used a range of tools, primarily to help with text enhancement activities (e.g. ChatGPT, Quillbot, Grammarly, autocompletion of sentences in emails, Reflect, Mem), automation (e.g. Zapier, Snaplogic), creative outputs (e.g. Dall-E, Midjourney, Adobe Firefly, Syntesia), and digital assistants (e.g. ChatGPT, Motion, Bixby).

Besides Grammarly, ChatGPT was the most common AI-powered tool used by 24 participants. When asked what they used it for, participants had three broad reasons: to help with writing tasks; to help with programming; and to generate and refine ideas. Writing emails was a particularly common task, with participants using prompts like "*Rewrite this email to be more concise*" or "*re-write this email...to make it seem less passive-aggressive*". As one participant stated, "*ChatGPT has been an incredible tool to instantly concise or summarise down my communication to the essential elements.*"

Untapped Benefits. Those who made use of AI tools were generally satisfied with it and mentioned how it has helped address some of the challenges we listed above. For example, one person stated "*I love AI tools, they help me immensely. They help me improve my work, get more done, help me get more out of my time and make me more efficient*", and another one who had only started using ChatGPT three weeks prior found "*it really is like having an assistant*".

It is no surprise that the unfamiliarity that many still have with AI, coupled with a reluctance to integrate a system that they are accustomed to presents an impediment to the widespread implementation of AI as a successful strategy for ADHD workers. Yet, the challenges that participants mentioned above suggest that automation, integration of tools and AI-powered assistants could help address some of the struggles around time management, task switching and prioritisation. We found that with managed support and a clearer outline of how AI could be used in a myriad of ways to assist them in their task management, it could remove many of the barriers that currently face ADHD individuals and free up time for other work.

5 Discussion and Conclusions

We have presented initial findings from a questionnaire with 49 knowledge workers on how they manage tasks, the challenges faced, the opportunities for designing more inclusive workplaces and technologies. This work contributes to the need to grow our understanding of ADHD in adults within the neurodiverse discourse [4] and expands the current productivity rhetoric to one that needs to be more inclusive.

It is important to mention that while the authors of this paper do not necessarily identify as neurodivergent, they do bring their own intersectional experiences of privilege and exclusion. Moreover, two authors have secondary experiences of family members with neurodiversity (ASD and ADHD). We recognise that to truly reach an inclusive productivity discourse shift it is fundamental to include people with disabilities in the meaning-shaping capacity, be this as participants or researchers [13, 25].

Our findings point to the need for a three-step multi-pronged approach to a more inclusive productivity discourse. Firstly, we call for co-designing inclusive productivity tools that account for *unintentional non-use* and help with integration. While the tools and strategies mentioned by participants are similar if not the same to those reported by neurotypical individuals, we found that these tools fail to account for their executive dysfunctions. For instance, the use of a digital calendar will be rendered redundant if key meetings and dates are not entered, lost instead in a fog of overwhelm and crushing workload.

Secondly, we emphasise the need for raising awareness about and further exploring the potential benefits of new AI tools, especially for individuals with ADHD. We saw a frustration that the plethora of tools used did not 'speak' to one another intuitively causing the user additional workload and time updating different apps and analogue systems concurrently. The use of AI, Chat GPT in particular, was highlighted as an underused resource by at least half of the participants. However, this should be coupled with digital literacy opportunities to minimise the burden of learning and managing a new productivity workflow.

Finally, we call for increasing understanding of the lived experience of ADHD in the workplace among line managers and colleagues. The complex social environment of a workplace presents many challenges to neurodiverse workers but particularly to those who have an ADHD diagnosis who are forced to conform to schedules which are often unachievable whilst often having to hide their lack of impulse control, inattention and hyperactivity from their colleagues [41]. Participants expressed a clear sense of anxiety surrounding workload, organisational issues and unsupportive management teams who lack better understanding of their needs. In fact, echoing prior work [3], most participants did not disclose their status at work. Yet, an enhanced appreciation of the ADHD worker as untapped potential to be realised, coupled with significant investment into the evolution of supportive tools is essential to integrate this under supported minority in our society.

References

1. Bouckley, C.: Neurotypical privilege in the labour market. LSE Business Review (2022). https://blogs.lse.ac.uk/businessreview/2022/02/24/neurotypical-privilege-in-the-lab our-market/ Retrieved 26 Oct 2023
2. Das, M., Tang, J., Ringland, K.E., Piper, A.M.: Towards accessible remote work: Understanding work-from-home practices of neurodivergent professionals. Proc. ACM Hum.-Comput. Interact. **5**(CSCW1), 1–30 (2021)
3. Morris, M.R., Begel, A., Wiedermann, B.: Understanding the challenges faced by Neurodiverse Software Engineering Employees. In: Proceedings of the 17th International ACM SIGACCESS Conference on Computers and Accessibility – ASSETS'15 (2015)
4. Spiel, K., Hornecker, E., Williams, R.M., Good, J.: Adhd and technology research–investigated by neurodivergent readers. In: Proceedings of the 2022 CHI Conference on Human Factors in Computing Systems, pp. 1–21 (2022)
5. Diamond, A.: Executive functions. Annu. Rev. Psychol. **64**, 135–168 (2013)
6. Abdelnour, E., Jansen, M.O., Gold, J.A.: ADHD diagnostic trends: increased recognition or overdiagnosis? Mo. Med. **119**(5), 467 (2022)
7. Topping, A.: ADHD services 'swamped', say experts as more UK women seek diagnosis. The Guardian (2023). https://www.theguardian.com/society/2023/jan/13/adhd-services-swamped-say-experts-as-more-uk-women-seek-diagnosis#:~:text=Dr%20Tony%20Lloyd%2C%20the%20chief,who%20do%20not%20use%20medication
8. Benton, L., Vasalou, A., Khaled, R., Johnson, H., Gooch, D.: Diversity for design: a framework for involving neurodiverse children in the technology design process. In: Proceedings of the SIGCHI conference on Human Factors in Computing Systems, pp. 3747–3756 (2014)
9. Börjesson, P., Barendregt, W., Eriksson, E., & Torgersson, O.: Designing technology for and with developmentally diverse children: a systematic literature review. In: Proceedings of the 14th International Conference on Interaction Design and Children, pp. 79–88 (2015)
10. Çorlu, D., Taşel, Ş., Turan, S.G., Gatos, A., Yantaç, A.E.: Involving autistics in user experience studies: A critical review. In Proceedings of the 2017 Conference on Designing Interactive Systems, pp. 43–55 (2017)
11. Motti, V.G.: Designing emerging technologies for and with neurodiverse users. In: Proceedings of the 37th ACM International Conference on the Design of Communication, pp. 1–10 (2019)
12. Wilson, C., Brereton, M., Ploderer, B., Sitbon, L.: Co-Design beyond words: 'moments of interaction' with minimally-verbal children on the autism spectrum. In: Proceedings of the 2019 CHI Conference on Human Factors in Computing Systems, pp. 1–15 (2019)
13. Spiel, K., Frauenberger, C., Keyes, O., Fitzpatrick, G.: Agency of autistic children in technology research—A critical literature review. ACM Trans. Comput.-Hum. Interact. (TOCHI) **26**(6), 1–40 (2019)
14. Sonne, T., Obel, C., Grønbæk, K.: Designing real time assistive technologies: a study of children with ADHD. In: Proceedings of the Annual Meeting of the Australian Special Interest Group for Computer Human Interaction, pp. 34–38 (2015)
15. Cibrian, F.L., Hayes, G.R., Lakes, K.D.: Research Advances in ADHD and Technology. Springer International Publishing, Cham (2021)
16. Stefanidi, E., Schöning, J., Feger, S.S., Marshall, P., Rogers, Y., Niess, J.: Designing for care ecosystems: a literature review of technologies for children with ADHD. In Interaction design and children, pp. 13–25 (2022)
17. Cibrian, F.L., Lakes, K.D., Tavakoulnia, A., Guzman, K., Schuck, S., Hayes, G.R.: Supporting self-regulation of children with ADHD using wearables: tensions and design challenges. In: Proceedings of the 2020 CHI conference on human factors in computing systems, pp. 1–13 (2020)

18. Stefanidi, E., Schöning, J., Rogers, Y., Niess, J.: Children with ADHD and their care ecosystem: designing beyond symptoms. In: Proceedings of the 2023 CHI Conference on Human Factors in Computing Systems, pp. 1–17 (2023)
19. Dalton, N.S.: Neurodiversity & HCI. In: CHI'13 Extended abstracts on human factors in computing systems (pp. 2295–2304) (2013)
20. Fletcher-Watson, S., De Jaegher, H., Van Dijk, J., Frauenberger, C., Magnée, M., Ye, J.: Diversity computing. Interactions 25(5), 28–33 (2018)
21. Fuchsberger, V., Dziabiola, M., Mešić, A., Nørskov, D., Vetter, R.: HCI taking turns. Interactions 28(5), 38–43 (2021)
22. Brulé, E., Spiel, K.: Negotiating gender and disability identities in participatory design. In: Proceedings of the 9th International Conference on Communities and Technologies-Transforming Communities, pp. 218–227 (2019)
23. Holthe, M.E., Langvik, E.: The strives, struggles, and successes of women diagnosed with ADHD as adults. SAGE Open 7(1), 215824401770179 (2017)
24. Young, S., et al.: Females with ADHD: an expert consensus statement taking a lifespan approach providing guidance for the identification and treatment of attention-deficit/hyperactivity disorder in girls and women. BMC Psychiatry 20(1), 1–27 (2020)
25. Spiel, K., et al.: Nothing about us without us: investigating the role of critical disability studies in HCI. In: Extended Abstracts of the 2020 CHI Conference on Human Factors in Computing Systems, pp. 1–8 (2020)
26. Bennett, C.L., Rosner, D.K.: The promise of empathy: design, disability, and knowing the "other". In: Proceedings of the 2019 CHI Conference on Human Factors in Computing Systems, pp. 1–13 (2019)
27. Annabi, H., Sundaresan, K., Zolyomi, A.: It's not just about attention to details: Redefining the talents autistic software developers bring to software development. In: Proceedings of the 50th Hawaii International Conference on System Sciences (2017)
28. Zolyomi, A., et al.: Managing stress: the needs of autistic adults in video calling. Proc. ACM Hum.-Comput. Interact. 3(CSCW), 1–29 (2019). https://doi.org/10.1145/3359236
29. Tang, J.: Understanding the telework experience of people with disabilities. Proc. ACM on Hum.-Comput. Interact. 5(CSCW1), 1–27 (2021)
30. Walkowiak, E.: Neurodiversity of the workforce and digital transformation: the case of inclusion of autistic workers at the Workplace. Technol. Forecast. Soc. Chang. 168, 120739 (2021)
31. Kalantari, N., Zheng, H., Graff, H.J., Evmenova, A.S., Genaro Motti, V.: Emotion regulation for neurodiversity through wearable technology. In: 2021 9th International Conference on Affective Computing and Intelligent Interaction (ACII) (2021)
32. Kim, J.G., et al.: The workplace playbook VR: exploring the design space of virtual reality to foster understanding of and support for autistic people. Proc. ACM Hum.-Comput. Interact. 6(CSCW2), 1–24 (2022)
33. Lowy, R., Gao, L., Hall, K., Kim, J.G.: Toward inclusive mindsets: design opportunities to represent neurodivergent work experiences to neurotypical co-workers in virtual reality. In: Proceedings of the 2023 CHI Conference on Human Factors in Computing Systems, pp. 1–17 (2023)
34. Alharbi, R., Tang, J., Henderson, K.: Accessibility barriers, conflicts, and repairs: understanding the experience of professionals with disabilities in hybrid meetings. In: Proceedings of the 2023 CHI Conference on Human Factors in Computing Systems, pp. 1–15 (2023)
35. Simpson, E., Dalal, S., Semaan, B.: Hey, can you add captions?": the critical infrastructuring practices of neurodiverse people on TikTok. Proc. ACM on Hum.-Comput. Interact. 7(CSCW1), 1–27 (2023)
36. Faraone, S.V., et al.: The world federation of ADHD international consensus statement: 208 evidence-based conclusions about the disorder. Neurosci. Biobehav. Rev. 128, 789–818 (2021)

37. Weyandt, L.L.: Neuropsychological performance in adults with attention deficit hyperactivity disorder. In: Attention Deficit Hyperactivity Disorder: From Genes to Patients, pp. 457–486. Humana Press, Totowa, NJ (2005)
38. de Graaf, R., et al.: The prevalence and effects of adult attention-deficit/hyperactivity disorder (ADHD) on the performance of workers: Results from the WHO world mental health survey initiative. Occup. Environ. Med. **65**(12), 835–842 (2008)
39. Williams, R.M., Boyd, L., Gilbert, J.E.: Counterventions: a reparative reflection on interventionist HCI. In: Proceedings of the 2023 CHI Conference on Human Factors in Computing Systems, pp. 1–11 (2023)
40. Braun, V., Clarke, V.: Using thematic analysis in psychology. Qual. Res. Psychol. **3**(2), 77–101 (2006)
41. Adamou, M., et al.: Occupational issues of adults with ADHD. BMC Psychiatry **13**(1), 1–7 (2013)

Co-design and Physical Computing with ADHD Learners: Preliminary Investigations

Elena Cicuto[1], Rosella Gennari[1] (iD), and Alessandra Meonio[2]($\boxtimes$) (iD)

[1] Free University of Bozen-Bolzano, Bolzano, Italy
elena.cicuto@unibz.it, gennari@inf.unibz.it
[2] Ca' Foscari University of Venice, Venezia, Italy
alessandra.melonio@unive.it

Abstract. Engaging young people with neurodevelopmental disorders in technology co-design and physical computing can empower them in different manners. This position paper focuses on Attention deficit/hyperactivity disorder (ADHD) children and physical computing for co-designing with them, to give them new expression means and promote their self-agency. It starts presenting recent research on tools for collaboratively engaging young learners in co-design with physical computing. Then the paper overviews characteristics of ADHD children that matter for enabling them to fully participate in co-design with physical computing, or which can hamper their engagement. It concludes with challenges for future research related to co-design with physical computing as an empowerment opportunity for ADHD children.

Keywords: ADHD · physical computing · co-design · engage · learn · technology

1 Introduction

Research in Human Computer Interaction (HCI) and Technology Enhanced Learning (TEL) has shown an increasing interest in the design of technologies for neurodivergent people, especially in the autism spectrum; in recent years, a newly increased interest in such communities targets people with Attention Deficit and Hyperactivity Disorders (ADHD) [1].

ADHD and other neurodivergent children have often been involved in the design of technologies, or their usage, mostly individually and from a clinical perspective, as information holders or testers, or anyhow their participation is subordinate to the goals of adults, for example, educators [2–8]. More research is needed concerning how to engage them in the design of technologies for promoting their well-being in general, and their self-agency in shaping their solutions in particular [1]. Co-design has been used for this aim with people with specific learning disabilities [6]. Generally speaking, co-design aims to include, right from the start of the design process, the perspectives of different people affected by a technology under design. Thereby, co-designing means

© IFIP International Federation for Information Processing 2024
Published by Springer Nature Switzerland AG 2024
A. Bramwell-Dicks et al. (Eds.): INTERACT 2023 Workshops, LNCS 14535, pp. 124–131, 2024.
https://doi.org/10.1007/978-3-031-61688-4_11

to collaboratively engage in a design process not only designers but also non-designers, especially end-users, besides other relevant stakeholders.

Moreover, research is needed concerning how to empower ADHD children with computing skills during a co-design process. Due to the unprecedented penetration of technology in every aspect of everyday life, understanding how computing works is considered a fundamental competence for *all* children: a primary responsibility when co-designing with them is to educate to it the citizens of tomorrow. This has been recently done by exposing children to computing with physical devices, such as programmable microcontrollers, sensors, and actuators, which have the advantage of making concrete abstract concepts and reasoning steps [9]. Effectively engaging ADHD children through co-design processes with physical computing toolkits could be a great empowerment opportunity for them, especially at crucial times such as the developmental age, during which they are often subject to social exclusion and marginalisation also in learning contexts [2].

So far, promoting co-design with ADHD children has been marginally considered. How to empower them with physical computing tools has received even less attention. Instead, we believe that this is a fundamental aspect for their education and responsible participation in our technology-driven societies: due to the unprecedented penetration of technology in our life, "a primary responsibility when teaching Computer Science is to educate the citizens of tomorrow"–all of them [9].

To promote their true participation in co-design with physical computing, it is fundamental to study how to best foster it and what might instead hinder it. This paper surveys existing literature on co-design and physical computing. It then zooms in on the specific characteristics of ADHD learners that matter for co-designing with physical computing. Starting from these, it starts envisioning possible directions for enabling them to participate, actively, in co-designing with physical computing.

2 Co-design and Physical Computing

Co-design means adopting a conceptual model that focuses on empowering a specific group of people, taking agency and power, *during* the co-design process itself [10]. This is especially important when the process focuses on giving powerless people, such as children, a voice in the co-creation of a service or product [11]. For this reason, co-designing even to create technologies with and for non-expert users implies responding to the various needs of the participants by giving them the opportunity to express their skills with the aim of empowering them to solve and investigate the socio-scientific issues of their community through genuine enquiry. In this way, adopting this approach it is possible to involve several stakeholders creating an ecosystem of partners who can contribute with their expertise in the entire process of design, aldo through the adoption of techniques for creating a collaborative environment and providing a pro-active exchange of information based on shared experiences.

In this area of research, physical-computing devices started to be used and thought as mediation elements that could also facilitate the learning of abstract concepts faced with the consideration that children might be more interested if technologies, concepts, and experiences were linked and made tangible. The physical-computing approach allows an everyday object to become a so-called "smart thing", i.e., a physical thing with embedded electronics, and which is capable of collecting, processing, reacting and exchanging data through input and output devices [12].

In order to frame co-design and physical computing with children, researchers, educators or practitioners have used paper-based toolkits, such as storyboards and role-playing games, besides physical-computing boards and companion electronics (e.g., sensors and actuators) for children, such as micro:bit, Arduino UNO or Raspberry Pi boards [9, 11, 13].

However, there are few toolkits that enable different children, e.g., with different age ranges and expertise, to rapidly appropriate physical computing and prototype meaningful design projects with them, starting with their ideation. Even fewer enable to do so in collaboration with others. For instance, the IoTgo toolkit includes collaborative game boards, physical cards, an app besides physical-computing tools such as micro:bit boards. By playing it together, different non-designers could design smart things for a context, rapidly prototype their ideas, reflect in the process from different perspectives, and revise iteratively their prototypes of smart things [9].

3   ADHD Learners

ADHD is a Neuro-Developmental Disorder (NDD), and as such it is characterized by severe co-occurring deficits in the cognitive, social, communicative, motor, behavioral, and emotional spheres (DSM-5) [14]. Circa 7–10% of minors are reported to show symptoms of this disorder with a continuous increase of this percentage over time, to the extent that it represents a social problem that also tends to affect their families and, in general, their care and educational ecosystems [15].

As for the educational ecosystems, it is in fact frequent that ADHD symptoms co-occur with learning disabilities, observable in school contexts. These range from a lack of organizational skills, lack of self-regulation capabilities, difficulty in maintaining concentration in class and achieving academic goals, to even having problems with reading and anxiety [16].

In some cases, male children manifest a trend to disruptive behaviors, a certain degree of obsessiveness, and decreased inhibition, while female children are characterized by depression [17].

All these aspects heavily influence the child's school and non-school performances. Since problems are mainly noticeable at school age, interventions for ADHD young learners have tended to focus on their poor time management, organization of tasks, memory and rule-following skills. This, in order to reduce the risk of a state of alienation and/or self-exclusion, especially in heterogeneous environments such as school classes, with repercussions on individual, social and relational functioning.

4   ADHD Learners and Co-design

Despite a number of studies that try to engage in co-design children within the autism spectrum, with dyslexia or other specific learning disabilities, there are few works that aim to include in co-design ADHD children, and even less ADHD teens [18–23]. In particular, "little HCI research in the area invites this population to co-construct the technologies or to leverage neurodivergent experiences in the construction of research aims" for promoting their empowerment, in the sense of self-agency [17].

At the same time, the number of studies that try to include ADHD young people in technology co-design is expected to increase, especially in the educational context. As mentioned above, ADHD becomes evident when children come up against a composite and heterogeneous system such as schools are [24]. In this scenario, the main issues for which it is most complicated to include these children in co-design actions result to be inattention, hyperactivity and impulsivity, often in co-morbidity with other conditions. Because of that, some researchers focused their efforts on finding a way to better include different learners by observing and working on their strengths, trying to organize activities according to their "coolabilities", as well as by creating an education complex system composed by various stakeholders for supporting the inclusion of children with neuro-disorders within traditional schools [25–27]. For this purpose, the involvement of teachers as well as parents, educators, and specialists is necessary for a co-design process to be successful. In this way, it may be possible to understand the needs and interests of all participants by encouraging both the exploration of problems and prototype solutions [28].

Alas, co-design interventions for children with neuro-developmental disorders are often very limited, firstly, due to a large number of necessary stakeholders and secondly, due to the fact that they do not have the capacity to generalize strategies with which it could be possible to measure the effective inclusion, contributions, and empowerment of children with ADHD in the several phases of design [1].

5 ADHD Learners and (Physical) Computing

Initiatives or tools for empowering ADHD children with computing means are relatively scarce. Technologies developed for ADHD children tend to focus on what they experience difficulties with, such as games to train short-term memory, smart toys and devices to support the learning process and suppress undesired behaviors, or tangibles to facilitate organization, time-management and planning [24].

To the best of our knowledge, there are very few environments or tools for introducing ADHD children to computing [29, 30]. In particular, one paper focuses on promoting co-design with fabrication and computing, requiring different rounds of revision with physical material: five middle school ADHD learners with designing and fabricating a personalized "fidge" by following the process of engineering design; "despite issues in measurement precision, students successfully optimized their design solution over time through multiple rounds of revision" [31].

That may also be due to the variability of the ADHD population, which has an impact on setting principles and guidelines for better including them in computing activities. Some ADHD learners may excel in some computing tasks when they are exceptionally interested in it and may hyper-focus, albeit also negatively so becoming rigid in their choices. Others, instead, may experience difficulties in staying focused on the computing task at hand, they may need to be constantly reminded of where they are in a task and what they are working towards, and they may need to be situated in a context which prevents competing stimuli and enables them to stay focused [32, 33].

In conclusion, despite the literature prays the benefit of early introducing all learners, also with learning disabilities, to computing with physical devices [34], to date, there are not enough empirical studies or evidence-based guidelines indicating how to introduce ADHD children to computing in general, and physical computing in particular.

6 Conclusions and Future Work

Resonating with recent exploratory research that advocates the need of designing technology for ADHD children which goes "beyond symptoms", this paper posits the challenge of including them in technology co-design and physical computing.

This approach to computing and design has been profitably applied with diverse learners in recent work, and it has the potential of also enabling ADHD children to acquire new expression means and increase their self-agency possibilities, in collaboration with others. The adoption of co-design with physical computing could be the right approach not only to foster relations between neurotypical and non-neurotypical children, but also to contribute to their mutual learning, giving all the possibility to increase their computing means.

Challenges are related to understanding what co-design methods can best support the engagement of ADHD children in design, or how to adapt them accordingly. For instance, story-telling as well as narrative framing, scenario sketching or story-boarding with tangible material and clear progression markers can help ADHD learners stay concentrated and focused, without getting lost across different co-design steps. Role-playing can help those who suffer from hyper-activity. Other challenges are related to what features of existing physical-computing toolkits can engage ADHD children, and what features may instead disengage them.

Moreover, being co-design a collaborative process, it is also important to investigate what features of co-design methods and physical-computing toolkits can improve their collaboration with peers, besides with designers and other education stakeholders, thereby possibly fostering their inclusion among peers in learning contexts.

References

1. Stefanidi, E., Schöning, J., Rogers, Y, Niess, J.: Children with ADHD and their Care Ecosystem: Designing Beyond Symptoms. In: Proceedings of the 2023 CHI Conference on Human Factors in Computing Systems (CHI '23). Association for Computing Machinery, New York, NY, USA, Article 558, 1–17 (2023). https://doi.org/10.1145/3544548.3581216
2. Dreessen Katrien, S.S., Bieke, Z.: Exploring user gains in participatory design processes with vulnerable children. In: Proceedings of the 15th Participatory Design Conference: Short Papers, Situated Actions, Workshops and Tutorial - Volume 2, 1–5. ACM, Hasselt and Genk Belgium (2018). https://doi.org/10.1145/3210604.3210617
3. Cibrian, F.L., et al.: Supporting Self-Regulation of Children with ADHD Using Wearables: Tensions and Design Challenges. CHI, April 25–30, 2020. Honolulu, HI, USA (2020). https://doi.org/10.1145/3313831.3376837
4. Zhu, R., Hardy, D., Myers, T.: Community led Co-design of a social networking platform with adolescents with autism spectrum disorder. J. Autism and Develop. Disord. 52, 38–51 (2022). https://doi.org/10.1007/s10803-021-04918-9

5. Powell, L., Wheeler, G., Redford, C., Parker, J.: The suitability and acceptability of a co-designed prototype psychoeducational activity book for seven- to eleven-year-olds with ADHD. Design for Health **5**(1), 4–25 (2021). https://doi.org/10.1080/24735132.2021.192 8380

6. Raman, S., French, T.: Enabling genuine participation in co-design with young people with learning disabilities. CoDesign **18**(4), 431–447 (2022). https://doi.org/10.1080/15710882. 2021.1877728

7. Potapov, K., Marshall, P.: LifeMosaic: co-design of a personal informatics tool for youth. In: Proceedings of the Interaction Design and Children Conference (IDC '20), pp. 519–531. Association for Computing Machinery, New York, NY, USA (2020). https://doi.org/10.1145/ 3392063.3394429

8. Litner, B.: Teens with ADHD: the challenge of high school. Child & Youth Care Forum. **32**, 137–158 (2003). https://doi.org/10.1023/A:1023350308485

9. Gennari, R., Matera, M., Morra, D., Melonio, A., Rizvi, M.: Design for social digital well-being with young generations: Engage them and make them reflect. Int. J. Human-Comp. Stud. **173** (2023). https://doi.org/10.1016/j.ijhcs.2023.103006

10. Yip, J.C., et al.: Examining adult-child interactions in intergenerational participatory design. In: Proceedings of the 2017 CHI Conference on Human Factors in Computing Systems (CHI '17), pp. 5742–5754. Association for Computing Machinery, New York, NY, USA (2017). https://doi.org/10.1145/3025453.3025787

11. Rubegni, E., Landoni, M., Malinverni, L., Jaccheri, L.: Raising awareness of stereotyping through collaborative digital storytelling: design for change with and for children. Int. J. Human-Comp. Stud. **157**, 102727 (2022). ISSN 1071-5819. https://doi.org/10.1016/j.ijhcs. 2021.102727

12. Gennari, R., Matera, M., Melonio, A., Rizvi, M., Roumelioti, E.: The evolution of a toolkit for smart-thing design with children through action research. Int. J. Child-Comp. Interact. **31**, 100359 (2022). ISSN 2212-8689. https://doi.org/10.1016/j.ijcci.2021.100359

13. Hodges, S., Sentance, S., Finney, J., Ball, T.: Physical computing: a key element of modern computer science education. Computer **53**(4), 20–30 (2020). https://doi.org/10.1109/MC. 2019.2935058

14. American Psychiatric Association: Diagnostic and Statistical manual of Mental Disorders (DSM-5) (2013)

15. Fekete, G., Lucero, A.: P(L)AY ATTENTION! Co-designing for and with Children with Attention Deficit Hyperactivity Disorder (ADHD). In: Human-Computer Interaction – INTERACT 2019: 17th IFIP TC 13 International Conference, Paphos, Cyprus, September 2–6, 2019, Proceedings, Part I, pp. 368–386. Springer-Verlag, Berlin, Heidelberg (2019). https://doi.org/10.1007/978-3-030-29381-9_23

16. Zheng, Q., Cheng, Y.Y., Sonuga-Barke, E., et al.: Do executive dysfunction, delay aversion, and time perception deficit predict ADHD symptoms and early academic performance in preschoolers. Res Child Adolesc Psychopathol **50**, 1381–1397 (2022). https://doi.org/10. 1007/s10802-022-00937-x

17. Spiel, K., Hornecker, E., Williams, R.M., Good, J.: ADHD and technology research – investigated by neurodivergent readers. In: Proceedings of the 2022 CHI Conference on Human Factors in Computing Systems (CHI '22), Article 547, pp. 1–21. Association for Computing Machinery, New York, NY, USA (2022). https://doi.org/10.1145/3491102.3517592

18. Motti, V.G.: Progettare tecnologie emergenti per e con utenti neurodiversi. In: Atti della 37a Conferenza Internazionale ACM sul Design della Comunicazione (SIGDOC '19), Articolo 11, pp. 1–10. Association for Computing Machinery, New York, NY, USA (2019). https:// doi.org/10.1145/3328020.3353946

19. Francés, L., et al.: Current state of knowledge on the prevalence of neurodevelopmental disorders in childhood according to the DSM-5: a systematic review in accordance with the PRISMA criteria. Child Adolesc Psychiatry Ment Health **16**, 27 (2022). https://doi.org/10.1186/s13034-022-00462-1

20. Soysa, A.I., Al Mahmud, A., Kuys, B.: Co-designing tablet computer applications with Sri Lankan practitioners to support children with ASD. In: Proceedings of the 17th ACM Conference on Interaction Design and Children (IDC '18), pp. 413–419. Association for Computing Machinery, New York, NY, USA (2018). https://doi.org/10.1145/3202185.3202764

21. Malinverni, L., et al.: Participatory design strategies to enhance the creative contribution of children with special needs. In: Proceedings of the 2014 conference on Interaction design and children (IDC '14), pp. 85–94. Association for Computing Machinery, New York, NY, USA (2014). https://doi.org/10.1145/2593968.2593981

22. Vasalou, A., Ibrahim, S., Clarke, M., Griffiths, Y.: On power and participation: reflections from design with developmentally diverse children. Int. J. Child-Comp. Interact. **27**, 100241. ISSN 2212-8689. https://doi.org/10.1016/j.ijcci.2020.100241

23. Frauenberger, C., Makhaeva, J., Spiel, K.: Blending methods: developing participatory design sessions for autistic children. In: Proceedings of the 2017 Conference on Interaction Design and Children (IDC '17), pp. 39–49. Association for Computing Machinery, New York, NY, USA (2017). https://doi.org/10.1145/3078072.3079727

24. Börjesson, P., Barendregt, W., Eriksson, E., Torgersson, O.: Designing technology for and with developmentally diverse children: a systematic literature review. In: Proceedings of the 14th International Conference on Interaction Design and Children (IDC '15), pp. 79–88. Association for Computing Machinery, New York, NY, USA (2015). https://doi.org/10.1145/2771839.2771848

25. Fekete, G., Lucero, A.: P(L)AY ATTENTION! Co-designing for and with Children with Attention Deficit Hyperactivity Disorder (ADHD). In: Lamas, D., Loizides, F., Nacke, L., Petrie, H., Winckler, M., Zaphiris, P. (eds.) Human-Computer Interaction – INTERACT 2019. INTERACT 2019. Lecture Notes in Computer Science(), vol 11746. Springer, Cham (2019). https://doi.org/10.1007/978-3-030-29381-9_23

26. Grundwag, C., Nordfors, D., Yirmiya, N.: Coolabilities–Enhanced Abilities in Disabling Conditions. SocArXiv. November 26 (2017). https://doi.org/10.31235/osf.io/stgd4

27. Garcia-Melgar, A., et al.: Collaborative team approaches to supporting inclusion of children with disability in mainstream schools: A co-design study. Research in Developmental Disabilities **126**, 104233 (2022). ISSN 0891-4222. https://doi.org/10.1016/j.ridd.2022.104233

28. Pinos Cisneros, T., Escobar Vega, F., Kröse, B., Schouten, B., Ludden, G.: Co-creating hybrid toys as an approach to understand children's needs in play experience. In: Holloway, D., Willson, M., Murcia, K., Archer, C., Stocco, F. (eds.) Young Children's Rights in a Digital World. Children's Well-Being: Indicators and Research, vol 23. Springer, Cham (2021). https://doi.org/10.1007/978-3-030-65916-5_17

29. Galeos, C., Karpouzis, K., Tsatiris, G.: Developing an educational programming game for children with ADHD. In: 15th International Workshop on Semantic and Social Media Adaptation and Personalization, pp. 1–6. SMA, Zakynthos, Greece (2020). https://doi.org/10.1109/SMAP49528.2020.9248458

30. McKnight, L.: Designing for ADHD: in Search of Guidelines. IDC 2010 Digital Technologies and Marginalized Youth. pp. Print (2010)

31. Hansen, A.K., Hansen, E.R., Hall, T., Fixler, M., Harlow, D.: Fidgeting with Fabrication: Students with ADHD Making Tools to Focus. In: Proceedings of the 7th Annual Conference on Creativity and Fabrication in Education (FabLearn '17), Article 13, pp. 1–4. Association for Computing Machinery, New York, NY, USA (2017). https://doi.org/10.1145/3141798.3141812

32. Koushik, V., Kane, S.K.: It Broadens My Mind: Empowering People with Cognitive Disabilities through Computing Education. In: Proceedings of the 2019 CHI Conference on Human Factors in Computing Systems (CHI '19), Paper 514, pp. 1–12. Association for Computing Machinery, New York, NY, USA (2019). https://doi.org/10.1145/3290605.3300744
33. Cerezo, E., et al.: Guidelines to design tangible tabletop activities for children with attention deficit hyperactivity disorder. Int. J. Human-Comp. Stud. **126**, 26–43 (2019). ISSN 1071-5819. https://doi.org/10.1016/j.ijhcs.2019.01.002
34. De Araújo, E.C.J., Andrade, W.L.: A systematic literature review on teaching programming to people with cognitive disabilities. In: IEEE Frontiers in Education Conference (FIE), pp. 1–8. Lincoln, NE, USA (2021). https://doi.org/10.1109/FIE49875.2021.9637361

Diversity-Centred Design: Thinking Through Video-Mediated Communication Systems for Disability and Neurodiversity

Rebekah Cupitt(✉) ⓘ

Birkbeck, University of London, London W1CH 0PD, UK
r.cupitt@bbk.ac.uk

Abstract. Video-mediated communication is often touted as opening up access for neurodiverse people and people with a range of disabilities. While previous research has shown that this claim needs to be tempered with an acknowledgement of ableist assumptions made at the design stage, this paper discusses a less clear-cut issue: what failure to communicate via video meeting technologies in situations where multiple neurodiverse conditions and disabilities are present, might teach us. Drawing on observational data as well as shared and personal experiences, it is argued that paying attention to technology's failures rather than automatically fixing them are important first steps in designing for diversity first.

Keywords: ableism · diversity · disability · neurodiversity · inclusion · accessibility · universal design · video meetings · video mediated communication disability-centred design

1 Video Meetings as Accessible Technology?

1.1 A Pre-pandemic Account

Many would say that holding a video meeting involves making a sacrifice - sacrificing that sense of being there and in the same room. Pre-pandemic, it was a question of travelling to meet in person versus saving time, the environment, and money. A choice of meeting online with high-end video meeting equipment or making do with low-end, sub-par systems that worked on laptops or mobile phones. Zoom, Skype, Google Video, Cisco Tandberg and other similar alternatives offered acceptable levels of service for the occasional video meeting, but these required a variety of compromises and accommodations [3].

Swedish Television's Division for Programming in Swedish Sign Language. In previous research, Cupitt demonstrated how the shortcomings of video meeting technologies were two-fold [6, 7]. The mismatch of different brands of equipment, cumulative constellations of a variety of technologies and incompatibilities between components made systems sub-optimal and prone to error. At Swedish television's Division for programming in Swedish Sign Language (*SVT Teckenspråk*), a video meeting system that had

© IFIP International Federation for Information Processing 2024
Published by Springer Nature Switzerland AG 2024
A. Bramwell-Dicks et al. (Eds.): INTERACT 2023 Workshops, LNCS 14535, pp. 132–138, 2024.
https://doi.org/10.1007/978-3-031-61688-4_12

been tailor-made for one location (Leksand and the old *Dövas TV* offices), had been transposed partially but never fully customised to a second office space in Falun [6]. The two-camera set-up designed to work for communication with interpreters, Ddeaf[1] and hearing co-workers, had been hastily assembled in a basement meeting room. This haphazard placement of video meeting cameras, microphones, monitors, and other equipment became something that people's bodies moved around to accommodate [7]. This need for human adaptation stands in opposition to the usual discussions on accessible technology and disability which figures technological solutions as accommodating a variety of modalities of communication and even facilitating (sometimes empowering) people with disabilities [18, 31].

Disabled by Design. In a long term ethnographic study, Cupitt problematised this notion that technology enabled and instead argued that there was an element of disabling occurring as video meeting technologies, designed by hearing and for hearing users, failed to meet the requirements of communication in Sign Language and with interpreters present [7]. Rather than support the well-established inclusive work environment that promoted the right for Swedish Ddeaf employees to use their first language, *teckenspråk*, video meeting technology undermined the pro-Sign Language ethos of the dual language workplace [7]. In effect, Ddeaf employees (who considered their deafness to be more-than disability), became simply disabled as video meeting systems failed to support their visual modes of communication in Sign Language.

When Visual Media Technologies Fail. It seems ironic that visual media technologies like video meeting systems should fail to support a visual language like Sign Language but a close examination of the affordances of video meeting systems reveal the hearing-centred biases and the lack of input at the design stage from Ddeaf users [7].

People Innovate. While the video meeting systems did not enable fluid communication in Swedish, Swedish Sign Language, and communication mediated via interpreters, it did however create an opportunity for Ddeaf employees to draw explicit attention to the nature of Sign Language communication[2]. In several meetings, employees (mainly Ddeaf but also hearing colleagues who were dedicated to creating an inclusive work environment) used the failures of the technology, the necessary human adaptations, and fine-tuning of the system components (particularly the camera and its angle) to point out how Sign Language communication required more of both people and technologies. Taking the time to correctly position the camera, to ask colleagues to move their

---

[1] Ddeaf or dDeaf is a relatively new term that building on previous ways of labelling various identities associated with a medical diagnosis of deafness. 'Deaf' refers to identifying as culturally deaf and being a Sign Language user [23]. 'deaf' refers to identifying with deafness as a disability, not a cultural identity. D/deaf acknowledges that a person might identify as one or the other and using this means the researcher avoids assigning an identity to their interlocutors. Ddeaf has emerged to recognise that it is not an either/or relationship (as suggested by the use of '/') and that people might identify as both 'deaf' and 'Deaf' at the same time or alternate between the two.

[2] More details on this articulation of Deaf identity and Sign Language user needs is explained in [6] and in a forthcoming article [8].

places and furniture to ensure they were in eye-sight of dDeaf and Sign Language-using (*teckenspråkiga döva* [10]) colleagues[3] [7].

1.2 Attending to Difference

During the pandemic some universities excluded travel for conferences for insurance reasons, and many conferences shifted to online only formats. This shift was welcomed by some as making conferences more accessible, for example, those with limited financial revenue could now easily attend and participate in some form[4]. Prior to the pandemic, researchers such as [26] had already pointed out how attendance via 'tele-robot' had afforded them access to a variety of conferences. From this perspective, the shift to online conferences via platforms such as Whova, Zoom and other tailor-made virtual conference environments promised to upend some of the ableist dimensions of academia [9].

Prior to a 'return to normal' and a re-prioritisation of in person attendance, Cupitt attended a panel at an online conference where it once more became clear just how important it is to accommodate difference when designing video communication technologies and how sometimes designing for accessibility means inaccessible access for others. During this panel, the discussion was disrupted by an audience member requesting that only the panelist speaking be 'spotlighted'. In other words, they found it distracting to see all panelists on the screen (as well as one or two audience members who still had their cameras on). The audience member had not been able to tailor their Zoom setup up to spotlight only certain people and the conference IT staff who was on hand to help with technical issues like this, had not overridden individual user set-ups in Zoom. The panelists had said they preferred to be able to see each other during the discussion. Reasons the panelists gave for wanting to see each other ranged from personal preference, to panel format considerations (it was a roundtable discussion and in order for it to be a discussion, panelists needed to be able to see each other, facial expressions, and body language). The panelists were representatives speaking about supporting each other in academia and a number of them shared that they were neurodiverse and/or disabled. They all did research on disability and were part of the critical disability studies field of anthropology. As an audience member who is not diagnosed as neurodiverse nor disabled, commenting on events or attempting to interpret the exchange without a discussion with the panelists, would only serve to confuse the multiple user-needs that clashed momentarily during this panel.[5] The important observation to make, however,

---

[3] The importance of visibility is something that has been problematised in media studies with reference to visibility on social media and how this affects minorities. In a previous article, I further discussed the notion of 'visibility explicitly in reference to dDeaf modes of communication and research on video-mediated communication [7].

[4] This was the author's personal experience as a UK-based, early career scholar with limited research funds to cover travel for work.

[5] There are issues of voice and representation underlying this short description. A paper co-written with these panelists is currently under review where I have contributed with an audience member voice, and the panelists have added their experiences to co-create a multi-perspective account of the tensions created by competing neurodiverse user needs [8].

is that the disruption caused by a conflict of needs that were tied to the wide range of neurodiverse and disabled attendees and panelists, created a moment where all present (and even those watching the recording after the event) could *attend to difference*. As [8] note, the momentary confusion and disorientation called out the illusion of seamless and universally accessible communication [18, 19] highlighting that, as other scholars have shown, guidelines and software features can not possibly cover all problems encountered by *all* users [2, 4, 25]. Something that has not yet been the matter of wide scholarly discussion is the opportunities failures afford people with disabilities and who are neurodiverse, to make explicit their needs known and demonstrate how ableism affects them daily. Further, these moments where the challenges of communicating via video when disability and/or neurodiversity become visible, can be turned into political acts where disability activists and scholars can call out ableism and share their experiences in tangible ways [8, 9, 15].

2   Accessibility and Inclusion

2.1   Intra-relations

This paper is in no way an argument for making technologies poorly in order to give people with disabilities and who are neurodiverse opportunities to educate their ableist colleagues. But it does aim to demonstrate human ingenuity and perseverance in the face of socio-technological and design-derived failures. There are moments where video technologies are not at fault, the people using them are (for instance at SVT Teckenspråk) human-originating failures. For example, a hearing colleague might fail to look at the monitor and miss noticing that their dDeaf colleague was signing to them [6, 7]. If we take video systems as a whole and understand them as intra-related webs of human and technological components, then we might want to consider the possibility of designing systems that not only articulate system status and give user feedback, but which more deftly allow for moments of human explanation. This might take the form of a video meeting system or even a panel format that allowed for a short statement on each person's preferred modes of communication in some way that did not a) disable a participant; b) force an identity onto a participant, be it gender-, ability-, or ethnicity-related identity; and c) allow for reconfigurations of modes of communication[6].

2.2   Questions to Take with Us

These suggestions are difficult to put into practice. For the purpose of discussion, the questions I am most interested in are firstly, a) can we design for all, and secondly, b) is this even a desirable outcome? Are we potentially making invisible difference through attempting to accommodate all possible permutations of cognitive, physical, and emotional ways of being? And are we aiming to eradicate the conflict of competing and changing user-needs and many different lived experiences.

---

[6] Here I am referring to the work of Lucy Suchman [29] who argued for how human-interactions with machines are reconfigurings of understandings of each other's affordances, modes of communication, structures, subjectivities/objectivities, but even perhaps capabilities [30],

Further, we could ask ourselves where we lie on the spectrum of being a disabled-centred designer to use a term borrowed from Nakamura [8]. Historically, designing technology for people with disabilities has worked to compensate for an apparent lack of ability - drawing on disability understood based on the medical model [29]. Garland Thomson points out that the term "...disability brings together traits that may have little in common in order to create a social class of people designated as defective and politically, economically, and socially discriminated against... grouped together under the medical-scientific rubric of abnormality and its accompanying cultural sentence of inferiority" [12, pp 1557–1587). [2] explains how recent paradigm shifts in how disability is understood in the fields of computer science lie behind a move to accessibility and even more-so, towards inclusive design. An acceptance of the relational [21, 22] and social models of disability [29], rather than an exclusive focus on medical models of disability is one of these shifts [2]. Even so, designing with disability in mind is somewhat different than designing from a disability-centred point of view.

While this paper and many other scholars [11, 12, 19] have noted the different lived experiences of people with disabilities, asking the question of what universal design takes away from us might just be an important first step in moving design from an accessibility-first state [5] to a diversity-first paradigm.

3 Conclusion

This paper started with an example founded on research with dDeaf filmmakers in Sweden, which was then contrast with a more recent example of a virtual conference panel that took place via Zoom (embedded within a custom online conference platform). These two examples although quite different, both speak to how people deal with and take advantage of instances where communication is disrupted by the values that have been encoded into digital media technologies at the design and development stage. Set in relation to each other they work to call into question the model of thinking where success is defined as a seamless, integrated use of technologies in all situations by all users, irregardless of their abilities and mental health. Success might just be a case where someone *without* a disability or who is neuro-normative realises that this is not the only way of being; thus continuing discussions initiated by [5, 23, 25] and others [2, 13–15] on the nature of inclusion and accessibility in HCI [16], interaction design and the anthropology of technology.

References

1. Acevedo, S.M., et al.: How do we show up for one another?: learning from disability justice and anthropology in conversation roundtable. Annual Meeting for the American Association of Anthropologists (AAA), Baltimore, MD Nov 17–21 (2021)
2. Begnum, M.E.N.: Universal Design of ICT: A Historical Journey from Specialized Adaptations Towards Designing for Diversity. In: Antona, M., Stephanidis, C. (eds.) Universal Access in Human-Computer Interaction. Design Approaches and Supporting Technologies. HCII 2020. Lecture Notes in Computer Science, vol. 12188. Springer, Cham (2020)

3. Börjesson Rivera, M., Cupitt, R., Henriksson, G.: Meetings, practice and beyond – environmental sustainability in meeting practices at work. In: Nielsen, M., Rittenhofer, I., Grove Ditlevsen, M., Esmann Andersen, S., Pollach, J. (eds.) Nachhaltigkeit in der Wirtschaftskommunikation Europäische Kulturen in der Wirtschaftskommunikation, pp. 159–190. Springer Fachmedien, Wiesbaden (2013)

4. Calvo, R., Seyedarabi, F., Savva, A.: Beyond Web Content Accessibility Guidelines. Expert Accessibility Reviews. In: Proceedings of the 7th International Conference on Software Development and technologies for Enhancing Accessibility and Fighting Info-exclusion, pp. 77–84. ACM (2016)

5. Churchill, E.: Putting accessibility first. Interactions **25**, 5 (2018)

6. Cupitt, R.: Make difference. Deafness and video technology at work. Doctoral Thesis No. 3, 2017, KTH Royal Institute of Technology, Stockholm (2017)

7. Cupitt, R., Forstorp, P.-A., Lantz, A.: Visuality without form: video-mediated communication and research practice across disciplinary contexts. Qual. Inq. **25**(4), 417–431 (2019)

8. Cupitt, R., et al.: Video meetings: access and disrupture. In: Fagan-Robinson, K., Carew, M., Noce, G. (eds.) Inaccessible access. Rutgers University Press (2024)

9. Durban, E.L.: Anthropology and Ableism. Am. Anthropol. **124**(4), 1–14 (2021)

10. Fredäng, P.: Teckenspråkiga döva. Gondolin, Sweden (2005)

11. Garland Thomson, R.: Extraordinary Bodies: Figuring Disability in American Culture and Literature. Columbia University Press, New York (1997)

12. Garland Thomson, R.: Feminist Disability Studies. Signs: J. Women in Cult. Soci. **30**(2), 1557–1587 (2005)

13. Hamraie, A., Fritsch, K.: Crip Technoscience Manifesto. Catalyst 5(1) Special Section on Crip Technoscience (2019). https://catalystjournal.org/index.php/catalyst/issue/view/2199 Last Accessed: 22 December 2020

14. Hamraie, A.: Designing collective access: a feminist disability theory of universal design. Disability Studies Quarterly **33**(4) (2013). https://dsq-sds.org/article/view/3871/3411 Last Accessed: 22 December 2021

15. Hartblay, C.: Disability expertise: claiming disability anthropology. Curr. Anthropol. **61**(21), 526–536 (2020)

16. Hayes, G.: Inclusive and Engaged HCI Interactions XXVII.2 March-April 2020:26 (2020). https://interactions.acm.org/archive/view/march-april-2020/inclusive-and-engaged-hci Last Accessed: 19 December 2021

17. Hollier, S., Brewer, J., White, J. Sajka, J., O'Connor, J., Noble, S.: Accessibility of Remote Meetings. W3C Editor's Draft (2021). https://raw.githack.com/w3c/apa/9c9109f52551b42 e27f77a61b30415602df39565/remote-meetings/index.html

18. Imrie, R.: From Universal to Inclusive Design in the Built Environment. In: Swain, J., French, S., Barnes, C., Thomas, C. (eds.) Disabling Barriers - Enabling Environments, 2nd edn., pp. 279–284. SAGE Publications, London (2004)

19. Mace, R., Hardie, G., Plaice, J.: Accessible environments: toward universal design. In: Preiser, W., Vischer, J., White, E. (eds.) Design Interventions: Toward a More Humane Architecture. Routledge, London (2015)

20. Monaghan, L.: A World's Eye View: Deaf Cultures in Global Perspective. In: Monaghan, L., Schmaling, C., Nakamura, K., Turner, G.H. (eds.) Many Ways to Be Deaf, pp. 1–24. Gallaudet University Press, Washington, USA, International Variation in Deaf Communities (2003)

21. Moser, I., Law, J.: Good passages, bad passages. The Sociological Review **47**(S1), 196–219 (1999)

22. Moser, I.: On becoming disabled and articulating alternatives: The multiple modes of ordering disability and their interferences. Cult. Stud. **19**(6), 667–700 (2005)

23. Padden, C., Humphries, T.: Deaf in America: Voices from a Culture. Harvard University Press, Cambridge, MA (1990)

24. Petrie, H., Savva, A., Power, C.: Towards a unified definition of web accessibility. In: Proceedings of the 12th Web for All Conference (W4A '15), Article 35, pp. 1–13. Association for Computing Machinery, New York, NY, USA (2015)
25. Power, C., Freire, A., Petrie, H., Swallow, D.: Guidelines are only half of the story: accessibility problems encountered by blind users on the web. In: Proceedings of the SIGCHI conference on human factors in computing systems, pp. 433–442 (2012)
26. Rode, J.A.: On Becoming A Cyborg: A Reflection On Articulation Work, Embodiment, Agency and Ableism. Breaking Down Barriers: Usability, Accessibility and Inclusive Design, pp. 239–249. Springer Verlag (2018). https://doi.org/10.1007/978-3-319-75028-6_21
27. Rømen, D., Svanæs, D.: Validating WCAG versions 1.0 and 2.0 through usability testing with disabled users. Universal Access in the Information Society **11**(4), 375–385 (2012)
28. Shakespeare, T.: Disability Rights and Wrongs Revisited. Routledge, London (2014)
29. Suchman, L.: Human-machine reconfigurations: Plans and situated actions, 2nd edn. Cambridge University Press, Cambridge (2007)
30. Taylor, A.: Becoming more capable. In: Cupitt, R. (ed.) Disabling Technology Series, Platypus, the CASTAC blog (2017). https://blog.castac.org/2017/04/becoming-more-capable/ Last Accessed: 19 December 2021
31. Vasquez, K.: Virtual Conferences Aren't as Accessible as You Might Think. Scientific American (2021). https://www.scientificamerican.com/article/virtual-conferences-arent-as-accessible-as-you-might-think/ Last Accessed: 19 December 2021

Co-design a Multisensory Tool to Support Collaborative Play with and for Autistic Children: A Methodological Approach

Mohamad Hassan Fadi Hijab[1]([⊠]) [iD], Nahwan Al Aswadi[2] [iD], Shaza Khatab[1] [iD],
Dena Al-Thani[1] [iD], Joselia Neves[2] [iD], Marwa Qaraqe[1] [iD], Achraf Othman[3] [iD],
and Noora Alsulaiti[4] [iD]

[1] Information and Computing Technology Division, College of Science and Engineering,
Hamad Bin Khalifa University, Doha, Qatar
{mhhijab,shkh41443,dalthani,mqaraqe}@hbku.edu.qa
[2] College of Humanities and Social Sciences, Hamad Bin Khalifa University, Doha, Qatar
{nalaswadi,jneves}@hbku.edu.qa
[3] Mada Qatar Assistive Technology Center, Doha, Qatar
aothman@mada.org.qa
[4] Shafallah Center, Doha, Qatar
noora.alsulaiti@shafallah.org.qa

Abstract. This paper introduces a co-design methodology aimed at the development of a multisensory tool to facilitate collaborative play among autistic children, a demographic traditionally underrepresented in the co-design process. Due to challenges in social and communication skills, autistic children may experience difficulties in engaging in collaborative play. Co-design is used to effectively incorporate the perspectives of all stakeholders, including researchers, developers, and end users when developing a new product. In this work, the co-design methodology was devised following an extensive contextual inquiry study involving interviews and observational sessions of 18 autistic children, based in a disability center and an inclusive school, in Qatar. The research method involves sequential and interconnected stages of logistics setup, familiarization, pair interaction, co-design, and testing, each laying the groundwork for the subsequent phase. Future endeavors should focus on validating and enhancing this co-design approach to ensure its efficacy and adaptability to varying contexts and user needs.

Keywords: co-design · autism · autistic children · collaborative play · multisensory tool · methodology

1 Introduction

Over the past few years, the number of children diagnosed with autism has increased significantly [1]. In Qatar, where this research is based, one in every 87 children have been diagnosed with Autism [2]. To uphold the identity-first language preferred by many in the

A. Bramwell-Dicks et al. (Eds.): INTERACT 2023 Workshops, LNCS 14535, pp. 139–145, 2024.
https://doi.org/10.1007/978-3-031-61688-4_13

autism community, this paper uses the term "autistic person" to refer to individuals with Autism Spectrum Disorder [3]. This terminology reflects an empowering perspective that respects and appreciates autistic individuals for who they are, rather than defining them by their diagnosis.

Embracing a neurodiversity perspective, autistic children may experience challenges in play, especially collaborative play [4]. Collaborative play, understood as an interaction between at least two children playing towards a common goal, is a crucial facet of children's developmental journey. Not only does it enable children to exercise empathy and negotiation skills, but it also offers a safe space for them to experiment with different conflict resolution strategies [5]. Given its significance, the exploration of how autistic children engage in this type of play can offer valuable insights into how to support their developmental growth.

Recent years have witnessed a progressive shift in the field of Human-Computer Interaction towards a more democratic approach in technology design. Co-design has been adopted as a key strategy to create interactive technologies, recognizing users as integral members of the design team [6, 7]. Originating from the Participatory Design method, this approach advocates for the user's right to participate in the design process at every stage, from the inception of an idea to its final assessment [8]. This shift underscores a more inclusive ethos, valuing diversity and promoting equality in technology design. Involving autistic children in the co-design process, however, brings its unique challenges. However, the benefits of adopting a strengths-based approach far outweigh them. This approach shifts the focus from perceived deficits to the unique strengths, experiences, and interests of autistic children [9]. Although some barriers may arise, especially when working with children who have limited communication abilities, the inclusion of indirect stakeholders, such as caregivers and teachers, can facilitate the process [10].

In the context of these observations, this paper is part of a larger project that aims to co-design, develop and evaluate a multisensory tool to support collaborative play for autistic and non-autistic children [11]. It presents a co-designing methodology, highlighting the importance of inclusive co-design methods that respect and value the unique experiences and abilities of autistic children. This paper starts by offering an overview of the contextual inquiry process, along with associated results. It then outlines the co-design phases, focusing on the first four stages, while noting that the fifth phase remains incomplete. Subsequently, the paper discusses the encountered challenges and their implications on the co-design process. The paper concludes with a synthesis of findings and directions for future work.

2 Requirements Gathering

This project involved ten autistic children from a disability center and eight from an international inclusive school, in Qatar. Prior to data collection, ethical approval was obtained from the Qatar Biomedical Research Institute Research Board. The project's aims and methodology were independently presented to therapists and teachers at both institutions. The team recruited autistic children aged between 7 to 12, ensuring they underwent comparable assessments, managed by the institutions. A contextual inquiry approach [12] was adopted, encompassing observations and interviews at both sites. The main goal was to discern behavioral patterns and elucidate the challenges and prospects of collaborative play among autistic children.

Both the center and the school collected consent forms from parents and confirmed their availability for interviews, which were conducted with 16 parents, 12 teachers, six speech and language therapists, four psychologists, six occupational therapists, and one physiotherapist across both institutions. Despite two parents being unable to participate, a total of 45 semi-structured interviews were carried out. As well, 48 collaborative play classes, led by teachers, were observed in both sites. Thematic analysis was employed to evaluate the transcribed interviews and video recordings [13].

Two sets of themes were generated separately from the interviews and observation sessions. From the interviews, themes emerged offering insights into autistic children and collaborative play, structured around a 5W-H model. This model addresses parameters to gather the "who," pertaining to the individuals involved; "where," exploring various play settings; "what," investigating technologies used; "why," discussing motivations; "which," addressing the sensory stimuli; and "how," detailing strategies for collaborative play. Observation sessions yielded themes of "collaborative play", "coordinated activity", "potential for collaboration", and "collaborative activity". Collaborative play implies shared goals and encompasses awareness, coordination, and communication [14, 15]. "Coordinated activity", often teacher-guided, was a dominant feature in the observed incidence, while "potential for collaboration" indicated activities that missed one of the collaborative play components with a potential for evolving into collaborative play. The theme of "collaborative activity" emphasized working collectively towards a common goal without adult's guidance.

Overall, this contextual inquiry provided valuable insights into understanding collaborative play among autistic children. The results shed light on the occurrence and nature of collaborative play in both sites. They also highlighted the potential benefits of collaborative activities for autistic children. These findings have implications for practitioners, educators, and researchers working with autistic children. They underscore the importance of creating environments that foster collaborative play and facilitate social interactions among autistic children.

3 Co-design Phases

This paper entails a step-by-step co-design process shown in Fig. 1. These stages are sequential and interconnected, each setting the foundation for the next. At the time of writing this paper, we find ourselves in phase 4.

3.1 Phase 1: Logistics Setup

The first phase was the 'setup of logistics'. The process was a collaborative effort involving the research team, therapists, and teachers from both institutions. These stakeholders were asked to assist in establishing a conducive environment that entailed a room familiar to the children participating in the study, equipped with toys that the children regularly

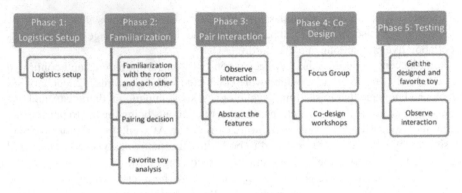

Fig. 1. Co-design study process

interacted with. Creating a familiar environment enables autistic children to feel comfortable and at ease, enabling them to freely express themselves. This room served as the setting for all subsequent phases of the study.

3.2 Phase 2: Familiarization

This phase comprised daily sessions of 30 min each, to help the children be accustomed to each other as well as the room setup. Over five days, the sessions were captured using three fixed and one moving camera operated by a researcher, while another two researchers were taking notes. Throughout the sessions, the children were allowed to play freely without adult interference. Following the fifth session, an analysis of the recorded footage was carried out, to group the children into pairs, in view of mutual attraction to the same toy during these initial sessions.

3.3 Phase 3: Pair Interaction

This phase aimed to foster rapport between children and researchers and promote collaborative play. Three 30-min sessions were held for each pair, focused on the mutually selected toy from the previous sessions. To eliminate distractions, no other toys were present. Each session, documented by two fixed cameras and annotated by a pair of researchers. The researchers initiating the session with verbal (i.e., "hi") and non-verbal (i.e., handshaking, waving, and AAC [16, 17]) greetings, utilizing the "circle of friends" technique [18]. Subsequently, a 'toy play' segment involved guided interaction with the chosen toy, transitioning gradually into 'free play'. Post-session, the recordings underwent analysis to discern children's interaction with the toy, extracting its features and sensory attributes for subsequent co-design phases.

3.4 Phase 4: Co-design

This phase aimed to initiate the prototyping process of a multisensory tool. It began with a focus group meeting involving therapists and teachers. The aim of this focus group was to explore the concepts and skills involved in collaborative play through open-ended questions and discuss the findings of previous stages. Such discussions were intended to foster a deeper understanding of collaborative play skills as observed among the children in previous phases. The next step involved the researchers sharing their plans for the forthcoming co-design sessions, facilitating a constructive dialogue to agree on a feasible structure. It is worth noting here that at the time of writing this paper, only the focus group meeting was carried out. Hence, modifications may arise later during co-design implementation. This co-design phase will encompass several workshops, each one focused on one of three main stages: features selection, prototyping, and collaborative play scenario design. In the features selection stage, a Paired Choice Preferences Assessment Procedure [19] will be used, a method that is known to be particularly effective in understanding the preferences of autistic children. This will involve displaying a variety of extracted feature options on an extendable tray. The options selected from this stage will then be compiled into a bag of stuff, which the children will utilize to create their own mascots. During the prototyping stage, the children will encounter 'start' and 'end' stations. Here, they will assemble a track that extends from the start to the end. Their self-designed mascots will be placed in a container at the start, which will traverse the path they have assembled towards the destination. As part of this journey, the children will have the opportunity to introduce obstacles requiring collaborative tasks, such as pressing a button, to facilitate the container's passage from start to end. Upon reaching the destination, the mascots will be released. Throughout this journey, the children will continuously receive auditory and visual feedback and stimuli, fostering an engaging and interactive experience.

3.5 Phase 5: Testing

In the final phase, the prototype will be tested to determine if it facilitates collaborative play among autistic children. The prototype will have undergone refinement to ensure it aligns with a high-level design. The resultant product will then be introduced to the same children who participated in the prior phases. The structure of these sessions will remain consistent with that of Phase 3. The behavior and interactions of the children will be observed during these sessions to identify any potential modification that could enhance their collaborative play experience with the developed tool. This phase will be vital to ensure that the co-designed prototype aligns with the intended goal of encouraging collaborative play, effectively integrating the insights and preferences gathered from the children throughout the process.

4 Challenges and Reflection on Co-design

The planning of the co-design sessions was based on the findings from the contextual inquiry and Phase 1 was relatively easy. However, facilitating the children's familiarity with the playroom presented a challenge, as the children were used to follow the guidance of the teacher in this space rather than to engage in free play. However, as Phase 2 approached its conclusion, the children began to perceive the room as a space for free play, resulting in an observable increase in enjoyment and spontaneous activity.

In Phase 3, the children initially displayed a lack of participation in the sessions. The implementation of the 'circle of friends' at the beginning and the subsequent sessions was instrumental in fostering this bond. In phase 4, a significant challenge arose in the technique of collecting the children's preferences. Given that the children were unable to draw, craft, or verbally articulate their imagined tool, the implementation of the paired choice preferences assessment became an indispensable solution to this impediment. As this assessment was already in use at the center to evaluate the children's stimuli, the children were accustomed to the process.

Another hurdle involved the limitation of variables in the choice preferences. Focusing exclusively on one feature while eliminating others proved to be a complex task. Hence, the proposed solution involves developing a 3D-printed extendable tray to simplify the children's selection process. Feature choices will be presented on a small board attachable to the tray, allowing variable options. This method will provide a consistent display of options, thereby effectively constraining variables.

5   Conclusion and Future Work

This paper proposes structured methodology to co-design a multisensory tool that enhances collaborative play among autistic children. Even though it builds upon pre-existing practices, the approach sets itself apart by tailoring these phases to the target demographics. The inclusion of autistic children in the design process sets a significant addition in inclusive design practices, underscoring the value of including their perspectives and experiences. Even though the methodology's individual components are not novel, their integration into a unified process provides a meaningful contribution to the field. Looking ahead, the methodology invites further application to other settings and across a wider spectrum of autistic children. Future work also includes the continued improvement of the designed tool, driven by ongoing cycles of user experiences and feedback. Such practices ultimately contribute to an increasingly inclusive and empathetic environment that promotes collaborative play for all children, regardless of their neurotype. This research not only contributes to new conceptualizations of practical tool design, but also encourages further discourse on the importance of inclusivity in play - critical aspects of childhood development.

Acknowledgement. This study was made possible by NPRP grant # NPRP13S-0108-200027 from the Qatar National Research Fund (a member of Qatar Foundation). The findings achieved here are solely the responsibility of the author[s].

References

1. Maenner, M.J., et al.: Prevalence and characteristics of autism spectrum disorder among children aged 8 years — autism and developmental disabilities monitoring network, 11 sites, United States, 2018. MMWR Surveill. Summ. **70**(11), 1–16 (2021). https://doi.org/10.15585/MMWR.SS7011A1

2. Alshaban, F., et al.: Prevalence and correlates of autism spectrum disorder in Qatar: a national study. J. Child Psychol. Psychiatry **60**(12), 1254–1268 (2019). https://doi.org/10.1111/jcpp.13066

3. Diagnostic and statistical manual of mental disorders: DSM-5^{TM}, 5th ed. Arlington, VA, US: American Psychiatric Publishing, Inc. (2013). https://doi.org/10.1176/appi.books.9780890425596

4. Dwyer, P.: The Neurodiversity Approach(es): What Are They and What Do They Mean for Researchers? Hum. Dev. **66**(2), 73–92 (2022). https://doi.org/10.1159/000523723

5. Whitman, E.C.: The impact of the social play on young children, PhD Thesis. Murray State University (2018). https://doi.org/10.12968/eyed.2005.6.11.17415

6. Harrison, S., Sengers, P., Tatar, D.: Making epistemological trouble: third-paradigm HCI as successor science. Interact. Comput. **23**(5), 385–392 (2011). https://doi.org/10.1016/j.intcom.2011.03.005

7. Bødker, S.: Third-wave HCI, 10 years later---participation and sharing. Interactions **22**(5), 24–31 (2015). https://doi.org/10.1145/2804405

8. Brown, V., Choi, J.H.: Refugee and the post-trauma journeys in the fuzzy front end of co-creative practices **2**, 1–11 (2018). https://doi.org/10.1145/3210586.3210598

9. Spiel, K., Frauenberger, C., Keyes, O.S., Fitzpatrick, G.: Agency of autistic children in technology research - A critical literature review. ACM Trans. Comp.-Hum. Interact. **26**(6) (2019). https://doi.org/10.1145/3344919

10. Druin: The role of children in the design of new technology, Behaviour & Infirmation Technology. Behaviour & Information Technology **21**(1), 1–25 (2002)

11. Hijab, M.H.F., Al-Thani, D.: En Route to Co-designing Inclusive Play With and For Autistic Children. In: 2022 9th International Conference on Behavioural and Social Computing (BESC), pp. 1–4. IEEE (2022). https://doi.org/10.1109/BESC57393.2022.9995240

12. Holtzblatt, K., Beyer, H.: Contextual design: defining customer-centered systems. Elsevier (1997)

13. Clarke, V., Braun, V.: Thematic analysis. Journal of Positive Psychology **12**(3), 297–298 (2017). https://doi.org/10.1080/17439760.2016.1262613

14. Gutwin, C., Greenberg, S.: A descriptive framework of workspace awareness for real-time groupware. Comp. Suppor. Cooper. Work (CSCW) **11**(3–4), 411–446 (2002). https://doi.org/10.1023/A:1021271517844

15. Dillenbourg, P.: What do you mean by collaborative learning?. In: Collaborative-learning: Cognitive and Computational Approaches, pp. 1–19. Elsevier, Oxford (1999). https://doi.org/10.4018/978-1-60566-786-7.ch012

16. Van Grunsven, J., Roeser, S.: AAC Technology, Autism, and the Empathic Turn. Soc. Epistemol. **36**(1), 95–110 (2022). https://doi.org/10.1080/02691728.2021.1897189

17. Hijab, M.H.F., Al-Thani, D., Banire, B.: A Multimodal Messaging App (MAAN) for Adults With Autism Spectrum Disorder: Mixed Methods Evaluation Study. JMIR Formative Research **5**(12), e33123 (2021). https://doi.org/10.2196/33123

18. Kalyva, E., Avramidis, E.: Improving communication between children with autism and their peers through the 'circle of friends': a small-scale intervention study. J. Appl. Res. Intellect. Disabil. **18**(3), 253–261 (2005). https://doi.org/10.1111/j.1468-3148.2005.00232.x

19. Fisher, W., Piazza, C.C., Bowman, L.G., Hagopian, L.P., Owens, J.C., Slevin, I.: A comparison of two approaches for identifying reinforcers for persons with severe and profound disabilities. J. Appl. Behav. Anal. **25**(2), 491–498 (1992). https://doi.org/10.1901/jaba.1992.25-491

Coping with Depression

Lukáš Novák, Miroslav Macík^(⊠) ⓘ, and Božena Mannová ⓘ

FEE, Czech Technical University in Prague, Prague, Czech Republic
macikmir@fel.cvut.cz

Abstract. Depression is a severe mood disorder that is frequent in the population and can negatively affect several aspects of life. This article summarizes the essential facts about depression, like frequent symptoms, risks, and treatment methods. Based on cognitive therapy, we propose an application that allows users to cope with depression, by activity planner and thought reliever. Both methods allow users to maintain an overview of their cognitive processes and subsequently potentially decrease the severity of their depressive symptoms.

Keywords: Depression · cognitive therapy · mental health · self help · software applications for coping with depression

1 Introduction

The global prevalence of depression during a lifetime ranges from 10% to 15% [11]. These numbers are even higher for adolescents, where the prevalence of elevated depressive symptoms increased from 24% between 2001 and 2010 to 37% between 2011 and 2020 [16]. The onset of COVID-19 pandemics even worsened the situation [13].

Depression is a severe mood disorder manifested primarily by long periods of sadness and significantly lowered joy from activities that under normal circumstances make the affected person happy. Different types exist, whereby sometimes depression is described as a symptom of another disease. The typical length of a single depression episode is between two weeks and several years. Most frequently, it ranges from three to six months [10]. Episodes of depression can recur [2]. At one moment, approximately 3.8% of the world population is affected by depression [4]. Recent studies from 2020 also show that 17% of US citizens between 18 and 25 years have dealt with depression in the previous year [1].

The medical diagnosis of clinical depression corresponds to continuous experiencing depressive symptoms every day for at least two weeks. At the same time, the symptoms must include depressive mood or loss of interest and joy in everyday activities. A study [12] shows that 59–87% of individuals that attempted suicide were affected by depressive disorder. About 15% of patients with mood disorders ended their life by suicide. This is approximately 500× higher than in the general population.

© IFIP International Federation for Information Processing 2024
Published by Springer Nature Switzerland AG 2024
A. Bramwell-Dicks et al. (Eds.): INTERACT 2023 Workshops, LNCS 14535, pp. 146–152, 2024.
https://doi.org/10.1007/978-3-031-61688-4_14

In this paper, we describe our work-in-progress on an application that applies selected cognitive therapy methods to contribute to coping with depression symptoms.

2   Related Work

Several methods to treat depression exist. For milder forms, a change in lifestyle and attendance at psychotherapy is often recommended, there the patient can confide their issues to the therapist and learns to deal with them and develop their thinking and their personality. There are different types of psychotherapy – individual, family, and group therapies. Some of the more well-known types of specialized psychotherapies include cognitive behavioral therapy (CBT) [9] or Gestalt therapy [17]. A useful aid to proper treatment is psycho-diagnostics, whose function is to use current expertise to analyse the patient's mental state and try to make a correct diagnosis. This way, the patient can learn more about their mental health and their doctors can direct their treatment more efficiently. For example, the patient may learn that their mental or physical issues are rooted in a different problem than they initially thought.

Only for severe forms of depression psychiatric care is also recommended [2], as psycho-pharmaceuticals can cause various side effects and thus be an additional burden on the patient's health. To treat depression, various antidepressants are most commonly prescribed, e.g. SSRIs, i.e. antidepressants with selective serotonin reuptake inhibition. The full onset of effects of antidepressants is expected to take between 4 and 6 weeks for most of them.

Apart from contact psychotherapy and psychiatric treatment there are several individual methods, some of them are based on modern technologies and apps. Zhang et al. [18] conducted a 8-week randomized trial of 13 mental health apps. They identified three clusters of app use behaviors: learning, goal setting and self-tracking. The reduction of depression symptoms was most notable for participants who engaged in self tracking, but improvement was achieved also for learning and goal setting engagements at moderate level of usage (not too much nor too little). Chandrashekar et al. [8] argue that mental health apps do have value in providing psychological treatment. They present four recommendations for high-efficacy mental health apps: high patient engagement, simple user interface, transdiagnostic capabilities, and self-monitoring features. Bowie-Dabreo et al. [6] focused on ethical issues of apps for tackling depression. They conducted thematic analysis of more than 2200 user reviews of 40 apps. Authors propose implications for ethical design based on principles of nonmaleficence, beneficence, justice, autonomy, and virtue.

An example of an app for emergency psychological help is *Don't panic* [3]. The app is a quick help for people with depression, anxiety, self-harm, suicidal thoughts, and eating disorders. Options here are breathing exercises to calm down, simple games to distract the mind, and planning or noting activities. The app is available in ten languages. Apps to mitigate the effects of depression are commonly available, and individuals with depression are frequently encouraged

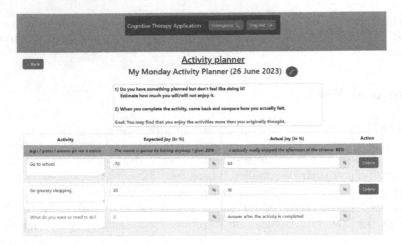

Fig. 1. Activity planner UI.

to use them. These apps are often quite complex – targeting multiple disorders and offering a multitude of coping techniques. However, it may be good for part of the users as suggested by [8], some users may struggle with the high complexity of the apps.

3   Supporting Cognitive Therapy

The causes of depression symptoms largely originate in the brain. So, even if a certain external action that would treat us from depression in the long term were to take place, there must naturally be an effect on the brain between these two events. One of the ways using which it is possible to get rid of depressive feelings, or at least alleviate them, is to change the way we think and thereby change the thoughts that deepen or perpetuate depression.

The human brain commonly uses associations – for example, if we hear a conversation on a certain topic, we tend to recall information that we have associated with said topic. In such a case, we can liken the brain's function to an artificial neural network that learns by acquiring inputs and then adjusting its internal structure based on assessing its outputs. In a similar way, however, the human brain can create negative behavioral patterns by, for example, learning using its expected outcomes rather than the actual ones.

The application uses the principles of cognitive therapy [7,14] that mainly focuses on thought patterns. Cognitive therapy is the predecessor of cognitive behavioral therapy. In this part we describe selected methods of cognitive therapy and how they can be supported by web or smartphone applications.

Activity planner with a retrospective assessment. This function as depicted in Fig. 1 uses the above mentioned ideas of cognitive therapy. Specifically, it presupposes that the expected activity in the future is less pleasant for people with depression than it actually is.

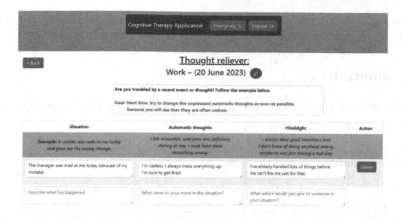

Fig. 2. Thought reliever UI.

First, a user writes down the activities they plan to carry out and a value in percentages expressing their expected joy from performing these activities and then they carry out these activities. Afterwards, they return to their planner and write down how much they really enjoyed each of the activities and see if they underestimated them in their prior evaluation.

The idea of this function is that the depressed user is going to see that their previous assessments can be skewed, which should improve their mood over time because they do not have to spend time on activities that they previously considered unpleasant [7].

Thought Reliever. Individuals with depression and anxiety often deal with negative thoughts [15]. These thoughts can occupy a significant part of consciousness, and due to the associative nature of the human brain, their memory trace is hardened over time [14].

In such difficult psychological situations, individuals with depression can record their thoughts and feelings and subsequently think about whether these thoughts reflect actual facts and possibly write down rational thoughts. This activity is supported by our design as depicted in Fig. 2. The goal is to realize that an individual that deals with depression has the tendency to interpret daily situations as worse and think about the worst possible scenarios. One must not reinforce the negative thoughts in the mind because that only makes them more frequent.

Safe and Calming Environment. The application design should reflect its therapeutic manner and support its primary function – psychical relief. The application should have calming appearance and be pleasant to use, following requirements should be reflected in the application design: Certain fonts and color combinations can contribute to the more that others [5]. The use of the application itself must not worsen patient's mood. It must be easy to use, clear and responsive. The sensitive personal data handled by the application must be stored securely in encrypted form. Moreover, the design should affirm users that their data are safe and they can delete the sensitive information at any time.

4 Evaluation

The purpose of the experiment was to evaluate usability of both user and administration parts of the application.

4.1 Participants

We recruited 15 participants from the group of fellow students and relatives. Firstly a screener was provided to them with questions regarding age, occupation, and computer and smartphone use. Furthermore, questions related to possible depression: Were you experiencing low mood during the past month? Have you recently lost interest in activities that you previously enjoyed? Would you say that you are experiencing depression?

Based on the results, the participants were split into three groups. The task of the most technology-enthusiastic *group C* was to evaluate the UI of the administrative part. *Groups A and B* focused on the evaluation of the main part of the application, while *group A* comprised individuals that use web applications on a daily basis and *group B* were less technology enthusiastic individuals with little experience in using web applications. Both *groups A and B* consisted of five participants, where only part of them experienced depressive symptoms.

4.2 Procedure

The individual test sessions were conducted individually in a calm environment using a laptop. A moderator was present at each test session providing participants with test scenarios. The moderator actively encouraged the participants to follow the thought-allow protocol.

4.3 Tasks and Results

Task 1 − Registration: 1. Create new user account using the assigned activation code and select year of birth or leave it empty. 2. Log-out after a successful registration. 3. Log-in again to verify creation of the account.

All participants from the *group A* completed the task successfully. Three participants from the *group B* had difficulties proceeding from the sign-in page to the registration page. The probable cause was unfamiliarity with the link labeled "Create new account" placed below the sign-in form.

Task 2 − Activity Planner: 1. Sign-in using the assigned login credentials. 2. Select item activity planner. 3. Create new activity planner, do-not enter any name. 4. Change name of the created activity planner. 5. Fill in two records accordingly to instructions on screen. 6. Delete one of the records. 7. Create a new activity planner and subsequently delete it.

All participants from the *group A* completed the task. There was an issue with comprehending the function of expected/experienced happiness. Some participants suggested using emoticons instead of percentages. Emoticons are more familiar to most users experienced with modern web applications. Some participants were surprised that the implicit name of a newly created planner is different from the input field placeholder.

Participants of the *group B* have difficulties to comprehend the last point (7.) of the task. The reason can be that the assignment of this point was hard to comprehend, also it was possible to delete the activity planer only from the list and not from the opened-planner screen.

The vast majority of participants expressed the desire to enter a value of real happiness larger than 100%, however, in the version that was subject to the experiment the value was limited to 100% upper limit.

Task 3 – Thought Reliever: 1. Sign-in using the assigned login credentials. 2. Select item thought diary. 3. Create new thought diary and enter any name you like. 4. Fill-in two diary entries accordingly to on-screen instructions.

Participants from both *groups A and B* encountered similar issues. Although all participants could finish the task, the evaluation revealed that the instructions were not clear enough. The question: "What comes to your mind in this situation, how did you feel?" was answered as "bad" (or by similar term) by most of the participants.

On the basis of the evaluation results, following modifications were implemented: In the *Though reliever*, the field label was changed to: "What came to your mind when you were in the situation and how did you feel?". The name of column was changed from "Original thoughts" to "Automatic thoughts". The extent of experienced happiness was changed to –100 to 200 (from 0–100%). An example entry was added for both activity planner and thought reliever.

5   Discussion

Depression is a severe mood disorder that affects a significant part of society and can negatively impact various aspects of the lives of those affected. This work desires work-in-progress on an application that aims to support coping with some symptoms of depression by leveraging selected cognitive therapy methods. In contrast to other solutions, our approach focuses on maximal simplicity and corresponding good usability. Although the evaluation showed that the direction could be promising, an assessment of the effect on depression symptoms needs to be conducted.

6   Conclusion and Future Work

In this paper, we presented a concept of an application that contributes to tackling depression symptoms by leveraging cognitive therapy methods. The application is intentionally simple and provides two main functions – activity planner and thought reliever. It is the subject of future work to involve more individuals that encounter depressive symptoms in the development process by co-design and evaluating the subjective and objective impact of the application on depression symptoms.

Acknowledgments. This research has been supported by research the project RCI (reg. no. CZ.02.1.01/0.0/0.0/16_019/0000765) supported by EU.

References

1. Major depression – statistics, (on-line). https://www.nimh.nih.gov/health/statistics/major-depression. Accessed 20 Dec 2022
2. What is depression?, (on-line). https://www.nimh.nih.gov/health/publications/depression. Accessed 20 Dec 2022
3. Nepanikař application, (on-line). https://nepanikar.eu/aplikace-nepanikar/. Accessed 09 Jan 2023
4. World health organisation – depression, (on-line). https://www.who.int/news-room/fact-sheets/detail/depression. Accessed 30 Jan 2023
5. Birren, F.: Color Psychology and Color Therapy; A Factual Study of the Influence of Color on Human Life. Pickle Partners Publishing, USA (2016)
6. Bowie-DaBreo, D., Sas, C., Iles-Smith, H., Sünram-Lea, S.: User perspectives and ethical experiences of apps for depression: a qualitative analysis of user reviews. In: Proceedings of the 2022 CHI Conference on Human Factors in Computing Systems, pp. 1–24 (2022)
7. Burns, D.D.: Feeling Good: The New Mood Therapy. Harper, Topanga (2008)
8. Chandrashekar, P.: Do mental health mobile apps work: evidence and recommendations for designing high-efficacy mental health mobile apps. Mhealth **4** (2018)
9. Driessen, E., Hollon, S.D.: Cognitive behavioral therapy for mood disorders: efficacy, moderators and mediators. Psychiatr. Clin. **33**(3), 537–555 (2010)
10. Gilmer, W.S., et al.: Factors associated with chronic depressive episodes: a preliminary report from the star-d project. Acta Psychiatr. Scand. **112**(6), 425–433 (2005)
11. Lépine, J.P., Briley, M.: The increasing burden of depression. Neuropsychiatr. Dis. Treat. **7**(sup1), 3–7 (2011)
12. Látalová, K.: Suicidalita u psychických poruch. Grada Publishing, první edn. (2015)
13. Mahmud, S., Mohsin, M., Dewan, M.N., Muyeed, A.: The global prevalence of depression, anxiety, stress, and insomnia among general population during COVID-19 pandemic: a systematic review and meta-analysis. Trends Psychol. **31**(1), 143–170 (2023)
14. Neenan, M., Dryden, W.: Cognitive Therapy in a Nutshell, January 2011. https://doi.org/10.4135/9781446288832
15. Pospos, S., et al.: Web-based tools and mobile applications to mitigate burnout, depression, and suicidality among healthcare students and professionals: a systematic review. Acad. Psychiatry **42**, 109–120 (2018)
16. Shorey, S., Ng, E.D., Wong, C.H.: Global prevalence of depression and elevated depressive symptoms among adolescents: a systematic review and meta-analysis. Br. J. Clin. Psychol. **61**(2), 287–305 (2022)
17. Yontef, G., Jacobs, L.: Gestalt therapy. Curr. Psychother. **4**, 59491012–604 (1989)
18. Zhang, R., et al.: Clinically meaningful use of mental health apps and its effects on depression: mixed methods study. J. Med. Internet Res. **21**(12), e15644 (2019)

"That's Our Game!": Reflections on Co-designing a Robotic Game with Neurodiverse Children

Patricia Piedade[1]([envelope]) [ORCID], Isabel Neto[2] [ORCID], Ana Pires[1] [ORCID], Rui Prada[2] [ORCID], and Hugo Nicolau[1] [ORCID]

[1] Interactive Technologies Institute, Instituto Superior Técnico, University of Lisbon, Lisbon, Portugal
{patricia.piedade,hugo.nicolau}@tecnico.ulisboa.pt
[2] INESC-ID, Instituto Superior Técnico, University of Lisbon, Lisbon, Portugal
{isabel.neto,rui.prada}@tecnico.ulisboa.pt

Abstract. Many neurodivergent (ND) children are integrated into mainstream schools alongside their neurotypical (NT) peers. However, they often face social exclusion, which may have lifelong effects. Inclusive play activities can be a strong driver of inclusion. Unfortunately, games designed for the specific needs of neurodiverse groups, those that include neurodivergent and neurotypical individuals, are scarce. Given the potential of robots as engaging devices, we led a 6-month co-design process to build an inclusive and entertaining robotic game for neurodiverse classrooms. We first interviewed neurodivergent adults and educators to identify the barriers and facilitators for including neurodivergent children in mainstream classrooms. Then, we conducted five co-design sessions, engaging four neurodiverse classrooms with 81 children (19 neurodivergent). We present a reflection on our co-design process and the resulting robotic game through the lens of Self-Determination Theory, discussing how our methodology supported the intrinsic motivations of neurodivergent children.

Keywords: Co-design · Classrooms · Children · Neurodivergent · Inclusion · Games · Neurodiversity

1 Introduction

Play is an essential factor for childhood development [21,31], aiding in the development of creativity, social skills and perception [7–11,14]. Moments of play are a source of fun and a space for self-expression and exploration [9,16]. In fact, the United Nations Convention on the Rights of the Child recognises play as a fundamental right [30]. Games, as a form of play, promote pleasurable engagement and players' well-being [15,17]. Furthermore, games have the potential to promote inclusive and engaging experiences in mixed-ability scenarios [5,12,13,22]. However, neurodivergent children still face significant barriers regarding access to inclusive play scenarios and their above-mentioned benefits [24,28]. In this

© IFIP International Federation for Information Processing 2024
Published by Springer Nature Switzerland AG 2024
A. Bramwell-Dicks et al. (Eds.): INTERACT 2023 Workshops, LNCS 14535, pp. 153–160, 2024.
https://doi.org/10.1007/978-3-031-61688-4_15

work, we take on the framework of the identity model of disability, using the concept of *neurodiversity* to encompass the multitude of neurological differences in human brains. Where most brains are *neurotypical*, and some diverge from these norms, thus, referred to as *neurodivergent* (e.g.: ADHD, autism, dyslexia, and intellectual disabilities) [6].

In a 2021 critical review of games developed by the HCI research community for neurodivergent players [28], Spiel and Gerling analysed 66 publications under the lens of Disability Studies and Self-Determination Theory. The authors conclude that serious games, designed for medical and training purposes, comprise most of the corpus. These games attempt to create an engaging facade for boring or repetitive tasks, tendentially prioritising training over enjoyment, and are driven by motivators outside neurodivergent interests. Furthermore, these games are often designed top-down, excluding the player from the design process and focusing on single-player dynamics, reducing opportunities for inclusive play and social interaction.

Though HRI is a growing field within HCI research, none of the games analysed by Spiel and Gerling [28] included robots as game elements. Previous works regarding mixed-ability gaming have successfully leveraged robotic devices as proponents for inclusive play [22,25]. Moreover, outside the framework of games research, robots have proved to be a viable tool to create engaging experiences for neurodivergent individuals [4,18–20]. Hence, there is unexplored potential for including robots in games geared towards neurodiverse groups.

Players' motivation is a central aspect of game design. Engaging gaming experiences require a motivated player [29]. With wide use within HCI Games research [29], Self-Determination Theory (SDT) is a theory that models human motivation [26,27] and the basis of Spiel and Gerling's critical review of HCI games for neurodivergent players [28]. SDT proposes three basic psychological needs that an activity must fulfil to promote intrinsic motivation: autonomy, competence and relatedness [26,27]. Autonomy pertains to an individual's ability to choose their actions and circumstances according to their values and preferences [26]. Competence describes a feeling of mastery over a particular subject and being met with appropriate challenges [26]. Finally, relatedness is a feeling of social connectedness, being part of a group where one is cared for and cares for others through significant contributions [26]. SDT argues that when an activity meets these three basic needs, it promotes motivation, which can lead to personal fulfilment and well- [26]. Therefore, it is imperative that we take such needs into account when designing user experiences, such as games, or even participatory design processes. Given the lack of games designed for a neurodiverse context and the potential of robots as game elements within this context, we set out to co-design a robotic game with and for neurodiverse classrooms. Throughout our co-design process, we aimed to centre neurodivergent interests and fill the research gap identified by Spiel and Gerling [28]. In this paper, we reflect upon our co-design process and resulting game through the lens of SDT, critically evaluating our process as a form of accountability and informing future research within this context on how to better support self-determination within neurodiverse groups.

2 Co-design Process

Aiming to bridge the gap within neurodiverse elementary school classrooms, we engaged in a multiple-methods co-design process by involving various stakeholders. Before engaging directly with the children, we engaged educators and neurodivergent adults in formative studies to better understand the barriers and facilitators to inclusion in a neurodiverse classroom.

Co-Design Workshops. We proceeded to the co-design workshops within neurodiverse classrooms (Fig. 1). We held these workshops at a local mainstream public elementary school. Four classrooms, two 2nd and two 4th grades, participated in the sessions. There were 81 students, aged 6 to 12, 19 of whom were neurodivergent (13 learning differences - G01ND3, G02ND1, G02ND6, G03ND3, G03ND4, G06ND1, G10ND5, G11ND3, G12ND1, G12ND3, G15ND2, G16ND1 and G16ND6, one dyslexia - G03ND4, two intellectual disabilities - G05ND1 and G05ND4, two ADHD - G06ND2 and G06ND3, one Down's Syndrome - G11ND5, and one Global Developmental Delay - G13ND1)[1].

Over the course of four months, we conducted five hour-long sessions with each class. Teachers divided their classrooms into groups of 4 to 6 students based on usual seating arrangements, interests, and friendships. Throughout the process, children kept a project portfolio to store worksheets, drawings, and other design artifacts. We chose the Ozbot Evo [3] as the robotic game element due to its target age range and proven efficacy in mixed-ability settings [22] and with neurodivergent children [19]. Each session started with a participative recap, where a researcher would prompt the children to recall events from past sessions. The first two sessions focused on building rapport with the children and familiarizing them with the robots. Children customized a folder to use as a project portfolio, decorated an Ozobot and partook in game-like activities to explore its features. Session three focused on game design elements. Using Expanded Proxy Design [23] and worksheets detailing essential game elements, children were asked to design games, themed around Oceans and Sustainability (curricular themes suggested by the teacher) for a stuffed animal friend with neurodivergent characteristics. Afterwards, we analysed the children's game concepts, identifying prominent game mechanics and themes and establishing the basic characteristics of our co-designed game. The final game concept consisted of a game of tag, where an Ozobot would chase players around a game board while the players attempted to complete mini-games to earn the most tokens and win the overall game. For the last two sessions, each group of children formalized a concept for a mini-game, prototyped it, and play-tested it. Each group was given one of four themes inspired by their creations in session three and the two curricular themes proposed by the teachers. Researchers provided them with worksheets detailing game mechanic elements and crafting materials to actualize their ideas. Most mini-games generated had a rich narrative but vague rules.

---

[1] each child within this project is represented by an id GXXNNY, where XX is a group number, NN indicates if a child is ND or NT, and Y is an in-group identifier.

Game Design Process. Following the end of the co-design sessions, we conducted an iterative game design process supported by the results of the co-design workshops, culminating in a final prototype. The game, entitled "The Shark Escape", was based around a classic "tag" mechanic (as this was the most popular among children's prototypes) where players moved animal shaped pieces around a gameboard, evading being caught by the Ozobot, decorated like a shark. To avoid frustration related to waiting for one's turn, all players move at once, according to an automatic digital dice. Each player attempted to gather the three coloured tokens needed to return to their start position and win the game. To win tokens, players must land on mini-game spaces and win the corresponding mini-games: (1) Recycling - a two-player finger-football-style game in which players attempted to score goals with small coloured styrofoam balls in the correct recycling bin; (2) Treasure - a single-player game in which those not playing placed fish figurines on a grid, and the player attempted to move the Ozobot with the Ozobot Evo app [1] remote control to reach the treasure without touching the fishes; (3) Animals - a classic multi-player memory game enhanced with AR, mapping the cards to opensource 3D models through the Halo AR app [2], in which players attempt to find the most pairs of marine animals. Winning a mini-game earned a player a corresponding token and a spin of the lucky prize wheel, which could earn them an extra reward (eg., the ability to move extra spaces). If caught by the shark (i.e. having their pawn knocked down by the Ozobot), players lose one token.

Game Evaluation. To evaluate our prototype, we conducted a play-test session in neurodiverse classrooms. We recruited the four classrooms who had participated in the co-design sessions and an additional class as a control group. In total, 100 students, 26 of which were neurodivergent, tested the game. Classrooms were once again split into groups of 4 to 6 children, and each group played the game for one hour, while a researcher facilitated gameplay and observed.

Fig. 1. Stages of the co-design process of a robotic game with neurodiverse children.

3   Findings/Analysis Through Self-Determination Theory

Individual motivation is often disregarded when designing games for neurodivergent players [28]. As a form of self-accountability, we analyse findings from our co-design process and game evaluation session under the lens of SDT. We focus this analysis on findings related to neurodivergent children, aiming to understand which practices best supported their self-determination.

Competence. Taking into account the educational setting in which we situated our design process, competence was a key aspect to balance when creating co-design activities. Crafting activities presented manageable and fulfilling challenges. For instance, during session five, G06ND2 created a detailed boat structure and G02ND6 diligently coloured a gameboard prototype, both showed pride in their work and received praise from group-mates. On the other hand, less engaging group decision-making activities, such as conceptualizing games, proved frustrating for some. For example, G05ND4 often disengaged from the activities, G06ND2 frequently stood up so see what other groups were doing, G03ND4 struggled to complete the game elements worksheets, and G15ND2 struggled to have opinions heard. Strategies, such as encouraging children to draw their ideas (G05ND4), encouraging consensus rather than a majority vote (G06ND2), reminding children they could draw rather than write (G03ND4), and making turn-taking mechanics explicit (G15ND2), promoted neurodivergent children's sense of competence in these less entertaining activities. During our last visit to the school, one neurodiverse pair (G06ND1 and G05NT2) shared with us they planned on taking the knowledge they acquired to create their own game, indicating they felt competent in the game design knowledge aquired through the process. Regarding the final prototype, we found that it provided enough of a challenge to keep the groups engaged while allowing everyone to succeed at a similar rate. Some neurodivergent children (eg., G05ND1, G05ND4, and G16ND6) struggled with counting spaces on the game board; however, they did not seem to perceive this as a lack of competence, simply moving in alternative ways around the gameboard and disregarding the dice.

Relatedness. Group work, especially within a school context, promotes socialisation, but not necessarily relatedness. We attempted to mitigate this issue by allowing teachers to form groups based on friendships and interests rather than enforcing a balance regarding the gender or neurodivergence of students within each group. We found that groups grew closer and learned to accomudate each other throughout the process. For instance, G02ND6's disruptive behaviour was initially perceived as bad, but, through the Expanded Proxy Design [23] activity, they found a positive framework to employ it: their game concept consisted on pranking polluting humans out of wildlife habitats. This activity also allowed for self advocacy, with G05ND1 proudly stating: "[The proxy] is like me! [...] She may not be able to read and write, but she has a good heart.". Regarding the game, we designed it to fit children's preference for competitive games (which most considered favorites due to being able to showcase competence), rather than inforcing socialization through a collaboration/cooperation mechanic. However, the presence of a common enemy - the Ozobot -led children to spontaneously collaborate. For example, G06ND1 and G06ND3 encouraged G06ND2 to find matching pairs in the memory game, and G16ND1 shared his extra tokens with group-mates.

Autonomy. Once again, the school and group work settings are not natural promoters of autonomy as tasks are often dictated. Furthermore, the context of neurodiverse groups having to make joint decisions can lead to neurodivergent interests being overshadowed by the neurotypical majority. We aimed to reduce this issue by emphasizing that group decisions should be based on overall agreement rather than a majority vote. For example, G06ND2 felt very strongly about his ideas being include in the group's game, leading the rest of the group to find a way to incorporate everyone's contributions (a game where the player would have to sequentially complete various mini-games). We found that activities that required the creation of multiple design artifacts promoted individual autonomy. For instance, during session 4, G05ND1 created the mini-game's narrative, while G05ND2 drew the different scenes within it, adding specific details. During the final play-test, children often bent the rules, which was accepted by their fellow group-mates. For example, whenever a group-mate landed on a mini-game spot G02ND6 would move his pawn there to play it as well, and lacking a proper place to store his token's G05ND2 started placing them on the Ozobot's plasticine shark fin. Players felt autonomous enough to play as they wished, we attribute this to a sense of ownership over the co-designed game. Still, the sit-down nature of the game left G06ND2 unfulfilled, seeking entertainment in unused game pieces, while other's played mini-games.

4   Conclusion

Having identified a need for gaming experiences designed for neurodiverse groups and the potential of robots to promote engagement, we set out to co-design a game with mainstream classrooms. We successfully co-designed a robotic board game with four neurodiverse classes, with a total of 80 students, 19 of which neurodivergent. We present a critical review of our design process under the lens of self-determination theory. Overall, we found that more entertaining activities with multiple resulting artifacts promototed promoted neurodivergent self-determination within the co-design process. And the game's common enemy and allowance for rule-bending motivated neurodivergent children during gameplay. However, group decision-making activities, and the sit-down nature of the board-game require reworking in order to better advocate for neurodivergent competence, relatedness and autonomy.

In future work, we aim to further explore how the sense of ownership provided by the co-design process can promote autonomy in gameplay, and relatedness and competence in neurodiverse groups.

Acknowledgements. This work was supported by the European project DCitizens: Fostering Digital Civics Research and Innovation in Lisbon (GA 101079116), by the Portuguese Recovery and Resilience Program (PRR), IAPMEI/ANI/FCT under Agenda C645022399-00000057 (eGamesLab) and the Foundation for Science and Technology (FCT) funds SFRH/BD/06452/2021 and UIDB/50021/2020.

References

1. Evo by ozobot - apps on google play (2023). https://play.google.com/store/apps/details?id=com.evollve.evo&gl=US&pli=1
2. Halo ar - 3d creator & scanner - apps on google play (2023). https://play.google.com/store/apps/details?id=io.lightup.lens&gl=US
3. Ozobot — robots to code and create with, April 2023. https://ozobot.com/
4. Balasuriya, S.S., Sitbon, L., Brereton, M., Koplick, S.: How can social robots spark collaboration and engagement among people with intellectual disability?, pp. 209–220. Association for Computing Machinery (2019). https://doi.org/10.1145/3369457.3370915
5. Brederode, B., Markopoulos, P., Gielen, M., Vermeeren, A., de Ridder, H.: Powerball: the design of a novel mixed-reality game for children with mixed abilities. In: Proceedings of the 2005 Conference on Interaction Design and Children, pp. 32–39. IDC '05, Association for Computing Machinery, New York, NY, USA (2005). https://doi.org/10.1145/1109540.1109545
6. Dalton, N.S.: Neurodiversity & HCI, pp. 2295–2304. Association for Computing Machinery (2013). https://doi.org/10.1145/2468356.2468752
7. Fromberg, D.: Play Issues in Early Childhood Education. Merrill Publishing Company, Merrill (1990)
8. Fromberg, D., Gullo, D.: Perspectives on Children. Routledge, London (1992)
9. Fromberg, D.P., Bergen, D.: Play from Birth to Twelve: Contexts, Perspectives, and Meanings. Routledge, London (2012)
10. Garvey, C.: Play, vol. 27. Harvard University Press, Cambridge (1990)
11. Ginsburg, K.R.: The importance of play in promoting healthy child development and maintaining strong parent-child bonds. Pediatrics **119**(1), 182–191 (2007). the Committee on Communications, the Committee on Psychosocial Aspects of Child, Health, F., https://doi.org/10.1542/peds.2006-2697
12. Gonçalves, D., Rodrigues, A., Richardson, M.L., de Sousa, A.A., Proulx, M.J., Guerreiro, T.: Exploring asymmetric roles in mixed-ability gaming. Association for Computing Machinery (2021). https://doi.org/10.1145/3411764.3445494
13. Graf, R., et al.: IGYM: an interactive floor projection system for inclusive exergame environments, pp. 31–43. Association for Computing Machinery (2019). https://doi.org/10.1145/3311350.3347161
14. Huizinga, J.: Homo Ludens: A Study of the Play-Element in Culture. Routledge, London (2014)
15. Iacovides, I., Mekler, E.D.: The role of gaming during difficult life experiences. In: Proceedings of the 2019 CHI Conference on Human Factors in Computing Systems, pp. 1–12. CHI '19, Association for Computing Machinery, New York, NY, USA (2019). https://doi.org/10.1145/3290605.3300453
16. Johnson, J.E., Christie, J.F., Yawkey, T.D.: Play and Early Childhood Development. Scott, Foresman & Co, New York (1987)
17. Jones, C., Scholes, L., Johnson, D., Katsikitis, M., Carras, M.: Gaming well: links between videogames and flourishing mental health. Front. Psychol. **5** (2014). https://doi.org/10.3389/fpsyg.2014.00260, https://www.frontiersin.org/articles/10.3389/fpsyg.2014.00260
18. Kewalramani, S., Palaiologou, I., Dardanou, M., Allen, K.A., Phillipson, S.: Using robotic toys in early childhood education to support children's social and emotional competencies. Australas. J. Early Child. **46**, 355–369 (2021). https://doi.org/10.1177/18369391211056668

19. Knight, V.F., Wright, J., DeFreese, A.: Teaching robotics coding to a student with ASD and severe problem behavior. J. Autism Dev. Disord. **49**, 2632–2636 (2019). https://doi.org/10.1007/s10803-019-03888-3

20. Laurie, M.H., Manches, A., Fletcher-Watson, S.: The role of robotic toys in shaping play and joint engagement in autistic children: implications for future design. Int. J. Child-Comput. Interact. 100384 (2021). https://doi.org/10.1016/j.ijcci.2021.100384, https://www.sciencedirect.com/science/article/pii/S2212868921000830

21. Liu, C., et al.: Neuroscience and Learning Through Play: A Review of the Evidence. The Lego Foundation, Dinamarca (2017)

22. Metatla, O., Bardot, S., Cullen, C., Serrano, M., Jouffrais, C.: Robots for inclusive play: co-designing an educational game with visually impaired and sighted children, pp. 1–13. Association for Computing Machinery (2020). https://doi.org/10.1145/3313831.3376270

23. Metatla, O., Read, J.C., Horton, M.: Enabling children to design for others with expanded proxy design, pp. 184–197. Association for Computing Machinery (2020). https://doi.org/10.1145/3392063.3394431

24. Morris, B.A., Havlucu, H., Oldfield, A., Metatla, O.: Double empathy as a lens to understand the design space for inclusive social play between autistic and neurotypical children. In: Extended Abstracts of the 2023 CHI Conference on Human Factors in Computing Systems. CHI EA '23, Association for Computing Machinery, New York, NY, USA (2023). https://doi.org/10.1145/3544549.3585828

25. Pires, A.C., et al.: TACTOPI: exploring play with an inclusive multisensory environment for children with mixed-visual abilities. In: Proceedings of the 2023 Interaction Design and Children. IDC '23, Association for Computing Machinery, Chicago, IL, USA (2023). https://doi.org/10.1145/3585088.3589389

26. Ryan, R.M., Deci, E.L.: Self-Determination Theory: Basic Psychological Needs in Motivation, Development, and Wellness. Guilford Publications, New York, February 2017. google-Books-ID: Bc_DDAAAQBAJ

27. Ryan, R.M., Deci, E.L.: Self-Determination Theory. In: Maggino, F. (ed.) Encyclopedia of Quality of Life and Well-Being Research, pp. 1–7. Springer International Publishing, Cham (2022). https://doi.org/10.1007/978-3-319-69909-7_2630-2

28. Spiel, K., Gerling, K.: The purpose of play: how HCI games research fails neurodivergent populations. ACM Trans. Comput.-Hum. Interact. **28** (2021). https://doi.org/10.1145/3432245

29. Tyack, A., Mekler, E.D.: Self-determination theory in HCI games research: current uses and open questions. In: Proceedings of the 2020 CHI Conference on Human Factors in Computing Systems, pp. 1–22. ACM, Honolulu HI USA, April 2020. https://doi.org/10.1145/3313831.3376723, https://dl.acm.org/doi/10.1145/3313831.3376723

30. UNICEF: Convention on the rights of the child (1989). https://www.unicef.org/child-rights-convention/convention-text

31. Zosh, J.M., et al.: Accessing the inaccessible: redefining play as a spectrum. Front. Psychol. **9** (2018).https://doi.org/10.3389/fpsyg.2018.01124, https://www.frontiersin.org/article/10.3389/fpsyg.2018.01124

Understanding the Concept of Cognitive Disability

Masood Rangraz$^{(\boxtimes)}$ ⓘ, Anne-Kathrin Peters ⓘ, and Jan Gulliksen ⓘ

KTH Royal Institute of Technology, Stockholm, Sweden
rangraz@kth.se

Abstract. This article provides a critical analysis of the current research terminology used to describe people with cognitive disability, intellectual impairment, neurodiversity, mental disorder, or psychological dysfunction. Medical diagnoses of the brain, nerves, mind, or psyche inform the use of these terms for describing behavior that is not deemed "normal" in humans. Cognitive disability is proposed as a more appropriate one than other similar terminologies after an analysis of diverse policy documents and academic publications.

Keywords: Cognitive Disability · ICF · DCM-5

1 Introduction

The 2030 Agenda for Sustainable Development and its Sustainable Development Goals (SDGs) rest on the transformative promise of "leave no one behind" (LNOB). One group of individuals who may face the risk of being left-behind are individuals with disabilities [1]. Among them, individuals with cognitive disabilities are often not acknowledged within the broader context of people with disabilities and discussions surrounding accessibility [2, 3]. The unresolved term "cognitive disability" appears to be one of the causes of such negligence, in our opinion. A quick review of the existing body of scholarly works and policy documents yields an array of terms that could be combined to form substitutes for cognitive disability (Table 1).

Table 1. Terms closely associated to Cognitive Disability

Alternatives for *cognitive*	Alternatives for *disability*
Intellectual, perceptual, psychological, mental, developmental, neurodevelopmental, neuropsychiatric, psychosocial, learning, neurocognitive, neurodiversity, behavioral	Health, disorder, illness, dysfunction, disorder, impairment, abnormality, handicap

Conditions including aphasia, autism, attention deficit, dyslexia, dyscalculia, and memory loss are examples of cognitive disability. The inconsistencies in the human

A. Bramwell-Dicks et al. (Eds.): INTERACT 2023 Workshops, LNCS 14535, pp. 161–167, 2024.
https://doi.org/10.1007/978-3-031-61688-4_16

mind, brain, neurological system, intelligence, or psyche go by a wide variety of labels. Cognitively disabled, intellectually impaired, neurodiversity users and mentally disordered are only a few of the terms coined, in use, and debated today. The semantic variability attests to the medical and social complexities of identifying the various aspects of human condition.

The root of the issue may be the source of knowledge that is rarely shared. Two branches of science, namely medical and social sciences, define and categorize variations in human psychology and behavior from their own vantage point [4]. It is a contentious process, with each field having its own perspective and understanding of what constitutes "normality". Addressing them requires defining normality and agreeing on the normal threshold. Such an endeavor is not straightforward, however. Shedding light on the range of human conditions, medical and social sciences sometimes work together (or against each other) to sharpen the normality argument, each deal with the topic in its own terms unnoticed by the other. Therefore, it becomes a challenging and time-consuming effort to classify varied conditions under mutually agreed upon labels.

In this short paper, the goal is to open the discussion and critically reflect on the terminologies used to label people with atypical mental/neurocognitive functioning. We address the following research question:

How is atypical mental/neurocognitive functioning conceptualized in policy documents and academic literature?

2   Purpose and Background

Recent discoveries have led to a rethinking of traditional norms and an acceptance of the diverse nature of human experience. At the same time, debates continue on what these various conditions should be called, with some arguing that labels are unnecessary and imprecise, while others argue they are vital in helping to understand and support those with unique needs. It is generally agreed that while words and labels could never fully capture the nuances of individual experiences, having a shared language is essential in creating an inclusive world where all people could be treated with respect and empathy.

Inquiries such as focused conceptualizations for different mental/neurocognitive functioning are not immediate preoccupations of the design science. In fact, new or improved concepts rarely are discussed in design science literature [5] which might make the topic of this paper rather inconsequential. Yet, we know that users with a different mental/neurocognitive functioning point to a certain complexity, i.e., complexity of the user. Such complexity, according to Janlert and Stolterman (2017), is "extraordinarily complex" and is usually treated as a fixed phenomena [6]. The analysis of the complexity of the systems or artifacts promises more insight and contribution, and this is why empirical and systemic studies, rather than inquiries about diversity on the user side, dominate in HCI.

It seems that design science is firmly invested in the idea of the 'psychic unity of mankind' considering how doing ethnography and designing is inseparable [7, 8]. The history and the prospect of analyzing how people with diverse mental/neurocognitive functioning systems/artifacts question the common interactive and operating assumptions. There is certainly a shortage of ethnographic studies on how such people engage in society [8] let alone the design oriented studies that solely target users with cognitive complexity. Our hope is that the results of this inquiry help to understand the user complexity with less confusion and in more accessible terms. To this end, we believe, designing for such users is a sensible and sensitive enterprise that needs development of simple portraits of concepts in the first place.

3   Method

The study begins by examining the terms used to describe cognitive disability in the two reference frameworks/models, the DCM-5 and ICF, as well as how these terms are used in selected academic literature. Following the methodology outlined by Isabelle Walsh and Frantz Rowe [9], a comprehensive literature search was conducted. To identify and analyze different conceptualizations of mental/neurocognitive functioning, the literature was searched using a mix of a wide variety of terms all having close ties to cognitive disability as it is outlined in the introduction (Table 1).

4   Results

After looking at a variety of policy documents and academic literature, it's evident that there is no universally accepted approach to identify cognitive issues. Two resources in particular stand out among the other works published on this subject. Advocating the rights of individuals with varying degrees of mental/neuro-cognitive functioning, many groups consult definitions and taxonomy of the following documents:

1. Diagnostic and Statistical Manual of Mental Disorders (DSM-5) by American Psychiatric Association (APA) and,
2. The International Classification of Functioning, Disability and Health (ICF) by World Health Organization (WHO)

DSM is a reference manual used to classify mental health illnesses. It uses a standardized vocabulary that aims to make healthcare professionals communicate more effectively. The DSM can be used to record and communicate a patient's diagnosis once such diagnosis has been made. Outside of the United States, DSM is only partially recognized. According to DSM-5 categorization (Table 2), mental disorder is a primary concept that encompasses other disorders. The first tier includes disorders such as,

- The neurodevelopmental disorders,
- Schizophrenia spectrum and other psychotic disorders,
- Bipolar and related disorders,
- Depressive disorders,
- Anxiety disorders
- Etc.

In the second tier, there are disorders and conditions that share some similarity. For example, intellectual disability, communication disorder, attention deficit/hyperactivity disorder fall under the first-tier category of neurodevelopmental disorders:

Table 2. Overview of DSM-5

	1st tier	2nd tier
Mental Disorder ⇒	neurodevelopmental disorder⇒	-intellectual disability
		-communication disorder
		-attention deficit/hyperactivity disorder
		-etc

WHO's (ICF) describes mental health or health-related states and means to standardise disability language and measurement (Fig. 1). For ICF, disability is an all-encompassing term that describes a condition with three main, rather general components of body functions and structures, activity, and participation. However, both personal and environmental factors help put the lives of people with various diagnosis into perspective.

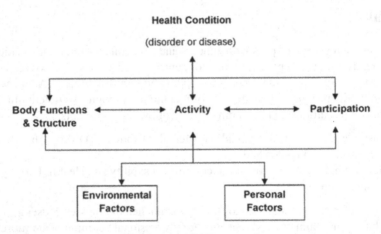

Fig. 1. The ICF Framework

The DSM-5 and the ICF are two well-known resources for classifying the mental/neurocognitive functions of people with cognitive disabilities. The DSM-5 uses a hierarchical approach to condition description, whereas ICF has a bottom-up approach and is more open to nuances. Some have claimed that ICF may benefit from additional data, such as individuals' facts, subjective experience, and recurrent patterns of experience [10]. Janlert and Stolterman (2017) contend that such additional data is unlimited and there are numerous user-complexity-related domains. Incorporation of these nuances makes analyzing the user complexity "less tractable" than analyzing objective (material) complexity, they argue. It is best to avoid incorporating them and focus on objective complexity instead, as the complexities of user could expand more quickly than complexity of systems and artifacts [6].

In light of the literature on cognitive disability, we share our initial result and analysis.

5   Synthesis of the Two Frameworks

The result shows that issues with cognition indicate difficulties with learning, remembering, and communicating. Along with cognition, disability is favored because oftentimes interventions to overcome and manage disabilities frequently involve lowering or eliminating environmental and social barriers [11]. The results show that treating user complexity in terms of cognitive disability could be a departure point for novel contributions in design science. The figure below displays different dimension of such complexity (Fig. 2). It rests on the two frameworks and their subsequent uses in academic literature.

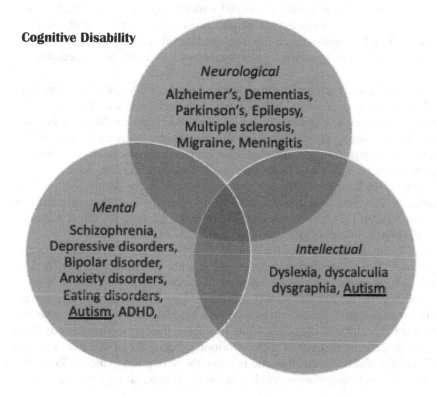

Cognitive Disability

Neurological

Alzheimer's, Dementias, Parkinson's, Epilepsy, Multiple sclerosis, Migraine, Meningitis

Mental

Schizophrenia, Depressive disorders, Bipolar disorder, Anxiety disorders, Eating disorders, Autism, ADHD,

Intellectual

Dyslexia, dyscalculia dysgraphia, Autism

Fig. 2. Conceptualization of Cognitive Disability

6   Discussion and Conclusions

Labeling is a simple, unavoidable, and powerful tool. The autism spectrum disorder is one example that has difficulties with labeling. It is believed that autism falls under the heading of mental disorders together with schizophrenia and the bipolar disorder. However, the World Report on Disability – which is a joint effort of the World Health

Organization and the World Bank – characterizes it as a developmental or learning disability (2011)[1]. Since, The United Nations Convention on The Rights of Persons with Disabilities (UNCRPD) and European Accessibility Act define disabilities as *"mental, intellectual or sensory impairments"*, two labels on autism become problematic in at least two ways. One is when in subsequent studies, particular labels get associated with certain outcomes. A prime example is when mental disorders are considered an important risk factor with certain consequences like committing suicide. Having described autism as a type of mental disorder, we may take such correlation for granted without considering whether autism could be a risk factor at all for such an outcome. The difficulty with regarding autism as an intellectual disability begets another type of problem since intellectual disability is usually associated with low IQ. However, suffering from low IQ is not always the case with autistic people. Such association is a falsely assumed co-occurrence. Similar arguments could be sketched for other conditions. For example, it is still a sensitive issue to treat ADHD as a psychosocial impairment or a neurological one [12].

Even the terms per se complicates the understanding of certain conditions. For example, UNCRPD ruled over a case in Mexico in which an individual with intellectual disability was denied access to tertiary education. The underlying condition was caused by a brain damage during childhood which was later diagnosed with delayed motor, perceptual and language development interfering with learning processes. What is interesting about this case is that it is likely that many readers of the case have not given much thought to the topic of the highest degree of education for people with intellectual disabilities. This is because intellectual disability is nearly typically connected with having a low IQ level [13]. This is one example of how a labeling has implications for the individuals' possibilities or granted opportunities in life.

Atypical mental/neurocognitive functioning is conceptualized differently for different purposes. The distinctions may appear to be without significance; nonetheless, we believe that the ways in which we respond to human conditions and the ways in which we distribute resources in society are profoundly influenced by these formulations. Incorrectly applying a definition based on incorrect identifying elements can cause unintended exclusions and accessibility problems, making it crucial to pay close attention to the defining features of these terminology. It could be that one is simply marginalized in social discourse, that one is given the wrong funds and facilities, that one is denied access to necessary psychological or environmental support, and so on.

References

1. WHO: Disability. https://www.who.int/news-room/fact-sheets/detail/disability-and-health. Last accessed 09 May 2023
2. Borg, J., Lantz, A., Gulliksen, J.: Accessibility to electronic communication for people with cognitive disabilities: a systematic search and review of empirical evidence. Univ. Access Inf. Soc. **14**, 547–562 (2015)
3. Borina, M., Kalister, E., Orehovački, T.: Web Accessibility for People with Cognitive Disabilities: A Systematic Literature Review from 2015 to 2021. In: Duffy, V.G., Gao, Q., Zhou,

---

[1] Neither *mental* nor *intellectual*.

J., Antona, M., Stephanidis, C. (eds.) HCI International 2022 – Late Breaking Papers: HCI for Health, Well-being, Universal Access and Healthy Aging. pp. 261–276. Springer Nature Switzerland, Cham (2022)

4. Vehmas, S., Kristiansen, K., Shakespeare, T.: The unavoidable alliance of disability studies and philosophy. In: Kristiansen, K., Vehmas, S., and Shakespeare, T. (eds.) Arguing about disability: philosophical perspectives. Routledge, London (2010)

5. Wobbrock, J.O., Kientz, J.A.: Research contributions in human-computer interaction. Interactions **23**, 38–44 (2016)

6. Janlert, L.-E., Stolterman, E.: Things That Keep Us Busy: The Elements of Interaction. The MIT Press (2017)

7. Pink, S., Fors, V., Lanzeni, D., Duque, M., Sumartojo, S., Strengers, Y.: Design Ethnography: Research, Responsibilities, and Futures. Routledge, London (2022)

8. McKearney, P., Zoanni, T.: Introduction: for an anthropology of Cognitive Disability. The Cambridge J. Anthropol. **36**, 1–22 (2018)

9. Walsh, I., Rowe, F.: BIBGT: combining bibliometrics and grounded theory to conduct a literature review. European Journal of Information Systems, 1–22 (2022)

10. Geyh, S., Schwegler, U., Peter, C., Müller, R.: Representing and organizing information to describe the lived experience of health from a personal factors perspective in the light of the International Classification of Functioning, Disability and Health (ICF): a discussion paper. Disabil. Rehabil. **41**, 1727–1738 (2019)

11. Miles, S.R., Averill, L.A.: Definitions of Abnormality. In: Cautin, R.L., Lilienfeld, S.O. (eds.) The Encyclopedia of Clinical Psychology, pp. 1–5. John Wiley & Sons Inc, Hoboken, NJ, USA (2015)

12. Williams, C.: ADHD: What's behind the recent explosion in diagnoses?, https://www.new scientist.com/article/mg25834372-000-adhd-whats-behind-the-recent-explosion-in-diagno ses/, last accessed 09 May 2023

13. Charman, T., Pickles, A., Simonoff, E., Chandler, S., Loucas, T., Baird, G.: IQ in children with autism spectrum disorders: data from the Special Needs and Autism Project (SNAP). Psychol. Med. **41**, 619–627 (2011)

Applying a User-Centered Design (UCD) Approach to the Increasing Number of Anxiety Disorders in Students and Workers

Anna Šebíková[✉]

Faculty of Architecture - Design, Czech Technical University in Prague, Prague, Czechia
sebikann@cvut.cz

Abstract. Anxiety disorders have a negative impact on work and academic performance, so it is important to look for new solutions to minimize the inequalities that can arise in the workplace or at university. Apps and design products targeting anxiety disorders can help reduce stress and improve mental well-being. Finding innovative solutions and, last but not least, testing these solutions and adapting them to users is key. The goal of the work is to examine existing designs and to test new ways that would respect the requirements of the selected target group.

Keywords: Anxiety · User-centered design · Product design

1 Introduction

1.1 Motivation

Anxiety is a mental disorder that affects people in their daily lives. Among other things, disorder can have an impact on their work and study performance, after which inequalities are created in the work environment or study environment between the healthy and the anxious. Anxious people then may experience difficulty maintaining concentration, social isolation, lack of motivation, difficulty solving problems and high levels of stress in the work or study environment.

Education, the provision of support by companies or institutions and, finally, the development of innovative solutions can improve the working and study life of anxious patients. Innovative solutions in the form of existing applications and in the form of design aids designed to treat mental illnesses can play an important role in reducing stress and promoting overall mental well-being.

The aim of this article is to explore and evaluate the advantages and disadvantages of these solutions aimed at anxiety disorders in the context of the work and study environment and, finally, to outline the methodology of designing the solution from the point of view of user-centered design (UCD) procedures as secondary element in treating anxiety disorders.

© IFIP International Federation for Information Processing 2024
Published by Springer Nature Switzerland AG 2024
A. Bramwell-Dicks et al. (Eds.): INTERACT 2023 Workshops, LNCS 14535, pp. 168–174, 2024.
https://doi.org/10.1007/978-3-031-61688-4_17

1.2 Anxiety Disorders

One of the most common psychological disorders are anxiety disorders, and anxiety is their most significant symptom. With significant physical symptoms, anxiety disorders are often unidentified and confused with physical illnesses in general practitioners' offices. Anxiety can be so-called trait anxiety or state anxiety. In the acute state anxiety form, physical symptoms of the "fight-or-flight" [1] reaction appear. On the other hand – in the state form, the prevailing element is overall increased excitement [2].

According to ICD-10, anxiety disorders are classified in the category of Neurotic, stress-related and somatoform disorders (F40–F48). Anxiety disorders are included in the subcategories of Phobic anxiety disorders (F40) and Other anxiety disorders (F41) [3].

As in the cases of other illnesses, people with anxiety can also experience stigmatization from the environment. In the case of the stigmatization of mental disorders, rejection is linked to the ongoing different behavior of individuals (fear of the possibility of endangering the environment) - however, patients with mental illnesses without obviously different behavior, such as anxiety disorders or somatoform disorders, also experience stigmatization. The stigmatization of these disorders is an unanswered question, and probably in this case the mere label "mental illness" is enough for stigmatization [4]. According to the Indigo research, in which 91 respondents with a mental disorder took part, 54% of them try to hide their illness, 20% experience evasive behavior from others and 18% feel rancor from their surroundings [5].

Treatment can be carried out using psychotherapy or pharmacotherapy, but preferably using a combination of both methods. The effectiveness of psychotherapy is long-term. Psychotherapeutic methods used to treat anxiety disorders include individual, group, or cognitive behavioral therapy (CBT), which specifically teaches the patient to manage their fears, avoidance behaviors, and panic attacks [6].

Principles of CBT (Cognitive Behavioral Therapy) are based on the work of Aaron Beck, who developed cognitive therapy in the 1960s [7]. Cognitive therapies aim to transform dysfunctional beliefs and erroneous information processing in specific mental disorders [8].

When using psychotropic drugs, antidepressants and benzodiazepines are most used. The choice of psychotropic drugs is influenced by the goal of treatment, the phase of treatment and other factors (preferences, contraindication, addictions) [9].

2 Research

2.1 Design Approach

The term "design" originates from the Latin word "designare" [10] and is commonly used today to refer to planning, intending, proposing, and projecting [11]. Designers are individuals dedicated to creating design. The concept of design as a profession emerged during the 18th and 19th centuries, particularly during the industrial revolution [12]. Previously, the term "designer" was associated with the theological notion of a Designer-God [13], possibly because of that society sees designers as solitary creators [14]. However, it is common for specialists from various fields to contribute to the design process alongside designers themselves. User-Centered Design (UCD) is an approach closely associated with psychologist and designer Donald Norman, who pioneered the development of user-friendly and intuitive designs to prevent user frustration [15]. UCD recognizes three types of users: primary, secondary, and tertiary. Primary users are those who directly use the object or service, while secondary users have occasional or indirect contact with it. Tertiary users are those affected by the object or service's use or those who financed its development. Considering all these user types is crucial in the design process [16]. UCD is applied in various design fields, including software application design.

2.2 Existing Solutions – Apps and Design Products

Thanks to existing experimental studies, the effectiveness of the two most popular applications used to reduce stress, depression and anxiety have been compared by authors. For anxiety, the Calm [17] app (founded 2012) needs more studies to evaluate its effectiveness. Headspace [18] (founded 2010) has been shown to be effective in the context of depression. In the context of anxiety, mindfulness, well-being and stress, the Headspace app showed improvement in at least 40% of experimental studies [19]. Both apps are used by 50% of anxiety and depression app users [20]. According to the seller, the Headspace application offers guided meditations, mindfulness exercises, movement exercises, etc. Headspace focuses on stress, anxiety, productivity, building resilience and better sleep. Similarly, Calm includes a selection of meditations, bedtime stories, songs, stretching exercises and mindfulness techniques for better sleep and relaxation. Other applications such as Sanvello [21], Wysa [22], Youper [23] or Moodnotes [24] use the principles of cognitive behavioral therapy.

Design products can be an effective tool in diverting attention from stressors, and there are various principles that these products function. At the same time, they can affect different senses. For example, CalmiGo [25] and essential oil diffusers [26] use the distraction of smell. Studies show that aromatherapy can have a suppressive effect on stress [27]. Other design solutions, such as weighted vests [28] and weighted blankets [29], use pressure, which can provide a sense of safety and comfort. There are also coloring books [30] for adults that allow people to relax and focus their attention on the creative process of drawing – it uses visual senses and motor movement, which is also used in anti-stress toys [31]. Devices using breathing regulation, such as the Beurer [32] or Breathing friend [33], focus on the correct breathing rhythm and can help to calm the nervous system. Solutions using the user's hearing also play a significant role in lowering the level of anxiety. Earplugs, such as Calmer [34], and the Apollo Neuro [35], which works with pulsations, can reduce external stimuli, and help people focus and relax.

3   Discussion

3.1   Evaluation of Existing Solutions

The mentioned aids often offer a quick solution for acute anxiety states, allowing immediate relief and distraction from stress. For example, devices using smell or pressure can help calm the body and mind in a moment of need. However, some of these researched designs may not be suitable for use in a work environment or in certain situations, which may limit their practicality. For example, the need of using hands while using the product, special position of the body that is required for the use of specific design, discretion etc. In this case, the use of a user-centered design approach is appropriate.

On the other hand, apps aimed at reducing anxiety often offer a longer-term solution. For example, applications based on the principles of cognitive-behavioral therapy can help people understand and manage the underlying causes of anxiety, thereby enabling lasting changes in their perception and responses to stress. These apps can provide educational materials, exercises, and support to help develop effective strategies for managing anxiety.

The optimal approach might be to combine the advantages of both approaches. The use of products to immediately relieve the symptoms of anxiety can be supplemented with applications that focus on long-term solutions to the problem. In this way, the acute symptoms of anxiety could be addressed while simultaneously working to identify and manage the deeper causes and problems. Combining these approaches could yield better results and help people reduce anxiety and improve their overall well-being in both the short and long term.

3.2   New Perspectives – Using Noninvasive VNS

There is also an interesting idea that anxiety symptoms can be reduced not only by regulating breathing or other methods mentioned above, but also by changing the temperature, especially the temperature on the vagus nerve [36, 37]. A new design for reducing anxiety symptoms could use this very principle (VNS). By being able to stimulate the vagus nerve through temperature changes, it could support the body's physiological response to anxiety and reduce its symptoms (heart rate).

The vagus nerve is one of the main nerves associated with relaxation and calmness, it is so called parasympathetic nerve [38]. Numerous studies are examining the technique of Vagus Nerve Stimulation (VNS) in the context of pharmacoresistant epilepsy and depression. For instance, in the treatment of refractory epilepsy using invasive VNS, an implanted device (pulse generator) is utilized in the upper left chest area, connected to electrodes placed on the left side of the neck. Invasive VNS presents limitations in the form of potential side effects, such as wound infections or dysphonia, that may arise during implantation [39]. Only a few studies are investigating the impact of VNS on anxiety disorders [40]. One such study from 2008 provides evidence of improvement in the condition of several patients with pharmacoresistant anxiety disorders in both acute and long-term periods through the use of VNS technique. However, it highlights the need for further future studies [41]. A study from 2022 explores the effect of VNS and its non-invasive forms on fear and anxiety in patients with autism spectrum disorder [42]. A potential limitation could lie in the difference in effectiveness between invasive and non-invasive methods.

By combining the ideas that the design would use temperature stimulation on the vagus nerve and the applications using CBT principles aimed at reducing anxiety, a comprehensive approach to anxiety management could be achieved. This would provide comprehensive and effective support for people in the workplace who suffer from anxiety, allowing them to reduce symptoms while addressing long-term and overall anxiety management through the incorporation of an application using CBT principles.

As there is no device on the market yet that uses thermal stimulation of the vagus nerve to reduce anxiety, testing is required to ensure its effectiveness and safety. The testing should include a clinical trial on human subjects with a prototype of the future product. The aim of these tests would be to evaluate whether a functional prototype using thermal nerve stimulation reduces anxiety symptoms.

Testing. The process of testing a new anxiety-reducing aid will involve several steps. It will begin by screening potential participants using a questionnaire that includes questions about the frequency, intensity, and restrictions because of anxiety in their lives.

The proband will be placed in front of the screen, which will be scanned by two cameras to record the results more accurately and will fill out a self-report questionnaire – Beck Anxiety Inventory [43]. This is followed by biofeedback scanning, during which the participant's stress is first increased using the Stroop test [44] and his performance is judged by the error rate in mathematical tasks.

This is followed by another filling in of the anxiety inventory. In the next phase, the proband's stress will be increased again using the Stroop test and subsequent mathematical tasks, during which in this part of the testing the proband will attach a Peltier module [45] (as a functional prototype of the future product) to the area of the vagus nerve. This is followed by filling in the anxiety scale.

Error rates in mathematical tasks, changes on the anxiety scale and scanned biodata will be evaluated and compared.

4   Conclusion

User-centered design plays a pivotal role in designing solutions that are not only effective but also accessible for individuals with anxiety disorders. By prioritizing the needs and desires of users, this approach ensures that design solutions address their specific challenges and promote mental well-being. Achieving this requires close collaboration between designers, psychological and sociological experts, and the users themselves. By combining their expertise and insights, it becomes possible to create user-friendly designs that minimize frustration and provide support for individuals with anxiety disorders. It is crucial to emphasize anxiety and mental health awareness, challenge stigma, and foster an environment that encourages the development of innovative solutions tailored to the needs of those suffering from anxiety disorders.

References

1. Cannon, W.B.: Bodily Changes in Pain, Hunger. Fear and Rage. Appleton, New York (1929)
2. Praško, J.: Interní medicína pro praxi, Mezioborové přehledy, Úzkostné poruchy. 500, via https://www.internimedicina.cz/pdfs/int/2004/10/07.pdf. Last accessed 15 February 2021
3. ICD-10, via https://icd.who.int/browse10/2019/en#/F41. Last accessed 29 June 2023

4. Hatzenbuehler, M.L., Phelan, J.C., Link, B.G.: Stigma as a fundamental cause of population health inequalities. Am. J. Public Health **103**(5), 813–821 (2013)
5. Wenigová, B.: Stigma a duševní poruchy. Sanquis **38**, 24–28 (2005)
6. Laňková, J., Praško, J.: Úzkostné poruchy - Doporučený diagnostický postup pro praktické lékaře; CDP-PL, Praha, 4 (2006) via https://www.svl.cz/files/files/Doporucene-postupy-2003-2007/Uzkostne-poruchy.pdf. Last accessed 15 February 2021
7. Becková, J.: Kognitivně behaviorální terapie. Základy a něco navíc, p. 17. Guilford press (2011)
8. Beck, A.T.: Cognitive therapy: Past, present, and future. J. Consult. Clin. Psychol. **61**(2), 194–198 (1993)
9. Farmakoterapie úzkostných poruch, Mudr. Sylva Racková, Mudr. Luboš Janků, Ph.D. [online]. 2006 [cit. 2023-21-06]. via https://www.psychiatriepropraxi.cz/pdfs/psy/2006/03/01.pdf. Last accessed 30 June 2023
10. http://www.latin-dictionary.net/search/latin/designare. Last accessed 30 June 2023
11. https://dictionary.cambridge.org/dictionary/english/design. Last accessed 30 June 2023
12. Walker, J.A.: Design History and the History of Design, New Ed. Pluto Press (1990)
13. Nahm, M.C.: The theological background of the theory of the artist as creator. The Journal of the History of Ideas VIII **3**, 363–372 (1947)
14. On seeing design as redesign, https://janmichl.com/eng.redesign.html. Last accessed 30 June 2023
15. Norman, D.: Psychology of everyday things (1988)
16. Eason, K.: Information technology and organizational change. Taylor and Francis, London (1987)
17. https://apps.apple.com/us/app/calm/id571800810. Last accessed 30 June 2023
18. https://apps.apple.com/us/app/headspace-mindful-meditation/id493145008. Last accessed 30 June 2023
19. O'Daffer, A., Colt, S.F., Wasil, A.R., Lau, N.: Efficacy and Conflicts of Interest in Randomized Controlled Trials Evaluating Headspace and Calm
20. Wasil, A.R., et al.: Examining the reach of smartphone apps for depression and anxiety. American Journal of Psychiatry **177**(5), 464–465 (2020)
21. https://apps.apple.com/us/app/sanvello-anxiety-depression/id922968861
22. https://apps.apple.com/us/app/wysa-mental-health-support/id1166585565
23. https://apps.apple.com/us/app/youper-cbt-therapy-chatbot/id1060691513
24. https://apps.apple.com/us/app/moodnotes-mood-tracker/id1019230398
25. https://calmigo.com/. Last accessed 30 June 2023
26. https://vitruvi.com/collections/essential-oil-diffusers. Last accessed 30 June 2023
27. Paula, D., Luis, P., Pereira, O.R., Maria Joao, S.: Aromatherapy in the Control of Stress and Anxiety. Alternative & Integrative Medicine **06**(04) (2017)
28. https://www.sensorydirect.com/weighted-compression-vest. Last accessed 30 June 2023
29. https://gravityblankets.com/products/new-gravity-cooling-weighted-blanket?_pos=1&_sid=bbf015698&_ss=r&clickId=4428234687&correlationId=dc23e198-9e11-4182-83f0-6463b836b0cf&utm_campaign=21181&utm_content=8-12847&utm_medium=affiliate&utm_source=partnerize. Last accessed 30 June 2023
30. https://printablefreecoloring.com/drawings/relaxation/anti-stress. Last accessed 30 June 2023
31. https://www.sensorydirect.com/candy-glitter-sensory-variety-pack. Last accessed 30 June 2023
32. https://www.beurer.com/web/gb/products/wellbeing/shiatsu-and-massage/stress-releazer/stress-releazer.php. Last accessed 30 June 2023
33. https://dcgi.fel.cvut.cz/publications/2015/prazakova-pdw-bf. Last accessed 30 June 2023
34. https://www.flareaudio.com/products/calmer. Last accessed 30 June 2023

35. https://apolloneuro.com/. Last accessed 30 June 2023
36. Jungmann, M., Vencatachellum, S., Van Ryckeghem, D., Vögele, C.: Effects of cold stimulation on cardiac-vagal activation in healthy participants: randomized controlled trial. JMIR Form Res. (2018)
37. Mäkinen, T.M., et al.: Autonomic nervous function during whole-body cold exposure before and after cold acclimation. Aviat Space Environ Med (2008)
38. Howland, R.H.: Vagus Nerve Stimulation. Curr. Behav. Neurosci. Rep. 1(2), 64–73 (2014). https://doi.org/10.1007/s40473-014-0010-5
39. Howland, R.H.: Vagus Nerve Stimulation (2014)
40. Chrastina, J., et al.: Možnosti vagové stimulace mimo epileptochirurgii (2012)
41. George, M.S., et al.: A pilot study of vagus nerve stimulation (VNS) for treatment-resistant anxiety disorders (2008)
42. Shivaswamy, T., et al.: Vagus Nerve Stimulation as a Treatment for Fear and Anxiety in Individuals with Autism Spectrum Disorder (2022)
43. https://www.psychiart.cz/testy/beck/. Last accessed 30 June 2023
44. Jensen, A.R., Rohwer, W.D., Jr.: The Stroop color-word test: a review. Acta Physiol. (Oxf) 25, 36–93 (1966)
45. Min, G., Rowe, D.: Improved model for calculating the coefficient of performance of a Peltier module. Energy Convers. Manage. 41(2), 163–171 (2000)

HCI-E2-2023: Second IFIP WG 2.7/13.4 Workshop on HCI Engineering Education

Editorial to the Second IFIP WG 2.7/13.4 Workshop on HCI Engineering Education

Lucio Davide Spano[1]([envelope]) [iD], José Creissac Campos[2] [iD], and Anke Dittmar[3] [iD]

[1] University of Cagliari, Cagliari, Italy
davide.spano@unica.it
[2] University of Minho & HASLab/INESC TEC, Braga, Portugal
jose.campos@di.uminho.pt
[3] University of Rostock, Rostock, Germany
anke.dittmar@uni-rostock.de

Abstract. The second workshop on HCI Engineering Education continued the effort of the IFIP Working Group 2.7/13.4 on User Interface Engineering by discussing the issues and identifying the opportunities in teaching and learning Human-Computer Interaction (HCI) Engineering. The workshop attracted eight papers covering different teaching contexts, ranging from massive university courses, passing through different teaching experiences in specific academic curricula, and even teaching engineering concepts to children. In addition, the workshop received input for improving and adapting the repository material to the dynamic nature of this field. The discussion after the presentation of the contributions focused on how to model competencies, the support to interdisciplinary work, the overall course design, the recruitment of the students and the provision of educational resources, paving the way for further editions of the workshop.

Keywords: HCI Engineering · education · teaching · case study · repository · Git · end-user development · model-based design of user interfaces

1 Introduction and Background

In the dynamic market of new interactive technologies and varying users' needs, in both professional and personal settings, the quest to bridge the gap between human interaction and computing systems stands as an ever-evolving challenge. The proliferation of interactive possibilities makes it difficult for traditional curricula to consistently cover the relationships between the interface design and the engineering aspects of an interactive system.

HCI Engineering stands at the intersection of numerous disciplines, each contributing to a facet of the complex mosaic representing an interactive system. It concerns the methods, techniques, and tools essential for the systematic design, development, testing, evaluation, and deployment of interactive systems

A. Bramwell-Dicks et al. (Eds.): INTERACT 2023 Workshops, LNCS 14535, pp. 177–182, 2024.
https://doi.org/10.1007/978-3-031-61688-4_18

across various application domains. However, traditional Computer Science or Computer Engineering curricula seldom include dedicated courses on this topic. On the one hand, traditional courses on Human-Computer Interaction (HCI) focus on the basics of the human-centred design approach. In contrast, traditional courses on Software Engineering often neglect interactive aspects of systems [1, 4, 8, 12].

To answer the question of how to address the topic of HCI Engineering in academic curricula, the first edition of the workshop, at INTERACT 2021 [3], aimed at identifying, examining, and structuring educational approaches and resources to empower the teaching and learning of HCI Engineering. During the first edition, participants discussed the various students' skills and experiences, exploring how to introduce and teach HCI Engineering in multiple contexts, whether within Computer Science programs or UI/UX Design curricula. In addition, the discussion covered also the diverse lecturing modalities, encompassing on-site lectures, project-based pedagogy, and online/remote lecturing.

Building upon the foundations laid by its predecessor, the second edition of the workshop, at INTERACT 2023, aimed at creating an organized compendium of educational resources presented in a standardized structure. This resource will be available online and serve as a hub for various educational materials, from slides and reference materials to exercises and exams. In addition to the educational resources, the goal was again to collect further experiences teaching HCI Engineering topics in an academic context and additional educational settings, including practitioners and professionals in related fields.

This paper summarises the results achieved during the second edition of the workshop, by introducing the different contributions and reporting on the discussion and the identified open issues. The paper is organised as follows. Section 2 provides details about the organization of the workshop, Sect. 3 summarizes the presented papers and, finally, Sect. 4 describes the discussion during the workshop and future work.

2   Workshop Organization

To have a starting point for the discussion and building the second edition results, we solicited contributions by distributing a Call for Papers on different channels, such as mailing lists on HCI and Software Engineering, social media and publicity on related conferences. Position papers should report experiences related to HCI Engineering (HCI-E) education such as curricula or teaching units dedicated to HCI-E, case studies/projects demonstrating aspects of HCI-E and evaluation of students' skills related to HCI-E. We received eight submissions from different authors, all considered to be of high quality and interesting for the workshop.

The workshop took place on August 28, 2023. Ten people participated in the workshop, four remotely and six on-site. The activities in the agenda included a morning session where authors presented the material, course, module or position described in their paper through a brief talk of 15 min. After each talk, participants had a 5-min slot for asking questions to clarify the presented contribution's scope. We introduce the papers discussed in this part in Sect. 3.

In the afternoon, the organisers moderated the discussion and reflection on common themes from the collected experiences. We organised it in two parts to keep it focused on the most important topics. The first part was a half-an-hour brainstorming session in which participants proposed topics they considered important to discuss. We spent the last 10 min establishing an order to discuss the topics. In the second part, participants discussed the topics identified. We report the main points resulting from the discussion in Sect. 4.

3   Presented Papers

The list of accepted papers at the workshop is the following:

An Online Repository for Collecting and Sharing HCI-Engineering Case-Studies (included into [11] after the workshop). This paper builds upon the first HCI Engineering Education workshop to create an online repository for sharing HCI-related content using Git versioning. It outlines the repository's structure and content addition process.

A Revised Presentation Format for Educational Resources in HCI Engineering (included into [11] after the workshop). This paper introduces a new teaching sample framework for the above mentioned online repository, emphasizing the practical application of conceptual knowledge and discusses its application using an end-user design tool example for mobile data collection.

Considering Modelling Techniques in HCI Engineering Education   [9]. This paper explores the importance of teaching modelling in HCI engineering, addressing students' perception challenges. It suggests strategies to engage students effectively with modelling techniques in evolving technologies and methodologies.

Human-Centred Engineering with Micro-Electronics for Pre-teens   [7]. This paper reports a study with ten pre-teens using the IoTgo educational toolkit for human-centred engineering with microelectronics. The research analyzes the experience and offers insights for future education and human-centered engineering work for young learners.

Teaching HCI to Hundreds of Undergraduate Software Engineering and Computer Science Students   [2]. This paper reports on the experience of moving an introductory HCI course from a postgraduate to an undergraduate program, resulting in a mandatory course with larger class sizes. It shares experiences and advice on teaching HCI to large classes, including adapting to online teaching during the COVID-19 pandemic, as well as students' assessment.

Using an HCI Perspective to Encourage Young Students to Pursue Computer Science & Engineering Careers: The "Envisioning the Digital City" Workshop [5]. The paper discusses two workshop formats for middle and high school students as part of a university program promoting STEM careers. It focuses on teaching basic HCI concepts and problem-solving to address real-world issues. Students are tasked with envisioning innovative mobile apps using design thinking, resulting in creative solutions and low-level prototypes, even without prior design and programming experience.

Teaching HCI in Multidisciplinary Situations: Experience report and Lessons learnt [6]. Technical Bachelor degrees in France are constrained by a national pedagogical program requiring thematic volumes and schedules for their implementation. The program now puts more emphasis on practical knowledge and interdisciplinary collaboration and requires degree programs in computer science to set up multidisciplinary projects for students. This paper highlights how Grenoble and Valenciennes Technical Institutes handle teaching HCI in multidisciplinary situations to prepare students to design and implement computing solutions for user needs. The authors share lessons from their experiences.

The User Interface Technologies Course at the University of Cagliari [10]. This paper discusses the teaching of HCI Engineering concepts within the User Interface Technologies course in the Master's Degree in Computer Science at the University of Cagliari. The course encompasses various aspects of User Interface technology, from desktop interface toolkits to information visualization, gestural interaction, eXtended Reality, and the intersection of Artificial Intelligence with User Interface development. The paper delves into the rationale behind the syllabus design, the assessment method, and the lessons learned over four years of offering the course.

Each accepted paper was first reviewed before the workshop presentation. Then, the authors were requested to update the submission considering the comments in the reviews and the discussion during the workshop. The updated version underwent a second round of reviews before being accepted for publication. All the papers have been improved and extended during this process and leveraged the collaboration during the workshop. In particular, the paper [11] is the result of merging the first two contributions in the list above initially submitted to the workshop into one, since they addressed the same topic of structuring the description of learning materials.

4   Discussion and Future Work

The focus in the workshop was on HCI Engineering education for students in computer science, software engineering and related subjects. Main themes that arose from the presentations and were discussed by the participants included modeling competencies, interdisciplinary work, overall course design, recruitment of students, and provision of educational resources.

The presentation of [2] raised a discussion on the challenges of teaching HCI Engineering at different stages of the students path, and the impact that has on the Syllabus. Additionally, the challenge of managing large classes was discussed, particularly the challenges faced when teaching work intensive topics like empirical usability evaluation to a large number of students.

A particular goal of HCI Engineering education is to promote systematic approaches to user interface design which require modeling competencies [9]. It is important that students understand the role of different models (e.g., contextual and task models) and learn to create and connect them. In this context, one participant pointed out that more reliable educational software tools are needed that support students in following such systematic development approaches to see their advantages.

The presentation of [6] started a discussion on how to prepare students for interdisciplinary collaboration as necessary in the development of interactive systems. Workshop participants pointed out the potential of HCI Engineering education in producing "belief-changing exercises" [2] for students that help them to learn switching between different design perspectives. Additionally, workshop formats such as those in [5,7] may attract school students with more diverse interests to study computer science or related disciplines as they depict them not as a "niche for stereotypical programmers" [5] but provide a human-centric and pragmatic perspective on these disciplines. However, the participants also discussed the challenges of designing courses for both undergraduate and graduate students that result from the broad range of topics and methods in HCI Engineering [10]. It was emphasized that a balance between the breadth and depth of topics has to be achieved that are covered in a course.

Based on the presentations of [11], participants exchanged views on how to improve the existing online repository for educational resources in HCI Engineering. One idea was to create an ontology that supports keyword-based search in the repository. Another idea informed by the presentation of [9] concerned the development Pedagogical Content Knowledge that is specific to HCI Engineering. Pedagogical Content Knowledge describes typical student misconceptions and proven teaching strategies to overcome them [13]. Future work will be dedicated to the further development of the online repository for a stronger integration with other HCI resources, to make it more flexible and richer in content but also support its maintenance.

References

1. ACM/IEEE-CS Joint Task Force on Computing Curricula: Computer Science Curricula 2013. Technical report, ACM Press and IEEE Computer Society Press (2013)
2. Andrews, K.: Teaching HCI to hundreds of undergraduate software engineering and computer science students. In: Bramwell-Dicks, A., Evans, A., Winckler, M., Petrie, H., Abdelnour-Nocera, J. (eds.) INTERACT 2023 Workshops. LNCS, vol. 14535, pp. 226–238. Springer, Cham (2024). https://doi.org/10.1007/978-3-031-61688-4_22
3. Caffiau, S., Campos, J.C., Martinie, C., Nigay, L., Palanque, P., Spano, L.D.: Teaching HCI engineering: four case studies. In: Ardito, C., et al. (eds.) INTERACT 2021. LNCS, vol. 13198, pp. 195–210. Springer, Cham (2022). https://doi.org/10.1007/978-3-030-98388-8_18
4. Churchill, E.F., Bowser, A., Preece, J.: Teaching and learning human-computer interaction: past, present, and future. Interactions 20(2), 44–53 (2013)

5. Díaz, P., Onorati, T., Montero, Á.: Using an HCI perspective to encourage young students to pursue computer science & engineering careers: the "Envisioning the Digital City" workshop. In: Bramwell-Dicks, A., Evans, A., Winckler, M., Petrie, H., Abdelnour-Nocera, J. (eds.) INTERACT 2023 Workshops. LNCS, vol. 14535, pp. 239–252. Springer, Cham (2024). https://doi.org/10.1007/978-3-031-61688-4_23

6. Dupuy-Chessa, S., Oliveira, K.M., Lepreux, S., Pruszko, L.: Teaching HCI in multidisciplinary situations: experience report and lessons learnt. In: Bramwell-Dicks, A., Evans, A., Winckler, M., Petrie, H., Abdelnour-Nocera, J. (eds.) INTERACT 2023 Workshops. LNCS, vol. 14535, pp. 253–259. Springer, Cham (2024). https://doi.org/10.1007/978-3-031-61688-4_24

7. Gennari, R., Soufiane, K., Melonio, A.: Human-Centered Engineering with Micro-Electronics for Pre-teens. In: Abdelnour Nocera, J., Kristin Larusdottir, M., Petrie, H., Piccinno, A., Winckler, M. (eds.) Human-Computer Interaction – INTERACT 2023. INTERACT 2023. LNCS, vol. 14145, pp. 281–285. Springer, Cham (2023). https://doi.org/10.1007/978-3-031-42293-5_22

8. Hewett, T.T., et al.: ACM SIGCHI curricula for human-computer interaction. Technical report, ACM New York, NY, USA (1996)

9. Martinie, C.: Considering modelling techniques in HCI engineering education. In: Bramwell-Dicks, A., Evans, A., Winckler, M., Petrie, H., Abdelnour-Nocera, J. (eds.) INTERACT 2023 Workshops. LNCS, vol. 14535, pp. 201–215. Springer, Cham (2024). https://doi.org/10.1007/978-3-031-61688-4_20

10. Spano, L.D.: The user interface technologies course at the University of Cagliari. In: Bramwell-Dicks, A., Evans, A., Winckler, M., Petrie, H., Abdelnour-Nocera, J. (eds.) INTERACT 2023 Workshops. LNCS, vol. 14535, pp. 260–269. Springer, Cham (2024). https://doi.org/10.1007/978-3-031-61688-4_25

11. Spano, L.D., Campos, J.C., Dittmar, A., Forbrig, P.: An online repository for educational resources in HCI-engineering. In: Bramwell-Dicks, A., Evans, A., Winckler, M., Petrie, H., Abdelnour-Nocera, J. (eds.) INTERACT 2023 Workshops. LNCS, vol. 14535, pp. 183–200. Springer, Cham (2024). https://doi.org/10.1007/978-3-031-61688-4_19

12. The Joint Task Force on Computing Curricula: Software Engineering 2014: Curriculum Guidelines for Undergraduate Degree Programs in Software Engineering. Technical report, ACM Press and IEEE Computer Society Press (2015)

13. Wiese, E.S., Wiese, J., Kogan, M., Dawson, J.: Lightweight methods for developing pedagogical content knowledge for HCI. EduChi 22, 4th (2022)

An Online Repository for Educational Resources in HCI-Engineering

Lucio Davide Spano[1]([ID]), José Creissac Campos[2][ID], Anke Dittmar[3][ID], and Peter Forbrig[3][ID]

[1] University of Cagliari, Cagliari, Italy
davide.spano@unica.it
[2] University of Minho and HASLab/INESC TEC, Braga, Portugal
jose.campos@di.uminho.pt
[3] University of Rostock, Rostock, Germany
{anke.dittmar,peter.forbrig}@uni-rostock.de

Abstract. This paper leverages the outcomes of the first workshop on HCI Engineering Education [4] to create an online repository where the community can share content relevant to HCI. The repository takes advantage of the functionalities of the Git file versioning system to support presenting and adding content. The paper describes the structure of the repository and the process for adding new content. In addition, we propose an adaptation of the framework for presenting teaching samples, supporting more flexibility in the application of educational material for different teaching objectives. The new presentation format starts with describing a design problem and emphasises the students' applied understanding of conceptual and theoretical knowledge. The presentation format is demonstrated and discussed by the example of an end-user design tool for mobile data collection.

Keywords: HCI Engineering · education · teaching · case study · repository · Git · end-user development · model-based design of user interfaces

1 Introduction and Background

The quality of an interactive computing system should be considered along various dimensions. For instance, we must consider the quality of the system from the perspective of its user interface's design. This is the focus of human-centred design processes [11] and leads us to think about the system in terms of its usability [10]. We also must consider how such design is implemented, which leads us to think about the quality of the system's implementation (e.g., its architecture and the technologies used). Each of the dimensions requires a distinct set of skills, making the design and engineering of this type of system an interdisciplinary effort. Interdisciplinary work is characterized by both distributed work by specialized sub-teams (e.g., software engineers, interaction designers,

A. Bramwell-Dicks et al. (Eds.): INTERACT 2023 Workshops, LNCS 14535, pp. 183–200, 2024.
https://doi.org/10.1007/978-3-031-61688-4_19

ergonomists) and collaboration in heterogeneous teams [1]. Accordingly, students need to be trained within their chosen discipline, but additionally they should also be exposed to assumptions, values and constraints in other disciplines and to design activities that cross disciplinary boundaries [15].

Research on design pedagogy in Human-Computer Interaction (HCI) has raised considerable interest in recent years (cf. the research agenda by Wilcox et al. [20]). Human-computer interaction engineering (HCI-E) education in particular aims at preparing students in computer science and related areas for collaborative design practices. In this context, McCrickard et al. [16] criticize HCI courses that merely provide an overview of various elements of interface design or have "students building cool interfaces". Oleson et al. [18] point out that computer science students often experience difficulties "to engage meaningfully with designerly aspects of HCI... or erroneously view design as easy, inessential work". In a previous workshop [2], several challenges of HCI-E education were identified, from keeping courses and curricula up to date with fast evolving technologies and methods, to ensuring that computer science students understand that different types of users will interpret and react to interactive systems differently, to the need to consider real-life systems in the learning process. The discussion was grounded on four concrete projects and exercises used in HCI Engineering courses lectured by the workshop participants, and taken as samples of relevant teaching materials to promote the learning of HCI Engineering concepts through practice. The rationale for this was an understanding that students will benefit from "realistic case studies that simultaneously exemplify HCI concepts and model the process of designing [but also developing] usable systems" [19]. An outcome of the discussion was the proposal of a common presentation framework for teaching samples [4]. The immediate goal of the framework was to help characterise and compare the different teaching samples. A medium-term goal was the creation of an online repository of educational resources for HCI-E.

This paper first presents an implementation of such an extensible online resource to where the materials from [4], and others, might be uploaded and made available. The implementation employs existing tools such as the Git file versioning system and the blogging engine Jekyll [12]. The paper describes how teaching samples can be added, modified, and navigated by using an illustrative example. The paper then reconsiders the presentation framework in [4] and proposes an adaptation which allows for more flexibility in the application of educational resources within different course settings. In the adapted presentation format, specific design problems are considered to be the central element. They ideally require theoretical background knowledge from different domains and have the potential to support various teaching objectives. Again, an example is used to illustrate the suggested ideas. The paper closes with a discussion and future work.

2   The Online Repository

The repository's success depends on the quantity and quality of the collected teaching material. On the one hand, the quality requires a detailed and consistent categorisation and description of each sample, including, for instance, its aims, the application domain, the target students, etc. On the other hand, to maximise the number of teaching samples described in the repository, we need a fast and straightforward procedure for uploading data and allowing the authors to update the description if required. Keeping in mind these two requirements, we support uploading a new sample and editing the existing description by leveraging a development tool HCI engineers are familiar with: the Git file versioning system. A first implementation of such a system is available at the following URL: https://github.com/IFIP-WG-2-7/Teaching-HCI-Engineering.

2.1   Implementation Overview

We host the repository on GitHub [9] which allows us to maintain the data, keeping track of the changes in the description of the teaching samples. In addition, we leverage the hosting support for code-project websites available on GitHub, called GitHub pages [8]. Such support exploits a blogging engine called Jekyll [12], which allows transforming text by using different common syntaxes (e.g., Markdown, HTML etc.) into static web pages. Our idea for supporting the repository was to leverage this to automatically create an online readable version of the repository data for easing the teaching material search and navigation without requiring the authors to produce it.

In summary, the teaching sample GitHub repository consists of the following elements:

- A basic Jekyll installation, containing the definition of the home page and the templates for rendering the teaching samples overview (by listing them) and details (reporting the sample's data in a human-readable way). We detail the generation process in Sect. 2.3.
- A folder containing the teaching samples data. It contains a sub-folder for each sample, and includes a structured description and optional assets (e.g., images, documents, code packages etc.) that may enhance the description. We describe such structure in Sect. 2.2.

We exploit standard pull requests to the repository to request the insertion of a new teaching sample and modify existing definitions. Such a mechanism allows us to review the proposed repository changes and fix possible problems before accepting the request. We detail such a process in Sect. 2.4.

2.2   Describing a Teaching Sample

Each teaching sample has a dedicated sub-folder, which must include at least the *description.md* file. As suggested by the name, it contains the description of the teaching sample, containing both meta-data and a textual explanation of the sample.

The file slightly enhances the presentation format discussed in [4] for identifying the relevant information about a teaching sample. It contains a header section, including a YAML[1] structure for metadata. The fields are the following:

- **layout:** A value allowing the engine to select the correct template for rendering the data. Currently, we have only one template for all samples, but this allows us to support sub-categories in the repository and to render the information using the appropriate structure.
- **permalink:** the repository sub-url the author would like to assign to the current sample;
- **title:** The teaching sample title.
- **authors:** a structured list including the information about the teaching sample authors. Each **author** entry contains the following information:
  - **name:** the author's name;
  - **surname:** the author's surname;
  - **url:** the author's homepage;
- **type:** the type of the teaching sample, either *project* (i.e., a piece of work developed throughout the course or as a final assignment) or *exercise* (i.e., a piece of work developed for a sub-part of the course);
- **application-domains:** A list of domains where we can apply the teaching sample.
- **interaction-techniques:** The list of interaction techniques supported in the teaching sample (e.g., WIMP, mobile, gestures etc.).
- **current-students:** The background of the students that currently use the teaching sample (e.g., Computer Science, Design etc.).
- **student-level:** The level of the students that currently use the sample (L1, L2, L3 for first, second and third Bachelor's year; M1 and M2 for the first and second year of the Master's).
- **HCI-theme:** A brief description of the covered HCI themes.
- **tools:** A list of tools used for teaching (e.g., Android toolkit, startup code etc.);
- **brief-description:** A brief abstract of the teaching sample.

The textual explanation of the teaching sample must contain a Markdown-formatted rich text, optionally including media elements (images, videos, links etc.). It must contain the following sections:

1. **Targeted students and prerequisites**. This section contains the description of the students and their pre-requisite levels in the disciplines involved in HCI-E, including HCI and Software Engineering (SE);
2. **Objectives**. A description of the pedagogical objectives of the teaching sample.
3. **Pedagogical steps/monitoring, initial materials and tools**. A description of the pedagogical management of the sample, including the tools used and the initial materials provided.

---

[1] https://yaml.org/, last visited October 09, 2023.

4. **Expected outputs and Evaluation**. A description of the expected outcomes and their evaluation.

   Figure 1 shows a concrete example of a *description.md* file describing a teaching sample. The header part, contained between the three minus (hyphen) characters (`---`), contains the YAML structured meta-data. The body part allows
formatting the content through headers, bullet lists, etc., using the Markdown
syntax. The ellipses in the example (represented by the `[...]` symbol) correspond
to parts of the text that have been truncated for brevity sake. The corresponding
human-readable rendering of the information is depicted in Fig. 3.

2.3 Navigating the Samples

The rendering of the teaching sample consists of two templates for generating an
HTML version of the data contained in the repository. The first template displays
the list of samples in the repository, showing an overview of their definition. It
basically consists of a card-based visualization of the following fields: title, brief
description and application domains. Figure 2 shows the layout of the list. People
can access the details of a teaching sample by clicking on the title.

   Currently, the navigation of the existing teaching samples does not support
any filtering or search. However, we have already planned changes to the current
listing template to support keyword-based searches. In addition, we plan to add
filters at least on the application domains, the student level and background,
leveraging on the description meta-data.

   The second template provides a detailed view of a teaching sample. It includes
the rendering of all the pieces of information in the *description.md* file, as shown
in Fig. 3. The layout consists of two columns. In the main one (on the left), we
show the title, the brief description and all the sections of the textual explanation, reporting the text and the media elements included in the description file.
In the sidebar on the right, we display the meta-data information as an "identity
card" of the current sample. It also includes the author list and a link to their
homepages for giving credit to the authors.

2.4 Adding or Modifying a Teaching Sample

Providing an easy yet effective way to propose new teaching samples or modify
the description of existing ones is crucial for the repository's success. As already
mentioned above, we leverage a well-known process for managing this process,
the *pull requests* provided by the Git versioning system.

   Usually, pull requests represent a notification to team members that a developer completed a feature, requesting its integration into the main development
branch. Adding a new feature may require adding new code files or changes to
existing ones. Thus a pull request may contain a combination of both. In open-
source code projects, developers often use pull requests to ask the community to
adopt some changes to the codebase, allowing "external" developers (i.e., people who are not the core maintainers) to contribute actively to the project. A

```
---
layout: case-study
title: Electronic Prescription System
authors:
    - author:
        name: José
        surname: Campos
        url: "https://www.di.uminho.pt/~jfc/index.shtml"
type: Project
application-domains:
    - Information systems
    - Health
interaction-techniques:
    - WIMP
current-students: "Computer Science"
student-level: L3
HCI-theme: "UI design and implementation"
tools:
    - None
brief-description: "The Project consists in developing a system to
↪   support doctors in prescribing medicines. [...] "
---


## Targeted students and prerequisites
The electronic prescription system project was first used in a third-year
↪   course on object-oriented analysis and design (OOAD).
[...]


## Objectives
As stated above, from an HCI Engineering perspective, one objective of
↪   the project is to raise students' awareness of user-centered
↪   concerns.
[...]


## Pedagogical steps/monitoring, initial materials and tools
The students self-organize in groups of 3 to 5 to carry out the project.
↪   The project is executed during the semester as the topics are worked
↪   on in class.
[...]


## Expected outputs and Evaluation
The expected outputs are the models mentioned above and the corresponding
↪   system implementation.
[...]
```

Fig. 1. A sample *description.md* file from the repository.

pull request must be accepted by the code repository owner(s) to be included in the codebase. All major code hosting services (e.g., GitHub) provide means for discussing such changes, asking for modifications to the originally proposed changes until a consensus for accepting or discarding the request is reached.

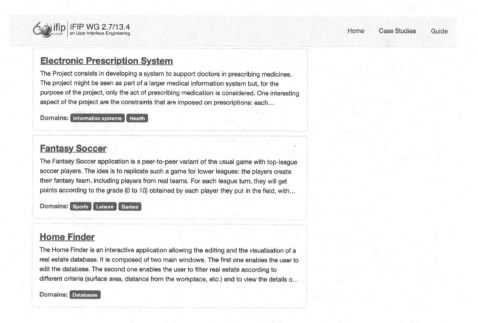

Fig. 2. Overview of the teaching samples in the repository.

Such a supervised process for incorporating changes proposed by the community fits well with our needs. On the one hand, it allows people to proactively suggest new content to be inserted into the repository collection. The only requirement is having a GitHub account. On the other hand, it allows us to enforce a quality standard on the published content by reviewing the proposed changes and discussing them with the author and the community before accepting them. Through such review, we ensure that all the proposed samples are relevant for the repository, contain the required meta-data, and the textual description is clear enough for the reader and other sanity checks on the content.

For proposing or changing the description of a teaching sample, who proposes new content (the *author* from now on) should perform the following steps:

1. *Fork the Teaching HCI Engineering repository on GitHub.* This creates a personal copy of the repository in the author's computer, where s/he will perform the changes. The author may use the same copy for more than one pull request.
2. *Create a new branch for the current request.* A branch is a separate version of the main Git repository, which allows working on different features without affecting the main project. In our case, we use it for working on a specific teaching sample.
3. *Create or edit the sample's content.* In the personal copy of the repository, the author adds a new sub-folder to create a teaching sample, or s/he edits the files to update the description of an existing one. In both cases, changes must be compliant with the structure introduced in Sect. 2.2.

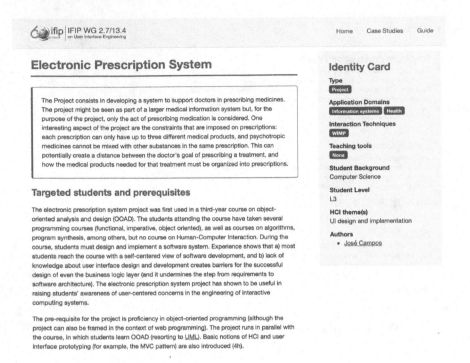

Fig. 3. Sample detailed visualization of a teaching sample.

4. *Commit the changes in the personal copy.* The author commits the changes in the personal copy, adding a small description of the new version.
5. *The author sends the pull request to the original project.* This notifies us, as the repository owners, that there is a new request.
6. *The owners review the requested changes.* In this phase, we review the changes contained in the request to ensure that the content meets the quality standards for being accepted. If needed, we initiate a discussion with the author through GitHub for clarification. We may propose changes to the request or ask the author to perform them. Eventually, we will make a decision about accepting or discarding the request.
7. *Merge on the main branch.* In case of a positive assessment, we accept the request, and the new content is merged into the main project branch. This results in the update of the readable version. discussed in Sect. 2.3.

3   The Presentation Framework Revisited

The above described implementation of the online repository builds on the framework in [4] with teaching samples being organised around student projects or exercises (see Sect. 2.2). In the process of providing a repository for maintaining and sharing the teaching samples, we also dedicated effort to reviewing their format. In this section, we examine, through an example, a modification of the presentation format in which specific design problems or design tasks are considered to be the central element of teaching samples. The design tasks ideally require theoretical background knowledge from different domains and have the potential to support various teaching objectives. The original template mentions application domain and HCI theme but these are not rich (detailed) enough to capture the fact that, from an educational perspective, we will be interested in conveying specific concepts and knowledge.

3.1 The New Format

We propose a new format for adapting the description of teaching samples to different educational usage scenarios, i.e., different ways for using the sample and the related material to reach specific pedagogical objectives. In addition, we propose also to explicit the conceptual and theoretical issues addressed or exemplified through the sample. In detail, the new format contains the following items:

1. Identity card with a title, a brief description of the design task, application domain, interaction techniques,
2. Description of the design problem,
3. Related conceptual and theoretical issues
   - Issue 1: description and references
   - Issue 2: ...
   - ...
4. Materials (provided to or created by the students),
5. Educational usage scenarios
   - Context 1: teaching format, participants and pre-requisites, pedagogical objectives, activities
   - Context 2: ...
   - ...

The original template in [4] characterises an application context but the same resource might be used in multiple educational usage scenarios. Currently to represent that the item would have to be replicated multiple times, one for each context. We argue that the adapted format allows for more flexibility in the application of teaching samples within different course settings. This is illustrated in the following example of a design tool for mobile data collections.

3.2 A Teaching Example Described Through the Revised Presentation Framework

Identity Card

- Title: MDC design tool,
- Design task: A design tool that allows end users to create mobile applications for in-situ data collections,

- Application domain: in-situ data collections,
- Interaction techniques: WIMP, WIMP mobile.

Description of the Design Problem

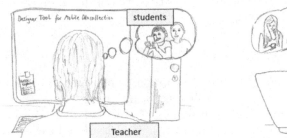 

Fig. 4. A teacher and a researcher using the MDC design tool to create an app for their students and study participants respectively.

In the example, we consider tool support for conducting in-situ data collections - a technique which can be used for diverse purposes. For example, a teacher may wish to ask students to collect data during a biology field trip or a researcher may want to apply the experience sampling method in their empirical study [14]. Mobile devices can facilitate such in-situ data collections. How can the teacher, the researcher or another questioner be supported in creating apps for their respondents according to the needs of the specific situation? In other words, what we are looking for is a design tool for mobile data collections (in short MDC design tool) that can be used by end-users. Figure 4 illustrates the use of the MDC tool (a desktop application) by the teacher and by the researcher.

Related Conceptual and Theoretical Issues

Understanding Roles in End-User Development. In the considered application domain (in-situ data collections), we can distinguish between questioners (e.g., the teacher and the researcher in Fig. 5) and respondents (e.g., the students and the study participants in Fig. 4). The MDC design tool supports end-user development and, more specifically, end-user design. A simple distinction between users, designers and developers is not sufficient and students need to understand the dual role of the questioners. They are end users of the MDC design tool, and at the same time, designers of MDC apps for the respondents (see Fig. 5). This dual role is referred to as designer-user in [6].

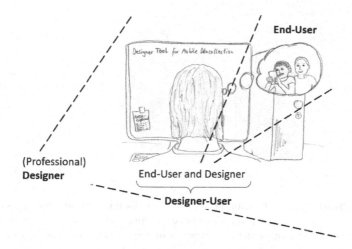

Fig. 5. The dual role of questioners and nested design spaces.

A key assumption in end-user development concerns the differences in the contexts and goals of people acting in the role of a professional developer or an end-user developer. Professional developers are responsible for the quality of the system under development, but typically they are not the users of the system. In contrast, end-user developers have less interest in or understanding of quality criteria, but want to modify or create a system for situated use [13]. A questioner/designer-user in our example wants to create a MDC app for a specific situation, for example, for a biology field trip with their school class.

Design Spaces. The concept of design space is considered to be a valuable tool for understanding design processes in terms of design options and design constraints. In the example, the professional designer needs to be aware of the nested design spaces that are indicated in Fig. 5. The designer-users move in their own more situated design spaces. The way the MCD design tool is shaped has a profound influence on how designer-users can shape the in-situ data collections and their interaction with the end users. The professional designer has to understand the goals and needs of the designer-users (both in their role as end-users and as designers), the goals and needs of the app users, and the relationships between them [6].

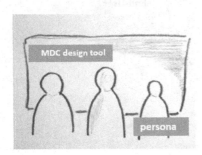 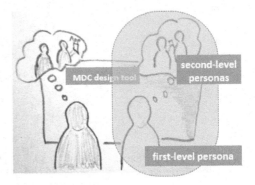

Fig. 6. Left hand side: application of "classical" persona method, right hand side: use of two-level personas - a first level persona represents a group of designer-users and its second-level personas represent the corresponding groups of end users (from [6]).

Design Representations for Multidisciplinary Work. Software development processes can be characterized as processes of creating, refining, modifying or discarding design representations or models. Basically, two types of models can be distinguished: system models describing the interactive software system under development itself and contextual models describing the context of use (both in current situations and in future). Among common system representations for multidisciplinary collaboration are user interface sketches and prototypes, popular contextual models are personas and scenarios. The example helps students to appreciate the value of shared design representations. Moreover, it can help them understand that contextual models also have to be adapted to address design problems more adequately. For example, two-level personas consisting of a first-level persona and some second-level personas (Fig. 6) are more effective in capturing design problems with nested design spaces [6].

End-User Software Engineering and Model-Based Approaches. End-user software engineering supports end-user developers by systematic and disciplined activities that address software quality issues. There are two general approaches: dictating proper design practices and injecting good design decisions, e.g., by a combination of constraints and generation mechanisms [3]. As for our example, the latter approach is interesting and can be implemented by a domain-specific model-based approach such as in [7] following the Cameleon Reference Framework [5].

Materials

Materials provided to or created by the students can include:

- description of the application domain (e.g., in-situ collections, question types)
- personas and scenarios (Fig. 7),
- user interface sketches of the MDC design tool and generated apps (Fig. 8),
- paper and software prototypes (Fig. 10),
- meta-models, transformation rules and models for generating apps (Fig. 9).

Educational Usage Scenarios

We show how the same teaching sample may serve two different educational scenarios by detailing two usage contexts. Each one has its specific participants, pedagogical goals and activities.

 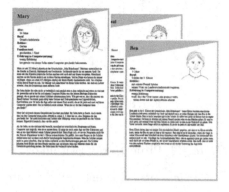

Fig. 7. Two two-level personas: Mark with Lisa and Tom (template format), Mary with Paul and Ben (narrative format).

Context 1. User-centred design courses consisting of a lecture part and an exercise part.

- *Participants:* Students of computer science and related engineering disciplines.
- *Pedagogical objectives:*
    - appreciation of user-oriented design approaches,
    - applied understanding of UCD methods and design representations.
- *Activities:* Topics in lecture include those described in Sect. 3.2. The example is used throughout the exercise part of the course.
    - introduction of the design task,
    - creation of two-level personas (Fig. 7),
    - brainstorming with scenarios and UI sketches of MDC apps for end users,
    - design ideas for the MDC design tool (how can the designer-user design the structure of MDC forms and MDC navigation?): individual UI sketching, sharing of ideas and consensus building by using the personas (Fig. 8),
    - refinement of scenarios,
    - creation of paper-prototype,
    - prototyping session.

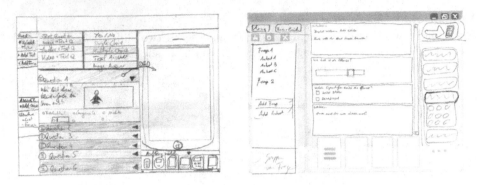

Fig. 8. Two individual UI sketches of the MDC design tool.

Context 2. Project work (within or in connection with HCI engineering course).

- *Participants:* Students of computer science and related engineering disciplines.
- *Prerequisites:* Students are familiar with ideas of model-based development of user interfaces and tool support (e.g., EMF[2], ATL[3]).
- Pedagogical objectives:
  - knowledge and skills in model-based development,
  - use and appreciation of contextual models.
- *Activities:*
  - introduction of the project task,
  - students are provided with (two-level) personas, scenarios, UI sketches,
  - creation of meta-models (domain, abstract UI, concrete UI, final UI) and transformation rules (Fig. 9),
  - embedding in simple UI (Fig. 10).

We used the example design task in scenarios as described above but other scenarios are possible. For example, interaction design students could use 'traditional' personas and two-level personas to reflect on the effectiveness of these variants (see also [6]).

---

[2] https://eclipse.dev/modeling/emf/.
[3] https://eclipse.dev/atl/.

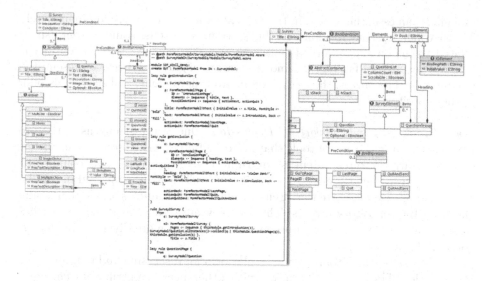

Fig. 9. Meta-models for domain models and abstract UI models (Ecore models in EMF) and some transformations rules (ATL).

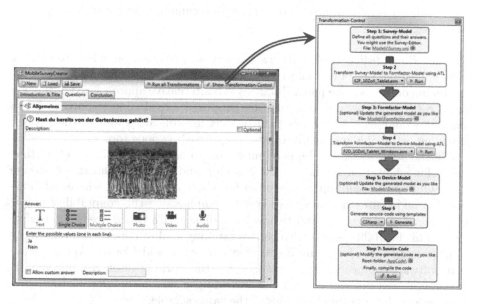

Fig. 10. Software prototype with implemented stepwise generation of apps (using Ecore models and ATL in the model-based approach).

4   Discussion and Future Work

The solution for managing the sample repository presented in this paper highlights the feasibility of implementing ideas from previous workshops with minimal effort, an essential aspect in the context of a repository predominantly relying on voluntary contributions. In this section, we discuss some further aspects related to the ongoing effort of collecting and sharing the samples, considering factors such as tool familiarity among software engineers, effective presentation of educational resources, the role of community discussions, and the extensibility of the repository.

Tools Familiarity and Support for Discussion. One of the strengths of the proposed solution is the use of tools that are readily familiar to software engineers. This familiarity ensures potential contributors can use these tools comfortably without a steep learning curve. The reviewing tools usually employed in collaborative coding also facilitate the discussion of teaching samples and a final quality check by the repository owners. This is a key advantage, as it lowers the barriers to entry for new contributors and encourages a more diverse and engaged community of participants.

Furthermore, these tools provide a platform for discussing and refining teaching samples. Through collaboration with other peers, contributors engage in discussions, share their insights, and collectively improve the quality of educational resources. This collaborative aspect is essential, particularly considering that voluntary contributors rely on a sense of community and shared purpose to drive progress.

Effective Presentation of Educational Resources. The question of how to present these educational resources effectively is another fundamental consideration for continuing our work. The paper discusses two alternative approaches. On the one hand, concrete ideas and examples are proposed as valuable resources. These concrete examples serve as practical models for educators and learners alike, providing actionable insights into how to approach various topics.

On the other hand, it is equally important to present material in a way that allows for adaptation to the specific teaching and learning contexts of diverse users. One-size-fits-all approaches often fall short in education, where individualisation and contextualisation are key. By emphasising the adaptability of our educational resources, we cater to a wider audience with varied needs and preferences. This flexibility aligns with the overarching goal of making the repository a valuable resource for many users. One idea we would like to leverage again from software engineering tools is *branching* the learning resources, allowing us to maintain the original content but providing means to develop further, personalise and share tailored versions of the same sample.

Semantic Navigation of the Teaching Samples. One noteworthy idea discussed during the workshop was the creation of an ontology for teaching examples. This ontology aims to enhance navigation within the repository by providing a structured and standardised way to categorise and discover educational resources. On the one hand, providing semantic relationships in the collected data helps find more significant content and navigation. However, building an ontology requires a considerable amount of work. Therefore, it may be worth considering adopting or adapting existing ones.

Extensibility and Format Adaptation. Beyond the initial implementation of ideas from the HCI-E^2 workshops, the repository needs to address the issue of the moving targets [17] evolving and adapting to the changes in the needs of the community. Two critical aspects of this evolution are content extensibility and format adaptability.

Content extensibility refers to the repository's capacity to grow by accommodating an increasing variety of teaching samples. The repository must remain open, updated and inviting to new contributions. The success of this effort lies in maintaining a welcoming and user-friendly environment, ensuring that potential contributors are encouraged to share their expertise and experiences.

Additionally, the repository's ability to adapt its format is paramount. As educational methodologies and technologies evolve, so should the repository's presentation and delivery methods. The proposal of a revised format in this paper is indeed an example of such need to adapt. By keeping the process of format adaptation relatively straightforward, we enable the repository to remain relevant and effective as educational practices and technologies continue to evolve.

References

1. Baker, M., Détienne, F., Burkhardt, J.M.: Quality of collaboration in design: articulating multiple dimensions and viewpoints. In: 1st Interdisciplinary Innovation Conference, Telecom ParisTech (2013)
2. Baumann, K., et al.: HCI-E2: HCI engineering education - for developers, designers and more. In: Ardito, C., et al. (eds.) INTERACT 2021. LNCS, vol. 12936, pp. 542–547. Springer, Cham (2021). https://doi.org/10.1007/978-3-030-85607-6_74
3. Burnett, M.: What is end-user software engineering and why does it matter? In: Pipek, V., Rosson, M.B., de Ruyter, B., Wulf, V. (eds.) IS-EUD 2009. LNCS, vol. 5435, pp. 15–28. Springer, Heidelberg (2009). https://doi.org/10.1007/978-3-642-00427-8_2
4. Caffiau, S., Campos, J.C., Martinie, C., Nigay, L., Palanque, P., Spano, L.D.: Teaching HCI engineering: four case studies. In: Ardito, C., et al. (eds.) INTERACT 2021. LNCS, vol. 13198, pp. 195–210. Springer, Cham (2022). https://doi.org/10.1007/978-3-030-98388-8_18
5. Calvary, G., Coutaz, J., Thevenin, D., Limbourg, Q., Bouillon, L., Vanderdonckt, J.: A unifying reference framework for multi-target user interfaces. Interact. Comput. **15**(3), 289–308 (2003)
6. Dittmar, A., Hensch, M.: Two-level personas for nested design spaces. In: Proceedings of the 33rd Annual ACM Conference on Human Factors in Computing Systems, pp. 3265–3274 (2015)
7. Dittmar, A., Kühn, M., Forbrig, P.: A domain-specific model-based design approach for end-user developers. In: Proceedings of the 2014 ACM SIGCHI Symposium on Engineering Interactive Computing Systems, pp. 161–166 (2014)
8. GitHub: GitHub Pages (2020). https://pages.github.com. Accessed 19 Apr 2023
9. IFIP WG2.7/13.4: Teaching HCI Engineering Repository (2022). https://github.com/IFIP-WG-2-7/Teaching-HCI-Engineering. Accessed 19 Apr 2023

10. ISO: ISO 9241-11: Ergonomics of human-system interaction—Part 11: Usability: Definitions and concepts. International Organization for Standardization (2018)
11. ISO: ISO 9241-210:2019 Ergonomics of human-system interaction – part 210: Human-centred design for interactive systems. International Organization for Standardization (2019)
12. Jekyll Team: Jekyll blog engine (2022). https://jekyllrb.com. Accessed 19 Apr 2023
13. Ko, A.J., et al.: The state of the art in end-user software engineering. ACM Comput. Surv. (CSUR) **43**(3), 1–44 (2011)
14. Larson, R., Csikszentmihalyi, M.: The experience sampling method. New Dir. Methodol. Soc. Behav. Sci. **15**, 41–56 (1983)
15. Mackay, W.E.: Educating multi-disciplinary design teams. In: Proceeding of Tales of the Disappearing Computer, pp. 105–118 (2003)
16. McCrickard, D.S., Chewar, C.M., Somervell, J.: Design, science, and engineering topics? Teaching HCI with a unified method. ACM SIGCSE Bull. **36**(1), 31–35 (2004)
17. Myers, B., Hudson, S.E., Pausch, R.: Past, present, and future of user interface software tools. ACM Trans. Comput.-Hum. Interact. **7**(1), 3–28 (2000). https://doi.org/10.1145/344949.344959
18. Oleson, A., Solomon, M., Ko, A.J.: Computing students' learning difficulties in HCI education. In: Proceedings of the 2020 CHI Conference on Human Factors in Computing Systems, pp. 1–14. ACM, New York (2020)
19. Rosson, M.B., Carroll, J.M., Rodi, C.M.: Case studies for teaching usability engineering. SIGCSE Bull. **36**(1), 36–40 (2004). https://doi.org/10.1145/1028174.971315
20. Wilcox, L., DiSalvo, B., Henneman, D., Wang, Q.: Design in the HCI classroom: setting a research agenda. In: Proceedings of the 2019 Designing Interactive Systems Conference (DIS 2019), pp. 871–883. ACM (2019). https://doi.org/10.1145/3322276.3322381

Considering Modelling Techniques in HCI Engineering Education

Célia Martinie(✉) 📵

ICS-IRIT, Université Toulouse III – Paul Sabatier, Toulouse, France
celia.martinie@irit.fr

Abstract. Teaching HCI engineering focuses on preparing students for the design, development, and implementation of usable and effective interactive computing systems. Amongst the engineering approaches that can be taught for that purpose, model-based techniques are interesting because they match the industry's needs for techniques to develop usable and reliable interactive computing systems. Beyond this concrete motivation for teaching students how to build and use models, models are also interesting because they help students to reason and understand problems, and can even make them better at identifying and solving problems. However, students do not always understand the benefits of using modelling techniques. They may find them abstract, cumbersome, and worthless. The purpose of this paper is to discuss the importance of teaching modelling for HCI engineering, especially in a context where new technologies and new methodology trends are continuously emerging. This paper proposes several strategies to increase the involvement of students with modelling techniques.

Keywords: HCI education · Engineering Interactive Computing Systems · Modelling techniques

1 Introduction

Teaching HCI requires taking into account the field's diverse perspectives (e.g. interaction design, human factors, software development...) [3]. Since the first curricula for Human-Computer Interaction [9], there have been constant evolutions: evolutions of the disciplines related to HCI (for example, the multi-user and collaboration paradigm made the computer-supported collaborative work field emerge), evolutions of the techniques, evolutions of the technologies and evolutions of the context of use. To consider these evolutions and maintain an up-to-date HCI education curriculum, members of the HCI community gathered and proposed regular symposiums on HCI education [5]. The name of this initiative namely "HCI living curriculum" emphasizes the fact that HCI curricula should constantly evolve. This is also the case for HCI engineering curricula because the range of interaction techniques and interactive systems has broadened a lot and so have the methods and tools for their design and development. The IFIP working group on UI engineering thus initiated a series of workshops on this topic a few years ago, to gather, analyze, structure, and share relevant educational resources [1].

© IFIP International Federation for Information Processing 2024
Published by Springer Nature Switzerland AG 2024
A. Bramwell-Dicks et al. (Eds.): INTERACT 2023 Workshops, LNCS 14535, pp. 201–215, 2024.
https://doi.org/10.1007/978-3-031-61688-4_20

Teaching HCI engineering focuses on preparing students for the design, development, and implementation of usable and effective interactive computing systems. Amongst the engineering approaches that can be taught for that purpose, model-based techniques are interesting because they match the industry's needs for techniques to develop usable and reliable interactive computing systems. Beyond this concrete motivation for teaching students how to build and use models, models are also interesting because they help students to reason and understand problems, and can even make them better at identifying and solving problems. In this paper, we highlight the benefits of teaching modelling techniques in HCI engineering courses. We also specially discuss the issue of students not always engaging with modelling techniques, and investigate the possible strategies to overcome this issue. The paper is structured as follows. Section 2 summarises the specificities of HCI engineering education. Section 3 highlights the benefits of teaching and the importance of teaching modelling. Section 4 presents the main aspects of modelling competence and the main issues encountered when teaching modelling to students. Section 5 presents a set of possible strategies to overcome these issues. Section 6 concludes the paper and presents a set of selected perspectives for the teaching of modelling in HCI engineering education.

2   Specificities of HCI Engineering Education

HCI Engineering education focuses on teaching how to design, develop, and implement interactive computing systems. The aim is to provide students with knowledge and competencies about systematic approaches, methods, and tools to make and deploy interactive systems that are usable and reliable.

Amongst the engineering approaches that can be taught to build usable and reliable interactive systems, models are very interesting because they enable engineers and developers to describe systematically a part or an aspect of an interactive system. There are different types of modelling techniques and each of them targets the description of an aspect of an interactive system [4] (e.g., user task models to describe the user tasks in a hierarchical and temporally ordered way, dialogue models to describe the possible states of the user interface and its behaviour according to the events that possibly occur). A modelling technique aims to gather the main concepts that underlie an aspect of the interactive system. These main concepts help to understand an aspect of the interactive system (e.g. user tasks, interaction behaviour) and thus to be able to describe this aspect. Models are also a means to ensure that an aspect of the interactive system reaches a property that the user expects (e.g. usability for user tasks, reliability for interaction behaviour). To summarize, the models of an interactive system can be used to identify, describe, understand, and reflect on an aspect of the system, as well as to practically apply verification techniques that take models as inputs.

To illustrate this point, we present and discuss the example of an exercise proposed to students following a master's in HCI (degree in computer science) [16]. This exercise aims to make the students understand that the design of the UI can be relatively independent of the functional core of the interactive system. This exercise also aims to provide them with a model-based technique to verify the properties of the interaction with an interactive system. The main goal of the exercise is to develop an application simulating a traffic light. This application, depicted in Fig. 1 b), is made up of three light bulbs (red, orange and green). The traffic light exhibits three different modes of operation: i) when it is stopped, ii) when it is working, and iii) when it is faulty. In the stopped mode, all the light bulbs are switched off (see Fig. 1 a). In the faulty mode, the orange light bulb is blinking (it is switched off during 400 ms and switched on during 600 ms). Finally, the working mode is different depending on the country in which it is deployed.

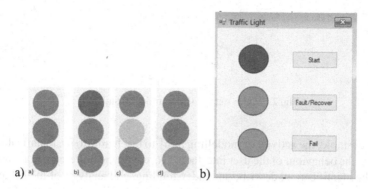

Fig. 1. Graphical rendering of the traffic lights desktop application from [16]

The students learn to program the presentation part of the UI (selecting appropriate widgets, programming widgets if needed, and preparing the layout of the widgets), as well as to program the behavioural part of the UI. Concerning the behavioural part of the UI, they have to apply the following method:

1. Identify all possible events.
2. Identify all possible actions.
3. Build the finite state machine model to describe the behaviour of the UI.
4. From the finite state machine model, produce the state/event matrix.
5. Program source code for event handlers.

Figure 2 shows the finite state machine model of the behaviour of the application that simulates traffic lights (French version). In the initial state (state A, pointed out by the black disc and arrow), the traffic light is in the Fail mode. When an event Start is received, the traffic light changes state to the R state in the diagram. During this state change, the red lightbulb is switched on ("r" action on the arc label from state "A" to state "R"). From that initial state of the working mode, the timer "tR" will be switched on starting the autonomous behaviour of the traffic light in this mode, alternating from Red to Green, from Green to Orange, and then back to Red.

The finite state machine model enables the students to get and understand the different possible states of the application, as well as to verify properties (usability and reliability in this example). For example, it is possible to check that red, green, and orange light bulbs will switch on and off alternatively at the expected predefined time (tR, tG, tO). Another example is that it is possible to check that whatever the current running state (R, O, or G) if a fault occurs, the traffic light will enter the faulty mode (red and green light bulbs switched to off and orange light bulb blinking).

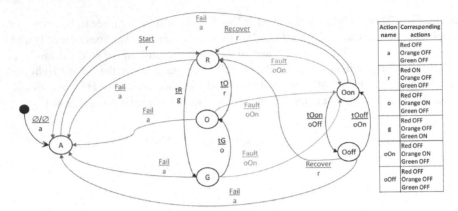

Fig. 2. Finite state machine model from [16]

In this example, the activity of modelling aims to teach how to systematically design and develop the behaviour of the user interface. Moreover, the finite state machine model supports the identification, description, understanding, and analysis of the behaviour of the application that simulates traffic lights. In this example, the finite state machine model also enables the verification of properties (usability, reliability) for the application.

3   The Importance of Teaching Modeling

When teaching science, scientific modelling is the iterative and cyclic process of developing and using models in science, and the produced models aim to investigate, represent, explain, and predict phenomena [6]. Models are central tools for communicating and reasoning in science. The modelling competence is emphasized in standards and curricula in many countries [7].

The teaching of modelling techniques is specifically important in HCI engineering education because we target that our students can apply systematic approaches and ensure properties for the interactive system they will develop and deploy. Furthermore, we target that our students can engineer software for user interfaces and user interactions (e.g. rendering software, dialogue software, input interaction software…).

Beyond arguing for the use of models in teaching HCI Engineering, we can even argue that not using models may be a problem. In the article of Leon Winslow [19] about programming pedagogy, Winslow argues that:

> "*Models are crucial to building understanding. Models of control, data structures and data representation, program design, and problem domain are all important. If the instructor omits them, the students will make up their own models of dubious quality.*"

If we don't teach modelling techniques to our students, they will themselves build their own mental models of the different aspects of the interactive system they are designing and developing. They will also build their own mental models of how to deal with the different aspects of the interactive system, without guidance. All of these self-made mental models may be wrong. This is why it is crucial to include modelling techniques in HCI engineering curricula.

4 The Modeling Competence and the Main Issues Encountered When Teaching Modeling to Students

The modelling competence decomposes in 3 aspects [7]: the meta-modelling knowledge, the modelling practice and the modelling product (presented in Fig. 3).

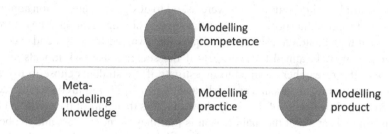

Fig. 3. The modelling competence (adapted from [7])

The modelling practice is the specific sequence of observable and distinguishable operations while being engaged in modelling [7]. The modelling practice can also be referred to as modelling process or modelling activities. The modelling practice includes data collection, such as gathering documentation and performing observations or inquiries.

A modelling product is a tangible, visible, and communicable artefact [7]. Its quality relates to the components and relationships that are required to accurately explain the object of the study. Its complexity relates to the number of components and relationships in the model.

The meta-modelling knowledge corresponds to how models are used, why they are used, and what their strengths and limitations are [7].

There are five aspects of the meta-modelling knowledge that can be learned [7]:

- The first aspect is the nature of models and corresponds to knowing if a model replicates or envisions a part of the interactive system
- The second aspect is named multiple models and corresponds to knowing different types of models and different foci of notations
- The third aspect is the purpose of models and corresponds to knowing if a model aims to describe, explain, or predict
- The fourth aspect is testing models which corresponds to the knowledge of how to test the model itself and how to compare the model with the analysed part of the system
- The fifth aspect is changing models and corresponds to the knowledge of how to correct a model, and how to revise it due to new insights or due to wrong hypothesis.

Several curricula, including HCI curricula, explicitly contain teaching units on the modelling practice and modelling product (e.g. [8, 16]). Students graduating from courses corresponding to these curricula are thus expected to master modelling practice and modelling products.

The meta-modelling knowledge seems to be the most difficult to acquire. Gonçalves et al. [8] reported on a study about the use of task modelling techniques by students who are pursuing a master's degree in computer sciences. This study was led a few years ago on students who had to produce a specification for a supervision application in a command-and-control room of an industrial mixing station [8]. Around 200 students have been taught different types of modelling techniques (including UML, Petri nets, and task modelling). They were then given information about the command-and-control room and the industrial mixing station. They were asked to design the supervision application as well as to produce the specifications of the supervision application. They were also informed that they could choose the techniques they wanted to design and specify the application. The study aimed to investigate if the students use task models and how. In particular, the researchers wanted to investigate if the students chose to use a task modelling technique to understand user tasks and to identify the required user interactions with the system. The results of the study show that less than half of the students choose to use task models and that the main reason is that they do not understand the benefits of using the models, even if these benefits have been taught and discussed before the design and development of the supervision application.

Such a result highlights that there is an open issue about the outcome of the teaching of modelling techniques in terms of meta-modelling knowledge. Students getting graduated may reach an acceptable level of modelling practice and of building modelling products. However, they may not apply the learned modelling techniques in their future practice, and then fail to deliver usable and reliable interactive systems.

5 Possible Strategies to Support the Acquisition of the Modelling Competence

Berre et al. [2] proposed ideas to help students understand the purpose and benefits of using models for software engineering. They are to:

- Ensure that the modelling course ends up with a working application/service/app
- Show the usage of connected models from the beginning of the activity to the production of the application with appropriate tools

Another possibility, as proposed by Wiese et al. [18] for HCI education is to develop Pedagogical Content Knowledge (PCK). Pedagogical Content Knowledge is the anticipation of student misconceptions and the knowledge of what teaching strategies are likely to be effective (or not).

In this section, we explore the possibility of applying these ideas to the teaching of HCI engineering.

5.1   Connected Models to Support the Acquisition of the Modelling Competence

In HCI engineering, and in particular in the EICS community [10], several contributions deal with models as *"EICS focuses on models, languages, notations, methods, techniques, and tools that support the development life-cycle of interactive systems at any stage, from specification and requirements elicitation to validation"*. Moreover, in the category of contributions dealing with models, a subset focuses on models that are connected to the interactive application, from a concrete software point of view. Such connection enables checking and ensuring consistency and coherence between the software of the implemented interactive application and the specification of an aspect of the interactive system. Several types of connections may be established between models and interactive applications:

- Task model driven generation of UI [17]: a toolkit automatically produces an instance of the user interface software from task models (description of user tasks).
- Runtime interpreter of dialogue models running with high-fidelity prototypes (the current dialogue model state displays close to the frame and widgets) [15]: an integrated modelling environment, which includes a runtime interpreter of dialogue models, provides support to produce a formal specification (model) of the user interface dialogue and to produce software for declaring the UI widgets and their relative layout (presentation part of the UI). The integrated modelling environment also enables running the user interface from the dialogue model, which makes a call to the presentation part of the UI.
- Co-execution of task models with an interactive application [11, 12]: an integrated modelling and development environment provides support to produce task models and user interface software, as well as to co-execute them in a synchronised way.

In the rest of the section, we present an example that focuses on the third type of connection, which is between models and an interactive application. This type of connection aims to check and ensure consistency between user tasks and an interactive application. We selected the example of the TOUCAN IDE [11] that supports the editing of task models, the editing of source code for the Java SWING interactive application, and the co-execution of the task models with the Java SWING interactive application. Fig. 4 presents a screenshot of the TOUCAN IDE where the upper left panel labelled "Projects" displays the Java program files and task models that compose a project. In Fig. 4, the main central area decomposes into two main scenes: the left one displays the code of a Java file and the right one displays task models.

The main steps to build an interactive application are to edit the task models and to program the interactive application. Both can be executed independently. Then, the goal is to co-execute them to ensure consistency between task models and interactive applications. Before co-executing task models with the Java SWING application, task model elements must be linked to the source code. In particular, task model elements that describe interactive actions with the application have to be linked to events in the application. Each interactive input task in the task model has to be linked to its corresponding event handler method in the application source code. Each interactive output task has to be linked to its corresponding rendering event in the application source code.

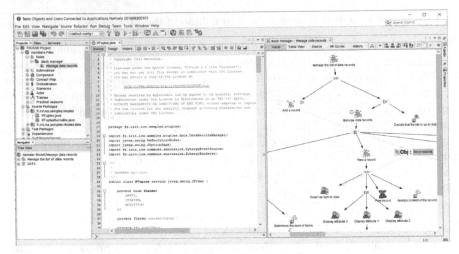

Fig. 4. The TOUCAN IDE

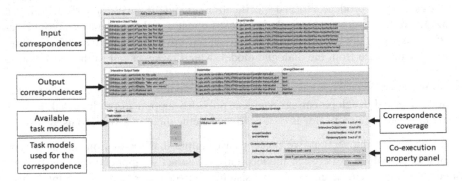

Fig. 5. The correspondence editor in TOUCAN

The TOUCAN IDE provides support to retrieve all the interactive tasks in the task model, as well as all the event handlers and rendering events in the source code. The TOUCAN IDE provides a graphical user interface (correspondence editor presented in Fig. 5) to link the interactive tasks to the event handlers and rendering events.

Once the task models are linked to the interactive application source code, the co-execution of the task model with the interactive application can be run in 2 ways:

– Task-model driven co-execution (presented in Fig. 6): from the task model, each task is executed one by one and the interactive input tasks described in the model will trigger events in the interactive application if the corresponding control is available and enabled. The co-execution panel, at the bottom in Fig. 6, presents a list of tasks that are doable by the user according to the current state of the interactive application (visible part of the interactive application displayed at the top right in Fig. 6). One of the available interactive input tasks can be chosen for execution. When chosen, the execution of an interactive input task will trigger the corresponding event in the interactive application.

– User interface driven co-execution: The second way is to execute the interactive application, and user interactions that happen will be tagged on interactive output tasks in the task model (through the forwarding of rendering events to identify the involved interactive output tasks).

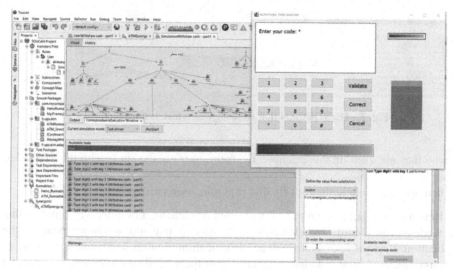

Fig. 6. The TOUCAN IDE with task-driven co-execution (from [11])

There is a direct connection between the task model and the running application, from a concrete software point of view. Using this type of technology, the students can run the application they developed and concretely see the tasks that are not doable by the user, either because something is missing in their application or because the required function is not available at the time it is needed by the user. Figure 7 presents a screenshot of the TOUCAN IDE with task-driven co-execution and with a user task that is not executable at runtime. The task "Type key 2 as first digit" is highlighted in orange, which means that this task should be doable by the user but that this task is currently not doable (whereas it should be possible as it belongs to the set of tasks that should be doable). This warning displayed by the TOUCAN IDE enables the identification a possible issue in the interactive application. In this case, we can see that the button "2" of the interactive application is not enabled, and this is the root cause of the issue. Such button deactivation may occur because of a programming fault and the student can then fix the issue.

In this example, the use of connected models can help the students to acquire meta-modelling knowledge, by supporting the learning of:

– how models are used (in this example, to compare tasks to perform with the current state of the app)

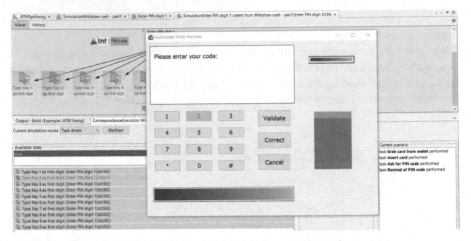

Fig. 7. The TOUCAN IDE showing that a task is not executable

- why they are used (in this example, to ensure user effectiveness with the developed app)
- their strengths and limitations (in this example, user satisfaction is out of scope)

Beyond this example, the use of connected models, in a broader way, implies that the students can identify the elements in the models that link to the elements in the application. Being able to make such an identification requires understanding the foundations of the modelling notation, which is part of the modelling competence. The use of the connected models also implies that students can make the relevant modifications to maintain consistency between models and applications if one of them, or both, evolves. Being able to make such maintenance activities is also part of the modelling competence.

5.2   Towards a Collection of PCK for Teaching Modelling in HCI

Pedagogical Content Knowledge is composed of a problem and a method to overcome the problem. Several examples of Pedagogical Content Knowledge for HCI can be found in the article of Wiese et al. [18]. An example extracted from their article is:

- Problem: *"In a previous semester, students didn't iterate on their prototypes enough because they scheduled usability tests back to back."*
- Proposed method to overcome this problem: *"As a course staff, we can prevent this by requiring separate deadlines for each test and revisions to the prototype in response."*

Hereafter is an example of Pedagogical Content Knowledge that is explicitly related to modelling. This example is about a recurrent problem we face when teaching task modelling to students who follow the master in HCI of the University Toulouse III – Paul Sabatier [16]. Task models are hierarchical representations of user tasks to reach a main goal [13]. This example of PCK related to modelling can be formulated in the following way:

- Problem: Each semester in task modelling courses, at least one student builds a task model in a "workflow-like" way (depicted in Fig. 8 a)) rather than in a hierarchical way (depicted in Fig. 8 b)).
- Proposed method to overcome this problem: As a course staff, we have to show to the students the wrong model that has been produced in a "workflow like" way. We have to make this presentation explicitly and use examples that help them to build a mental model of the result they should not reach.

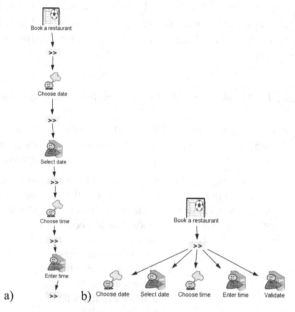

Fig. 8. Types of task models produced by students of the master in HCI

There is thus also a need to develop Pedagogical Content Knowledge for teaching modelling in HCI. We have to systematically identify the common problems we face when teaching modelling in HCI and systematically identify the possible solutions to overcome these problems. The development of PCK for teaching modelling in HCI requires taking into account the different types of modelling techniques in HCI, as well as the different types of modelling knowledge (modelling practice, modelling product and meta-modelling knowledge). The goal is to develop and organize pedagogical material for teaching about models, teaching techniques that rely on models, and guiding to conduct modelling activities.

Table 1 presents an example of classification that could be relevant to organize PCK. For each PCK, we describe the type of modelling technique (first column), the description of the problem (second column), the proposed method to overcome the problem (third column) and the aspect(s) of the modelling competence involved (fourth column), which could be modelling practice, modelling product or meta-modelling as explained in Sect. 4 in this article. The PCK gathered in Table 1 particularly focus on teaching task modelling. Rows one to four are outcomes from the experiences of recurrent problems we face when teaching task modelling to students who follow the master in HCI of the University Toulouse III – Paul Sabatier [16]. Row five is an outcome of the results of a study led at the University of Valenciennes [8]. Such a classification for the PCK enables to organize the grouping of PCK, as well as to identify which aspects of the modelling competence are managed. The example presented in Table 1 could be extended to other types of modelling techniques.

Furthermore, as far as there are several types of modelling techniques in HCI, there is also a need to identify if there are some PCK that are common to several modelling techniques and if there are some PCK that only relate to a specific modelling technique.

Such a classification would support the analysis of coverage of the modelling competence, as well as the systematic identification of problems according to each aspect of the modelling competence.

Table 1. Classification of the PCK for teaching task modelling

Type of modelling technique	Description of the problem	Proposed method to overcome the problem	Aspect(s) of the modelling competence involved
Task modelling	Some students build a task model in a "workflow-like" way rather than in a hierarchical way	As a course staff, we have to show to the students the wrong model that has been produced in a "workflow like" way. We have to make this presentation explicitly and use examples that help them build a mental model of the result they should not reach	Modelling product (hierarchical relationships)
Task modelling	Some students identify a task type that does not match the task they want to describe	As a course staff, we can propose some intermediate exercises (before building models) to make students establish relationships between human actions and predefined types of tasks in task modelling notations	Meta-modelling (1st aspect)

(continued)

Table 1. (*continued*)

Type of modelling technique	Description of the problem	Proposed method to overcome the problem	Aspect(s) of the modelling competence involved
Task modelling	Some students, after having identified and represented an input interaction, forget to describe the feedback from the system that should be perceptible by the user	As a course staff, we teach to the students the theories of human information processing (e.g. Norman's Seven Stages of Action [14]) before starting the exercises of modelling interactive tasks	Modelling product (human information processing representation)
Task modelling	Some students struggle with finding the main goals of the users and focus more on the low-level interactions between the user and the interactive system than on why the user is interacting with the system	As a course staff, we can provide examples of tasks performed by users with different roles who use the same interactive application	Modelling practice (extraction of relevant information from data collection)
Task modelling	Some students do not identify the relevance of building task models [8]	As a course staff, we can propose exercises that present concrete design problems and that aim to map these design problems with types of modelling techniques	Meta-modelling (1st and 2nd aspects)

6 Conclusion and Perspectives

Modelling techniques have to be included in HCI engineering curricula because graduate professional engineers and developers have to be able to build correct mental models of the different aspects of the interactive systems they build. A wrong mental model of one of several aspects of the interactive system may jeopardize the usability and reliability of the deployed interactive system.

The HCI engineering community needs to investigate how to better support the acquisition of modelling competence. HCI students master quite well the collection of information to build models and the production of models from this collected information. However, they hardly acquire meta-modelling knowledge, meaning that most of them do not understand the benefits of using the models, and may not use modelling techniques when relevant.

The main perspectives to overcome these issues are to explore strategies to foster the engagement of students with modelling techniques and to increase the acquisition of meta-modelling knowledge. We proposed two strategies for that purpose: the use of connected models and the creation of a collection of Pedagogical Content Knowledge for teaching modelling in HCI.

Concerning the use of connected models, the main perspectives are to investigate what should be connected models for teaching HCI Engineering and how to tackle the following questions:

– Are there connections between types of models and interactive systems that are more relevant than others to teach modelling? We have to take into account the diverse parts or views on the interactive system to be able to connect different types of models with a produced interactive system (user, tasks, system behaviour…)
– Could we build teaching tools for connecting models to interactive systems? Using connected models in our daily teaching practice requires several means: Integrated Development Environments that embed support for model editing and simulation, as well as toolkits to connect models to interactive systems.
– As we face the constant state of change in user contexts and technologies, how to take into account this evolving trend and be able to maintain the possibility of connecting models to interactive systems that are based on new languages and new technologies.

Concerning the creation of a collection of Pedagogical Content Knowledge on modelling for HCI engineering, the main perspective is to investigate the possible ways to gather and structure the problems and possible solutions. We may need to use several categories for the structuring: type of modelling techniques, modelling purpose, target application domain, and aspect of the modelling competence (meta-modelling, modelling practice, modelling product).

References

1. Baumann, K., et al.: HCI-E2: HCI engineering education: for developers, designers and more. In: Ardito, C., et al. (eds.) Human-Computer Interaction – INTERACT 2021: 18th IFIP TC 13 International Conference, Bari, Italy, August 30 – September 3, 2021, Proceedings, Part V, pp. 542–547. Springer International Publishing, Cham (2021). https://doi.org/10.1007/978-3-030-85607-6_74
2. Berre, A.J., Huang, S., Murad, H., Alibakhsh, H.: Teaching modelling for requirements engineering and model-driven software development courses. Comput. Sci. Educ. 28(1), 42–64 (2018)
3. Churchill, E.F., Bowser, A., Preece, J.: Teaching and learning human-computer interaction: past, present, and future. Interactions 20(2), 44–53 (2013). https://doi.org/10.1145/2427076.2427086
4. Dix, A., Finlay, J., Abowd, G.D., Beale, R.: Human-computer interaction. Pearson Educ. (2003)
5. EduCHI living curriculum. https://hcilivingcurriculum.org/. Last accessed May 2023
6. Giere, R. N., Bickle, J., Mauldin, R.: Understanding scientific reasoning. Thomson Wadsworth (2006)

7. Göhner, M.F., Bielik, T., Krell, M.: Investigating the dimensions of modelling competence among preservice science teachers: meta-modeling knowledge, modelling practice, and modelling product. J. Res. Sci. Teach. **59**(8), 1354–1387 (2022)
8. Gonçalves, T.G., de Oliveira, K.M., Kolski, C.: The use of task modelling in interactive system specification. Cogn. Tech. Work **19**, 493–515 (2017)
9. Hewett, T.T., et al.: ACM SIGCHI Curricula for Human-Computer Interaction. Technical Report. Association for Computing Machinery, New York, NY, USA (1992)
10. López Jaquero, V.M., Vatavu, R.D., Panach, J.I., Pastor, O., Vanderdonckt, J.: A newcomer's guide to EICS, the engineering interactive computing systems community. Proc. ACM Hum.-Comput. Interact. **3**(EICS), 1–9 (2019). https://doi.org/10.1145/3300960
11. Martinie, C., Navarre, D., Palanque, P., Barboni, E., Canny, A.: TOUCAN: an IDE supporting the development of effective interactive Java applications. In: EICS, pp. 4:1–4:7 (2018)
12. Martinie, C., Navarre, N., Palanque, P., Fayollas, C.: A generic tool-supported framework for coupling task models and interactive applications. In: EICS, pp. 244–253 (2015)
13. Martinie, C., Palanque, P., Barboni, E.: Principles of task analysis and modelling: understanding activity, modeling tasks, and analyzing models. In: Handbook of Human Computer Interaction. Springer, Cham (2022). https://doi.org/10.1007/978-3-319-27648-9_57-1
14. Norman, D.A.: Psychology of Everyday Action. Basic Book, The Design of Everyday Things, New York (1988)
15. Palanque, P., Ladry, J.-F., Navarre, D., Barboni, Ei.: High-fidelity prototyping of interactive systems can be formal too. In: Jacko, J.A. (ed.) Human-Computer Interaction. New Trends: 13th International Conference, HCI International 2009, San Diego, CA, USA, July 19–24, 2009, Proceedings, Part I, pp. 667–676. Springer Berlin Heidelberg, Berlin, Heidelberg (2009). https://doi.org/10.1007/978-3-642-02574-7_75
16. Palanque, P., Martinie, C.: The curriculum for education in engineering interactive systems at the master in HCI of the University Toulouse III – Paul Sabatier. In: Ardito, C., et al. (eds.) Sense, Feel, Design: INTERACT 2021 IFIP TC 13 Workshops, Bari, Italy, August 30 – September 3, 2021, Revised Selected Papers, pp. 211–220. Springer International Publishing, Cham (2022). https://doi.org/10.1007/978-3-030-98388-8_19
17. Tran, V., Vanderdonckt, J., Tesoriero, R., Beuvens, F.: Systematic generation of abstract user interfaces. In: EICS 101–110 (2012)
18. Wiese, E.S., Wiese, J., Kogan, M., Dawson, J.: Lightweight methods for developing pedagogical content knowledge for HCI. In: 4th Annual Symposium on HCI Education. 4th Annual Symposium on HCI Education (2022)
19. Winslow, L.E.: Programming pedagogy—a psychological overview. SIGCSE Bull. **28**(3), 17–22 (1996)

Human-Centred Engineering
with Micro-electronics for Pre-teens

Rosella Gennari[1]([⊠])[iD], Soufiane Krik[1][iD], and Alessandra Melonio[2][iD]

[1] Faculty of Engineering, Piazza Domenicani 3, 39100 Bolzano, Italy
gennari@inf.unibz.it, soufiane.krik@unibz.it
[2] Ca' Foscari University of Venice, Via Torino 155, 30170 Venezia Mestre, Italy
alessandra.melonio@unive.it

Abstract. This paper reports a study with 10 pre-teens using the IoTgo educational toolkit for human-centred engineering with micro-electronics. The toolkit guided pre-teens from the exploration of the inner workings of sensors and actuators to the development of their own smart things for interacting with people with sensors, actuators, and wireless communication. The study triangulates multiple sources and analyses the experience for stirring future work at the intersection of education and human-centred engineering for young generations.

Keywords: Human centred design · electronics · education · learning · pre-teen · smart thing

1 Introduction and Related Work

People, especially children and teens, daily interact with smart things, such as smart watches. These interact through micro-electronic physical devices, like sensors and actuators, and data that is exchanged via wireless communication. Programmable microcontrollers, like micro:bit, can help engineer with electronics a functional prototype of a "smart thing" interacting with people, e.g., to detect if its user's temperature is increasing and send an alert to a nearby peer wearing a similar smart watch [12]. Ad-hoc toolkits with micro-electronics can enable also non-experts to engineer prototypes of smart things interacting with people, e.g., [14]. However, this and other similar toolkits are mainly used with researchers or practitioners from other fields than engineering, or for promoting design or critical thinking when used with children or teens, e.g., [3,5,9,16].

To the best of our knowledge, few initiatives educate pre-teens to engineer smart things with micro-electronics, after deeply exploring how it works [11]. Fewer invite pre-teens to engineer smart things by adopting a human- or user-centred perspective, in which it is relevant to consider who uses smart things (*persona*), what goal these tackle (a.k.a., *mission*), where they are mainly used (a.k.a., *location*) [5,15]. This paper deals with it.

The paper reports a case study of a camp with pre-teens to engineer, with micro-electronics, smart thing prototypes for personas, using them in certain

A. Bramwell-Dicks et al. (Eds.): INTERACT 2023 Workshops, LNCS 14535, pp. 216–225, 2024.
https://doi.org/10.1007/978-3-031-61688-4_21

locations, for achieving well-defined missions. Pre-teens used the IoTgo toolkit, which structures the educational path, guiding them from the exploration of the inner workings of sensors and actuators through hands-on experiments, to the design of their smart things for interacting with people with sensors, actuators, and data which is exchanged via wireless communication. The toolkit was presented as demo at INTERACT. This paper focuses instead on the study itself: it reports the study design and results that were not published in the demo paper [4]. It only reports the parts of the IoTgo toolkit, focusing on the novel ones, which matter for explaining the study itself. The camp involved 10 pre-teens from the last year of primary school to middle school. The study is analysed by considering multiple data sources and reporting the sweet and pain points of the experience for stirring future work for educating different learners and practitioners to human-centred engineering with micro-electronics.

2 Toolkit for Human Centred Design with Electronics

IoTgo consists of physical elements, digital and electronic elements. The former include paper-based cards and boards for playing cards and conceptualising ideas of smart things. The latter include programmable open-source microcontrollers, related physical devices, and a dedicated app. Similar versions have been used in past experiences, especially with high-school learners and university students with no programming or electronics background, e.g., [6,8].

The IoTgo kit of this paper was adapted to pre-teens, for enabling them to experiment with micro-electronics and wireless communication, and then engineer smart things with a human-centred perspective. Its main novel components are sketched in the following.

2.1 Exploring and Experimenting

Similar kits only used micro:bit microcontrollers to program, e.g., [8]. For enabling younger learners to explore and experiment with basic electronic circuits, IoTgo also uses Arduino UNO boards and related physical devices (e.g., light sensors, LEDs, banana clips, digital multi-meters) [1].

It also has companion cards that have explanatory illustrations and wiring schemes for creating circuits, step by step, first without Arduino UNO for exploring sensors, and then with it for triggering actuators according to signals read by sensors. See examples in Figs. 1 and 2.

2.2 Exploring a Context and Conceptualising Ideas

IoTgo has also two main boards for exploring a human-centred context, with a problematic situation to tackle, and engineering smart things for it, instead of three or more boards as with older learners [6–8]. Cards, to place on boards, decompose smart things along their non-technical components (e.g., personas), and technical components (e.g., sensors and actuators).

Fig. 1. Parts of the toolkit for: (1) exploring and experimenting with how a light sensor works with a multi-meter and flashlight (left); (2) explaining how to create the related circuit (right)

Specifically, the context board helps empathise with a problematic context and find a solution for it: it starts with a story presenting the context, acting as scenario; it guides to choose non-technical cards for things to make smart ("what"), personas using them ("for whom"), locations where persona use them ("where"), and missions that personas tackle with them ("for what") in relation to the given context. The other board is for communication and technical cards, to use in either one of two manners: to sense and send data via wireless; to interact with such data. Part of the former communication board is in Fig. 3.

2.3   Programming the Interaction and Communication

IoTgo also contains micro:bit microcontrollers [12]. These are chosen because they have onboard Bluetooth antennas and are easy to embed in things to make smart. Moreover, the IoTgo app enables non-experts to automatically generate a MakeCode block-based programs for micro:bit, starting from the chosen combinations of cards on the communication boards [13]. Participants can then further edit and upload programs on micro:bit microcontrollers. In this manner, participants can rapidly test their ideas of smart things in action, then share and reflect on them, and revise them rapidly.

3   Study Design

3.1   Participants and Context

The study involved 10 pre-teens, aged 10–13 years old (9 males, 1 female). Three were from the last year of primary school, whereas all others were from the first two years of middle school. Only one of them had past programming experience

 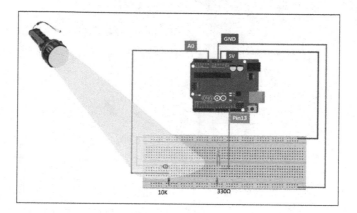

Fig. 2. Parts of the toolkit for: (1) exploring and experimenting with how LEDs work, via an Arduino UNO and again a light sensor and a flashlight (left); (2) explaining how to create the related circuit (right)

with the micro:bit and programming in MakeCode. The study was organised over three days (Day 1–3), for 3–4 hours per day, in August and September 2022. It was held in a dedicated open space for young learners. Participants worked in pairs. Each pair was provided with a laptop computer and the IoTgo toolkit.

3.2 Research Question and Data Collection

The main research question was as follows: *what would pre-teens learn through the experience?* Data were collected in relation to it *after* and *during* the experience from multiple sources. After the experience, data were collected via (1) an ad-hoc questionnaire, (2) and by considering prototypes by pre-teens. The questionnaire was adopted in other similar studies with micro-electronics toolkits and it is under standardisation [7]. Prototypes by pre-teens are those developed on the last day, and they are taken as indicators of learning as common in the literature, e.g., [6]. Specifically, the conceptualisations of prototypes were documented in the IoTgo board illustrated in Fig. 3, and complemented with MakeCode programs. Data, related to what might promote or hamper learning in the experience, were collected via observations, and tracked in written notes and videos. The data processing was approved by the ethics committee of the authors' university.

3.3 Protocol and Tasks

The protocol is detailed in the following per day of the camp.

Day 1. On Day 1, participants explored sensors and actuators with the material of IoTgo described in Subsect. 2.1. Firstly, participants built circuits without Arduino UNO boards to explore the inner working of sensors, that is, light

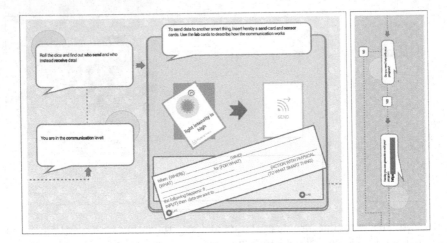

Fig. 3. Parts of the communication board: conceptualisation part concerning sensors and how to send data (left); IoTgo link to the app for generating a program (right).

sensors, temperature, and soil moisture sensors. Stronger with an understanding of how they worked, they built circuits to explore the inner working of actuators, LEDs, liquid-crystal displays (LCDs), and buzzers.

Day 2. On Day 2, participants experimented with micro:bit microcontrollers, part of IoTgo, and the same sensors and actuators as Day 1 except LCDs. First, a researcher introduced a micro:bit, and explained the differences with the Arduino UNO board. Afterwards, participants experimented with how to program the boards with MakeCode and connect sensors and actuators to them.

Day 3. On Day 3, participants designed personas' interactions with smart things and their communication by using the material of IoTgo, illustrated in Subsect. 2.2, and the companion app illustrated in Subsect. 2.3. The first half of the day was for exploring how to conceptualise and program the interaction and wireless communication with micro:bit boards. Then pairs and a group of three were created to design their own smart things for personas and their missions in locations (e.g., town). These were then matched in 3 groups of 4–5 members. At the end, each group shared their prototypes with all others and researchers.

4   Results

This section analyses participants' answers to the questionnaire, the prototypes they delivered at the end of the experience, and researchers' observations of the entire experience to answer the leading research question (see Subsect. 3.2).

4.1 Questionnaire

The questionnaire was the same independently of whether participants came from the last year of primary school (younger), or the first two years of middle school (older). Each item came with a score of 1. The total score across items, divided per age group (younger, older), is reported in Table 1. The same table also reports the total score across participants, divided per item.

The total scores across items denote a generally positive result of the learning experience, with $Mean = 8.11$ and standard deviation $SD = 2.46$. Differences are noticeable between the **younger and older group**. The total score across participants was anyhow generally positive, with $Mean = 8.7$ and $SD = 1.57$. The first four items are related to knowledge of the working of sensors and actuators: almost all participants replied correctly to them.

The other items are related to the conceptualisation of ideas with sensors, actuators, and MakeCode programs. In particular, Item 10, which created most differences (5 out of 10 tackled it, correctly), was related to **the programming of the communication**, explored as last during the experience.

Table 1. Results of the learning questionnaire (score from 0 to 10)

age group	total score across items	item	total score across participants
older	10	1	10
older	8.89	2	10
younger	6.66	3	8
younger	10	4	9
older	6.67	5	10
younger	2.22	6	8
older	7.78	7	10
older	10	8	8
older	10	9	9
older	8.89	10	*5*

4.2 Prototypes

Every group managed to deliver a prototype at the end of the experience, which was **functioning**, using sensors and actuators **correctly**, and communicating at a distance as shown in Fig. 4. A group also managed to insert their prototype into a physical thing to better convey their idea, as shown in the same figure.

Each prototype embedded a **human-centred perspective**: it was coherent with the chosen thing to make smart for a persona, in a given location, and for a given mission. For instance, a group delivered a prototype related to a *smart watch* (the "what" part) for them and their grandmothers (the "who" part) who needed to *relate* (the "for what" part) to them in *town* (the "where" part). The interaction and communication were as follows:

When the child was supposed to come home, the grandmother pressed a button and a notification and a sound appeared on the child's watch.

Originally, the sound was grandmother's voice saying "come home" but this turned out to be unfeasible to develop in the short time of the experience.

Interestingly, all participants decided to **explore a novel sensor, actuator or programming feature** for their project, e.g., a motion sensor, not introduced during Days 2 and 3, and which they decided to learn how to use on their own starting with what they had done during the experience concerning digital sensors.

Fig. 4. Prototypes by participants, shared at the end of the experience: embedded in a physical thing (left); enacting the wireless communication (right)

4.3   Observations

Pain Points. On Day 1, when participants explored how sensors and actuators worked with Arduino micro-controllers, the following emerged. They needed further **assistance in connecting** the components of circuits. There were also issues in **reading and using the measured values with the digital multi-meter** especially for measuring ohm and Kohm. All were quickly sorted out and provided indications for updating the material of the toolkit for future work.

On Days 2 and 3, younger participants tended to **get lost with the different boards**, e.g., two 10-year old participants constantly needed help in finding the right board, and they became fearful of "getting it wrong" the more material they had to master. Furthermore, even though the majority of participants were all engaged when the board and programs for wireless communication were introduced, when they started their own design, then they mostly focussed on exploring new physical input or output devices, **without paying attention to how communication worked** and the program to make it work.

Sweet Points. On Day 1, most participants were **able to connect the change in the sensed data with what measured** and returned via actuators. Moreover, all participants **engaged in exploring how sensors and actuators worked with Arduino micro-controllers**, especially in relation to a plant in need of water. For instance, they asked many questions concerning the usage of the soil-moisture sensors, which then they enjoyed using again on Days 2 and 3. They also reacted happily when a sound alarm was activated in case the plant was asking for water.

On Days 2 and 3, participants tended to **rapidly pick up on their own the required micro-electronic components for their prototypes**, further indicating the efficacy of exploring them in dedicated parts of the experience on Day 1. As reported above, all participants engaged with the programming part related to the interaction with sensors or actuators, and less with the communication. The only exception was a pair with the participant who had some programming experience, e.g., he was willing to go beyond the MakeCode block-based environment and facilities, and he asked for help on how to replicate the same program for the communication in micro:python "for the fun of it".

5 Discussion and Conclusions

According to the available literature, ad-hoc toolkits, which consider the skills of participants, can educate them to engineer prototypes of smart solutions. The IoTgo toolkit version, presented in this paper, aimed at educating pre-teens to engineer smart things and embed a human-centred perspective in the process. Specifically, the toolkit guided pre-teens to empathise with a context that is problematic for certain human beings, and then to develop related smart-thing prototype solutions with micro-electronic physical devices (sensors, actuators, programmable microcontrollers) and communicating via wireless.

This paper presents a case study with 10 pre-teens using IoTgo. On the first day, the toolkit invited all to experiment with the inner workings of basic sensors and actuators. On the second day, guided by IoTgo, pre-teens explored microcontrollers and how to program their interactions with sensors and actuators. On the third day, pre-teens used IoTgo to engineer prototypes of their ideas of smart things interacting with people, to tackle a problematic context. The study presented in this paper explored a research question—*what would pre-teens learn?* To answer it, data were processed from multiple sources (answers to the learning questionnaire in Subsect. 4.1, prototypes in Subsect. 4.2, observations in Subsect. 4.3), and they are hereby triangulated.

According to the analyses of prototypes by pre-teens, all of them managed to engineer working prototypes of smart things and adopt a human-centred perspective. According to observations, in relation to pain points, future toolkits will need to scaffold how to connect components of circuits and measure data differently than with cards with depictions and wiring schemes, e.g., [2,10]. However, all pre-teens seem to have benefited from exploring sensors and actuators before engineering their own smart things. This reading of observations is supported by the analysis of the prototypes, which correctly used sensors and actuators, and questionnaire results, besides similar literature findings [11]. In other similar experiences which did not invest time in exploring the inner workings of sensors and actuators first, participants with no experience were confused about how sensors and actuators worked, and this required rounds of feedback [8].

Differences in the questionnaire answers emerged between older and younger pre-teens, albeit the limited sample size does not allow for generalisations. According to observations, difficulties emerged especially in relation to the usage of more than one board by younger learners, as well as in the programming part of the communication. Independently of their age group, all tended to explore sensors and actuators, and not to focus on programs for communication. This result may have been also due to the fact that the IoTgo app automatically generated programs for communication and the limited time of the experience. Future work should replicate the study in different contexts, and give more time to training programming skills for the communication of smart things.

Acknowledgements. Authors acknowledge the contributions to past versions of IoTgo of co-authors and co-developers, especially M. Matera and M. Rizvi.

References

1. Arduino-Official-Store: Arduino UNO. https://store.arduino.cc/products/arduino-uno-rev3. Accessed 18 Apr 2023
2. Bellucci, A., Ruiz, A., Díaz, P., Aedo, I.: Investigating augmented reality support for novice users in circuit prototyping. In: Proceedings of the 2018 International Conference on Advanced Visual Interfaces, AVI 2018. ACM, New York (2018). https://doi.org/10.1145/3206505.3206508
3. De Roeck, D., Tanghe, J., Jacoby, A., Moons, I., Slegers, K.: Ideas of Things: the IOT design kit. In: Companion Publication of the 2019 on Designing Interactive Systems Conference 2019 Companion, DIS 2019, Companion, pp. 159–163. ACM, New York (2019). https://doi.org/10.1145/3301019.3323888
4. Gennari, R., Krik, S., Melonio, A.: A toolkit for human-centred engineering: an experience with pre-teens. In: Abdelnour Nocera, J., Kristin Larusdottir, M., Petrie, H., Piccinno, A., Winckler, M. (eds.) INTERACT 2023. LNCS, vol. 14145, pp. 281–285. Springer, Cham (2023). https://doi.org/10.1007/978-3-031-42293-5_22
5. Gennari, R., Matera, M., Melonio, A., Rizvi, M., Roumelioti, E.: Reflection and awareness in the design process: children ideating, programming and prototyping smart objects. Multimed. Tools Appl. (2020). https://doi.org/10.1007/s11042-020-09927-x
6. Gennari, R., Matera, M., Morra, D., Melonio, A., Rizvi, M.: Design for social digital well-being with young generations: engage them and make them reflect. Int. J. Hum. Comput. Stud. **173**, 103006 (2023). https://doi.org/10.1016/j.ijhcs.2023.103006
7. Gennari, R., Matera, M., Morra, D., Rizvi, M.: A phygital toolkit for rapidly designing smart things at school. In: Bottoni, P., Panizzi, E. (eds.) AVI 2022: International Conference on Advanced Visual Interfaces, Frascati, Rome, Italy, 6–10 June 2022, pp. 27:1–27:5. ACM (2022). https://doi.org/10.1145/3531073.3531119
8. Gennari, R., Melonio, A., Rizvi, M.: A tool for guiding teachers and their learners: the case study of an art class. In: CHI EA 2023, pp. 707–718. ACM, New York (2023). https://doi.org/10.1145/2559206.2578870
9. Herro, D., Quigley, C., Plank, H., Abimbade, O., Owens, A.: Instructional practices promoting computational thinking in STEAM elementary classrooms. J. Digit.

Learn. Teach. Educ. **38**(4), 158–172 (2022). https://doi.org/10.1080/21532974.2022.2087125

10. Kim, Y., et al.: SchemaBoard: supporting correct assembly of schematic circuits using dynamic in-situ visualization. In: Proceedings of the 33rd Annual ACM Symposium on User Interface Software and Technology, UIST 2020, pp. 987–998. ACM, New York (2020). https://doi.org/10.1145/3379337.3415887

11. Lechelt, S., Rogers, Y., Marquardt, N.: Coming to your senses: promoting critical thinking about sensors through playful interaction in classrooms. In: Proceedings of the Interaction Design and Children Conference, IDC 2020, pp. 11–22. ACM, New York (2020). https://doi.org/10.1145/3392063.3394401

12. Micro:bit-Educational-Foundation: Micro:bit Educational Foundation | micro:bit. https://microbit.org. Accessed 18 Apr 2023

13. Microsoft-micro:bit: MakeCode. https://makecode.microbit.org/. Accessed 18 Apr 2023

14. Mora, S., Gianni, F., Divitini, M.: Tiles: a card-based ideation toolkit for the Internet of Things. In: Proceedings of the 2017 Conference on Designing Interactive Systems, DIS 2017, pp. 587–598. ACM, New York (2017). https://doi.org/10.1145/3064663.3064699

15. Norman, D.: Human-Centered Design. https://www.interaction-design.org/literature/topics/human-centered-design. Accessed 18 Apr 2023

16. Schaper, M.M., et al.: Computational empowerment in practice: scaffolding teenagers' learning about emerging technologies and their ethical and societal impact. Int. J. Child-Comput. Interact. **34**, 100537 (2022). https://doi.org/10.1016/j.ijcci.2022.100537

Teaching HCI to Hundreds of Undergraduate Software Engineering and Computer Science Students

Keith Andrews[✉]

Graz University of Technology, Graz, Austria
kandrews@tugraz.at
https://isds.tugraz.at/keith

Abstract. As HCI has become more mainstream, introductory HCI courses have transitioned in many universities from more specialised elective courses taught in postgraduate degree programmes to compulsory courses taught in the first or second year of undergraduate degree programmes. At many universities, this transition means that class sizes can jump from one or two dozen students to many hundreds of students. This paper collects some of my experiences and advice for teaching HCI to such large class sizes, including redesigning the course to an online environment during the COVID pandemic.

Keywords: human-computer interaction · education · teaching · large class size · high enrolment · thinking aloud · heuristic evaluation · Sapphire

1 Introduction

In summer semester 1990, Human-Computer Interaction (HCI) was first offered at Graz University of Technology as an elective course for Master's students in Technical Mathematics/Computer Science (TM), which was a five-year straight Master's degree (Diplomstudium). Ludwig Reinsperger and Peter Sammer taught the first iterations of the course, using Ben Shneiderman's classic textbook [1].

I began teaching part of the course in 1992 and have been solely responsible for it since 1997 [2], as can be seen in Table 1. As time progressed, I wrote my own set of lecture notes, now comprising some 242 pages (PDF) [3], which have been used by dozens of other HCI educators around the world. For specific parts of the course, I recommend a variety of books and resources.

During the 1990s, I came to the realisation that it would be beneficial for students to come into contact with the principles of HCI much earlier in their academic careers, rather than just prior to finishing their Master's degree. As planning got underway at the university for the introduction of separate Bachelor's and Master's degrees (a result of Austria's participation in the Bologna

Published by Springer Nature Switzerland AG 2024
A. Bramwell-Dicks et al. (Eds.): INTERACT 2023 Workshops, LNCS 14535, pp. 226–238, 2024.
https://doi.org/10.1007/978-3-031-61688-4_22

Fig. 1. The first lecture of the HCI course in summer semester 2019.

Process), I successfully argued that HCI should be taught much earlier: in the first year of the Bachelor's degree.

Starting in the summer semester of 2003, I taught the HCI course as a compulsory course for first-year Bachelor students of Software Engineering and Management (SEM), scheduled as 3 contact hours per week in the 2nd semester and worth 4.5 ECTS credits. Throughout the 1990s, the numbers of students had remained relatively manageable, typically a few dozen (say 30–50) participants. With its new placement as a compulsory course in the second semester of the Bachelor's degree, at a stroke, in 2003, the number of participants jumped tenfold: from a few dozen to several hundred, as can be seen in Table 1.

Upto 2003, the HCI course had been formally structured into separate but linked lectures and practicals, with students technically able to take one without the other, although they were strongly encouraged to take both together. In 2004, the course was formally unified into a single entity: lectures with integrated practicals, with 3 contact hours (3VU). In 2006, the HCI course was included as a compulsory course into the newly introduced Bachelor's degree in Computer Science (CS), also in the 2nd semester.

2 Handling the Numbers

Early considerations included how to handle the supervision of practical work and how to manage the grading of hundreds of students. Since it would be

Table 1. Evolution of the HCI course at Graz University of Technology. SS indicates summer semester, WS indicates winter semester. The three lecturers involved are Ludwig Reinsperger (LR), Peter Sammer (PS), and Keith Andrews (KA). The three degree programmes are the Master's degree in Technical Mathematics / Computer Science (TM), and the Bachelor's degrees in Software Engineering and Management (SEM) and in Computer Science (CS). The number of students is derived from the number of issued certificates (both passes and fails).

Year	Lecturer(s)	Degree	Semester	Students	Remarks
1990 SS	LR	TM	8		
1991 SS	LR, PS	TM	8	37	
1992 SS	LR, PS, KA	TM	8	18	
1993 SS	PS, KA	TM	8	59	
1994 SS	PS, KA	TM	8	52	
1995 SS	PS, KA	TM	8	46	
1996 SS	PS, KA	TM	8	44	
1997 SS	KA	TM	8	49	
1997 WS	KA	TM	8	27	
1998 SS	KA	TM	8	28	
1998 WS	KA	TM	8	31	
1999 SS	KA	TM	8	46	
1999 WS	KA	TM	8	29	
2000 SS	KA	TM	8	40	
2000 WS	KA	TM	8	36	
2001 SS	KA	TM	8	52	
2001 WS	KA	TM	8	47	
2002 SS	KA	TM	8	64	
2002 WS	KA	TM	8	66	
2003 SS	KA	SEM	2	293	→ BSc
2004 SS	KA	SEM	2	250	→ 3VU
2005 SS	KA	SEM	2	203	
2006 SS	KA	SEM + CS	2	245	
2007 SS	KA	SEM + CS	2	237	
2008 SS	KA	SEM + CS	2	217	
2009 SS	KA	SEM + CS	2	205	
2010 SS	KA	SEM + CS	2	212	
2011 SS	KA	SEM + CS	2	218	
2012 SS	KA	SEM + CS	2	222	
2013 SS	KA	SEM + CS	2	229	
2014 SS	KA	SEM + CS	2	250	→ Sapphire
2015 SS	KA	SEM + CS	2	282	
2016 SS	KA	SEM + CS	2	263	
2017 SS	KA	SEM + CS	2	344	
2018 SS	KA	SEM + CS	2	307	
2019 SS	KA	SEM + CS	2	313	
2020 SS	KA	SEM + CS	4	30	74 → COVID
2021 SS	KA	SEM + CS	4	222	COVID
2022 SS	KA	SEM + CS	4	252	COVID
2023 SS	KA	SEM + CS	4	278	

impossible for a single lecturer to handle such large numbers, it was decided that a number of tutors (teaching assistants) would be assigned to the course. In addition, grouping students into groups of four for the practical exercises, rather than dealing with individual submissions, also helps keep the logistics more manageable. In summer semester of 2019, the last regular iteration of the course before the COVID restrictions, at the start of the course there were 330 students, in 91 groups of 4 (or 3), with 9 tutors (see Fig. 1); 313 completed the course, in terms of being issued a certificate at the end of the course, including both passes and fails.

Part of the logistics of dealing with large numbers of participants is responding to changes. Some students drop out a few days or sometimes even several weeks into the course. Sometimes, students are unresponsive, leaving their group colleagues in the lurch. Other times, members of a group simply do not get on with each other and request to move to another group. Managing these changes is often more time-consuming than preparing the lectures. Having a small first exercise towards the beginning of the course helps ameliorate this by forcing students to meet up in their groups, collaborate, and hand in some work. Those inclined to potentially drop out, then at least do so early on, causing less disruption.

I usually meet my tutors once a week for two hours, with extra meetings scheduled as required, particularly around grading after submission deadlines. Each tutor typically supervises around 10 groups of 4 students, responding to questions by email and holding three face-to-face meetings with each group as the term progresses. The final exam (MC Test) is held in tutorial groups, in-person, in a large lecture theatre at the end of the course.

3 Course Coverage

The HCI course at Graz University of Technology is an introductory course, aimed at providing an overview of the field to computer science and software engineering students. The field of HCI is extremely broad, as illustrated in Fig. 2, so choices regarding scope and focus had to be made. I chose to focus the theoretical part of the course (the lectures) on the bottom right corner ("Development Process" and "Computer") of Fig. 2, while only touching the other two areas ("Human" and "Use and Context"). This seemed to be a good match to the computer science and software engineering students at the university.

In terms of the practical part of the course (the practical exercises), two possible avenues were explored:

1. Have the students design and build an interface.
2. Have the students evaluate an existing interface.

I decided to focus on evaluation rather than design for the following reasons. Firstly, second semester students could not be assumed to have a solid enough background in programming to build user interfaces, which would require provision of significant extra support. Secondly, grading evaluation reports seemed

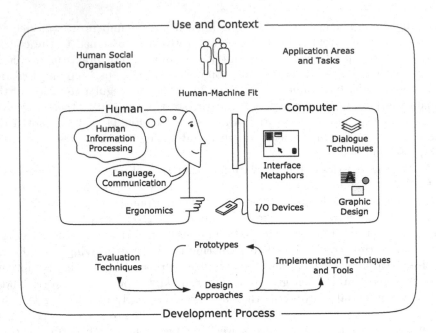

Fig. 2. The broad field of HCI. Redrawn and adapted from Fig. 1 of the classic ACM SIGCHI Curricula for Human-Computer Interaction [4, page 16].

to be easier and less subjective than grading user interface designs, particularly with large numbers of students. Thirdly, having students run user tests at this early stage of their studies would give them the potentially belief-changing experience of users thinking and acting differently to their own expectations, and the practical experience of running a user test would hopefully remain with them for the rest of their studies and careers.

4   Practical Exercises

A real-life scenario is used to make the practical work more realistic. Each student group plays the role of usability consultants who have been contracted to evaluate a web site. The tutor plays the role of their client, the manager of the assigned web site. At the start of the semester, each tutor suggests two publicly available web sites, which are suitable for evaluation in the course. They must be a) neither too good nor too bad in terms of their usability, i.e. offering enough issues to find, whilst not being disastrously poor, and b) not too small, offering enough scope to explore.

The five practical exercises used in the HCI course are shown in Table 2. In essence, the exercises can be boiled down to three tasks:

- Heuristic Evaluation (HE): Plan and Report.
- Thinking Aloud Test (TA): Plan and Report.

Table 2. The five practical exercises which contribute to the final grade, as used in summer semester 2023.

Ex	Title	Type	Points	%
1	Heuristic Evaluation Plan (HE Plan)	group	43	6.5
2a	Heuristic Evaluation (Individual Evaluations)	individual	70	10.6
2b	Heuristic Evaluation Report (HE Report)	group	116	17.5
3	Thinking Aloud Test Plan (TA Plan)	group	58	8.7
4a	Thinking Aloud Test (TA Report)	group	192	29.0
4b	Thinking Aloud Test (TA Full Videos)	group	84	12.7
5	Multiple Choice Test (MC)	individual	100	15.1
			663	**100.0**

– Multiple Choice Test (MC).

For each of these, detailed instructions [5] and an extensive set of materials [6] are provided. Each group presents their work at three face-to-face meetings: M1 (HE Plan), M2 (HE Report and TA Plan) and M3 (T3 Report).

At the start of the semester, students perform a heuristic evaluation [7,8] (HE) of a (publicly available) web site. The first task is to write a HE Plan (Ex1) [9]. This also functions as a starting point to ensure that group members make contact with one another and are serious about participating in the course. Then, each of the students in the group serves individually as an evaluator and assembles a list of positive and negative findings accompanied by short video clips (Ex2a). Finally, the students come together to aggregate their individual findings and write the HE Report (Ex2b) [10].

In the middle of the semester, students run a face-to-face thinking aloud test (TA) [11,12] of the same web site with five test users, who they recruit from among their friends, family, and colleagues. Again, the first task is to write a TA Plan (Ex3) [13]. Then, the group performs a pilot test with one user followed by the real test with four users. Five usability kits with recording equipment are available for students to borrow, one is shown in Fig. 3a. A typical test setup is shown Fig. 3b. Screen recording is done on the laptop with a webcam. Additionally, the external video camera records the screen, keyboard, mouse, and user's facial reactions in the mirror placed next to the laptop. Finally, the students analyse their results, formulate findings, produce video clips to illustrate each finding, and write their TA Report (Ex4a) [14]. Full session recordings are handed in offline and graded separately (Ex4b).

The multiple choice test (MC Test) at the end of the semester (Ex5) assesses knowledge of the theoretical material contained in the lecture notes and covered in class. Ten questions are asked, each with four parts. Rather than one of the four parts being true and the others false (where, on average, simply guessing would obtain 25% of the points), any of the four parts can be either true or false, and the exact combination has to be achieved in order to gain the points for that question. Sample test are available on the course web site [15]. Students must

(a) One of the usability kits available for students to borrow.

(b) The test setup used by one of the groups in summer semester 2017 [14].

Fig. 3. Usability kit and test setup. The image in (b) is used under the terms of a Creative Commons Attribution 4.0 International (CC BY 4.0) licence.

answer at least two of the ten questions correctly, in order to pass the course. After the multiple choice test has been marked, a grading review is scheduled, where students can optionally receive detailed face-to-face feedback and ask any questions they may have. Students then have one chance to retake the MC Test.

5   Grading Management with Sapphire

For the first 10 years of running the HCI course for undergraduates (2003–2013), grading was managed using a spreadsheet, one per tutor, as shown in Fig. 4. The grading system is based on individual ratings grouped into rating blocks. Each rating block is assigned an initial number of points, and deductions are made depending on individual rating criteria. Most of the ratings involve a binary decision as to whether or not the corresponding criterion applies. If so, an x is entered into the corresponding cell. This helps maintain consistency in grading across the tutors. Both fixed and percentage deductions are possible, and in some cases, a per-item deduction can be applied. It is also possible to define ratings which deduct a variable number of points or assign a variable number of bonus points, within a certain range, based on the assessment of the tutor.

Maintaining the spreadsheets and making adjustments to ratings or rating groups involved a significant amount of work and great care had to be taken not to damage the cell formulae. It was also impossible to provide detailed incremental feedback on a student-by-student basis as the term and grading progressed.

In 2014, a new web-based submission and grading management system called Sapphire [16] entered service. Sapphire was custom-built in Ruby/Rails and HTML/CSS/JavaScript [17,18] and is available as an open-source project [19]. Sapphire reproduces the concept of ratings and rating groups in a shared online environment with user accounts, roles, and permissions. Students register for the

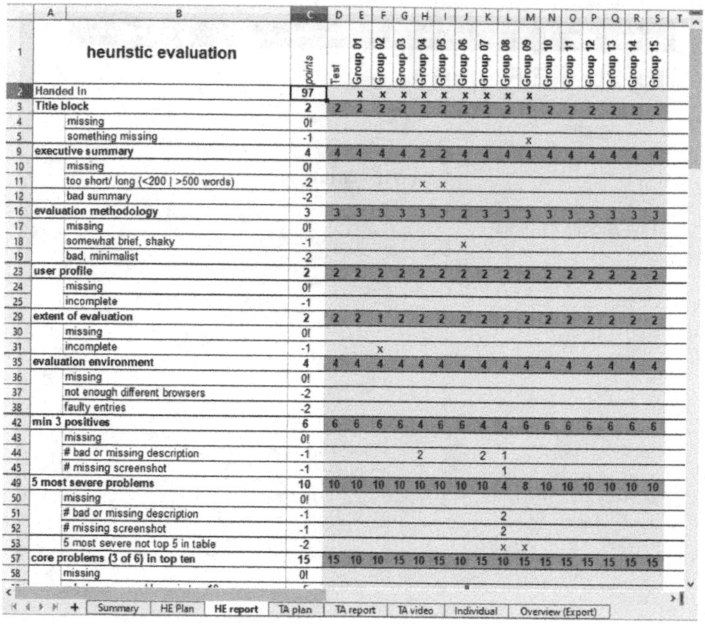

	heuristic evaluation	points	Test	Group 01	Group 02	Group 03	Group 04	Group 05	Group 06	Group 07	Group 08	Group 09	Group 10	Group 11	Group 12	Group 13	Group 14	Group 15
2	Handed In	97	x	x	x	x	x	x	x	x	x							
3	Title block	2	2	2	2	2	2	2	2	2	1	2	2	2	2	2	2	
4	missing	0!																
5	something missing	-1										x						
9	executive summary	4	4	4	4	4	2	2	4	4	4	4	4	4	4	4	4	
10	missing	0!																
11	too short/ long (<200 | >500 words)	-2					x	x										
12	bad summary	-2																
16	evaluation methodology	3	3	3	3	3	3	3	2	3	3	3	3	3	3	3	3	
17	missing	0!																
18	somewhat brief, shaky	-1						x										
19	bad, minimalist	-2																
23	user profile	2	2	2	2	2	2	2	2	2	2	2	2	2	2	2	2	
24	missing	0!																
25	incomplete	-1																
29	extent of evaluation	2	2	2	1	2	2	2	2	2	2	2	2	2	2	2	2	
30	missing	0!																
31	incomplete	-1			x													
35	evaluation environment	4	4	4	4	4	4	4	4	4	4	4	4	4	4	4	4	
36	missing	0!																
37	not enough different browsers	-2																
38	faulty entries	-2																
42	min 3 positives	6	6	6	6	6	4	6	6	4	6	6	6	6	6	6	6	
43	missing	0!																
44	# bad or missing description	-1						2		2	1							
45	# missing screenshot	-1									1							
49	5 most severe problems	10	10	10	10	10	10	10	10	4	8	10	10	10	10	10	10	
50	missing	0!																
51	# bad or missing description	-1								2								
52	# missing screenshot	-1								2								
53	5 most severe not top 5 in table	-2								x	x							
57	core problems (3 of 6) in top ten	15	15	10	10	15	10	15	10	15	10	15	15	15	15	15	15	
58	missing	0!																

Summary | HE Plan | HE report | TA plan | TA report | TA video | Individual | Overview (Export)

Fig. 4. Part of the spreadsheet used for grading for the first ten years of the Bachelor's course.

course on the university's campus management system, TUGRAZonline, and are then imported into Sapphire using a CSV file. In addition, a lecturer can create, edit, or delete students and student groups through Sapphire's user interface. Both individual and group exercises are supported. A submission component allows students and student groups to upload their exercise submissions online to Sapphire. Submission deadlines and late deadlines can be set and managed.

Sapphire's ratings editor, shown in Fig. 5, is used by the lecturer to configure points, ratings, and rating groups. The grading interface, shown in Fig. 6, is used by tutors to grade submissions. The interface is responsive and can comfortably be used on a tablet while simultaneously viewing a submission on a laptop. If a rating is changed after some grading has already taken place, tutors are notified of such changes in the interface.

Viewers can be configured for specific file types, such as PDF or HTML, and are opened within Sapphire as required. It is also possible to configure automated checkers for specific files, say for HTML validation or to run (part of) a file through an external plagiarism detection service. Finally, Sapphire provides export facilities for exporting both submissions (for archival purposes) and detailed grading reports (as spreadsheets).

One of the main benefits of Sapphire is that it is now possible to publish fine-grained intermediate results for each individual student online, as grading progresses during the term. In addition, Sapphire's commenting system allows a textual explanation to be attached to any applied rating, and written feedback

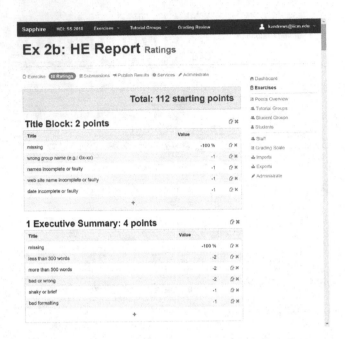

Fig. 5. Part of Sapphire's ratings editor, used by the lecturer to configure points, ratings, and rating groups.

Fig. 6. Part of Sapphire's grading interface, used by a tutor to grade a submission.

to be attached per exercise. Once grading of a particular exercise is finished, the lecturer can publish the provisional grading of all (or some) tutorial groups at the push of a button. Each student is notified by email when their own grading results become available, and only has access to these.

For the final grades, Sapphire's grading scale editor provides a graphical tool for the lecturer to set and review grade boundaries, as shown in Fig. 7. At least 50% of the points must be achieved for a pass, in this case 332 of the 663 points available. The grade boundaries can be adjusted up or down with the mouse.

6   Adapting to COVID

With the rapid spread of COVID, the HCI course in summer semester 2020 had to be suspended after the first lecture. Initially, 74 students had signed up for the course (rather than the usual 300+), an artefact of the course having been moved from the 2nd to the 4th semester, resulting in a temporary one-year dip, as can be seen in Table 1.

Moving the course entirely online was challenging for a number of reasons:

- The course is built around students running face-to-face thinking aloud tests with external test users. COVID-19 restrictions made this impossible.
- We looked at switching to remote user testing, but that would require significantly more resources for supervision and grading, since each student would essentially be running their own remote test(s) and we would have to view every one of them, rather than selecting one of the test videos from each group to view.
- Replacing user testing with something else would mean completely redesigning a large part of the course.
- Furthermore, I show a large number of videos and video clips in class, which are integral to explaining and illustrating the course material and practical exercises. Some of the videos are from published or broadcast video material: these can be shown in class under an exemption in Austrian copyright law, but cannot be streamed or republished. Other video clips are from previous user tests, where I have permission from the test users to show (parts of) them in class, but do not have permission to stream or publish them.

In the end, since there was no end in sight to the pandemic, I had to design a special COVID version of the course for an (almost) entirely online environment. Lectures were moved online with Webex. I could only show those videos which were already publicly available on the internet. There were no thinking aloud tests. Instead, the heuristic evaluation was extended, with each student evaluating with two devices (desktop and mobile) rather than just one. The three client meetings with the tutors were reduced to two and were also moved online with Webex. Solely the multiple choice test was held face-to-face, under the university's special COVID arrangements (face coverings, social distancing, check of COVID green status, cleaning and airing between exam sittings, etc.).

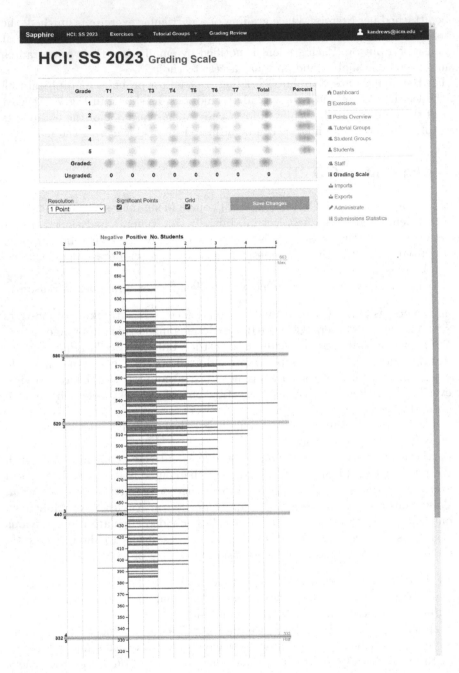

Fig. 7. Part of Sapphire's grading scale editor, used by the lecturer to set and review grade boundaries. The grade boundaries can be adjusted up or down with the mouse. In the Austrian system, grades 1 to 4 are passes and grade 5 is a fail. The summary statistics have been deliberately blurred.

The COVID version of the course was taught in Sep 2020 as a block course, with 30 students eventually participating. The persistence of COVID made it necessary to teach the COVID version of the course in summer semester 2021 and summer semester 2022 too. In summer semester 2023, the course reverted back to its previous format with in-person lectures and meetings, and face-to-face thinking aloud testing. In 2023, there were 278 students in 71 groups with 7 tutors.

7   Concluding Remarks

Teaching HCI as a compulsory undergraduate course is a challenging undertaking when many hundreds of participants are involved. However, with careful planning, logistics, and technical support it can be managed successfully, even if a global pandemic throws a spanner in the works.

Acknowledgements. Many tutors, former students, and colleagues have contributed to the success of the HCI course at Graz University of Technology over the years. I would especially like to acknowledge the contributions of the following people. Ludwig Reinsperger and Peter Sammer taught the first HCI course at the university, before passing the flame on to me. Karl Voit built the first version of the grading spreadsheet. Patrick Hackl maintained and extended the spreadsheet over five years, followed by Vesna Krnjic, Sabrina Huber, Laura Bom, and Christoph Bichler. Thomas Kriechbaumer and Matthias Link built Sapphire over several years and a Bachelor's and Master's thesis. Stefan Pranger maintained the Sapphire server for many years, followed by Amel Smajic. It is currently maintained by Duaa Nakshbandi and Bakir Haljevac.

References

1. Shneiderman, B.: Designing the User Interface: Strategies for Effective Human-Computer Interaction. Addison-Wesley (1986)
2. Andrews, K.: Human-Computer Interaction (2023). https://courses.isds.tugraz.at/hci/
3. Andrews, K.: Human-Computer Interaction: Course Notes (2023). https://courses.isds.tugraz.at/hci/hci.pdf
4. Hewett, T.T., et al.: ACM SIGCHI curricula for human-computer interaction. Technical Report. ACM (1992). https://doi.org/10.1145/2594128
5. Andrews, K.: HCI Practical Exercises (2023). https://courses.isds.tugraz.at/hci/practicals/
6. Andrews, K.: Materials for HCI Practicals (2023). https://courses.isds.tugraz.at/hci/practicals/materials/
7. Nielsen, J.: Heuristic evaluation. In: Nielsen, J., Mack, R.L. (eds.) Usability Inspection Methods, pp. 25–62. Wiley (1994)
8. Nielsen, J., Molich, R.: Heuristic evaluation of user interfaces. In: Proceedings of the Conference on Human Factors in Computing Systems (CHI 1990), Seattle, Washington, USA, pp. 249–256 (1990). https://doi.org/10.1145/97243.97281

9. Leski, F., Mandl, F., Weber, M., Ganster, P.: Heuristic Evaluation Plan (2017). https://cdn.isds.tugraz.at/hci/reports/ss2017/g3-02-tugraz-en/heplan/heplan. html

10. Leski, F., Mandl, F., Weber, M., Ganster, P.: Heuristic Evaluation Report (2017). https://cdn.isds.tugraz.at/hci/reports/ss2017/g3-02-tugraz-en/he/he.html

11. Krug, S.: Rocket Surgery Made Easy. New Riders (2009)

12. Nielsen, J., Clemmensen, T., Yssing, C.: Getting access to what goes on in people's heads?: reflections on the think-aloud technique. In: Proceedings of the 2nd Nordic Conference on Human-Computer Interaction, Aarhus, Denmark, pp. 101–110. ACM Press (2002). https://doi.org/10.1145/572020.572033

13. Leski, F., Mandl, F., Weber, M., Ganster, P.: Thinking Aloud Test Plan (2017). https://cdn.isds.tugraz.at/hci/reports/ss2017/g3-02-tugraz-en/taplan/taplan. html

14. Leski, F., Mandl, F., Weber, M., Ganster, P.: Thinking Aloud Test Report (2017). https://cdn.isds.tugraz.at/hci/reports/ss2017/g3-02-tugraz-en/ta/ta.html

15. Andrews, K.: HCI Sample Tests (2023). https://courses.isds.tugraz.at/hci/ practicals/test/

16. Sapphire. Sapphire Course Grading Management System (2023). https://sapphire. isds.tugraz.at/

17. Kriechbaumer, T.: Sapphire back-end: a web-based course grading management system. Bachelor's thesis, Graz University of Technology, Austria (2014). https:// ftp.isds.tugraz.at/pub/theses/kriechbaumer-2014-bsc.pdf

18. Link, M.: Sapphire frontend: a web-based course grading management system. Master's thesis, Graz University of Technology, Austria, p. 194 (2021). https:// ftp.isds.tugraz.at/pub/theses/mlink-2021-msc.pdf

19. Link, M., Kriechbaumer, T.: Sapphire – Course Management System, Graz University of Technology (2023). https://github.com/Sapphire-CM/Sapphire/

Using an HCI Perspective to Encourage Young Students to Pursue Computer Science and Engineering Careers: The "Envisioning the Digital City" Workshop

Paloma Díaz(✉) , Teresa Onorati , and Álvaro Montero

Computer Science Department, Universidad Carlos III de Madrid, Madrid, Spain
{pdp,tonorati,ammontes}@inf.uc3m.es

Abstract. In recent decades, the demand for STEM professionals has increased, and consequently, the effort of educational institutions to sponsor their STEM degrees. In the context of a university program promoting STEM careers among high-school students, we designed a workshop for middle and high-school students to show them a different perspective of computing as a pragmatic, social, and people-centered profession. We focus on teaching basic concepts of Human-Computer Interaction (HCI) as part of a problem-solving strategy to offer creative solutions to real problems of real people. The workshop proposes a list of well-known problems in urban environments, like social integration, elderly loneliness, or recycling, and asks the students to solve them envisioning an innovative mobile app by following a design thinking approach and applying several design artifacts, like scenario boards, user personas, thematic cards, and paper-based sketches. The results show that with little or no experience in designing and programming, participants engage in fruitful brainstorming sessions, offer creative solutions, and even implement low-level prototypes.

Keywords: Design Thinking · Design Workshop · STEM · Computer Science & Engineering

1 Introduction

One of the key factors of the fourth industrial revolution is the adoption of digital technologies to improve distinct aspects of the production process in fields like manufacturing, communication, and science, [1], and, more in general, to support our daily activities. According to the Digital Education Action Plan 2021–2027 by the European Commission, science, technology, engineering, and mathematics (STEM) skills are crucial for reaching the needed digital competencies and facing digital transformation [2]. However, the number of European students pursuing STEM degrees is relatively low, even lower if we focus on Computer Science and Engineering (CSE). Hence, the number of expected graduates will probably not cover the needs of a vibrant job market. Indeed,

© IFIP International Federation for Information Processing 2024
Published by Springer Nature Switzerland AG 2024
A. Bramwell-Dicks et al. (Eds.): INTERACT 2023 Workshops, LNCS 14535, pp. 239–252, 2024.
https://doi.org/10.1007/978-3-031-61688-4_23

according to the 2022 Digital Economy and Society Index, in 2020 a 55% of enterprises couldn't fill all their vacancies in information and communication technologies [3]. A potential way to make CSE more interesting for young students might rely upon motivating such passion instead on focusing only on coding. CSE needs to be perceived not as a niche for stereotypical programmers but as a pragmatic professional career that prepares you to architect the digital future through sustainable, valuable, and accessible solutions to relevant problems of our society, and with that aim diverse types of students, with different interests and passions, are required.

In this context, we describe an educational workshop called "Envisioning the Digital City," which engages K9-K12 students in a teamwork activity to ideate, design, and prototype mobile apps to support the needs of the future digital city. The workshop aims at applying basic concepts and methods from the field of Human-Computer Interaction (HCI) to build problem-solving strategies that offer creative solutions to real problems of real people. Through the practice, we encourage the participants to shift their perspective on CSE studies and orientate it towards a more pragmatic, social, and user-centered one. With no need for previous experience or knowledge in programming, the students practice with several HCI artifacts and learn how to apply them for problem-solving whilst developing empathy, and fostering creativity.

The workshop follows a four-step methodology inspired by the stages of the design thinking approach [4]: *empathize*, *define*, *ideate*, and *prototype*. The students organize in groups whose size depends on the number of participants, and work on predefined problems collaboratively. The workshop has been held 14 times offered in the promotion program of the university. To fit the requirements of the program, two formats that differ in the duration of the session are offered: two- and five-hours long. Compared to the shorter version, the five-hour workshop has a stronger focus on the ideation phase involving the students in more divergent and convergent design activities to foster collective creativity.

The remainder of this paper is structured as follows. Section 2 describes the proposed workshop by explaining how each phase is carried out. Section 3 presents the main results from running the different workshop editions, with the list of problems and technologies selected to solve or mitigate the proposal problems and the opinions collected from the students. Finally, conclusions and future lines are presented.

2 Related Works and Context

As discussed in the introduction, there is a compelling need to recruit more young students in CSE studies to prepare a diverse workforce that will lead the construction of a responsible and sustainable digital transformation. Though the CSE degree of Universidad Carlos III de Madrid is quite popular among young students and it always attract enough candidacies, the cohort of students is not quite diverse, having only a 14% of women. We also are facing, or expected to face in the near future, the effects of the demographic changes in Europe where the natality has dropped in the last decades. With a view to attract more students and more diverse, our University started a program to bring engineering closer to young students through hands-on workshops that could provide them with a real perspective of what an engineer does in the real practice. In this section we review some studies and approaches that inspired the creation of the workshop describe in this paper, "Envisioning the digital city" aimed at inspiring more young students and more women to CSE degrees.

In a recent study done with young students and employees in 6 European countries [5], the main reason to discard STEM studies is the perception of *being more difficult*, and the one to select them is *passion*. The study also found that stereotypes strongly influence the young student's interest towards STEM degrees and that such stereotypes are not always positive. Indeed, the prevailing stereotype of computer scientist in media and society goes around programming freaks and hackers with scarce social abilities, letting aside the fact that creativity and groupwork are the hearth of any computing project aiming at having impact in society. Misconceptions or lack of knowledge of what CSE is and what CSE professionals do can be related to the prospective students' interest in these careers [5, 6].

Akbulut and Looney introduced an interesting conceptual framework to understand how to inspire young generations to CSE studies [7]. According to the framework there are three factors that can act as precursors of final choices: *self-efficacy*, *outcome expectations*, and *interest*.

Self-efficacy is the personal perception of the capability to perform well and effectively in CSE studies. This could be the main factor of self-exclusion for students who do not see themselves as too brilliant in math as to pursue any STEM career and, particularly, could be the factor influencing many young women students to discard CSE as a professional career [8]. The framework proposes to offer activities that help younger students to experience immediate and frequent success in key concepts in CSE. In the last years, courses for teaching young students how to code using visual languages such as Scratch[1], AppInventor[2], Alice[3], and even including artificial intelligence modules with Machine Learning For Kids[4], have proliferated. This type of visual tools makes it easier to grasp computing concepts and algorithmic abilities by quickly creating prototypes without being a professional programmer. However, being programming a key skill in CSE, it is not the unique one, and probably not the most important if you aim at ideating innovative, useful, usable, sustainable, and responsible solutions that deal with our society challenges. Programming courses and competitions will probably fit those students that already are inclined to choose CSE as a major or degree but to deal with the needs of the digital transformation, more students and with more diverse interests are required. Unplugged activities that do not use computers but other physical artifacts, such as boards and games, have also become popular to introduce and practice complex math and computing concepts to K-12 students. A critical review of this kind of unplugged activities and their impact in the development of computational skills can be found at [9]. The workshop here described is a hybrid approach that mixes unplugged activities for ideation and design, and visual tools for programming to try and provide a more comprehensive perspective of a CSE project.

Outcome expectations is related with the personal judgement of the rewards that will be obtained by following a CSE degree. Typical expectations might be salary, high

---

[1] https://scratch.mit.edu.

[2] https://appinventor.mit.edu/.

[3] http://www.alice.org/.

[4] https://machinelearningforkids.co.uk/.

employability, social recognition, or sense of accomplishment. However, the GenZ who are considered as the first digital natives generation have different expectations about their professional career are more inclined towards careers that help them to grow as a persona, fit their values and where they can exert some social impact [10–12]. In this case, what is required is to engage young students in experiences whose core is understanding CSE as more than simply programming algorithms, but as a career to ideate and innovate to solve real world problems. The workshop here reported offers a design thinking approach to architect the digital world putting the stress in the problems that will be solved, the personas that are affected by such problem and the scenarios where the problem arises. In this way, participants start focusing on their environment and how a computing project could make it better, so they can perceive other kinds of outcomes that could be more aligned with the expectations of cohorts of young students who currently do not chose CSE.

Interest is related with the personal student interests and with "*an emotion that arouses attention to, curiosity about, and concern with*" a CSE career [7]. The *interest* factor aligns with the *passion* mentioned by the participants in the study reported in [5] and, similarly, the study in [7] shows that it is the factor that, influenced by self-efficacy and outcome expectations, has more influence in the choice goals of prospective students. To raise interest, four strategies are proposed: define activities aligned with current contents and aligned with students' values; use innovative pedagogic techniques; propose attainable challenges and increase the level of difficulty gradually. A way to engage more young students in CSE might rely upon motivating a passion for what CSE is by focusing on how it prepares you to architect the digital future through sustainable, valuable, and accessible solutions to relevant problems of our society. This is the goal we pursue with the "Envisioning the Digital City workshop" that provides hands-on activities to motivate students and to develop also the so-called soft or traversal skills, which include teamwork, critical thinking, empathy, innovation, creativity, and problem-solving. These are the kind of abilities a CSE student who wants to develop socially relevant solutions has to cultivate and that are valued by the companies [5].

3   Workshop Methodology

The workshop "Envisioning the digital city" is an activity for students with different profiles and backgrounds that is part of the initiatives proposed at the School of Engineering of Universidad Carlos III de Madrid to try and improve the attraction of young generations to STEM disciplines. The School of Engineering offers degrees in industrial, mechanical, electrical, electronic, communications, aerospace, biomedical, computing, robotics, data, and physics engineering as well as other STEM areas such as applied mathematics and sciences. In particular, the activity reported in this paper is included within the computer science courses and it embraces a HCI perspective for showing students that creativity, teamwork and problem-solving are fundamental skills for finding innovative solutions to real world problems.

The workshop is designed in two different formats, two- and five-hour long, in the context of two different university programs to promote STEM careers high-school students. One of them is the STEM Fridays[5] that offer a number of 2 h workshops held at the university classrooms from 18:00 to 20:00. The second is a TecnoCamp[6] a summer camp lasting one week where students get immersed into the university experience by staying in the university dorms and attending each day a 5-h technological hands-on workshop. They spend the rest of the day in cultural, sport and social activities. In both programs we have been running for several years the "Envisioning the digital city" workshop to inspire them to pursue CSE studies.

Participation in both activities is voluntary and depends on the interest these activities raise in young students. STEM Fridays are free and the TecnoCamp week has a very competitive cost to cover expenses of students. Tutors sign a release permission form that makes it possible to use the pictures taken during the workshops.

At the beginning of the workshop, we offer the students a different perspective on studying CSE that goes beyond programming and emphasizes the central role of users and users' needs to define creative strategies to solve real problems for real people. The workshop motto is "We are not programmers, we are architects of the digital future" trying to stress the multidisciplinary role of architecture where not only technical knowledge is required but also a sensibility to understand the needs of people and the opportunities and limitations of the environment. This change of perspective allows us to introduce the relevant role of HCI in enhancing soft skills like curiosity, empathy, and creativity, as reflected by the different phases of the workshop. The final goal of the workshops is to ideate and prototype a mobile app to solve a relevant problem within the context of the future digital city.

As shown in Fig. 1, after the initial *Presentation*, the workshop has four steps inspired by the Design Thinking approach [4]: *Empathize, Define, Ideation,* and *Prototype*. The workshop aims to guide the participants in designing a real *scenario* [13] and using *rapid prototyping* to check how ideas could work [14], two key cornerstones of HCI. In the scenario, participants have to identify and shape the problem of interest, the context where the problem occurs, the user personas affected by the problem, and the technologies that could be used to develop a solution. During the rapid prototyping phase, they will make use of different techniques and tools to get a first and very early idea of a mobile app.

To support the active discussion of the participants about each of these elements (i.e., problems, contexts, personas, and technologies), we have designed a set of visual cards and a board to follow an unplugged approach [9]. The cards are used as inspirational resources that help to break the ice by providing potential elements to use for each of the categories, but to avoid any fixation process, blank cards are also provided to choose your own problem, context, or technology. Figure 2 shows an example of each one of them. The cards give a graphical and textual representation of a list of problems (see Fig. 2a), contexts where the problem arises (see Fig. 2b), and technologies that could be involved (see Fig. 2c). The personas are represented as blank cards to let participants model the desired characteristics about potential users of the scenario, including age, skills, goals, and motivations (see Fig. 2d). The participants can manipulate the cards creating physical connections among them and, in this way, understand each represented

---

[5] https://www.uc3m.es/secundaria/divulgacion-ciencia/viernes-tecnologicos.

[6] https://www.uc3m.es/secundaria/divulgacion-ciencia/tecnocamp.

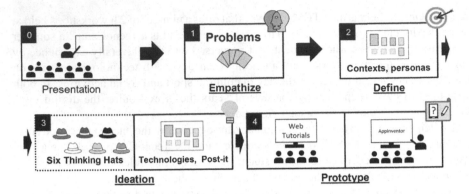

Fig. 1. The four phases of the workshop after the initial *Presentation* (0): *Empathize* (1), *Define* (2), *Ideation* (3), and *Prototype* (4).

concept and make sharing opinions and ideas with the other group members easier. In the next subsections we describe how we use the cards, the board and other tools to reach the workshop goals.

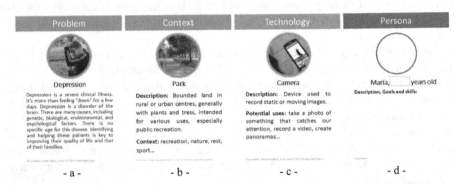

Fig. 2. Examples of the visual cards used in the workshop: *Problem* (a), *Context* (b), *Technology* (c), and *Persona* (d).

3.1 Empathize

The *Empathize* phase focuses on choosing and deeply understanding the problem or a combination of problems of interest for the group. Here, it is crucial to avoid any biases or previous beliefs that could affect the participants' choice and discussion. Considering the limitation in terms of time, especially for the two-hour session, we facilitate this step by suggesting six recurrent problems in urban environments that the participants can use as a starting point for further discussions on which way they want to contribute to making daily life more accessible. Inspired by the Sustainable Development Goals[7]

---

[7] https://sdgs.un.org/.

(SDG) followed by the European Commission to guide future directives for funding research and innovation, we have pointed out the following six categories of problems: environmental issues, emergencies, infrastructures, health habits, recycling, and social cohesion. The problems are listed in Table 1, the category is not made explicit in the cards.

Table 1. Available problems

EM Phase	Top-down/command and control
Environmental issues	Environmental commitment
	Learning about the environment
Emergencies	Emergency alerts for all
	Early warning of emergencies
	Emergency protocols
Infrastructures	Urban incidents
	Infrastructure needs
	Accessibility of infrastructures
Health habits	Physical exercise
	Eating habits
	Depression
Recycling	Recycling awareness
	Recycling places
	Recycling classification
Social cohesion	Intercultural learning
	Elder's solitude
	Social integration

The visual cards for the problems (see Fig. 2a) show an image and a short description of each of them. Participants can read this content and gain knowledge about each proposed problem as well as using Internet to look for more information. Using both textual and graphical information helps to empathize with each described situation. Additionally, blank cards are made available to define a different problem.

3.2 Define

Once the students have identified the challenge they want to deal with, the *Define* phase asks them to describe a scenario as a real example of what they have in mind. This activity is strictly related to the previous stage and requires raising empathy with the problem but trying to frame better where the problem is experienced and who is involved in the problem. In this case, a helpful suggestion is to get inspired by similar situations they know first-hand. To this scope, they work with context and persona cards.

The contexts represent where the identified problem could occur. To facilitate the discussion, we have included some cards as suggestions (see Fig. 2b), such as home, park, public transportation, streets, or squares. Again, blank cards are provided to identify other places such as the school, medical centers, etc. Participants are reminded that the problem might happen in different places, what could imply or not different technological interventions. For instance, in public spaces, privacy or the level of noise are relevant concerns to take into account during the design.

Personas are a typical design artifact of design thinking that was introduced by Alan Cooper in *"The inmates are running the asylum"* [15] as fictional characters that help at humanizing the concept of user by providing detailed descriptions with which designers create an emotional link that contributes to remember them during the whole process. In this case, we introduce the concept and goal of identifying personas and we provide blank cards (see Fig. 2d) that participants can fill with a description of the different characteristics of the stakeholders of the future mobile app, including a photo, name, age, hobbies, goals, and skills. Some stickers are provided to fill the gaps, including blank stickers.

The selected cards are organized on a scenario board where each element is associated with a color (see left side of Fig. 3): blue for problems, green for contexts, and red for personas. Participants organize their options in this space as shown in the example in the right side of Fig. 3.

The space at the bottom of the board allows the participants to add post-its with additional ideas or information they want to keep in mind from the brainstorming sessions. The populated board represents the user scenario [13] that the participants will use to describe the expected contribution they want to make and to generate ideas of potential solutions.

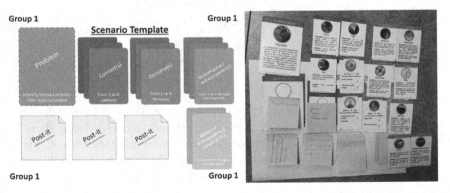

Fig. 3. The scenario board (left) to place the visual cards and an example of its use (right).

3.3 Ideation

Following the Design Thinking approach, the ideation phase has two main parts: divergent and convergent thinking. In divergent thinking, the participants are asked to creatively and spontaneously propose all the ideas that came to their minds without boundaries or limitations. They engage in a brainstorming activity with three main rules [16]: no criticism is allowed yet, unlimited ideas generated freewheeling, and the possibility to combine ideas. During the brainstorming, the participants can explore the cards on the board, creating relations among them and stepping into the personas' shoes to better understand their needs.

The second part of the *Ideation* phase consists of converging all the ideas generated previously in a unique proposal (i.e., convergent thinking). During the two-hour sessions, due to the short time, this part is included in the previous brainstorming activity, asking students to reach a consensus after the discussion. During the five-hour sessions, we use the Six Thinking Hats [17] technique to help them adopt different perspectives to understand better the generated ideas' limitations and benefits. To this scope, we provide each team with six hats of different colors, each focusing on a specific direction: yellow on benefits, green on creativity, white on data, red on emotion and intuition, black on negative outcomes, and blue on processes. We ask the students to put on a hat and participate in the discussion adopting that particular point of view (see Fig. 4). We assign the hats randomly, changing them several times during this phase. In this way, they have to make an effort to understand the other points of view in the group with a view to becoming more flexible and stepping outside their usual thinking. To encourage seeing the idea from different perspectives we also provide a SWOT matrix where they are invited to identify strengths, weaknesses, opportunities, and threats of their ideas.

Fig. 4. Working with six hats and SWOT matrix to evaluate ideas.

After the divergent and convergent thinking sessions, participants start working with the last set of visual cards to select the most appropriate technologies for the solution they want to propose (see Fig. 2c). There are two types of cards for technologies, the orange and the gray ones (see Fig. 3). The orange technologies, like cameras, maps, social networks, multimedia, and augmented reality, are easily implementable and could be part of the final prototype. The gray ones are additional components, like the Internet of Things and iBeacon, considered too complex to be included in the prototype. At this point, it is important to let the participants think outside the box without any limitations given by the specific language chosen for implementing the solution and that's why more complex technologies are also included even though they won't be able to include it in the first prototype. We also highlight during the whole workshop that design of new technologies is an iterative process made up or quick cycles of ideation-implementation-validation.

3.4 Prototype

In the last phase of the workshop, participants design and develop the prototype of mobile app they want to propose as a solution for the user scenario finally defined. With this purpose they use two tools: paper-based wireframes and AppInventor[8], a web development environment, to create mobile apps (see Fig. 5). Paper-based wireframes help to ideate the interface and functionalities offered by the app before going to the actual coding phase. Wireframing is another technique participants learn during the workshop.

Fig. 5. Working with wireframes and appInventor to create an early prototype.

The first three phases of the workshop guide the participants to ideate the proposed solution through different design artifacts. The visual cues, like the cards and the scenario board, that present the needed information to make decisions, so they do not require knowledge of HCI to understand the activity. In the prototype phase, it is important to consider that the workshop is open to technical and non-technical profiles from different education levels. For this reason, for students unfamiliar with the AppInventor tool, we give them some basic tutorials to learn the most common components for building a user interface, including images, labels, vertical/horizontal layouts, text fields, and buttons.

After spending some time with the tutorials, the students are ready to start implementing their mobile application or part of it, depending on its complexity and scope. During this phase, we support them with code tips and suggestions about how to adapt their idea to a low-level working prototype.

---

[8] https://appinventor.mit.edu/.

4 Workshop Results

The workshop has been conducted 14 times since 2019 in two- and five-hour formats. The five-hour sessions were carried out in a summer technical camp, and the two-hour sessions were Friday afternoon activities promoting STEM careers. Each year, we have also organized a special session to celebrate the International Day of Women and Girls in Science on the 11th of February, opening the workshop only to girl students. It is worth noting that these special sessions haven't pointed out any additional difficulty or initial rejection, and the participation and results have been similar to the general ones.

The participation was voluntary and oriented to high-school students. Furthermore, we replicated the two-hour workshop as part of one of the courses offered by the University as a learning program to improve the digital skills of undergraduate and graduate students from Social Sciences.

In total, more than 190 participants have attended our workshop, grouped into more than 50 groups. We have collected 53 projects addressing different problems and designing various solutions. Figure 6 represents the projects as paths connecting problems (first column on the left with blue lines), technologies (middle column with orange lines), and contexts (last column on the right with green lines). Next to each problem is the number of times the groups have chosen it. The labels with a star symbol indicate that the virtual card was not included in the visual card set provided, and the student decided to create it using a blank card provided for this proposal. The thickest path can easily recognize the problems, technologies, and contexts that have attracted more attention.

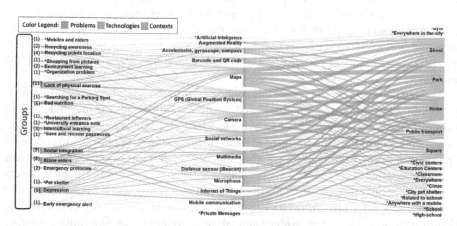

Fig. 6. The collected projects represented as paths connecting problems (on the left, blue), technologies (in the middle, orange), and contexts (on the right, green). (Color figure online)

Observing the visualization in Fig. 6, we can draw some interesting conclusions about the chosen problems, technologies, and contexts. In some scenarios, the students have decided to work on a combination of multiple problems (see the number of projects in the problem column in Fig. 6). While there is a balanced distribution among the chosen technologies and contexts, four problems stand out: lack of physical exercise, social integration, alone elders, and depression. This result highlights a shared concern among young students for mental health and elders' future.

During the workshop sessions, three researchers supported the groups in case they needed it and observed the participants' behaviors as individuals and as part of the group dynamic. In particular, we have noticed that during the Empathize phase, they adopted mainly two strategies to select a problem of interest. In the first strategy, the students already felt empathy for a problem, and in case it was not included in the cards, we invited them to keep working on it, adding a description in one of the available blank cards. In this case, they had first-hand knowledge about the users' needs and extra motivation for the activity. In the second strategy, the students lacked personal motivation, so they went through each one of the problem cards, discarding the ones that did not match their interests and finally keeping the one that received the most consensus. This strategy needed an extra effort to empathize with the challenge and understand the contexts and the personas.

After each workshop session, the participants answered a short survey about their experience. Nevertheless, we have limited access to the collected information because, to comply with privacy regulations, the University cannot store any personal data about the participants. For this reason, we cannot keep a follow-up to understand how attending the workshop influenced the students' decision on which career to pursue.

However, the workshop surveys indicate a high satisfaction of the participants with how the workshop was conducted (M = 4.58 out of 5, SD = .23) as an instrument to put in common ideas, exchange perspectives, and understand each other points of view. They found the used material and, in particular, the visual cards helpful (M = 4.69 out of 5, SD = .16) to have a global idea of the project while maintaining focus on each one of the steps of the workshop and to work with the contained information more interactively. Moreover, almost 94% (SD = .11) of the students would recommend the activity and 91% (SD = .18) thought participating in the workshop had arisen interest in STEM disciplines.

Another interesting comment we have collected over the workshop sessions is about the possibility of proposing innovative and creative solutions even if the students had to simplify them during implementation due to a lack of time and technical knowledge. For example, one of the teams decided to focus on proposing an application to cope with depression and prevent animals from feeling lonely until they are adopted. They ideated a social network that puts in contact people diagnosed with depression and animal shelters to carry out animal therapy sessions. Implementing an actual social network could be a complex and time-consuming challenge. For this reason, they finally prototyped an application to access information about animal shelters and a pet picture gallery. Another project developed during one of the workshop sessions aimed at helping the recycling process and raising people's awareness about its importance. The system would allow taking a picture of an object to be thrown into the garbage and show the proper colored bin and a street map with the closest one. The application would also include images of the effects of not recycling that object on the environment. In this case, during the implementation phase, the prototype was simplified to read the products' bar code and show the proper bin color and a map with the bin position.

5   Conclusions

The workshop "Envisioning the digital city" aims to highlight the influence of HCI concepts and techniques to enhance soft skills like creativity, empathy, and curiosity. The students are engaged in a design project where they have to work together to define a problem and propose a solution using artifacts like scenarios, personas, contexts, and technologies.

The workshop was first offered in 2019, receiving a great acceptance that made us repeat it yearly afterward and propose a more extended version as part of a summer camp for high schools. The participants appreciate the possibility of working on a topic they find interesting or empathize with, giving an idea of what they are more passionate about or worried about. This possibility follows the approach described in [7] to try and connect with prospective students personal interests by proposing cognitively affordable experiences. The workshop promotes self-efficacy perception as all participants took active part in all the activities. After 14 editions and with 190 participants, we never had any frustrated participant. The workshop is taught in Spanish, and all material is in Spanish, and we had a couple of occasions in which one or more participants who were on a visiting program didn't speak Spanish fluently. The team always reacted positively by facilitating translation and integrating non-Spanish speakers. Also, even though most of participants did not know their team partners, they didn't experience any trouble to work together. To improve outcome expectations, we focused on the fact that CSE is not only about programming, but about devising innovative uses of technology that can lead with current problems of our society. Finally, to improve interest the complexity of the activities was increased gradually, and we tried to use innovative methods like design thinking and the physicalization of design constituents (like the cards, boards or hats) to make the process funnier and more active.

As shown in a previous contribution where we used the workshop methodology to teach gender inclusion in design courses [18], this is a mind-opening activity where the students can learn by following their own path and taking advantage of the experience of the other team members. Moreover, considering that most students come alone, this methodology helps them share their opinions and make others listen to their voices. In this way, we are also giving them an alternative perspective on CSE studies, more oriented to putting people and their needs at the center of the decision-making and problem-solving process, where collaboration, creativity, and empathy are keys to finding real solutions for real problems.

Acknowledgment. This work is supported by the project sense2MakeSense, funded by the Spanish State Agency of Research (PID2019-109388GB-I00).

References

1. Zhou, K., Liu, T., Zhou, L.: Industry 4.0: towards future industrial opportunities and challenges. In: 2015 12th International Conference on Fuzzy Systems and Knowledge Discovery (FSKD), pp. 2147–2152 (2015)

2. European Comission. Digital Education Action Plan 2021–2027: Resetting education and training for the digital age (2020). https://education.ec.europa.eu/focus-topics/digital-education/action-plan
3. European Commission. Digital Economy and Society Index (DESI) (2022). https://digital-strategy.ec.europa.eu/en/policies/desi
4. Brown, T., Wyatt, J.: Design thinking for social innovation. Dev. Outreach **12**, 29–43 (2010)
5. Pompei, F., Borsani, G.: Rethink STE(A)M education: a sustainable future through scientific, tech and humanistic skills. In: EU STEM Observatory-Deloitte (2022)
6. Sochacka, N., Walther, J., Wilson, J., Brewer, M.: Stories 'Told' about engineering in the media: implications for attracting diverse groups to the profession. In: 2014 IEEE Frontiers in Education Conference (FIE) Proceedings, pp. 1–9. IEEE (2014)
7. Akbulut, A.Y., Looney, C.A.: Inspiring students to pursue computing degrees. Commun. ACM **50**(10), 67–71 (2007)
8. Sáinz, M., Eccles, J.: Self-concept of computer and math ability: gender implications across time and within ICT studies. J. Vocat. Behav. **80**(2), 486–499 (2012)
9. Huang, W., Looi, C.K.: A critical review of literature on "unplugged" pedagogies in K-12 computer science and computational thinking education. Comput. Sci. Educ. **31**(1), 83–111 (2021)
10. Bohdziewicz, P.: Career anchors of representatives of generation Z: some conclusions for managing the younger generation of employees. Zarzadzanie Zasobami Ludzkimi, (6 (113)-"Managing Diversity in the Context of International HRM"), pp. 57–74 (2016)
11. Fodor, M., Jaeckel, K.: What does it take to have a successful career through the eyes of generation z-based on the results of a primary qualitative research. Int. J. Lifelong Educ. Leadership **4**(1), 1–7 (2018)
12. Szlavi, A., Versino, S., Zanardi, I., Bolesta, K., Jaccheri, L.: Bridging values: the inclusion of young generations in computing. In: Antona, M., Stephanidis, C. (eds.) HCII 2023, pp. 154–170. Springer, Cham (2023). https://doi.org/10.1007/978-3-031-35681-0_10
13. Carroll, J.M., Rosson, M.B.: Human-computer interaction scenarios as a design representation. In: Twenty-Third Annual Hawaii International Conference on System Sciences, vol. 2, pp. 555–561. IEEE Computer Society (1990)
14. Hartson, H.R., Smith, E.C.: Rapid prototyping in human-computer interface development. Interact. Comput. **3**(1), 51–91 (1991)
15. Cooper, A.: The Inmates are Running the Asylum. Vieweg+ Teubner Verlag (1999)
16. Osborn, A.F.: How to think up (1942)
17. de Bono, E.: Six thinking hats: an essential approach to business management (1985)
18. Onorati, T., Díaz, P.: Integrating gender inclusion in web design courses through design workshops. In: Proceedings of the XXI International Conference on Human Computer Interaction, pp. 1–8 (2021)

Teaching HCI in Multidisciplinary Situations: Experience Report and Lessons Learnt

Sophie Dupuy-Chessa[1][✉], Kathia Marçal de Oliveira[2], Sophie Lepreux[2], and Laura Pruszko[1]

[1] IUT2, LIG, Univ. Grenoble Alpes, 2 Place Doyen Gosse, 38000 Grenoble, France
{sophie.dupuy-chessa,laura.pruszko}@univ-grenoble-alpes.fr
[2] Univ. Polytechnique Hauts de France, LAMIH, CNRS UMR8201, Le Mont-Houy Cedex 9, 59313 Valenciennes, France
{kathia.oliveira,sophie.lepreux}@uphf.fr

Abstract. The Computer Science Technical Bachelor degree in France aims at training professionals who participate in the design, production and implementation of computing solutions corresponding to users' needs. Its program contains realistic situations where knowledge from several disciplines must be put in practice within the context of transversal student projects. This paper focuses on knowledge related to Human-Computer Interaction (HCI) and its interrelationship with other courses. It presents how the Grenoble and Valenciennes Technical Institutes manage the multidisciplinarity and discusses some lessons learnt from these experiences.

Keywords: user interfaces · Technical Bachelor degree · work situations · multidisciplinary

1 Introduction

In France, Technical Institutes (IUT) aim at training technicians and provide a Technical Bachelor degree. The degree is constrained by the existence of a national pedagogical program requiring thematic volumes and schedules for the implementation of this degree. To train professionals able of transferring the knowledge acquired in their courses to the professional world, a degree always contains knowledge related to the working context such as economy, communication, or English. The program includes lectures, tutorials and practical work. It also proposes realistic work situations, i.e. projects in which the skills acquired during different courses are put into practice, thus requiring a multidisciplinary approach of teaching. For the computer science degree, human computer interaction is taught in several courses to address both the design and the development of user interfaces. The acquired knowledge must also be used and put into practice in work situations at every semester. This requires that the HCI teachers work regularly with teachers from other disciplines, not only in computer science but also in « humanities», such as communication and management.

A. Bramwell-Dicks et al. (Eds.): INTERACT 2023 Workshops, LNCS 14535, pp. 253–259, 2024.
https://doi.org/10.1007/978-3-031-61688-4_24

This paper presents the place of HCI within the Computer Science Bachelor degree in French Technical Institutes. It discusses the way it was implemented in two different IUT, Grenoble and Valenciennes. These experiences put in evidence the complementary work of HCI issues with different disciplines such as communication, law, management and computer science itself. We report our experiences, and propose the lessons we learnt.

Section 2 of this paper presents a more detailed description of the context: the Technical Bachelor degree in Computer Science. Section 3 focuses on the courses related to HCI in the degree. Then, Sect. 4 describes some lessons learnt from the experiences of multidisciplinarity in teaching HCI. At last, the paper ends with a conclusion (Sect. 5).

2 Context

This work centers around a three-year technological bachelor's degree program in computer science offered by Technical Institutes (IUT) in France. The general objective of the Computer Science technical degree is to train professionals who participate in the design, production and implementation of Information Technologies (IT) solutions corresponding to users' needs.

The national pedagogical program is divided in traditional business areas: 1) "computing" disciplinary fields, like Algorithms, Hardware architecture, Database management systems, Human-Computer Interaction, or Analysis, design and applications development, and 2) disciplinary fields covering scientific, social and human culture, like Mathematics, Economy, Law, Communication, Information System management, Project Management and English. Teachers work in teams by speciality areas, with a small overlap.

The program also contains «**Learning and Assessment Situations**» (LAS) which are realistic professional situations in which student puts their disciplinary knowledge into practice, and allow them to demonstrate their skill acquisition in a larger-scale project. The goal of LAS is to avoid the disciplinary fragmentation, which could in turn make some students (1) lacking a global understanding of IT techniques and (2) encountering some difficulties for articulating and efficiently linking the various approaches. The students are organized in groups and works in one or more projects defined to address the LAS of the specific semester. To this end, students benefit from supervised hours, in which a teacher is available to support them in each specific disciplinary issues; and autonomous hours, dedicated to group work towards the realization of the project.

Although the program was defined for three years, it has now been implemented for the first two years. Thereafter, we will focus on the first two years (4 semesters) to show the multidisciplinary nature of our teaching.

3 Teaching HCI in Multidisciplinary Situations

In this section, we describe how we have been teaching HCI in two different IUT, Grenoble and Valenciennes, considering the previously presented national pedagogical program followed by both sites. It is worth noting that these two institutes have professors involved in HCI research, which is not the case in all institutes across France. Our goal is to highlight how HCI issues impact and are used in different disciplines in student curriculum, such as communication, law, management and computer science itself. Figure 1 presents the main HCI courses taught per semester (in blue, top), as well as the courses from other disciplines that are directly related to the HCI knowledge acquired in the HCI courses (in yellow, center), and the Learning Assessment Situations (LAS) where both types of courses are complementary applied in a realistic situation (in green, bottom). Courses represented overlapping two areas of the figure means that they include both an HCI part as well as a technical programming part. Next sections present our lessons learnt within the scope of this general organization.

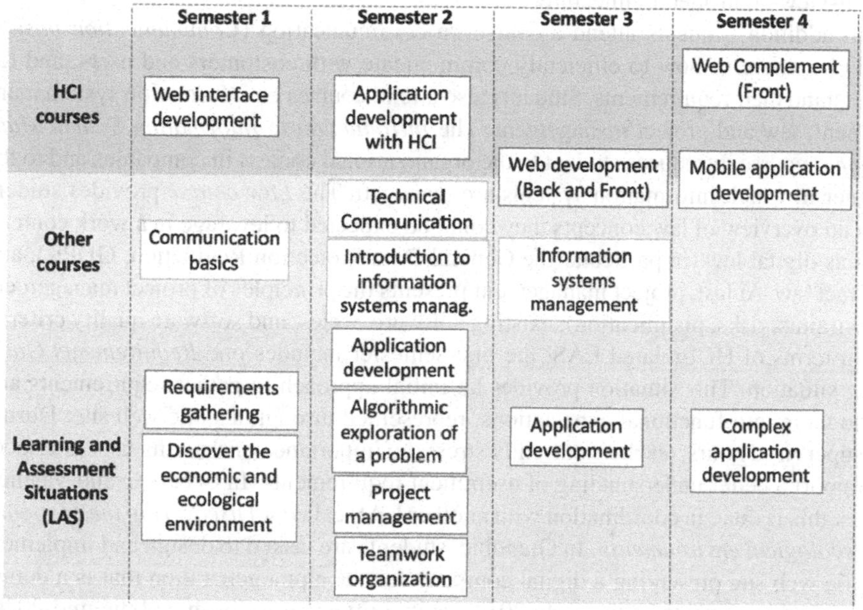

	Semester 1	Semester 2	Semester 3	Semester 4
HCI courses	Web interface development	Application development with HCI	Web development (Back and Front)	Web Complement (Front)
				Mobile application development
Other courses	Communication basics	Technical Communication	Information systems management	
		Introduction to information systems manag.		
Learning and Assessment Situations (LAS)	Requirements gathering	Application development	Application development	Complex application development
	Discover the economic and ecological environment	Algorithmic exploration of a problem		
		Project management		
		Teamwork organization		

Fig. 1. HCI Teaching in multidisciplinary situations. (Color figure online)

3.1 First-Year Courses

During the first year, two main courses are related to HCI: *Web interface development* and *Application development with HCI*. The first one takes place during the first semester and is related to the development of web interfaces. It mainly focuses on web display technologies (Hypertext Markup Language (HTML), Cascading Style Sheet (CSS)) It also introduces user interface specifications with simple representations, such as mockup. This course aims at (1) apprehending user interfaces development and (2) understanding customer and user requirements.

The second course is taught during the second semester. Its entire content focuses on HCI, and particularly addresses the technical and ergonomic viewpoint of user interfaces design. From the technical viewpoint, it introduces event-driven programming, user interfaces programming using graphical components (i.e., JavaFX in Grenoble and Valenciennes) and implementing software architecture consideration, such as the separation between the view and the model. This course must also raise awareness in ergonomics for the students. In Grenoble, the user-centered design cycle is presented with some associated techniques (e.g., persona, usability criteria, zoning, wireframing). In Valenciennes, task analysis. [1, 2], mock-up design (with Balsamiq[1] mockups and ergonomics concepts [3, 4] are introduced. In both sites, this *"Application development with HCI"* course is complementary to another course related to object-oriented design and programming. This allows students to build upon existing skills in modeling and programing, and allows teachers to further explain event-driven programing and the model-view-controller architecture.

In addition, students attend a course on communication (*Communication basics*) to (1) be aware of how to efficiently communicate with customers and users, and (2) understand their requirements. Students also attend courses on information system management, law and project management. The *Introduction to Information System Management* course introduces student to the organizational context in companies and to the manner in which information systems are managed. The *Law course* provides student with an overview of law concepts they could be expected to leverage in a work context, such as digital law (in particular the General Data Protection Regulation, GDPR), and contract law. At last, project management presents the principles of project management (constraints, risks, planification), existing software cycles, and software quality criteria.

In terms of HCI-related LAS, the first semester includes one *Requirements Gathering* situation. This situation provides an initial approach to gather requirements and refine them into functional expectations, represented through a static web site. During the supervised hours, teachers currently stress the importance of showing user interfaces to support a better understanding of user/client requirements. In Grenoble and Valenciennes, this is done in coordination with another LAS called « *Discovering the economic and ecological environment*». In Grenoble, students are tasked to design and implement a static web site presenting a digital company for the alpha generation that is a demographic cohort starting in the early 2010s as its initial year of birth and the mid-2020s as its final year of birth. In Valenciennes, the website showcases an event (e.g., wedding or rock festival). As the assignment requires students to understand informations related to the digital business field, the teaching team includes both web development teachers and economics teachers. The rest of the teaching team is comprised of communication teachers and computer science teachers in order to design and develop the web interfaces. The communication teachers help groups of 3–4 students to target their audience, and teach them how to adapt their content to this audience. Then, the computer science teachers guide student groups in the design and development of their web pages.

During the second semester, the program contains six LAS: (i) development of an application; (ii) algorithmic exploration of a problem; (iii) installation of network services; (iv) database exploitation; (v) project management and (vi) teamwork. In Grenoble, four situations ((i), (ii), (v) and (vi)) (presented in Fig. 1) were gathered into one large-scale project which addresses the development of an application facing some algorithmic problem, and which requires team work and project management. In Grenoble,

---

[1] https://balsamiq.com/wireframes/.

students are tasked to design and develop a software for social event management in groups of 5–6 students. In Valenciennes, two LAS ((i) and (ii)) were gathered together in a project whose goal is a grid-based game. In both sites, the teaching team includes the software development and HCI teachers for the design and development of the graphical interfaces, as well as the communication team and the teacher in charge of project management. The project management teacher guides students in the management of their project (e.g., identification of constraints and risks, planification). The communication team works with students on the value of their application and its customers. The HCI team supervises students in the design of their application's interfaces (persona, zoning, wireframing of interfaces). Then, jointly with the software development teachers, they guide students in realizing the application in Java and JavaFX following a MVC architecture.

3.2 Second-Year Courses

During the second year of the technical bachelor's degree, the HCI courses continue to explore the design and implementation of user interfaces for the Web in two courses: *Web development* and *Web Complement*. The aim is to further learn web technologies and programming, and to apply web accessibility and ergonomics principles. Both Grenoble and Valenciennes focus on PHP for the third semester course, and on Javascript with Ajax for the fourth semester (*Web Complement*).

Moreover, HCI is directly associated in two other courses. The first one, *Information System Management*, explores agile methods practices with Scrum [5], and the principles of digital ethics. Agile practices emphasize collaboration between self-organised, multidisciplinary teams and their customers. They are based on the use of a light but sufficient methodological framework centered on people and communication during a series of sprints. Each sprint is akin to a one- to four-week development phase, and each is designed so that the project team focuses on a limited part of the product or service to be delivered. At the end of each sprint, a sprint review is organized to (i) analyze the project's progress with the customer, (ii) examine any adaptation that needs to be made, and (iii) identify the objectives for the next sprint. For these meetings to be productive and effective, it is usually recommended to present the functionalities through a user interface (even if not definitive). This facilitates communication between the team and the user and better support requirements validation, as well as the identification of potential improvements and new requirements.

In the second course, *Mobile application development*, students are confronted with the back-end and front-end development of mobile applications. HCI issues are therefore explored while learning front-end aspects. HCI design principles and ergonomic rules are therefore taken into account.

During the second year, only one LAS is set for each semester: *Application Development* for the third semester, and *Complex application development* for the fourth semester. Each LAS leverages knowledge from all of the courses followed during the semester, as well as during the previous semesters. In Grenoble, two projects are carried out, i.e. one for each semester. In the third semester project, Grenoble students put into practice their knowledge of GDPR rules and of accessibility acquired in the first year HCI courses, and choose specific quality criteria to implement. They can choose any software process cycle model to develop their application. Moreover, one of the LAS supervised classes is dedicated to the evaluation of the quality of the user interface through the SUS questionnaire [4]. In the fourth semester project, a very bad software application with serious user interface problems is provided. The students are asked to criticize the application constructively, and to leverage their knowledge to propose a redesign of both the user interface and the application itself (that is done in Android/Javascript).

In Valenciennes, a sole two-semester guiding project is developed during the whole year, focusing on different issues each semester. In the third semester, the focus is on customer requirements gathering and validation. SCRUM agile mythology is mandatory, with a fixed number and size of sprints (3 weeks). The proposed project features a real customer interacting with one teacher, who in turn plays the role of product owner. At the end of each sprint, a product review centered on a small demonstration of the functionality is performed. The students organize the information considering task analysis models learnt in the previous semester. In the fourth semester, the goal is to a build a robust mobile application by developing a well-documented and good quality backend, and well-designed frontend considering HCI best principles learnt in the previous semesters.

4 Lessons Learnt from Multidisciplinarity

From a teaching point of view, setting up a multidisciplinary project necessitates to reach a consensus on (i) translating pedagogical objectives into projects assignments (e.g., through software domain, evaluation criterias,...) and (ii) producing resources for students. Interestingly, we observed points of convergence between the different subjects. Sometimes, the objectives are the same: for instance, the communication team and the HCI team both ask students to understand their target audience, and to think about how to provide a message in an appropriate manner. The points of view of other domains can help the HCI teachers in their practice. In the second year, the use of the « six hats» creativity method is directly inspired from the management domain, but can be used in many different contexts. In fact, many domains follow principles close to user centered design. It is then necessary to well coordinate everyone's activities to avoid redundancy and make better use of similar activities.

Moreover, the identification of customer needs, and the validation of good understanding by the development team, require the integration of communication techniques. An appropriate user interface design then becomes a mean of knowing and validating the requirements.

With some teaching teams, the points of views are complementary and need to be coordinated with the HCI teachers. In particular, implementing the MVC architecture, requires an alignment of practices between the development and HCI teams. This leads to discussions and changes in implementations every year.

Some HCI requirements may also be related to other domains. The GDPR requires the development of specific interfaces to collect users' consent. It is thus necessary that the law teachers can supervise students in the design of this kind of interfaces. Moreover, these consent forms are very similar to each other and could be generated automatically depending on the data collected and their treatment. This automatic generation could be a specific case for research in interfaces generation.

Furthermore, the current development of applications is in a short time-to-market requiring a strong interaction with customers, who should be completely integrated in the software development. Agile methodologies seek to address this need with short and fixed periods of development, as well as continuous validation with the customers. In this context, HCI is a key element towards a customer satisfaction.

5 Conclusion

This paper presents the experience of Grenoble and Valenciennes Technical Institutes in teaching HCI in multidisciplinary situations. It is shown how HCI issues are relevant, not only for computer science discipline, but also for communication, management and law. These experiences span over the two first years of a bachelor's degree in computer science. Both institutes are currently working towards the installation of the third year, which introduces two different specializations. Valenciennes will focus on user-centered design where HCI issues are in the core of the development. In this case, some particularities will be studied for people with disabilities. In Grenoble, most of the students will be enrolled in a work-study program. The work on HCI will be based on students' feedback in connection with project management. Feedbacks will be used to discuss both (i) how users are involved in the projects and (ii) how software quality criteria are implemented in students' tasks, in particular ergonomic criteria and maintainability criteria linked to software architecture. This will help to better position HCI issues within the practices of future IT technicians.

References

1. Marçal de Oliveira, K., Girard, P., Guidini Gonçalves, T., Lepreux, S., Kolski, C.: Teaching task analysis for user interface design: lessons learned from three pilot studies. In: Proceedings of the 27th Conference on l'Interaction Homme-Machine, IHM 2015, vol. 31, pp. 1–6. ACM (2015). https://doi.org/10.1145/2820619.2825011
2. Thomas, L., Patrick, G., Laurent, G., Allan, F.: ProtoTask, new task model simulator. In: Winckler, M., Forbrig, P., Bernhaupt, R. (eds.) HCSE 2012. LNCS, vol. 7623, pp. 323–330. Springer, Heidelberg (2012). https://doi.org/10.1007/978-3-642-34347-6_24
3. Scapin, D.L., Bastien, J.M.C.: Ergonomic criteria for evaluating the ergonomic quality of interactive systems. Behav. Inf. Technol. 6(4–5), 220–231 (1997)
4. Brooke, J.: SUS: a quick and dirty usability scale. Usability Eval. Ind. 189 (1995)
5. Scrum.org. https://www.scrum.org/. Accessed 30 May 2023

The User Interface Technologies Course at the University of Cagliari

Lucio Davide Spano[✉][iD]

Department of Mathematics and Computer Science, University of Cagliari,
Via Ospedale 72, 09124 Cagliari, Italy
davide.spano@unica.it

Abstract. This paper describes the experience of teaching Human Computer Interaction Engineering (HCI-E) concepts in the User Interface Technologies course for the Master's Degree in Computer Science at the University of Cagliari. The course covers the general traits of technologies for building User Interfaces for different platforms and modalities, including the architecture of classical desktop interface toolkits, the fundamentals of information visualization, gestural interaction, eXtended Reality and seminars about the interplay between Artificial Intelligence and the development of User Interfaces. We motivate the syllabus design for this course and the assessment method, discussing the issues and the success points we registered in four years since we started giving this course.

Keywords: User Interface Technologies · HCI Engineering · UI Toolkits · Information Visualization · Gestural Interaction · eXtended Reality

1 Introduction

After different revisions and ongoing discussions, academics and practitioners agreed on core Human-Computer Interaction (HCI) topics to be included in an undergraduate Computer Science Degree Curriculum [15]. For advanced courses at Master Degrees, the combination and balance between the various disciplines involved in the design, development and assessment of an interactive system require considering the goals of the Master Curriculum (or Curricula) where the course is included and the strengths and the interests of the research groups in the Department. In this paper, we discuss the structure of the syllabus, the teaching experience, the assessment, the issues, and the positive points of the "User Interface Technology" (UIT) course at Master Degree in Computer Science at the University of Cagliari, Italy.

We designed the course to provide students with a solid foundation in understanding and leveraging various technologies for developing User Interfaces (UIs). Through a combination of lectures and hands-on lab sessions, we explore a wide spectrum of UIs, discussing their architectures, structure and the design choices

A. Bramwell-Dicks et al. (Eds.): INTERACT 2023 Workshops, LNCS 14535, pp. 260–269, 2024.
https://doi.org/10.1007/978-3-031-61688-4_25

behind the toolkits supporting their development. They range from simple form-based interfaces to complex multi-device setups, Augmented and Virtual Reality experiences, and seminars on the interplay between Artificial Intelligence (AI) and user interaction. The course tries to convey the theoretical knowledge on how to solve relevant HCI-Engineering problems starting from the challenges posed by specific interaction techniques or modalities. For instance, we explain the Entity-Component-System architectural pattern [21] by showing the limitations in representing Virtual Reality (VR) objects through inheritance hierarchies. By solving this problem, we generalise the pattern for similar circumstances. Students are exposed to real-world challenges for understanding the engineering behind advanced interactive systems. The overall goal of the course is to show how modern UI development involves the integration of different development technologies, requiring the management of their complexity while striving to ensure the overall usability of the entire application.

The paper is organised as follows. We first describe the background of the students typically attending the course in Sect. 2, then we discuss the course syllabus in Sect. 3, and next we describe the method we use for grading our students in Sect. 4. Finally, we discuss the positive points and the issues we encountered in Sect. 5 and the conclusions in Sect. 6.

2   Students' Background

Most students attending the UIT course are first-year students of the Master's Degree in Computer Science at the University of Cagliari, Italy. They have the skills commonly defined for people having a Bachelor's Degree in Computer Science [15]: programming proficiency, database management, software engineering, computer architecture, operating systems, networking and, in general, problem-solving. As for the knowledge and skills related to Human-Computer Interaction, the Bachelor's programme includes an introductory course covering the foundations of the discipline: the historical evolution of HCI, human perception, memory and reasoning skills, user-centred design methods, usability principles, user-interface prototyping and evaluation. The course also includes laboratory activities, split into basics of UI programming in the first half and practical UI prototyping in the second. The organisation of the introductory HCI course, and more in general of the entire Bachelor Curriculum, allows only to teach how to use UI libraries and toolkits for building standard UIs and to focus on teaching our students how to avoid the most common design mistakes. At the Master's level, our goal is to enrich their background towards designing and programming more advanced interaction techniques and the ability to engineer libraries and solutions for enabling *others* to build interactive systems of different types.

3   Course Syllabus

The course consists of four chapters and a final emergent topic seminar. It includes 24 h of lectures plus 36 h of lab lessons. The duration is 12 weeks, each including a 2 h lecture and a 3 h lab lesson. The course is organised as follows:

User Interface Architecture. This chapter consists of 4 weeks and covers the basics of a window system implementation. We start introducing the main patterns, such as the View Tree, Observer and Model-View-Controller. Then we discuss the paradigms for defining the views (procedural, declarative and direct manipulation). After that, we cover the basics of the view drawing and rasterisation, explaining the basics of (re)painting, including damaged-area handling, z-ordering, and the simplest algorithms for managing clipping (Cohen-Sutherland [34]) and rasterisation (Bresenham [2]). Next, we discuss the management of the input devices, including the event loop definition, the state-machine representation of input devices [3] and how to manage (and design) UI animations. After that, we introduce the most recent evolutions of the Model-View-Controller pattern that currently allows expressing web-based UI views as pure functions of the application state and managing updates through the virtual DOM [10]. Finally, we discuss the evaluation of user interface toolkits, covering their evaluation criteria in the literature [20,29,30]. The lab lessons show the implementation details of the patterns described during the lectures through a proof-of-concept library we developed for teaching purposes called BurdUI [31]. It provides an HTML5 canvas-based implementation of a straightforward window system.

Information Visualization. The second chapter introduces the principles for creating data visualisation (2 weeks). The first lesson covers the basics of the Munzner's framework [28] and the criteria for defining static visualisations. The second lesson covers the interaction as a way to reduce the complexity. Lab lessons show concrete coding samples using D3.js [11], which is useful to demonstrate how to map data into marks and channels, and it provides simple but effective means for defining interactions in the visualisation.

Gestural Interaction. The third chapter of the course focuses on the gestural interaction modality (2 weeks). We start by defining the characteristics of gestural communication among humans, and then we discuss the problems and opportunities in exploiting it for interaction. We discuss the trade-off in designing gestural vocabularies between recognition techniques and expressiveness. Finally, we discuss how we can model and recognise gestures in user interface toolkits, discussing the advantages and limitations of compositional gesture modelling [16,17,32,33], machine learning [9] and hybrid approaches [4,5,12], pointing out the mismatches between the information required for building appropriate feedback and feedforward [35]. The lab lessons discuss the development toolkit abstraction based on skeleton joints and require the students to develop motivating examples in [5] using the recognition approaches discussed during lectures.

eXtended Reality. The fourth chapter introduces the techniques and toolkits for developing eXtended Reality experiences, focusing on immersive settings. First, we discuss the techniques for implementing common interaction tasks in 3D like selection, manipulation, navigation and indirect control [18]. After that, we discuss similarities and differences between holographic (Microsoft

Hololens) and passthrough-based (Meta Quest Pro) headsets supporting immersive eXtended Reality (XR) experiences, including the requirements for making the virtual content aware of the surrounding environment. The lab lessons focus on the development of XR experiences. We briefly cover some basic Unity concepts (e.g., the entity-component-system pattern), and then we discuss how to implement spatial-aware interactions through MRKT3 [26].

Closing Seminar. The last week of the course includes a seminar on a hot topic and a hands-on lab on related technologies. Currently, we discuss the implementation of explanations in AI decision support systems and the effects of supporting different reasoning styles (deductive, inductive and abductive) through such explanations [6, 7].

4   Assessment and Grading

The learning outcome of the course includes the knowledge and the understanding of the course syllabus that, as shown in Sect. 3 has as its main objective covering different technologies for developing user interfaces, starting from the simplest to the more complex ones (multi-device, augmented and virtual reality etc.). We assess this through a written test on the course topics.

Besides this, we require students to apply such knowledge to the concrete engineering and development of advanced user interfaces (e.g., by integrating different development technologies), managing the project complexity while guaranteeing the overall application usability. We assess such abilities through a project assignment. The student needs to autonomously analyse the technical requirements and the development cost for the engineering choices and to provide a working proof of concept prototype of the project idea.

We are also interested in assessing the communication skills the student acquired during the course. For this purpose, we ask them to explain the project through a (short) paper and a presentation, which must highlight the encountered design and engineering problems, show the proposed solutions and put them into the wider background of the course topics.

In summary, the exam grading consists of four activities:

- A written test on the course topics (20% of the final grade)
- Completing a project assignment on one of the course chapters (40% of the final grade)
- Writing a short paper describing the project assignment (20% of the final grade)
- Discuss the project through a presentation (20% of the final grade)

The procedure for defining the project assignment requires the student to propose an idea of an advanced UI or a toolkit supporting the development of specific UI parts. Starting from the initial idea, the student and the lecturer agree on the project's requirements and the points where a stub implementation is sufficient. After that, the student goes on with the engineering and the implementation of the solution, discussing the decision with the lecturer when needed. Finally, students deliver the paper and make an appointment to present the project.

5   Discussion

This section discusses some choices and trade-offs we balanced while organising the course.

Topic Breadth vs Depth. Each year, before the deadline for updating the course syllabus, we consider the opportunity to narrow the scope of the topics discussed in this course. The original idea was to organise it as a set of introductory seminars on different HCI branches to provide a curated introduction to different advanced topics. The project assignment was meant to provide the students with a chance to deepen their skills in their preferred topic. Then, after the first two years, we removed some chapters and limited the scope of others, e.g., by including them in other parts of the course. For instance, we removed the chapter on Computational Interaction from the original syllabus, which included a single lecture and one lab-lesson. There needed to be more than the available lessons for going beyond a seminar presentation, while the extent of the topic required more depth. We decided to drop the topic and use the time to deepen the chapter on XR. The original syllabus also included a week on designing and implementing animations, covering the usability principles, how to define them in different UI toolkits and (briefly) how they internally manage the updates. We decided to reduce this part since we noticed that students struggled to understand the animation internals, which leveraged the original description of the windowing toolkit architecture, which was clearly too short. So, we shrunk the extent of the animation discussion, and we increased the time on the windowing toolkit basics.

After these adaptations, we think we have reached the right balance between the topics we cover and the level of detail, at least in the context of our Master's Degree curriculum, i.e., when there are no further HCI courses. It contains lessons aiming at strengthening their background on windowing systems and UI engineering in general, and then introduces the most important traits of different advanced interaction techniques. However, we would not suggest our approach when the curriculum includes more than one HCI-related course: each of our chapters may result in a single, focused course on a specific topic.

The Programming Side of the Course. The lab lessons for each chapter require selecting specific toolkits for demonstrating the concepts. Candidate technologies may work on specific operating systems or require the knowledge of specific programming languages, which may be a barrier to teaching. Even though we are dealing with Master's students, who can learn new languages and switch between them, this requires more effort, and we try to avoid using too many languages. Ideally, we would need to select only a toolkit working on all operating systems and use a single programming language.

We preferred web-based toolkits in most chapters for these reasons: they work in all operating systems and use JavaScript. This choice is ideal for the information visualisation chapter and requires creativity for building the BurdUI library [31] in the user interface architecture chapter. Instead, it is partially working for the chapter on gestures, where we can cover Google MediaPipe hand tracking [22], a discontinued API for LeapMotion [27]. Still, we skip entirely the Microsoft Kinect API [25] that is not accessible in Javascript. Finally, we used to cover the XR concepts using the A-Frame library [15]. However, we recently relaxed the language requirement and decided to use Unity3D and Microsoft MRTK [26] to cover the interactions and the quality of the library design.

Besides the programming language, the main barrier we identified in the coding parts of the course is a low familiarity with the internals of graphical toolkits, i.e., drawing, elements layouts and updates. This increases the effort to follow the lab-lessons and the final project assignment. We decided to deepen the first chapter for this reason after the first two editions of the course. We believe that the basic knowledge of window systems should be among the fundamental skills for a Bachelor in Computer Science. However, such a topic seldom finds its space in introductory HCI courses, which focus on UI design, somehow neglecting technical parts. Other courses that may include such topics are either elective (e.g., Computer Graphics courses are usually not mandatory when included in the study plans), or they simply decide not to cover it (e.g., Operating Systems courses explain how to manage all resources but the screen). Our bachelor HCI course includes coding lab lessons, but they are enough to cover only the basics of using widgets and responding to events. More complex engineering topics are postponed to the UIT course.

Project Assignment. We give the students the freedom to propose ideas for their project assignment. They can select any of the course chapters, and they may also broaden the scope. We do not provide them with a list of possible projects, but we give them some suggestions and input for ideas during the lectures. Such an approach stimulates their curiosity and engages them with their work. However, while such freedom is usually well accepted by the most motivated students, some would always prefer a proper assignment by the lecturer. Given that the course is elective, we are keeping this method, paying extra-mentoring time for those needing more guidance. The process for defining the assignment teaches different things to our students. First, they learn to identify a problem or an opportunity where they can apply their acquired skills. Second, they learn to focus on the important aspects of demonstrating the solution, removing the less relevant parts. Indeed, many project ideas require too much effort to code them entirely. So they must find a way to prove their concept, putting reasonable effort into the development. Third, they learn to explain and defend their ideas against the lecturer's criticism and to adapt them according to the received comments. Through the definition of the project assignment, students usually understand what it is important for us as teachers to assess, and, as a consequence, they better understand the goal of the course.

We are used to submitting a demo or poster paper about projects having sufficient quality to HCI conferences. This commitment encouraged many students to polish their project work to ensure adequate submission quality. Some examples are the following:

- A toolkit for creating task tutorials in AR [23]
- An End-User development solution for creating merchandising showcases in Virtual Reality [24]
- A method for recognising stroke gestures in real-time through Long-Short Memory Term models [19]
- A toolkit for managing haptic feedback on VR controllers [1]
- An End-User development tool for video games [13]
- A workout visualisation for running coaches [8]
- An browser for medical records in XR [14]

Core vs Elective Course. From next year, the UIT course will be promoted from elective to core courses in our Master's Degree. This is a great opportunity to increase awareness among our students of the HCI Engineering importance. However, it will require a course redesign to fit this new role.

In the original planning, we aimed to cover hot topics in the field, combining our interests and experiences with the latest results and technologies available. Transforming it into a core course, we need to emphasise *core* elements that may be useful even for students who will not tailor their careers in the HCI field. In our opinion, core elements of HCI engineering are related with the understanding of the window toolkits internals. On the one hand, this allows people attending the course to master and better predict the behaviour of the code they develop for building a UI. On the other hand, such a discussion allows to cover different basic but relevant engineering solutions for managing resources (screen, memory, computation time etc.) and separating concerns (organisation, look and feel, behaviour etc.) through a set of concrete examples.

In addition, we will double the number of students, so the discussion on the project assignment will require more effort. Different solutions are possible for this problem, and all them would require validation during the next editions. One solution may be proposing projects at different levels of difficulties and leading to different maximum grades. For reaching the higher grades students should take open-ended assignments (i.e. the description of an interaction problem) and propose an innovative idea, while for lower levels the teacher can provide a full-specification of the assignment. Another solution is having a set of two or three possible projects (full-specified) for topic and let the student choose from such a predefined list. The current intent is trying to stimulate the students' creativity and interests, so we will start from an implementation of the first idea.

6   Conclusion and Future Work

This paper discussed our experience in teaching the "User Interface Technologies" course at the Master in Computer Science at the University of Cagliari.

We described the syllabus and the assessment method, and we reported the positive points and the issues we encountered, together with the improvements we made to the course through the years. Finally, we discussed the planned changes and the opportunities in transforming the course from elective to core for our Master's Degree.

References

1. Artizzu, V., Fara, D., Macis, R., Spano, L.D.: FeedBucket: simplified haptic feedback for VR and MR. In: Tortora, G., Vitiello, G., Winckler, M. (eds.) AVI '20: International Conference on Advanced Visual Interfaces, Island of Ischia, Italy, September 28 - October 2 2020, pp. 1–3. ACM (2020). https://doi.org/10.1145/3399715.3399947
2. Bresenham, J.E.: Algorithm for computer control of a digital plotter. IBM Syst. J. **4**(1), 25–30 (1965). https://doi.org/10.1147/sj.41.0025
3. Buxton, W.: A three-state model of graphical input. In: Diaper, D., Gilmore, D.J., Cockton, G., Shackel, B. (eds.) Human-Computer Interaction, INTERACT '90, Proceedings of the IFIP TC13 Third Interantional Conference on Human-Computer Interaction, Cambridge, UK, 27-31 August 1990, pp. 449–456. North-Holland (1990)
4. Carcangiu, A., Spano, L.D.: G-Gene: a Gene alignment method for online partial stroke gestures recognition. Proc. ACM Hum.-Comput. Interact. **2**(EICS) (2018). https://doi.org/10.1145/3229095
5. Carcangiu, A., Spano, L.D., Fumera, G., Roli, F.: DEICTIC: a compositional and declarative gesture description based on hidden Markov models. Int. J. Hum Comput Stud. **122**, 113–132 (2019)
6. Cau, F.M., Hauptmann, H., Spano, L.D., Tintarev, N.: Effects of AI and logic-style explanations on users' decisions under different levels of uncertainty. ACM Trans. Interact. Intell. Syst. (2023). https://doi.org/10.1145/3588320. just Accepted
7. Cau, F.M., Hauptmann, H., Spano, L.D., Tintarev, N.: Supporting high-uncertainty decisions through AI and logic-style explanations. In: Proceedings of the 28th International Conference on Intelligent User Interfaces, IUI '23, pp. 251-263. Association for Computing Machinery, New York (2023). https://doi.org/10.1145/3581641.3584080
8. Cau, F.M., Mancosu, M.S., Mulas, F., Pilloni, P., Spano, L.D.: An interface for explaining the automatic classification of runners' trainings. In: Proceedings of the 24th International Conference on Intelligent User Interfaces: Companion, Marina del Ray, CA, USA, 16-20 March 2019, pp. 41–42. ACM (2019). https://doi.org/10.1145/3308557.3308664
9. Cheng, H., Yang, L., Liu, Z.: Survey on 3D hand gesture recognition. IEEE Trans. Circuits Syst. Video Technol. **26**(9), 1659–1673 (2015)
10. Cheng, J., Wang, Z.: Inside fiber: in-depth overview of the new reconciliation algorithm in react (2017). https://indepth.dev/inside-fiber-in-depth-overview-of-the-new-reconciliation-algorithm-in-react/. Accessed 29 May 2023
11. D3.js Contributors: D3.js: Data-Driven Documents. GitHub Repository (2023). https://github.com/d3/d3. Accessed 29 May 2023
12. Dessì, S., Spano, L.D.: DG3: exploiting gesture declarative models for sample generation and online recognition. Proc. ACM Hum.-Comput. Interact. **4**(EICS) (2020). https://doi.org/10.1145/3397870

13. Fanni, F.A., et al.: PAC-PAC: end user development of immersive point and click games. In: Malizia, A., Valtolina, S., Mørch, A.I., Serrano, A., Stratton, A. (eds.) End-User Development - 7th International Symposium, IS-EUD 2019, Hatfield, UK, July 10-12, 2019, Proceedings. Lecture Notes in Computer Science, vol. 11553, pp. 225–229. Springer (2019). https://doi.org/10.1007/978-3-030-24781-2_20

14. Frau, V., Cuccu, C., Spano, L.D.: Mr^2: a mixed reality interface for navigating medical records. In: Khamis, M., Sorce, S., Cauchard, J.R., Gentile, V. (eds.) Proceedings of the 8th ACM International Symposium on Pervasive Displays, PerDis 2019, Palermo, Italy, 12–14 June 2019, pp. 1–2. ACM (2019). https://doi.org/10.1145/3321335.3329684

15. Joint Task Force on Computing Curricula: Computer Science Curricula 2013. Association for Computing Machinery (ACM) (2013)

16. Kin, K., Hartmann, B., DeRose, T., Agrawala, M.: Proton++: a customizable declarative multitouch framework. In: Proceedings of the 25th Annual ACM Symposium on User Interface Software and Technology, UIST '12, pp. 477-486. Association for Computing Machinery, New York (2012). https://doi.org/10.1145/2380116.2380176

17. Kin, K., Hartmann, B., DeRose, T., Agrawala, M.: Proton: multitouch gestures as regular expressions. In: Proceedings of the SIGCHI Conference on Human Factors in Computing Systems, CHI '12, pp. 2885-2894. Association for Computing Machinery, New York (2012). https://doi.org/10.1145/2207676.2208694

18. LaViola, J.J., Jr., Kruijff, E., McMahan, R.P., Bowman, D., Poupyrev, I.P.: 3D User Interfaces: Theory and Practice. Addison-Wesley Professional, Boston (2017)

19. Ledda, E., Spano, L.D.: Applying long-short term memory recurrent neural networks for real-time stroke recognition. In: Markopoulos, P., Hu, J., Palanque, P.A. (eds.) EICS '21: ACM SIGCHI Symposium on Engineering Interactive Computing Systems, Virtual Event, The Netherlands, 8-11 June 2021, pp. 50–55. ACM (2021). https://doi.org/10.1145/3459926.3464754

20. Ledo, D., Houben, S., Vermeulen, J., Marquardt, N., Oehlberg, L., Greenberg, S.: Evaluation strategies for HCI toolkit research. In: Proceedings of the 2018 CHI Conference on Human Factors in Computing Systems, CHI '18, pp. 1-17. Association for Computing Machinery, New York (2018). https://doi.org/10.1145/3173574.3173610

21. Martin, A.: Entity systems are the future of MMOG development – part 1 (2007). http://t-machine.org/index.php/2007/09/03/entity-systems-are-the-future-of-mmog-development-part-1/

22. MediaPipe, G.: Hand landmarks detection guide (2023). https://developers.google.com/mediapipe/solutions/vision/hand_landmarker. Accessed 31 May 2023

23. Meloni, F., Perniciano, A., Cerniglia, G., Frau, V., Spano, L.D.: AR tutorialkit: an augmented reality toolkit to create tutorials. In: Bellucci, A., Russis, L.D., Díaz, P., Mørch, A.I., Fogli, D., Paternò, F. (eds.) Joint Proceedings of the Workshops, Work in Progress Demos and Doctoral Consortium at the IS-EUD 2023 co-located with the 9th International Symposium on End-User Development (IS-EUD 2023), Cagliari, Italy, June 6-8, 2023. CEUR Workshop Proceedings, vol. 3408. CEURWS.org (2023). https://ceur-ws.org/Vol-3408/short-s0-02.pdf

24. Menale, A., Mereu, J., Nuvole, C., Pannuti, L., Spano, E.M., Spano, L.D.: VMXR: a EUD environment for virtual merchandizing in XR. In: Bellucci, A., Russis, L.D., Díaz, P., Mørch, A.I., Fogli, D., Paternò, F. (eds.) Joint Proceedings of the Workshops, Work in Progress Demos and Doctoral Consortium at the IS-EUD 2023 co-located with the 9th International Symposium on End-User Development (IS-

EUD 2023), Cagliari, Italy, 6-8 June 2023. CEUR Workshop Proceedings, vol. 3408. CEUR-WS.org (2023). https://ceur-ws.org/Vol-3408/short-s0-03.pdf

25. Microsoft: Kinect for windows sdk 2.0 (2014). https://learn.microsoft.com/en-us/windows/apps/design/devices/kinect-for-windows. Accessed 31 May 2023
26. Microsoft Inc.: Mixed Reality Toolkit 3 (2023). https://learn.microsoft.com/en-us/windows/mixed-reality/mrtk-unity/mrtk3-overview/. Accessed 29 May 2023
27. Motion, L.: Leap motion JavaScript API (2021). https://developer-archive.leapmotion.com/documentation/javascript/index.html. Accessed 31 May 2023
28. Munzner, T.: Visualization Analysis and Design. CRC Press, Boca Raton (2014)
29. Myers, B., Hudson, S.E., Pausch, R.: Past, present, and future of user interface software tools. ACM Trans. Comput.-Hum. Interact. **7**(1), 3-28 (2000). https://doi.org/10.1145/344949.344959
30. Olsen, D.R.: Evaluating user interface systems research. In: Proceedings of the 20th Annual ACM Symposium on User Interface Software and Technology, UIST '07, pp. 251-258. Association for Computing Machinery, New York (2007). https://doi.org/10.1145/1294211.1294256
31. Spano, L.D.: Burdui (2023). https://github.com/davidespano/burdui. Accessed 29 May 2023
32. Spano, L.D., Cisternino, A., Paternò, F.: A compositional model for gesture definition. In: Winckler, M., Forbrig, P., Bernhaupt, R. (eds.) Human-Centered Software Engineering. Lecture Notes in Computer Science, vol. 7623, pp. 34–52. Springer, Berlin (2012). https://doi.org/10.1007/978-3-642-34347-6_3
33. Spano, L.D., Cisternino, A., Paternò, F., Fenu, G.: GestIT: a declarative and compositional framework for multiplatform gesture definition. In: Proceedings of the 5th ACM SIGCHI Symposium on Engineering Interactive Computing Systems, EICS '13, pp. 187-196. Association for Computing Machinery, New York (2013). https://doi.org/10.1145/2494603.2480307
34. Sutherland, I.E., Hodgman, G.W.: Reentrant polygon clipping. Commun. ACM **10**(10), 554–562 (1967). https://doi.org/10.1145/363162.363163
35. Vermeulen, J., Luyten, K., van den Hoven, E., Coninx, K.: Crossing the bridge over Norman's Gulf of execution: revealing feedforward's true identity. In: Proceedings of the SIGCHI Conference on Human Factors in Computing Systems, CHI '13, pp. 1931-1940. Association for Computing Machinery, New York (2013). https://doi.org/10.1145/2470654.2466255

On Land, at Sea, and in the Air: Human-Computer Interaction in Safety-Critical Spaces of Control

From One to Many, from Onsite to Remote: Control Rooms as Diverse Contexts of Use

Tilo Mentler[1]([✉]), Philippe Palanque[2], Kristof Van Laerhoven[3],
Margareta Holtensdotter Lützhöft[4], and Nadine Flegel[1]

[1] Trier University of Applied Sciences, Trier, Germany
{T.Mentler,N.Flegel}@inf.hochschule-trier.de
[2] Université Toulouse III - Paul Sabatier, Toulouse, France
palanque@irit.fr
[3] University of Siegen, Siegen, Germany
kvl@eti.uni-siegen.de
[4] Western Norway University of Applied Sciences, Bergen, Norway
Margareta.Holtensdotter.Luetzhoeft@hvl.no

Abstract. In many contexts, control rooms are safety-relevant and, from the point of view of HCI research, complex socio-technical systems. This article first summarizes the contributions of the IFIP WG 13.5 Workshop at INTERACT 2023 entitled "On Land, at Sea, and in the Air: Human-Computer Interaction in Safety-Critical Spaces of Control". The process and results of a group work phase during the workshop will then be discussed. A variety of examples (e.g. offshore operation centers, traffic light control rooms) and characteristics (e.g. level of automation, number of operators) in connection with control rooms were identified. Finally, it is pointed out that the diversity of usage contexts should not tempt us to lose sight of cross-domain perspectives, but rather to integrate them through appropriate levels of consideration.

Keywords: Safety-Critical Systems · Control Rooms · Cockpits · Usable Safety · Usable Security · Resilience · Dependability

1 Introduction

The part "on land, at sea, and in the air" in the title of [3] already indicates that "location[s] designed for an entity to be in control of a process" [2] can be found in many contexts and many forms. This diversity and its relevance for consideration in the context of HCI research is also illustrated by the workshop contributions summarized in Sect. 2 and the group activities in the context of the IFIP WG 13.5 Workshop at INTERACT 2023 entitled "On Land, at Sea, and in the Air: Human-Computer Interaction in Safety-Critical Spaces of Control" (see Sect. 3). Finally, conclusions with regard to domain-specific and cross-domain research on spaces of control are summarized.

A. Bramwell-Dicks et al. (Eds.): INTERACT 2023 Workshops, LNCS 14535, pp. 273–278, 2024.
https://doi.org/10.1007/978-3-031-61688-4_26

2   Workshop Contributions

The authors of the contribution "Towards a Pattern Language for Scalable Interaction Design in Control Rooms as Human-Centered Pervasive Computing Environments", Flegel, Poehler, Van Laerhoven, and Mentler [1], examine the use of reusable solutions to design interaction in control room environments. In most control rooms, demands on operators are increasing and at the same time there is often a lack in support of the operators' tasks, goals and well-being. The authors argue that new technology solutions in this area are often domain-specific and focus on specific functionalities only, so in answer to this they have developed a cross-domain pattern language for control rooms as pervasive computing environments within a human-centered design process. This pattern language consists of eight hierarchical levels, which combine the perspectives of human computer interaction and pervasive computing environments, and is made available for the public through a web-based pattern platform with feedback and comment functions. The contribution ends with a set of discussion points and an outlook on this project.

A paper contribution by Wallmyr and Sitompul entitled "On the Interaction between Construction Vehicles and Humans in Close Cooperation" [6], focuses on the interaction with an increasingly automated robotic workforce, which is typically also working in cooperation with humans for industrial applications. Using the specific example of the construction industry, they illustrate how workers in this industry tend to control specific vehicles such as excavators and mobile cranes as operators. The authors report that it can be observed that such vehicles are increasingly automated, which in turn leads to novel types of interactions where humans work together with robot-like machinery. The authors of this paper then analyze the examples of excavators and mobile cranes and discuss a set of observations, such as the importance of gestures, the need of systems to adapt to new types of actions, and the requirements of such systems being reliable and trustworthy.

In the contribution "Towards Modelling Cooperation in Future Maritime Remote-Control Center" by Saager, Harre, and Hahn [4], the authors identify that the emergence of Maritime Autonomous Systems and Remote-Control Centers poses challenges in understanding and managing cooperation among actors in harbor berthing maneuvers. This paper introduces systematic methods to analyze cooperation from a human factors perspective to provide a basis for investigating these challenges, and provides a review that highlights four key aspects: task analysis, information analysis, social network analysis, and analysis of artifacts and physical layout within the Remote Control Centre and on board the Maritime Autonomous Systems. The authors mention as future work the combination of these methods into an approach and the application of these to the specific use case, to proactively address the increasing complexity of cooperation between all actors involved in the control of Maritime Autonomous Systems. A further aim is to integrate these considerations into the design phase of future Remote Control Centres.

The fourth contribution, "Analyzing Online Videos to Create a List of User Interface Elements: A Case for OpenCrane Design System", by Sitompul, Park, and Alsos [5], presents an ongoing process of developing the OpenCrane design system, which aims to provide open-source user interface elements to build graphical user interfaces for operating cranes. Focusing on remote rubber-tired gantry cranes, which are also known as yard cranes and are used for moving containers, this contribution presents a novel method for creating a list of user interface elements by analyzing online videos published by the crane manufacturers that fully or partially show the crane's graphical user interfaces. By using 11 online videos published by three crane manufacturers that met the authors' selection criteria, the analysis of the online videos resulted in 29 extracted user interface elements. This method's feasibility was evaluated by comparing these results with 27 user interface elements that were elicited from a field study at a port that employed such remote cranes, displaying a significant overlap between the two sets of user interface elements, as well as some differences, indicating the need of both methods a complementary ones.

3 Group Work

This section first explains the workshop procedure. The results of a group work phase by the participants are then discussed.

3.1 Method

After the individual presentation of the workshop contributions summarized in the previous section, the workshop continued with approximately 4 h of group work. An online whiteboard tool (Miro) was used for this purpose because some of the participants were on site and others were connected remotely. First, examples of control rooms were compiled. These were then discussed in terms of their similarities and differences. Based on this, special characteristics and classification options were derived.

3.2 Results

As Fig. 1 shows, the online whiteboard was used extensively and numerous key points and notes were compiled. The following were cited as examples of control rooms or control room-like facilities (see Fig. 2):

- control rooms for wind turbines,
- drone control & UAV control rooms,
- electricity grid control rooms,
- "financial" control rooms,
- control rooms of fire and rescue forces,
- intensive care units,
- offshore operation centers,

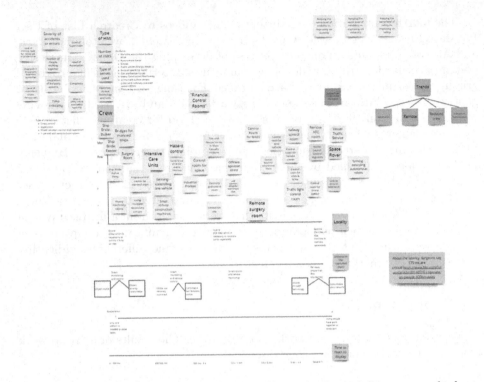

Fig. 1. Overview of the collected and organized contributions of the group work phase

- railway control rooms,
- rocket launch ground segments,
- satellite ground segments,
- ship bridges,
- traffic light control rooms.

   With regard to the comparability of these and other control room contexts, various criteria and characteristics were subsequently compiled, including:

- severity of accidents or errors,
- level of supervision,
- level of training need, for native use or professional,
- number of people working together,
- level of automation,
- integration in eco-system and extension possibilities,
- integration of 3rd party systems,
- complexity,
- level of investment (costs, resources),
- what is safety critical and (safety) supporting,
- time criticality,

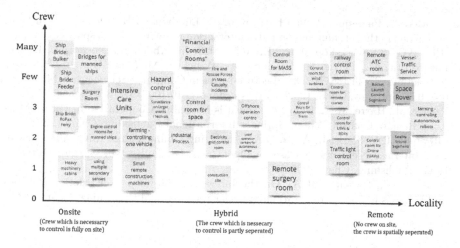

Fig. 2. Overview of the collected control room examples

- type of interaction (direct control, supervision, mixed between control and supervision, in parallel with autonomous system).

This revealed a variety of characteristics, for example with regard to the people involved (one or dozens) or the distance between the control room and the monitored processes (in the immediate vicinity or far away).

4   Conclusion

As can be seen from the workshop contributions and group work, the definition of control rooms as "location[s] designed for an entity to be in control of a process" [2] given at the beginning conceals a variety of specific usage contexts. This applies both with regard to the location (one? several? on site? far away?), the "entity" (one? several?) and many other factors such as the time frame. However, this finding should not lead to the assumption that only domain-specific considerations should be possible with regard to human-computer interaction. Rather, research should be intensified, especially with regard to cross-domain aspects - in recognition of the complexity and specificity of each domain.

References

1. Flegel, N., Poehler, J., Van Laerhoven, K., Mentler, T.: Towards a Pattern Language for Scalable Interaction Design in Control Rooms as Human-Centered Pervasive Computing Environments. Springer International Publishing, Cham (2023)
2. Hollnagel, E., Woods, D.D.: Joint Cognitive Systems: Foundations of Cognitive Systems Engineering. CRC Press, Boca Raton (2005)

3. Mentler, T., Palanque, P., Van Laerhoven, K., Lützhöft, M.H., Flegel, N.: On land, at sea, and in the air: human-computer interaction in safety-critical spaces of control: IFIP WG 13.5 workshop at INTERACT 2023. In: Abdelnour Nocera, J., Kristin Larusdottir, M., Petrie, H., Piccinno, A., Winckler, M. (eds.) Human-Computer Interaction – INTERACT 2023. Lecture Notes in Computer Science, vol. 14145, pp. 657–661. Springer, Cham (2023). https://doi.org/10.1007/978-3-031-42293-5_89
4. Saager, M., Harre, M.C., Hahn, A.: Towards Modelling Cooperation in Future Maritime Remote-Control Center. Springer International Publishing, Cham (2023)
5. Sitompul, T.A., Park, J., Alsos, O.A.: Analyzing Online Videos to Create a List of User Interface Elements: A Case for OpenCrane Design System. Springer International Publishing, Cham (2023)
6. Wallmyr, M., Sitompul, T.A.: On the Interaction between Construction Vehicles and Humans in Close Cooperation. Springer International Publishing, Cham (2023)

Towards a Pattern Language for Scalable Interaction Design in Control Rooms as Human-Centered Pervasive Computing Environments

Nadine Flegel[1]([⊠])[iD], Jonas Pöhler[2][iD], Kristof Van Laerhoven[2][iD], and Tilo Mentler[1][iD]

[1] Trier University of Applied Sciences, Schneidershof, 54293 Trier, Germany
{n.flegel,mentler}@hochschule-trier.de
[2] University of Siegen, Adolf-Reichwein-Straße 2a, 57076 Siegen, Germany

Abstract. Control rooms are central for well-being and safety of people in many domains (e.g., emergency response, ship bridge, public utilities). In most of these domains, demands on operators are increasing. At the same time tasks, goals and well-being of the operators is rarely proactively supported. New technology solutions are often domain-specific and focus on specific functionalities. What is urgently needed to meet the increasing demands are reusable solutions. We develop a cross-domain pattern language for control rooms as pervasive computing environments within a human-centered design process. The pattern language consists of eight hierarchical levels, which combine the perspectives of human computer interaction (HCI) and pervasive computing environments. It will be made available for the public through a web-based pattern platform with feedback and comment functions. This research will contribute to a better understanding of suitable interaction paradigms for control rooms and safety-critical pervasive computing environments.

Keywords: Pattern Language · Design Patterns · Safety-Critical Systems · Control Rooms · Interaction Design · Pervasive Computing Environments

1 Introduction

Control rooms are central to the well-being and safety of people. Whether it's everyday things like electricity, water and gas supply, the transport of people or goods (aircraft cockpit, ship bridge, etc.) or emergencies and accidents where immediate medical help is needed, control room operators bear major responsibility for monitoring and controlling such processes under extremely stressful conditions (e.g., decision-making in short time periods). While pervasive technologies (e.g., wearables, smart home solutions) are increasingly becoming part of private and professional life, where "people and devices are mobile and

© IFIP International Federation for Information Processing 2024
Published by Springer Nature Switzerland AG 2024
A. Bramwell-Dicks et al. (Eds.): INTERACT 2023 Workshops, LNCS 14535, pp. 279–291, 2024.
https://doi.org/10.1007/978-3-031-61688-4_27

use various wireless networking technologies to discover and access services and devices in their vicinity" [24], state of the art control rooms are still character-ized by stationary work on single-user workstations with several screens [13,23]. The different types of control rooms (see Sect. 2) mentioned in the beginning, appear different at first, but from a socio-technical perspective, generic problems can be identified that occur in most domains (e.g., limited cooperation activi-ties, information overload) (see Sect. 4). As demands on operators are increasing (e.g., private photo-voltaic systems influence energy grids, number of emergen-cies increase due to demographic and climate change) reusable approaches are needed so that it is not necessary to start from scratch in each domain. So far, only a few approaches exist that deal with "smart control rooms" [20,23] or "control rooms as pervasive computing environments" from a holistic perspec-tive [14]. New insights in the design of scalable interaction paradigms where safety critical operation processes are not only pivotal on the systems level inte-gration (e.g., in the control rooms' digital processes), but extended to the human operators and their interaction are required.

The aim of our research is to develop a cross-domain pattern language for scalable interaction design in control rooms as pervasive computing environments following a human-centered design process. A strict methodology is followed to gather and select candidate design patterns, following an evolution process with feedback loops [28]. The patterns are based on tasks, workflows and operators' needs in a variety of control room domains with respect to daily routine and critical situations, different levels of automation as well as individual and coop-erative work. The pattern language is structured hierarchically on eight levels and will be made available for the public within a web-based platform with feed-back functions for evaluation, development and discussion. This research will contribute to a better understanding of suitable interaction paradigms for con-trol rooms and safety-critical pervasive computing environments in general (e.g., intensive care units or operating rooms).

The paper is structured as follows: In Sect. 2 we take a look on control rooms and pattern languages in safety-critical domains and pervasive computing envi-ronments. In Sect. 3 we provide details on the development process of the pattern language. Results (see Sect. 4) are presented focusing on the structure of the pat-tern language and example patterns. This is followed by a discussion in Sect. 5. Finally, plans for future work are presented (see Sect. 6).

2   Related Work

The taxonomy of Mentler et al. [22] provides a differentiation of control room types focusing on location and number of operators acting in parallel (see Fig. 1). It points out a key difference between control rooms at "fixed" locations (e.g., emergency response, public utilities) and "mobile" control rooms (e.g., ship bridges, aircraft cockpits). In all types generic HCI-related issues can be found (e.g., monitoring of process states, decision making, etc.).

Pattern languages, in terms of collections of related patterns, have been defined for different purposes (e.g. website development; cf. [17]). With respect

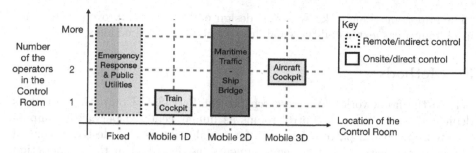

Fig. 1. Types of control rooms according to location and number of operators (Illustration based on [22]. Highlighted areas (green, yellow, dark grey) indicate the 3 domains considered in this study. (Color figure online)

to control rooms up to the authors' knowledge, there exists no specific pattern language for interaction design in control rooms from a holistic viewpoint. Romero-Gómez and Díaz [29] developed a pattern language to assist the design of alarm visualizations for operating control systems with 29 design patterns.

With respect to pervasive computing environments or ubiquitous computing research, there have been several suggestions and studies. For example, Chung et al. [5] developed a ubiquitous computing pattern language consisting of 45 patterns and addressing 4 topics (application domains, physical-virtual spaces, privacy management, fluid interaction). One of the few safety-specific pattern languages, in this case for frontline firefighters, has been presented by Denef and Keyson [9]. Wilde et al. [31] argue that long-range acceptance of design patterns it might be difficult but are convinced that developers of pervasive computing environments will require and refer to them in the future to a greater degree. Knote et al. [19] state that research on this topic is focussed rather on aspects like adaptivity or context-awareness than on "transparency, trust, privacy and informational self-determination". Using the example of personal data collection, one of the design pattern they describe is called "emergency button": "After pressing the [easily accessible] button, the system stops immediately collecting and using personal data" [19].

With respect to safety-critical domains, research on design pattern is mainly devoted to hardware- or software-related technical reliability [3]. Pap and Petri [27] describe one design pattern for safety-critical user interfaces based on the software engineering pattern Model-View-Controller (MVC). Therefore, it is related rather to software architecture than to interaction design. Grill und Blauhut [18] mention a pattern repository for user interfaces in safety-critical environments but no further information or public access has been provided since then. One of the more fine-grained approaches is presented by Mahemoff et al. [21] and Connelly et al. [6]. Their pattern language consists of 19 design patterns in 4 categories (task management, task execution, information, machine control). So far, design patterns with special consideration of scalability have been primarily related to software engineering issues like real-time applications or specific programming frameworks [11,25]. As Kaplan and Crawford [7] state:

"The important thing to know is that design patterns can improve performance in all four areas [extensibility, scalability, reliability, and timeliness]".

3   Methods

Within the framework of the research project PervaSafe Computing, which is dedicated to the topic of control rooms as human-centered pervasive computing environments, a pattern language for scalable interaction design in control rooms as pervasive computing environments, as described in the introduction (see Sect. 1), is under development. Subsequently, the development of the design patterns and the authoring process of the pattern language are presented.

3.1   Development of the Design Patterns

The collection of single design patterns is composed following the pattern evolution process by Reiners et al. [28] in which the patterns pass different states (just created, under consideration, pattern candidate, approved). According to Reiners et al. [28] the design patterns are derived from three sources:

- **Derived from project:** Patterns are directly derived from results of several studies conducted in the project as well as literature on control rooms focusing on HCI-related problems. In order to gain a common understanding of control rooms as future pervasive computing environments as well as to identify patterns (behaviours, needs, tasks, workflows) and individual variations, workshops at three different control rooms (emergency response, public utilities and ship bridge simulator) from two different types of control rooms (see Sect. 2) were conducted, in which challenges in the daily life of the operators according to the components of an interactive system [26] were analyzed and conceivable scenarios for future control rooms (e.g., autonomously carries out identified tasks, filters messages and forwards them to other operators if an operator is busy or stressed at the time, ensures that a message reaches the operator, suggests actions to maintain the operator's health) were discussed. In addition, 9 control room operators were asked about their opinion about the ideal control room using an interaction vocabulary and a free description [15] and an online-survey on digitalization in control rooms with 155 control room operators of the three aforementioned different control room domains [16].
- **Adapted to project:** Well-known patterns in the field of software engineering and software development [1,2] are explored by the project team, because so far, design patterns with special consideration of scalability have been primarily related to software engineering issues (see Sect. 2). The patterns are reviewed whether these are related to scalability and if they could be transferred to the context.
- **Project-external:** As some approaches to interaction design addressing parts of the described challenges (see Sect. 1) already exists for future pervasive computing environments (see Sect. 2), patterns from related pattern

collections (e.g., smart spaces, ubiquitous computing, pervasive computing) are adopted after reviewing whether these are related to the topic. The extent to which the patterns are suitable for safety-critical domains must be examined.

The pattern structure is based on the pattern language model by Borchers [4]. The pattern layout contains a name, an illustration showing the current problem, a context, problem, examples, a solution and a diagram which explains the solution. The patterns and the pattern language are developed within a human-centered design process in close cooperation with experts, therefore tools and formats for online and in-person evaluations, such as workshops, surveys, etc., are necessary. Pattern cards were chosen as a form of presentation reminiscent of playing cards, which makes it possible to present graphic and textual elements coherently. These pattern cards will be specifically designed for the control room domain. They are created for presenting, discussing and structuring design patterns within interdisciplinary workgroups.

3.2 Authoring Process of the Pattern Language

The collection of single design patterns needs to be organized in terms of relationships, purposes, scopes, levels or even contradictions in order to be comprehensible and an efficient aid for designers. The design patterns form the basis for the development of a pattern language. The authoring process consists of the following methods:

- **Pattern Hierarchy:** The design patterns are arranged hierarchically at different abstraction levels, which are derived from the concept of "control rooms as human-centered pervasive computing environments". The patterns are collected and organised in an online whiteboard.
- **Pattern Management Tool:** The design patterns, cards and pattern language will be made available to the public via an web-based interactive design pattern platform with tools for pattern management [10]. On the one hand, the platform should enable the authors of the patterns to manage them, on the other hand, it should be a living platform that is used throughout the entire development process in order to obtain feedback from experts in control room domains through appropriate feedback functions.

4 Results

In the following, first results of the development process are presented with selected design patterns as examples.

4.1 Development of the Design Patterns

In the following, two patterns of the aforementioned sources in Sect. 3.1 are introduced as well as two pattern cards.

The pattern "Ensure that a message/alarm reaches the operator." (see Table 1) is a guideline which is derived from interviews with control room operators and literature describing the problem of alarm and information management in control rooms (e.g., [8, 32]).

Table 1. Design pattern derived from project: Ensure that a message/alarm reaches the operator

Ensure that a message/alarm reaches the operator.	
Context	During a work shift, the operator has to deal with a large number of messages and alarms
Problem	In most control rooms, the visualization of messages and alarms is tied to stationary workstations. If the operator moves away from the workstation or does not have the screens in focus, messages and alarms can be lost. This can cost valuable time and, in the worst case, lead to accidents and disasters
Examples	When an operator goes to the coffee kitchen, messages and alarms are no longer in view or the person can only see from a distance if something is flashing on the workstation/public screen. In some cases, this is currently solved by placing another stationary screen for important messages and alarms in the coffee kitchen
Solution	It should be ensured and verified that operators perceive relevant information. The targeted presentation of messages and alarms should be made dependent on various factors related to the operator: location, focus, activity, status, resources. A check whether the person addressed has perceived the alarm and not just "blindly" acknowledged it should be automatically derived from these factors

The pattern "Load and State Balancer" described in Table 2 and Fig. 2 has been derived from software engineering patterns for scalability in terms of performance and technical reliability. In this context, scalable interaction design means that, on the one hand, users must be able to use a variety of possible interaction options with wearable, mobile, and stationary devices efficiently and securely. On the other hand, it means that users must still be able to cope with the increasing number of alarms and other messages by filtering, summarizing and automated processing.

The design pattern cards (see Fig. 2) contain the name and a graphical representation on the "front" side of the design pattern. The "reverse" side shows further information (problem and solution description). The graphical representation is developed systematically. A basic layout was developed for all design patterns. It depicts a control room with three control room operators on duty. Although the analysis of the context of use showed that the number of operators

Table 2. Design pattern adapted to project from the field of software engineering: Load and State Balancer.

Load and State Balancer	
Context	The flow of information is independent of the activities and states of the operator
Problem	Information is provided to many control room operators in different ways at the same time ignoring their individual current workload or affective state
Examples	While a human operator is for instance highly concentrated on solving an urgent problem in the control room, less relevant alarms that cannot be dealt with at the moment are still demanding attention through audio messages or via screen flashing
Solution	Control room operators' cognitive load and affective state (stress in particular) are modelled on a operator-worn computer. A dispatcher determines which operator will handle the request based on different policies

varies both within a control room, due to different shift staffing, and between control rooms, due to different tasks and responsibilities, this simplified representation can address both individual and cooperative aspects of the work.

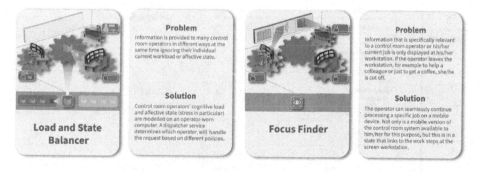

Fig. 2. Excerpt of the pattern language showing the patterns "Load and State Balancer" and "Focus Finder" in the format of design pattern cards.

4.2 Authoring Process of the Pattern Language

In the following, the results of the hierarchical structuring of the pattern language and the development of the web-based design pattern platform are presented.

The structure of the pattern language is based on the hierarchy concept of patterns by Reiners et al. [28]. The structure contains eight levels of abstraction (see Fig. 3). The four highest levels build the foundation of the pattern language. The Vision-Level contains the concept of "control rooms as human-centered pervasive computing environments" [14], which contains that the control room is "aware of operators' activities, cognitive load, and affective state as well as workflows and modes of operation." The challenge of this concept is to combine the research perspectives of the fields human computer interaction and pervasive computing. Therefore, the next level is devided in the perspectives on control rooms as human-centered environments as well as pervasive computing environments. The next two levels contain components of the two sub-visions. For human computer interaction the components are according to frameworks for the deisgn of interactive systems (e.g., [26]) tasks, operators, interactive system, organization and environment. Components of the pervasive computing environment are according to Satyanarayanan [12,30], e.g., mobility support, invisibility, localized scalability, context-awareness and user intent.

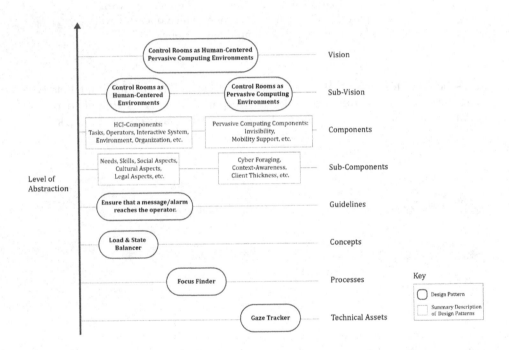

Fig. 3. Draft of a hierarchy scheme of the pattern language for scalable interaction design in control rooms with example patterns (based on the scheme of Reiners et al. [28]).

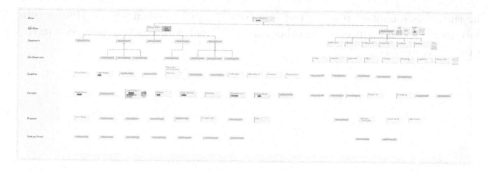

Fig. 4. Collection and hierarchical structure of the pattern language for scalable interaction design in control rooms in an online-whiteboard.

The next level contains guidelines for wide-ranging problems. One example is presented in Table 1, others are for instance that the control room should support the cooperation between operators, the operators' health and well-being and take into account the skills and states of the operators. The following level is about concepts like the "Load and State Balancer" introduced in Table 2. An example of the next level about processes, the "Focus Finder" is illustrated in the pattern card format in Fig. 2. The last level are technical asstes, important for pervasive computing environments, like the "Gaze Tracker", which is neccessary for patterns in the higher levels, for instance the "Focus Finder". At the current stage of development the pattern language consists of 80 patterns, organized in the online-whiteboard (see Fig. 4).

The web-based design pattern platform contains all patterns in the compact card format for a quick view (see Fig. 5) as well as a detailed view of the entire pattern layout. It is possible to rate a pattern and add comments. The rating is based on two questions: (1) How understandable is the pattern? (2) How relevant is the pattern?.

5   Discussion

Several discussion points arise regarding the vision of the control room as a human-centered pervasive computing environment, the different control room types, the development of a living pattern language and the transferability to related domains.

Is it Possible to Combine the Perspectives of HCI and Pervasive Computing Completely? In the development process, it is important to explore the relationships between patterns, with particular attention to patterns associated with the different perspectives. It is conceivable that some patterns contradict each other in their solutions.

Is the Pattern Language the Same for all Control Room Types? More specifically, it needs to be investigated whether the pattern language also differs in the mobile control room types (see Sect. 2) and to what extent the pattern language can be transferred to other safety-critical domains (e.g. surgeons in the operating room)?

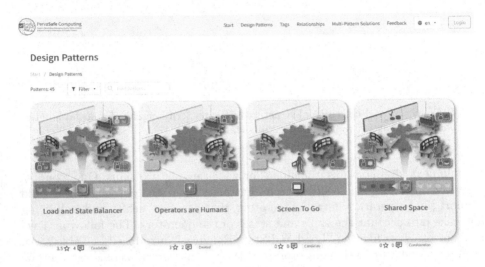

Fig. 5. Screenshot of the web-based design pattern library.

How can the Pattern Language be Designed in a Living Way? The question is whether the web-based platform and its functions to collect feedback can be used for evaluations and whether experts use it to give feedback.

6   Future Work

Within the framework of the project PervaSafe Computing, a wearable control room assistance system is under development, which serves as a central component of the vision of a control room as a "human-centered pervasive computing environment". The assistance system models the control room operators' cognitive load and affective state to influence information flow to the operator, which is guided by the work-related design patterns [14].

Future work on the pattern language includes the evaluation of individual design patterns with the help of the design pattern cards as well as the overall structuring of the entire pattern language (e.g., hierarchy, levels, relationships). For this purpose, expert interviews are planned with experts in the field of pattern languages, safety-critical HCI, pervasive computing environments and control rooms.

Acknowledgements. This project is funded by the Deutsche Forschungsgemeinschaft (DFG, German Research Foundation) - 425868829 and is part of Priority Program SPP2199 Scalable Interaction Paradigms for Pervasive Computing Environments.

References

1. Ahluwalia, K.S.: Scalability design patterns. In: Proceedings of the 14th Conference on Pattern Languages of Programs, PLOP '07. Association for Computing Machinery, New York (2007). https://doi.org/10.1145/1772070.1772073
2. Ardagna, C.A., Damiani, E., Frati, F., Rebeccani, D., Ughetti, M.: Scalability patterns for platform-as-a-service. In: 2012 IEEE Fifth International Conference on Cloud Computing, pp. 718–725 (2012). https://doi.org/10.1109/CLOUD.2012.41
3. Armoush, A., Kowalewski, S.: Safety recommendations for safety-critical design patterns (2009)
4. Borchers, J.O.: A pattern approach to interaction design. In: Proceedings of the 3rd Conference on Designing Interactive Systems: Processes, Practices, Methods, and Techniques, DIS '00, pp. 369-378. Association for Computing Machinery, New York (2000). https://doi.org/10.1145/347642.347795
5. Chung, E.S., Hong, J.I., Lin, J., Prabaker, M.K., Landay, J.A., Liu, A.L.: Development and evaluation of emerging design patterns for ubiquitous computing. In: Proceedings of the 5th Conference on Designing Interactive Systems: Processes, Practices, Methods, and Techniques, DIS '04, pp. 233-242. Association for Computing Machinery, New York (2004). https://doi.org/10.1145/1013115.1013148
6. Connelly, S., Burmeister, J., MacDonald, A., Hussey, A.: Extending and evaluating a pattern language for safety-critical user interfaces. In: Proceedings of the Sixth Australian Workshop on Safety Critical Systems and Software - Volume 3, SCS '01, pp. 39-49. Australian Computer Society, Inc., AUS (2001)
7. Crawford, W., Kaplan, J.: J2EE Design Patterns: Patterns in the Real World. O'Reilly Media Inc., Sebastopol (2003)
8. Dadashi, N., Golightly, D., Sharples, S.: Seeing the woods for the trees: the problem of information inefficiency and information overload on operator performance. Cogn. Technol. Work 19(4), 561–570 (2017). https://doi.org/10.1007/s10111-017-0451-1
9. Denef, S., Keyson, D.: Talking about implications for design in pattern language. In: Proceedings of the SIGCHI Conference on Human Factors in Computing Systems, CHI '12, pp. 2509-2518. Association for Computing Machinery, New York (2012). https://doi.org/10.1145/2207676.2208418
10. Deng, J., Kemp, E., Todd, E.G.: Managing UI pattern collections. In: Proceedings of the 6th ACM SIGCHI New Zealand Chapter's International Conference on Computer-Human Interaction: Making CHI Natural, CHINZ '05, pp. 31-38. Association for Computing Machinery, New York (2005). https://doi.org/10.1145/1073943.1073951
11. Douglass, B.P.: Real-Time Design Patterns: Robust Scalable Architecture for Real-time Systems. Addison-Wesley Professional, Boston (2003)
12. Ebling, M.R., Want, R.: Satya revisits "pervasive computing: Vision and challenges". IEEE Pervasive Comput. 16(3), 20–23 (2017). https://doi.org/10.1109/MPRV.2017.2940965
13. Flegel, N., Pick, C., Mentler, T.: A gaze-supported mouse interaction design concept for state-of-the-art control rooms. In: Ahram, T., Taiar, R., Groff, F. (eds.) Human Interaction, Emerging Technologies and Future Applications IV, pp. 208–216. Springer, Cham (2021). https://doi.org/10.1007/978-3-030-74009-2_26
14. Flegel, N., Poehler, J., Van Laerhoven, K., Mentler, T.: Towards control rooms as human-centered pervasive computing environments. In: Sense, Feel, Design:

INTERACT 2021 IFIP TC 13 Workshops, Bari, Italy, August 30 - September 3, 2021, Revised Selected Papers, pp. 329-344. Springer-Verlag, Berlin, Heidelberg (2021). https://doi.org/10.1007/978-3-030-98388-8_29

15. Flegel, N., Pöhler, J., Van Laerhoven, K., Mentler, T.: "i want my control room to be...": on the aesthetics of interaction in a safety-critical working environment. In: Proceedings of Mensch Und Computer 2022, MuC '22, pp. 488-492. Association for Computing Machinery, New York (2022). https://doi.org/10.1145/3543758.3547562

16. Flegel, N., Wessel, D., Pöhler, J., Van Laerhoven, K., Mentler, T.: Autonomy and safety: a quantitative study with control room operators on affinity for technology interaction and wish for pervasive computing solutions. In: Extended Abstracts of the 2023 CHI Conference on Human Factors in Computing Systems, CHI EA '23. Association for Computing Machinery, New York (2023). https://doi.org/10.1145/3544549.3585822

17. Graham, I.: A Pattern Language for Web Usability. Addison-Wesley Longman Publishing Co., Inc., USA (2002)

18. Grill, T., Blauhut, M.: Design patterns applied in a user interface design (UID) process for safety critical environments (SCEs). In: Holzinger, A. (ed.) HCI and Usability for Education and Work, pp. 459–474. Springer, Berlin Heidelberg, Berlin, Heidelberg (2008). https://doi.org/10.1007/978-3-540-89350-9_32

19. Knote, R., Baraki, H., Söllner, M., Geihs, K., Leimeister, J.M.: From requirement to design patterns for ubiquitous computing applications. In: Proceedings of the 21st European Conference on Pattern Languages of Programs, EuroPlop '16. Association for Computing Machinery, New York (2016). https://doi.org/10.1145/3011784.3011812

20. Koskinen, H., Laarni, J., Norros, L.: Activity-driven design approach to the novel control room environments. In: European Conference on Cognitive Ergonomics: Designing beyond the Product — Understanding Activity and User Experience in Ubiquitous Environments, ECCE '09, VTT Technical Research Centre of Finland, FI-02044 VTT, FIN (2009)

21. Mahemoff, M., Hussey, A., Johnston, L.: Pattern-based reuse of successful designs: usability of safety-critical systems. In: Proceedings 2001 Australian Software Engineering Conference, pp. 31–39 (2001). https://doi.org/10.1109/ASWEC.2001.948495

22. Mentler, T., Palanque, P., Harrison, M.D., van Laerhoven, K., Masci, P.: Control rooms from a human-computer interaction perspective. In: Ardito, C., et al. (eds.) Sense, Feel, Design, pp. 281–289. Springer International Publishing, Cham (2022). https://doi.org/10.1007/978-3-030-98388-8_25

23. Mentler, T., Rasim, T., Müßiggang, M., Herczeg, M.: Ensuring usability of future smart energy control room systems. Energy Inform. 1(1), 167–182 (2018)

24. Mezgár, I., Grabner-Kräuter, S.: Role of privacy and trust in mobile business social networks. In: Handbook of Research on Business Social Networking: Organizational, Managerial, and Technological Dimensions, pp. 287–313. IGI Global, USA (2012)

25. Nikolov, I.: Scala Design Patterns: Design Modular, Clean, and Scalable Applications by Applying Proven Design Patterns in Scala. Packt Publishing Ltd., Birmingham (2018)

26. Palanque, P.: POISE: a framework for designing perfect interactive systems with and for imperfect people. In: Ardito, C., et al. (eds.) Human-Computer Interaction - INTERACT 2021, pp. 39–59. Springer International Publishing, Cham (2021). https://doi.org/10.1007/978-3-030-85623-6_5

27. Pap, Z., Petri, D.: A design pattern of the user interface of safety-critical systems. In: International PhD Students' Workshop Control & Information Technology (2001)
28. Reiners, R., Halvorsrud, R., Eide, A.W., Pohl, D.: An approach to evolutionary design pattern engineering. In: Proceedings of the 19th Conference on Pattern Languages of Programs, PLoP '12. The Hillside Group, USA (2012)
29. Romero-Gómez, R., Díaz, P.: Towards a design pattern language to assist the design of alarm visualizations for operating control systems. In: Caporarello, L., Cesaroni, F., Giesecke, R., Missikoff, M. (eds.) Digitally Supported Innovation, pp. 249–264. Springer International Publishing, Cham (2016). https://doi.org/10.1007/978-3-319-40265-9_18
30. Satyanarayanan, M.: Pervasive computing: vision and challenges. IEEE Pers. Commun. 8(4), 10–17 (2001)
31. Wilde, A.G., Bruegger, P., Hirsbrunner, B.: An overview of human-computer interaction patterns in pervasive systems. In: 2010 International Conference on User Science and Engineering (i-USEr), pp. 145–150 (2010). https://doi.org/10.1109/IUSER.2010.5716740
32. Wilkinson, J., Lucas, D.: Better alarm handling-a practical application of human factors. Meas. Control 35(2), 52–54 (2002)

On the Interaction Between Construction Vehicles and Humans in Close Cooperation

Markus Wallmyr[1] and Taufik Akbar Sitompul[2(✉)]

[1] CrossControl AB, Uppsala, Sweden
`markus.wallmyr@crosscontrol.com`
[2] Department of Design, Norwegian University of Science and Technology, Trondheim, Norway
`taufik.a.sitompul@ntnu.no`

Abstract. In the spirit of the Czech translation of the word "robota" as the forced labor or worker, this paper discusses the interaction with increasingly automated robotic workforce working in cooperation with humans for industrial applications, for example, the construction industry. Nowadays, workers in the construction industry control their vehicles as operators. As their vehicles get increasingly automated, development leads to new types of interactions, where humans work together with robot-like machinery. We propose that such development will fundamentally change the type of interaction and decision-support systems needed to collaborate with increasingly automated construction vehicles.

Keywords: robotics vehicles · construction vehicles · collaborative interaction · human-machine teaming

1 Introduction

Robotic systems are common in the assembly lines of industrial production plants. Recent advancements are starting to take them out of fenced areas, and into acting safely and collaborative with humans [14,22]. However, robotic systems are less common in other industrial settings, such as construction sites, mining, forestry, or agriculture. Nevertheless, the machines used today are becoming increasingly automated, computer-controlled, and robot-like. An example that illustrates this is the combine harvester used in agriculture, which successfully changed the proportion of farmers in the US workforce from 38% to 3% within a century [4]. These machines have evolved from being only mechanical and directly controlled, to using systems with increasing levels of automation and computerization. Their systems adjust production and movement speed to supply the requested quality and level of harvesting using sensors, cameras, and image analysis [3].

Research prototypes of even more robotic vehicles are presented in both academia and industry, where robotic systems have demonstrated the potential

© IFIP International Federation for Information Processing 2024
Published by Springer Nature Switzerland AG 2024
A. Bramwell-Dicks et al. (Eds.): INTERACT 2023 Workshops, LNCS 14535, pp. 292–298, 2024.
https://doi.org/10.1007/978-3-031-61688-4_28

benefits for certain tasks, for example, mass excavation and material loading [1, 20], weed control [19], fertilizing or moving [12], wall building [7], mining [11], and material transportation [23]. However, despite the huge benefits of using automated machinery, Pedersen et al. [13] conclude that more complex tasks are nearly impossible to automate due to the required accuracy of the specification of the task. Humans are still more versatile and better at adapting to changing conditions, while machines still must be programmed specifically for each task [6]. Therefore, it is of interest to investigate the interplay between humans and robots fulfilling tasks in collaboration by utilizing each other's strengths.

2   Evolving Interaction

The interaction with manual or semi-automatic systems that we have nowadays is done via input devices, such as joysticks, buttons, pedals, and output devices, such as instruments, displays, and audio cues for specific events [24]. As systems get more automated, operators spend increasingly more time monitoring and ensuring system performance than performing actual operation [16]. The increasingly automated operation performed by the robotic system will likely also require higher coordination between the robotic system and another human. Operators need to know what the machine is doing now, why the machine is doing that, and what the machine will do after that.

One scenario is that the human is traveling with the machine, monitoring and assisting the machine or performing parallel tasks. Here, there are opportunities for information exchange that could convey the robot's understanding of the world and its intentions using, for example, using augmented reality or interactive windscreens [18], as well as other embodied means of communication such as haptics [9] or acoustic communication [10]. Different forms of instruments and display information would also be beneficial when interacting with highly autonomous systems. Displays are useful for showing complex and granular information, as well as allowing input to the system using touch control. In addition, the robotic system and humans can share a common visualization of the work area and the task to be performed, in the same way humans use blueprints and sketches. Display-based systems can also be used to communicate and be constantly informed on the status of the vehicle, such as its position and work plan.

More embodied interaction with humans, including voice, gesture, facial expressions, etc., is more common in personal or professional service robots [21], such as the rich interaction with ASIMO [15] or ERICA [8]. Moreover, Sheridan [17], in his list of status and challenges for human-robot interaction, concludes that the intimate collaboration with humans in manipulation tasks, as well as having mutual models between humans and computers is still a research challenge. Villani et al. [22] also highlight that collaborative robots in the industry are still underused.

It is not uncommon that industrial robotic systems target fully automated systems, which do not require any human intervention. Although this approach could potentially improve productivity, Goodrich et al. [5] note that it is likely that the usefulness and safety of robots in many of these domains would increase if human-robotic interaction considerations are included in their design. Nowadays, a machine operator at a construction site might work together with one or more human workers. They collaborate to accomplish a task using verbal and gestural communication, which is critical to perform the task efficiently. Following are two examples that we derived from our field studies:

2.1   Excavators

The first example is from a construction site, where an excavator and a ground worker are preparing a trench for underground piping (see Fig. 1). The excavator does the heavy lifting of moving and distributing gravel material to make a flat base in the trench. The co-worker works in the trench to check the actual height and correct slope, instructs the excavator operator where to pour additional gravel, and makes fine-grained adjustments. The excavator operator must pay attention to the location of the ground worker, to avoid pouring gravel over the ground worker, or hitting the ground worker with the bucket when he steps in to make a measurement. When more gravel is needed, the ground worker makes a waving gesture to indicate that more gravel is needed and points out where to pour the gravel. As long as the waving continues, more gravel is poured. There is even communication on increasing or decreasing the amount poured

Fig. 1. The picture taken from the cabin of an excavator, which shows the ground worker giving instructions to the excavator operator about where and how much the gravel should be poured.

by alternating waving behavior. Upon oral communication between the ground worker and the excavator operator, the operator moves the excavator's boom away from the ground worker to avoid the risk of injury, but also to get the operator's cabin closer to the worker.

2.2   Mobile Cranes

The second example of collaborative work between the construction vehicle and human workers is a mobile crane working at a construction site (see Fig. 2). The main task shown in Fig. 2 is to lift prefabricated wall panels from a truck to the correct location at the property. In general, how the communication is done in this context follows a similar pattern as in the previous excavator example, where the crane operator and the two ground workers communicating with gestures. Moreover, before lifting the wall panels from the truck, the operator monitors that the straps carrying the wall panels are properly attached to the crane wire. The operator can also see whether the ground workers at the site are ready for the next wall by observing their work. Upon unloading the wall panel, there is also a collaboration between the ground workers and the operator in placing the wall panel. The ground workers advice the operator to make a small movement needed to place the wall element at the exact right location. The ground workers are also actively moving the wall panel by rotating and pushing it to the right place.

Fig. 2. The picture taken from the cabin of a mobile crane, which shows two ground workers ensuring the prefabricated wall panel is placed correctly.

3   Discussions

The two examples presented in Sects. 2.1 and 2.2 can be used as the scenarios to discuss the interaction between robotic systems and humans. For example, replacing the machine controlled by an operator with a fully robotic system that would aid the human worker in fulfilling the same task. In both examples, it is obvious that gestures are the crucial type of communication. The robotic system needs to detect the gestures, understand the meaning of the gestures, and determine whether such gestures were intended for the robot or someone else at the worksite. The robotic system must also be aware of the operations performed by the human and be able to collaborate with human workers, such as the case of the fine-grained interaction during the placement of wall panels (see Fig. 2). In addition, vehicles nowadays also perform tasks that were not specified when they were manufactured [2]. Therefore, to provide full support at the workplace and natural interaction, the system might also need to interpret instructions to do new types of actions.

To allow the operator work closely with the machine, the system must also be reliable and trustworthy. This involves safety and security standards, as well as a well-implemented interaction preventing dangerous situations. For example, the robot stops its movement when humans are in close vicinity or performs more subtle communication, such as slowing movement or changing the engine's revolution per minute (RPM), which indicates that the machine is aware of the human nearby and intention of action. Since the context is in the professional setting, one option is to establish new types of interaction different from the ones currently used between human workers and operators. Although this could be a plausible solution, it would also require a lot of training for the involved users.

Moreover, it is also expected that more work would be increasingly performed by robots, for example, by having a robot perform the tasks of the ground worker as well. Such a case would require even more critical decision-making from the robotic system, such as adapting and managing unforeseen problems, occurring obstacles, or adjusting to changing conditions. This also puts requirements on critical interpretation, decision making, and communication by the robotic system. A human co-worker might want the robotic system to do something that might be out of the robot's physical capability or something that might harm the robot or its surroundings. The robotic system must be able to interact with its human counterpart and express why a task cannot be performed. Alternatively, the robotic system could also provide prediction to the human worker, which indicates how the robot will perform the task and what the end result will be.

4   Concluding Remark

There are many potential benefits from robots and humans working in collaboration. In this paper, we have shown two examples of current practices in construction vehicles to derive potential interaction, where robots and humans work together to solve tasks that are critical in terms of maintaining the safety of human workers and the quality of the end result. Making the interaction between robots and human workers natural and smooth is a timely and relevant research problem.

References

1. Blom, J.: Autonomous Hauler Loading. Master's thesis, Mälardalen University (2013). https://urn.kb.se/resolve?urn=urn%3Anbn%3Ase%3Amdh%3Adiva-21921
2. Buur, J., Caglio, A., Jensen, L.C.: Human actions made tangible: analysing the temporal organization of activities. In: Proceedings of the 2014 Conference on Designing Interactive Systems, pp. 1065–1073. DIS 2014, ACM, New York, NY, USA (2014). https://doi.org/10.1145/2598510.2598602
3. CLAAS Group: Seven awards in one go - one gold medal and six silver medals for CLAAS (2013). https://www.claas-group.com/press-corporate-communications/press-releases/seven-awards-in-one-go---one-gold-medal-and-six-silver-medals-for-claas/243688. Accessed 24 May 2023
4. Constable, G., Somerville, B.: A Century of Innovation: Twenty Engineering Achievements that Transformed our Lives. The National Academies Press, Washington, DC, USA (2003). https://doi.org/10.17226/10726
5. Goodrich, M.A., Schultz, A.C.: Human-robot interaction: a survey. Found. Trends® Hum. Comput. Interact. **1**(3), 203–275 (2008). https://doi.org/10.1561/1100000005
6. Greenfield, D.: Inside the human-robot collaboration trend (2015). https://www.automationworld.com/factory/robotics/blog/13313385/inside-the-humanrobot-collaboration-trend. Accessed 24 May 2023
7. Hager, I., Golonka, A., Putanowicz, R.: 3d printing of buildings and building components as the future of sustainable construction? Procedia Eng. **151**, 292–299 (2016). https://doi.org/10.1016/j.proeng.2016.07.357
8. Ishi, C.T., Machiyashiki, D., Mikata, R., Ishiguro, H.: A speech-driven hand gesture generation method and evaluation in android robots. IEEE Robot. Autom. Lett. **3**(4), 3757–3764 (2018). https://doi.org/10.1109/LRA.2018.2856281
9. Koehn, J.K., Kuchenbecker, K.J.: Surgeons and non-surgeons prefer haptic feedback of instrument vibrations during robotic surgery. Surg. Endosc. **29**, 2970–2983 (2015). https://doi.org/10.1007/s00464-014-4030-8
10. Löllmann, H.W., Barfuss, H., Deleforge, A., Meier, S., Kellermann, W.: Challenges in acoustic signal enhancement for human-robot communication. In: Speech Communication; 11. ITG Symposium, pp. 1–4. VDE Verlag, Berlin, Germany (2014)
11. Marshall, J.A., Bonchis, A., Nebot, E., Scheding, S.: Robotics in mining. In: Siciliano, B., Khatib, O. (eds.) Springer Handbook of Robotics, pp. 1549–1576. Springer, Cham (2016). https://doi.org/10.1007/978-3-319-32552-1_59
12. Moorehead, S.J., Kise, M., Reid, J.F.: Autonomous tractors for citrus grove operations. In: Proceedings of the 2nd International Conference on Machine Control & Guidance, pp. 309–313. University of Bonn, Bonn, Germany (2010). https://d-nb.info/1199005282/34#page=315
13. Pedersen, S.M., Fountas, S., Have, H., Blackmore, B.S.: Agricultural robots-system analysis and economic feasibility. Precis. Agric. **7**, 295-308 (2006). https://doi.org/10.1007/s11119-006-9014-9

14. Robla-Gómez, S., Becerra, V.M., Llata, J.R., González-Sarabia, E., Torre-Ferrero, C., Pérez-Oria, J.: Working together: a review on safe human-robot collaboration in industrial environments. IEEE Access **5**, 26754–26773 (2017). https://doi.org/10.1109/ACCESS.2017.2773127
15. Sakagami, Y., Watanabe, R., Aoyama, C., Matsunaga, S., Higaki, N., Fujimura, K.: The intelligent ASIMO: system overview and integration. In: IEEE/RSJ International Conference on Intelligent Robots and Systems, vol. 3, pp. 2478–2483. IEEE (2002). https://doi.org/10.1109/IRDS.2002.1041641
16. Sanchez, J., Duncan, J.R.: Operator-automation interaction in agricultural vehicles. Ergon. Des. **17**(1), 14–19 (2009). https://doi.org/10.1518/106480409X415161
17. Sheridan, T.B.: Human-robot interaction: status and challenges. Hum. Factors **58**(4), 525–532 (2016). https://doi.org/10.1177/0018720816644364
18. Sitompul, T.A., Wallmyr, M.: Using augmented reality to improve productivity and safety for heavy machinery operators: state of the art. In: Proceedings of the 17th International Conference on Virtual-Reality Continuum and Its Applications in Industry, pp. 8:1–8:9. VRCAI 2019, ACM, New York, NY, USA (2019). https://doi.org/10.1145/3359997.3365689
19. Slaughter, D., Giles, D., Downey, D.: Autonomous robotic weed control systems: a review. Comput. Electron. Agric. **61**(1), 63–78 (2008). https://doi.org/10.1016/j.compag.2007.05.008
20. Stentz, A.: Robotic technologies for outdoor industrial vehicles. In: Unmanned Ground Vehicle Technology III, pp. 192–199. SPIE (2001). https://doi.org/10.1117/12.439978
21. Thrun, S.: Toward a framework for human-robot interaction. Hum. Comput. Interact. **19**(1–2), 9–24 (2004). https://doi.org/10.1080/07370024.2004.9667338
22. Villani, V., Pini, F., Leali, F., Secchi, C.: Survey on human-robot collaboration in industrial settings: safety, intuitive interfaces and applications. Mechatronics **55**, 248–266 (2018). https://doi.org/10.1016/j.mechatronics.2018.02.009
23. Volvo CE: Volvo CE unveils the next generation of its electric load carrier concept (2017). https://www.volvoce.com/united-states/en-us/about-us/news/2017/volvo-ce-unveils-the-next-generation-of-its-electric-load-carrier-concept/. Accessed 24 May 2023
24. Wallmyr, M.: Seeing through the eyes of heavy vehicle operators. In: Bernhaupt, R., Dalvi, G., Joshi, A., Balkrishan, D.K., O'Neill, J., Winckler, M. (eds.) INTERACT 2017. LNCS, vol. 10514, pp. 263–282. Springer, Cham (2017). https://doi.org/10.1007/978-3-319-67684-5_16

Towards Modelling Cooperation in Future Maritime Remote-Control Center

Marcel Saager[1]([✉]) [iD], Marie-Christin Harre[2] [iD], and Axel Hahn[1,3] [iD]

[1] DLR Institute of Systems Engineering for Future Mobility, 26121 Oldenburg, Germany
marcel.saager@dlr.de
[2] Humatects GmbH, Marie-Curie-Str. 1, 26129 Oldenburg, Germany
harre@humatects.de
[3] Carl von Ossietzky University, Ammerländer Heerstraße 114-118, 26129 Oldenburg, Germany
axel.hahn@dlr.de, axel.hahn@uni-oldenburg.de

Abstract. The emergence of Maritime Autonomous Systems (MASS) and Remote-Control Centers (RCC) poses challenges in understanding and managing cooperation among actors in harbor berthing maneuvers. Systematic methods analyzing cooperation from a human factors perspective are essential. To address these challenges, a systematic approach is needed, focusing on human factors and analyzing cooperation comprehensively. This paper briefly introduces such methods to lay the groundwork for investigating these challenges. The review highlights four key aspects: task analysis, information analysis, social network analysis, and analysis of artifacts and physical layout within the RCC and on board the MASS. Considerations will be integrated into the design phase of future RCCs, effectively tackling upcoming challenges. This approach shows how cooperation between actors in RCC can be designed.

Keywords: Remote-Control Center · Human Factors · Modelling Cooperation

1 Introduction

In the era of maritime autonomy, the automation of ships in form of maritime autonomous surface ships (MASS) is becoming increasingly important. This development promises efficiency gains and cost savings, but also poses new challenges in terms of cooperation between the operator and actors involved. This paper focuses on a specific use case where cooperation becomes more complex and discusses possible methodological approaches for designing cooperation to solve complex situations.

Remote-Control Center (RCC) have emerged in research as central communication and control hubs [16]. There is currently a lively debate about the feasibility of transferring personnel from ships to land-based RCC. This shift aims to improve efficiency and safety by reducing human intervention on board. However, the human factor remains an aspect, be it in the form of a fallback level for the AI or the fact that there are still some people on board, for example technicians or passengers. Nevertheless, it should be ensured that a successful support of the human factor is still implemented [17].

A. Bramwell-Dicks et al. (Eds.): INTERACT 2023 Workshops, LNCS 14535, pp. 299–309, 2024.
https://doi.org/10.1007/978-3-031-61688-4_29

The relocation of the operator would affect cooperation between all actors. The face-to-face interactions common on traditional vessels would be replaced by digital communication tools. Effective and coordinated real-time cooperation will be essential to ensure smooth and safe operations. In order to systematically design and set up RCC, whether for safe deployment or certification purposes, it is necessary to develop a systematic approach on how operators can collaborate to solve tasks within the RCC, either individually or with other key actors. Therefore, in this paper, methods for modelling cooperation and an initial examination of future RCC in the maritime domain are described. A use case from a berthing manoeuvre in a harbor area is presented to identify the needs for research in modelling cooperation in RCCs. Based on this use case, a recommendation is developed on which modelling components are needed to model cooperation. The main objective is to design efficient cooperation between actors in future RCCs and consequently improve the performance and efficiency in the maritime sector.

The paper is structured as follows: In Sect. 2, the current state of research on RCCs is presented. The main characteristics of an RCC are derived from selected sources and assumptions are made about how an RCC is generally designed. In Sect. 3, the use case of a berthing manoeuvre in a harbor without and with RCC is presented. For this case, the findings from the state of the art are used and further refined in order to make clear which roles and tasks for cooperation can exist in an RCC in the future. This will also raise problems in this section that come with the restructuring of shipping through the advent of automation and thus the emergence of RCCs. Section 4 deals with methods that address cooperation. The methods were selected with regard to a set of predefined criteria, which are briefly presented in the section. Finally, the methods are discussed in the context of the RCC use case and what aspects they can add value to. A conclusion follows in Sect. 6.

2 Related Work in Maritime Remote-Control Center

Part of this work is to create a use case in the context of RCC and to identify the important factors for modelling corporation. Therefore, this section provides an overview of current trends, research and technologies related to RCC. From this, commonalities will be identified and presented, which will be used for the use case. Therefore, it was decided, that the presented research and practical examples address MASS and their associated RCC (especially their tasks, roles, structure).

A company, named Seafar operates MASS (Maritime Autonomous Surface Ships) and opened a shore control center in Antwerp in 2022. It consists of a control center and a traffic control center with two operators [8]. The IBM-equipped Mayflower is an example of a MASS capable of autonomous navigation. However, there is currently no dedicated RCC for this vessel [5]. Rolls-Royce presents a conceptual RCC in their presentations, with different workstations for different roles. It is clear that, there is a leadership role, a monitoring role and a role capable of interfacing with the AI of a MASS [4]. The RCC-CERT report of the Belgian Ministry models and ergonomically designs an RCC step by step. The focus of the work is to use and improve the modelling process described in the RCC-CERT report [3]. Porathe et al. set up an experimental RCC and discussed certain behaviors of ship operators. They emphasized the need for operators to have "ship sense", i.e. an understanding of the behavior of the ship. In addition, they pursued the concept of keeping the operator "in the loop" to enable him to carry out his duties without impairment [1, 2].

The following assumptions were identified:

- An RCC is shore-based, which means that navigation, monitoring and control no longer takes place on the ship.
- An operator in an RCC can monitor several MASS and, in case of an emergency, also take over control and steer them.
- Different RCC operators' roles have different tasks (since cooperation between these roles are the focus of this work, the individual roles will be mentioned in this chapter (c.f. reference to Table below).
- A MASS has an autonomy that mainly takes over maneuvering the vessel. The Remote Operator can override this autonomy and take over control of the MASS themselves.
- The workstations of the RCC operators are modeled similar to ship's bridge in the widest sense.

Additionally, the authors of the RCC-CERT study [3] describe a ten-step method for modeling and building a remote-control center. The steps are: 1. Task analysis, 2. Classification of tasks into high-level tasks, 3. Assignment of tasks to roles, 4. Description of the division of tasks between humans and automation, 5. Staffing: assigning the number of people to roles, 6. Definition of the interaction and cooperation between roles, 7. Specification of the information needed for each task, 8. Assignment of roles to workstations, 9. Design of the control room including human-machine interaction, room design, lighting, acoustics, and HVAC, 10. Checking the design against the higher-level requirements. As shown in this ten-step procedure, it is evident that in Step 6, the modeling of cooperation among all actors is a significant part in designing RCC. Furthermore, it is apparent that determining tasks and roles is also necessary for modeling cooperation. Therefore, Sect. 4 delves further into the methodical modeling of cooperation and gathers additional insights, which will then be compared to the use case from Sect. 3 in Sect. 5.

3 Use Case: Berthing in Harbor Region

Harbor regions are busy areas where various maneuvers take place. Nowadays, mooring maneuvers are complex situations involving different actors. The captain and the harbor pilot are on board and cooperate to moor the ship safely. The captain has the task of steering the ship and is responsible for it. He is also the one who knows the ship and its behaviour in detail. The harbor pilot gives instructions to the captain and benefits from knowing the area exactly. The two are in constant communication with each other and exchange information on different levels, be it verbally or non-verbally. In addition, the Vessel Traffic Service (VTS) can be involved in such maneuvers, as this is where the observation of the situation from an organizational point of view takes place. Other actors in the port and other vessels may also be involved, for example if they are in the way or have to wait. Due to the permanent changes on board and in the port during the maneuver, the cooperation among each other is already quite complex today.

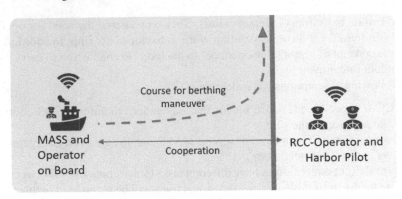

Fig. 1. 3 Possible Use Case: Berthing in Harbor Region

Nowadays, ship automation is advancing in the form of the Maritime Autonomous Surface Ship (MASS). MASS are divided into different levels according to the definition of the International Maritime Organization (IMO) [15], we use the definition of level 2–3 here as this best reflects the mixed traffic and the development of automation. Level 1 means only navigational assistance systems and at level 4, humans are no longer necessary, as the AI of the MASS can handle everything perfectly. Level 2–3 means that the ship can be controlled autonomously, but there may still be humans on board, for example in the engine room, and there must be at least one fallback level in the form of a remote-control center (RCC) (see Fig. 1). For this purpose, the findings from the related work (see Sect. 2) were used to specify RCCs. In particular, the results of the RCC-CERT report provide insights into what future roles and their tasks in an RCC could look like. For this purpose, we have analysed the individual work processes that could be relevant for a berthing manoeuvre from previous work and suggestions from the RCC-CERT study and distributed them among the new possible roles in an RCC (derived from the findings of the related work and the RCC-CERT study). This results in the following table (Table 1).

It should be noted, however, that these roles and the tasks assigned to them are only an initial suggestion. A remote-control operator can take over control of the MASS if autonomy is incapable to perform the berthing maneuver independently or if it fails. With regard to development of artificial intelligence, it is likely that the degree of automation on board will be gradually increased. In addition, it can be assumed that there are varying MASSs that need to be controlled by an RCC in port. This makes the underlying use case even more complex. The captain and the harbor pilot (not necessarily) will no longer be on board, but the maneuver must still be executed. Another actor emerges, the AI in the form of the MASS itself. Now the question is how the actors are rearranged and how they can work together to carry out the maneuver. The question is how the captain gets the same information at his disposition when steering remotely as on board, so that he still knows the ship precisely and can carry out the manoeuvre safely. Furthermore, it is unclear how the handover from the AI of the MASS to manual control is proceeded. In addition, the emergence of an RCC raises the question of what role the VTS now plays and whether additional port personnel are needed on board. The role of the harbor pilot

Table 1. Tasks and Roles in an RCC during Use Case while a Critical berthing maneuver

Role	Description of the Role	Main Task
Fleet Supervisor	Managing the entire organization of the RCC and has responsibility over various MASS. Accountable for the MASS	1.1 Communication regarding voyage planning and tracking of the MASS (and their changes) 1.2 Communication to coordinate malfunctions and emergencies
Remote Navigator Direct control	Takes over all tasks related to the direct control of the MASS, focuses on one vessel at a time	2.1 Maneuvering in Departure/de-berthing/berthing/arrival 2.2 Navigation pilotage 2.3 Maneuvering mass during malfunctions and emergencies 2.4 Communication with other ships, VTS, piloting 2.5 Handling information regarding malfunctions and emergencies 2.6 Taking care of changes in the voyage and track
Remote navigator monitoring	Monitors the MASS during operation	3.1 Monitoring the situation at sea and in port 3.2 Monitoring navigation and anchoring 3. Detecting malfunctions, emergencies, anomalies, hazards 3.4 Monitoring sensors and their functionalities
MASS	Operates autonomously (or widely autonomously), is monitored and supervised by an RCC	4.1 Operating navigation, including steering, autonomous 4.2 Give signals to the Remote Operator about its own limitations in special situations 4.3 Detects emergencies, malfunctions etc

is also uncertain. It is questionable whether the harbor pilot will come on board or be present in the RCC. It is possible that the harbor pilot as port expert and Remote Operator combines both functions. However, this would open up the question of who is then the vessel expert. It is unlikely that the Remote Operator is an expert on the harbor area AND every MASS and its behaviour. This would place greater requirements on the Remote Operator. It would be necessary to examine how the actors interact with each other, what their responsibilities are, what technologies they use and how they cooperate overall. A systematic approach to modelling cooperation could help, as these problems can then be considered and pointed out in a structured way. This would have several advantages: The work processes and the RCC itself could be better certified by defining what the cooperation should look like. Appropriate technologies for optimising human-machine interaction could be derived to improve cooperation. In addition, roles and tasks could be redefined and followed to enhance or overthink regulatory like STCW which defines training of seafarers.

4 Existing Cooperation Methods

In brief, cooperation after Hoc can be described as the process of two or more individuals working together towards a common goal [18]. For this, some questions that became apparent from the above use case are derived: Are Which tasks are addressed? Which actors are identified? Which responsibilities or roles are defined in the system? Are information and tasks identified? To what degree do technical resources need to be used? Is there collaboration with third parties? For this reason, methodological procedures were sought that address the aspects mentioned as far as possible. These are described roughly in the upcoming sections.

4.1 Method U

Method - U is an approach to design and evaluate the ergonomics of a system. It focuses on the human actors and their interactions with assistance systems. Method U aims to reconcile the influence of humans and machines in terms of cooperative behavior. Pecaux-Lemoine et al. adapted and extended the method to make it applicable to domains such as automotive and railway to develop assistance systems [6, 7].

In the extended method U, the modeler follows an 8-step descending phase of design.

This phase begins with Step 1, which involves setting new objectives and conducting a process analysis in Step 2. This is followed by Step 3, where human and technical resources are identified. Step 4 brings these resources together to examine activities.

Building on this foundation, Step 5 focuses on investigating human tasks and current support systems. Step 6 is the part that deals with cooperation, in the form of modifying the human tasks, establishing a common workspace, and adjusting the assistance systems. Step 7 complements the activity levels, while step 8 deals with the integration of a human-machine system and the associated training. These 8 steps are followed by a 4-step ascending evaluation phase. This includes step 9, which defines the experiment, step 10, the execution in a real or simulated environment, and step 11, a cognitive activity analysis. Step 12 describes the set of results obtained from the study. These findings can then be fed back into Steps 4, 6 and 8 in the form of human models, modifications or training adjustments. The main element of cooperation modeling is to reduce matrix, which is developed in step 6, of tasks from different levels. This will be conducted in Step 6 (Modification of Human tasks, Common Workspace Task allocation/Rules and Modification of assistance systems).

For each agent, this becomes the necessary know-how, i.e., the agent's ability to control and interact, and the know-how to cooperate, i.e., the ability to communicate and interact with each other. To see how two agents (human and human, or human and AI) cooperate with each other, their respective know how and know how to cooperate are put into a matrix to analyze their overlap [6, 7].

4.2 DiCoT

The DiCoT method is a structural approach to investigate distributed cognition. With this, it can be derived, how teamwork in a distributed cognition system could be designed. A basis for this is the work from Hutchins about distributed cognitions literature [13]. The DiCoT Method can be used to analyze interactive systems from the point of view of distributed teamwork [9, 10]. DiCot follows several principles which are summarized after Morand et al. [11]. The Dicot method can be divided into 5 models:

1. Physical Model: shows how the physical layout of the context is, for example through a room design. Some aspects like space horizon of observation (of the individual) or also the arrangements of the equipment are considered.
2. Information flow model: this model shows how information is passed through a team, including by whom and how.
3. Artefact model: includes all the artefacts, displays and tools that are used to retrieve, transform and second-guess information.
4. Social model: indicates the roles and responsibilities of the people in the system, pointing out that a higher level of experience leads to a higher level of responsibility.
5. Evolutionary model: shows how the system has evolved over time so that conclusions can be made about the reasons for change [9, 10].

An example of the application of the DiCoT method is provided by Morand et al. The authors investigated the effects of having an assistive function in the process of reanimating a person via cardiac massage. For this purpose, a study was conducted in which subjects acted as bystanders and had to resuscitate a human being. They received information from a dispatcher, with whom they are also connected via audio. In addition, the bystander receives a video on how to perform a cardiac massage. Furthermore, after some time, the first responders arrive with a defibrillator, and after the situation is under control, the simulation ends [11].

4.3 EAST Event Analysis of Systemic Teamwork

The EAST method includes a twelve-step program that has the objective to create three network models for modelling distributed situation awareness (DSA). These network models are divided into task network, information network and social network (see Fig. 2). In addition, the combinations of the individual networks are considered.

The original twelve steps of the EAST methodology were shortened by Stanton et al. to a five-step method [12]. These five steps limit the EAST method to the elementary diagram types and leave free space for other diagrams. The steps are:

1. determine scenario,
2. plan observation for the scenario,
3. perform observation,
4. create networks (diagram types) based on the observation,
5. combine and analyze the networks.

The task network describes the tasks and their schedule for execution. The agents must perform the tasks in the defined scenario. The social network represents the relationship between the agents, as well as necessary artifacts. They are connected to each other with edges representing the communication between the agents. The information network is created to show which information is relevant during the scenario, e. g. the communication between the agents. The aim is the combination of three network types as Task Network, Social Network and Information Network to show the distribution of task among the agents and the needed information.

4.4 WESTT – Workload, Error, Situation Awareness, Timing and Teamwork

WESTT is mainly a software to estimate and evaluate possible solutions that support cooperation between agents developed by Houghton et al. [14]. This software includes for instance a data table with ordered list of events over time together with the agents that are involved in these events. The tool can calculate workload, time and error metrics and thus offers an analytical prototyping tool to rapidly compare different approaches and solutions. Similar to EAST, WESTT takes three perspectives of analyzing cooperation into account: Task network structure, social network structure and knowledge network structure. It especially analyzes the following relations between these perspectives: command and operational structure needed for task performance, efficiency of distribution and spread of knowledge within the team and knowledge required to achieve success in carrying out tasks.

5 Modelling Cooperation in an RCC

For the berthing use case described in Sect. 3, several aspects need to be analysed in order to model the cooperation of the actors. These extracted aspects from the use case are described in the following perspectives and linked to the existing methods described in section four:

1. *Task analysis*: In the present use case (berthing), different tasks have to be performed, such as the assessment of distances to the quay or the steering of the ship. These tasks may need to be performed in cooperation by actors. The task analysis provides a basis for deriving the required information needs, responsibilities and physical artefacts and resources needed within these tasks in subsequent steps. Methods such as Method U, EAST and the RCC-CERT Belgian study provide approaches to systematically derive the tasks.
2. *Information Analysis* (Actors' information and information flow in the team): In addition to the tasks to be performed in the berthing manoeuvre, it is important to understand the information needed to perform necessary tasks and the flow of information between the actors. It is also important to analyse how this information is communicated. For example, the operator in an RCC needs to receive information about the berthing maneuver from the port personnel. Method U, EAST, DiCoT WESTT (Workload, Error, and Situation Awareness Taxonomy) and the Belgium Study may be relevant here and they provide approaches for identifying information and how it is exchanged among actors.

3. *Analysis of Social Network*: This perspective describes the relationships between actors and defines responsibilities for specific tasks or teams. For example, it is important to clarify which operator is responsible for the team they are working with when remotely controlling a MASS. This perspective also addresses who should perform which tasks in an RCC. The social aspect of this analysis looks at the relationships between two or more actors. Method U, DiCoT, EAST and WESTT can be applied here. The RACI model (Responsible, Accountable, Consulted, Informed) helps identify and define the roles and responsibilities of team members by categorizing them

4. *Artefacts & Physical Arrangement*: This perspective focuses on identifying the necessary artifacts that are required to perform tasks using essential information by the actors in the RCC. For example, an artifact could be the human-machine interface required by the operator to assess the state of the ship and the decision of the MASS AI during the berthing manoeuvre. Subsequently, action recommendations can be derived for the operator to work with a potential harbor pilot to berth the MASS if the AI is unable to do so. Here, methods such as DiCoT and Method U can be helpful. For the use case new artefacts, screens, sensors etc. which are needed in the RCC can be identified. From the DiCoT analysis, it can also be interesting to examine the physical structure of the RCC. This can answer further relevant questions of how future RCCs must be e.g. spatially structured and also where which person is located. Is the pilot on board? Is he or she in the RCC and has direct eye contact with the

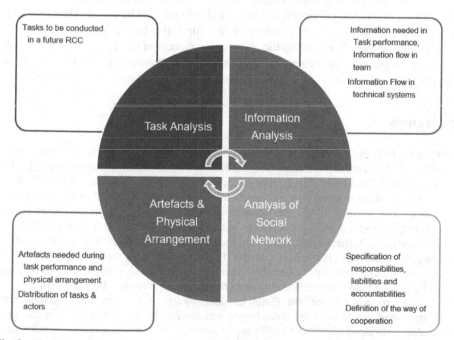

Fig. 2. The four main perspectives for analyzing & modelling cooperation for maneuvering MASS (in future RCC & onboard).

operator? From Method U it is interesting to look at how the know-how and the know how to cooperate is defined between the actors.

These four presented aspects can be visualized in the following figure.

It should be noted that additional information may support the aspects mentioned. This proposal represents a first approximation of how the berthing manoeuvre in the context of RCC can be systematically modelled from a cooperation perspective.

6 Conclusion

The advent of Maritime Autonomous Systems (MASS) and Remote-Control Centers (RCC) presents new challenges in terms of cooperation and understanding which actors communicate with whom and how. In order to analyse and manage the complex interrelationships involved, it is essential to rely on systematic methods that analyses cooperation from a human factors' perspective. In this paper, such methods were briefly introduced to provide a basis for investigating these challenges. The review of these methods revealed that four perspectives are particularly relevant for a comprehensive analysis: task analysis, information analysis, social network analysis, and analysis of artefacts and physical layout both within the RCC and on board the MASS. In order to proactively address the increasing complexity of cooperation between actors involved in the control of MASS, subsequent work will combine these methods into an approach and apply them to the specific use case. The aim is to integrate these considerations into the design phase of future RCCs in order to effectively address the challenges that lie ahead. The methodology enables the analysis and optimization of the cooperation between the actors involved in the control of MASS. By taking these aspects into account at an early stage, the complexity of cooperation can be successfully managed. This contributes to improving the efficiency and effectiveness of RCCs and maximizing the full potential of MASS.

References

1. Porathe, T.: Remote monitoring of autonomous ships: quickly getting into the loop display (QGILD). In: Plant, K., Praetorius, G., (eds.) Human Factors in Transportation. AHFE (2022) International Conference. AHFE Open Access, vol 60. AHFE International, USA (2022)
2. Porathe, T.: Remote monitoring and control of unmanned vessels: the MUNIN shore control centre. In: Proceedings of the 13th International Conference on Computer Applications and Information Technology in the Maritime Industries (COMPIT 2014), 12–14 May 2014 in Redworth, UK. V. Bertram (Ed.) Hamburg, Technische Universität Hamburg- Harburg. (2014)
3. Jung, T., Luedtke, A., Harre, M.-C., Javaux, D.: RCC-CERT - the drafting of a study on the definition and organisation of a Remote Control Centre (RCC) with a view to its CERTification . FPS Federal Public Service Mobility and Transport – DG Shipping. Belgium. (2023)
4. Rolls-Royce. Rolls-Royce and Finferries demonstrate world's first Fully Autonomous Ferry. News article from the Rolls-Royce website (2018). https://www.rolls-royce.com/media/press-releases/2018/03-12-2018-rr-and-finferries-demonstrate-worlds-first-fully-autonomous-ferry.aspx. Accessed 25 May 2023
5. Taylor, J., Give your business its own AI captain. Article. In: Decision Management Solutions (2021)

6. Pacaux-Lemoine, M.-P., Simon, P., Popieul, J.-C.: Human-machine cooperation principles to support driving automation systems design. In Conference: Fast Zero 2015, Gothenburg, Sweden (2015)
7. Gadmer, Q., Pacaux-Lemoine, M.-P., Richard, P.: Huma-automation – railway remote control: how to define shared information and functions? In: 16th Symposium on Control in Transportation Systems (IFAC 2021). Lille, France (2021)
8. MASS World. SEAFAR is expanding to Germany. Blog article (2022). https://massworld.news/seafar-expanding-germany. Accessed 25 May 2023
9. Blandford, A., Furniss, D.: DiCoT: a methodology for applying distributed cognition to the design of teamworking systems. In: Gilroy, S.W., Harrison, M.D. (eds.) DSV-IS 2005. LNCS, vol. 3941, pp. 26–38. Springer, Heidelberg (2006). https://doi.org/10.1007/11752707_3
10. Furniss, D., Blandford, A.: DiCoT modeling: from analysis to design. In: Presented at: CHI 2010 workshop: 'Contextual Analysis and Design', Atlanta, US (2010)
11. Morand, O., Safin, S., Caroline Rizza, C., Larribau, R., Pages., R.: Analyzing the challenges of an assistive application' integration in a complex emergency interaction using a distributed cognition perspective. In: Proceedings of the 33rd European Conference on Cognitive Ergonomics (ECCE 2022). Association for Computing Machinery, New York, NY, USA, Article 16, 1–9. (2022). https://doi.org/10.1145/3552327.3552332
12. Stanton, N.A.: Representing distributed cognition in complex systems: how a submarine returns to periscope depth (2014). https://doi.org/10.1080/00140139.2013.772244
13. Hutchins, E.: Cognition in the Wild. MIT Press, Cambridge, MA, USA (1995)
14. Houghton, R.J., Baber, C., Cowton, M., Walker, G.H., Stanton, N.A.: WESTT (workload, error, situational awareness, time and teamwork): an analytical prototyping system for command and control. Cogn. Technol. Work 10, 199–207 (2008)
15. IMO Autonomous Shipping. Blog article (2022). https://www.imo.org/en/MediaCentre/Hot Topics/Pages/Autonomous-shipping.aspx. Accessed 26 June 23
16. Dittmann, K., et al.: Autonomous surface vessel with remote human on the loop: System design for STCW compliance 54 (16), 224–231 (2021). https://doi.org/10.1016/j.ifacol.2021.10.097
17. Lutzhoft, M., Hynnekleiv, A., Earthy, J.V., Petersen, E.S.: Human-centred maritime autonomy - An ethnography of the future. In: IOP Conference Series: Journal of Physics: Conference Series, vol. 1357, p. 012032 (2019)
18. Hoc, J.-M.: Towards a cognitive approach to human–machine cooperation in dynamic situations. Int. J. Hum. Comput. Stud. 54(4), 509–540 (2001). https://doi.org/10.1006/ijhc.2000.0454

Analyzing Online Videos to Create a List of User Interface Elements: A Case for OpenCrane Design System

Taufik Akbar Sitompul$^{(\boxtimes)}$ ⓘ, Jooyoung Park, and Ole Andreas Alsos ⓘ

Department of Design, Norwegian University of Science and Technology (NTNU),
Trondheim, Norway
{taufik.a.sitompul,jooyoung.park,oleanda}@ntnu.no

Abstract. One of the first steps in developing a design system is to make a list of user interface (UI) elements, which is usually done by reviewing existing graphical user interfaces (GUIs). Doing so can be difficult depending on the context, since designers may not have access to a sufficient number of different GUIs. This paper presents a complementary method for creating a list of UI elements and the context is an ongoing work of developing a design system for remote rubber-tired gantry (RTG) cranes. We analyzed online videos published by the crane manufacturers that fully or partially show the crane GUIs. We included 11 online videos published by three crane manufacturers that met our selection criteria. The analysis of the online videos resulted in 29 UI elements. To evaluate the feasibility of this method, we compared the results with 27 UI elements elicited from a field study at a port that employed remote RTG cranes. The comparison shows that there is a significant overlap between the two sets of UI elements, but also some differences. This suggests that the two methods can complement each other instead of being alternatives. Regarding the order, we recommend conducting a field study first to obtain the necessary domain knowledge to better understand the content of online videos.

Keywords: Graphical user interface · Crane · Field study · Online video · YouTube · OpenCrane design system

1 Introduction

Graphical user interfaces (GUIs) for operating heavy machinery, such as cranes, could be quite different among various machine manufacturers, even though they are designed for the same type of machines [22]. This situation leads to diverse GUIs, which require operators to train themselves every time they use a machine from another manufacturer, since their knowledge with one GUI may not be entirely applicable to the other GUI. In addition, the diverse GUIs may also increase the risk of human error, since different GUIs may have different rules or mechanisms that operators should adhere to [15].

© IFIP International Federation for Information Processing 2024
Published by Springer Nature Switzerland AG 2024
A. Bramwell-Dicks et al. (Eds.): INTERACT 2023 Workshops, LNCS 14535, pp. 310–320, 2024.
https://doi.org/10.1007/978-3-031-61688-4_30

This paper presents an ongoing process of developing OpenCrane design system, which will provide open-source user interface (UI) elements to build GUIs for operating cranes. A design system is a collection of documented UI elements, visual guidelines, and design principles that one can reuse when designing digital products [21]. A design system could improve consistency across different digital products, since it serves as a single source of reference that different user interface designers and software developers could refer to when designing their digital products [5]. The motivation behind developing OpenCrane design system is the lack of standardization of GUIs used for operating cranes.

Since there are many types of cranes, this paper focuses on remote rubber-tired gantry (RTG) cranes, which are also known as yard cranes (see the left image in Fig. 1). RTG cranes are primarily used for moving containers between trucks and the storage yard. Although many RTG cranes are still controlled by operators who work from inside the cabin, there are newer RTG cranes that can be operated remotely from a control room [17]. The shift from on-site operation to remote operation is mainly driven by the increasing demand for better safety and productivity [11], since operators would not harmed in case of accidents and they can also operate any cranes within the port from the control room (see the right image in Fig. 1).

Fig. 1. The left image shows an example of remote RTG cranes. The right image shows the remote control station used by the operator to control any of RTG cranes within the port.

One of the early phases in developing a design system is to make a list of UI elements that will be made available, which is usually done by reviewing existing GUIs [21]. We reviewed existing GUIs for operating remote RTG cranes to create a list of UI elements that will be made available in our design system. We first conducted a field study at a port to see examples of GUIs for operating remote RTG cranes. The field study provided us with details about one example of such GUIs. However, we quickly realized that our source of information was still limited because the remote RTG cranes used at that port were made by one manufacturer only. To expand our source of information, we used online videos uploaded by different crane manufacturers that produce remote RTG cranes.

The objective of this paper is to discuss the feasibility of using online videos uploaded by crane manufacturers as a complementary method to create a list of UI elements when developing a design system. The feasibility of this method was evaluated by comparing the list of UI elements collected by analyzing online videos with the list of UI elements gathered from conducting a field study.

2   Related Work

As of 2022, there were 500 h of videos uploaded on YouTube every minute [19]. Due to its abundance of user-generated data, YouTube has attracted researchers to use it as the source of data for conducting research [7]. Research using data collected from YouTube can generally be categorized into two: (1) analyzing the content of the videos and (2) analyzing users' responses, such as comments and likes, on certain types of videos [16]. However, considering the focus of this paper, this section focuses on the research that analyzes the content of the videos.

The category of research that analyzes the content of the videos can have different objectives depending on who uploaded the videos on YouTube. The majority of research that analyzes videos uploaded by individuals tend to focus on gaining an understanding of certain aspects of human behaviors, for example, how people with motor disability use smartphones and tablets [3], how people behave when driving cars with assisted driving [4], and detecting symptoms of autism on children [6], just to name a few. The majority of research that analyzes videos uploaded by organizations tends to focus on understanding organizational-related goals that are implicitly conveyed through the videos, for example, how companies promote gambling as a completely harmless activity [20] or how companies envision the future of augmented reality in manufacturing and construction industries [23].

Among the research that analyzes videos uploaded by individuals, Sitompul and Wallmyr [18] specifically investigate the analysis of online videos as an alternative method to conducting a field study for understanding how operators of forest harvesters perform their work in natural settings. Using the work of Sitompul and Wallmyr [18] as a source of inspiration, we took a similar path by analyzing available videos on the internet. However, instead of gaining an understanding of certain aspects of human behaviors, we analyzed online videos to see different GUIs for operating remote RTG cranes and create the list of UI elements, which will be made available in OpenCrane design system.

3   Methods

In this study, we compiled two lists of UI elements through (1) a field study at a port that employed remote RTG cranes and (2) by analyzing eleven videos from three crane manufacturers. The two lists were then compared to find similarities and differences among them.

3.1 Conducting a Field Study to Elicit UI Elements

The field study was conducted at a port that employed remote RTG cranes made by Konecranes (see the left image in Fig. 1). The remote RTG cranes were operated from a control room that contained multiple operator stations. Each operator station was equipped with one large monitor and one small touchscreen monitor that present the video streams and the GUI (see Fig. 1).

The field study was conducted by the first author, since he spoke the same language as the crane operators. During the field study, he separately asked four crane operators to describe the meaning or function of the UI elements shown on both monitors in order to obtain a better understanding of the existing GUI. To make sure no details were missed, he also video recorded the monitors when the crane operators described the meaning of the UI elements. This activity took around two hours. He then spent a couple of hours just for observing the operators to make sure he completely understood the meaning and functionality of each UI element. During the observation, he also took multiple photos of the monitors, since the content of the GUI was continuously changing based on the crane operation.

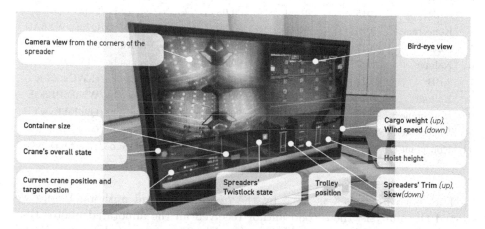

Fig. 2. An example of how the list of UI elements was extracted from the GUI observed during the field study.

The analysis was conducted by the first author by manually inspecting what kind of UI elements that were seen in the photos taken from the field study based on the information provided by the crane operators. The photos were used as the medium of the analysis instead of the videos, since photos are static and easier to annotate. The process was repeated until all the photos have been inspected and annotated. The results of the analysis are the list of UI elements found from the field study and the photos that have been annotated (see Fig. 2 for an example).

3.2 Analyzing Online Videos to Elicit UI Elements

To the authors' best knowledge, there are three companies that produce remote RTG cranes, namely ABB, Kalmar, and Konecranes. The relevant videos were collected from official YouTube accounts of those companies [1,10,12]. When this paper was written, the total uploaded videos from those three accounts were 863 videos. We applied two inclusion criteria to filter the uploaded videos: (1) the videos must be about remote RTG cranes and (2) the GUIs to control remote RTG cranes must be fully or partially visible in the videos. A total of 11 videos fulfilled the inclusion criteria (see Table 1 for the list of videos).

Table 1. The list of videos that were analyzed in this study. The video duration is measured in minutes and seconds. Relevant scenes are defined as the parts where the GUIs to control remote RTG cranes, are fully or partially visible.

No	Crane manufacturer	Year of publication	Video duration	Duration of relevant scenes	Link
1	Konecranes	2013	04:15	00:14	youtu.be/IaJU1baPd0E
2	Konecranes	2013	01:20	00:07	youtu.be/gJDquydoQMQ
3	ABB	2015	01:30	00:08	youtu.be/2-quWT5BCqU
4	Konecranes	2016	05:41	00:09	youtu.be/Q7oforWX6AU
5	ABB	2017	04:01	00:24	youtu.be/JIrPWW6r1uo
6	Kalmar	2017	02:04	00:19	youtu.be/YPbCJL_vPLI
7	ABB	2018	02:09	00:31	youtu.be/ehWQz_Z3-ic
8	Kalmar	2019	03:36	01:12	youtu.be/W2uFoP12ksE
9	Konecranes	2019	00:50	00:05	youtu.be/Q9bFiSEvwYU
10	Konecranes	2019	00:53	00:09	youtu.be/6-oap4pcqIk
11	Konecranes	2019	01:12	00:05	youtu.be/1AQJ9xDQxGE

The video analysis was done by the first and second authors. Before we started the analysis, the second author received all the annotated photos that have been produced from the field study (see Fig. 2 for an example), since she did not participate in the previous field study and she also had no prior experience in this domain. The video analysis was started after the second author has studied the results from the field study.

The analysis was done by separately watching the videos listed in Table 1. We did so to ensure that we would not influence each other's analysis. Since the videos were made for commercial purposes, we only analyzed the scenes where the GUIs were fully or partially visible and ignored the remaining parts of the videos. We used the clipping tool available on YouTube to take screenshots of the scenes that fully or partially showed the GUIs for controlling remote RTG cranes. The screenshots were then manually analyzed and annotated by inspecting what kinds of UI elements existed in the visible parts of the GUIs. The inspection and annotation process was similar to what we did when analyzing the GUI from the field study (see Fig. 2). The process was repeated until all the screenshots were inspected and annotated. We then met and compared our annotated screenshots. For different findings, we watched the videos once again to decide if they should be accepted or discarded. The results of this activity is the list of UI elements obtained from analyzing the online videos uploaded by crane manufacturers.

4 Results

The combined results from the field study and analyzing the online videos produced a total of 34 UI elements that are relevant for operating remote RTG cranes (see Table 2). If we look at the results from each method, the field study generated a list of 27 UI elements, while analyzing online videos produced a list of 29 UI elements. Comparing the results between both methods, we found 23 (or about 67%) overlapping UI elements.

After comparing the results from both methods, we found five UI elements that could only be found by analyzing online videos (see No. 1, 8, 10, 12, and 13 in Table 2). The reason why these five UI elements could not be found through the field study is that they were only found in the videos uploaded by ABB and Kalmar. In other words, we could not find these UI elements from the field study, since the GUI from Konecranes (see Fig. 2 for an example) did not have such UI elements.

If we look at the UI elements that could only be found from field study (see No. 26, 27, 32, 33, and 34 in Table 2), they are the graphical buttons that operators could use to control certain parts of remote RTG cranes. The main reason why these UI elements could not be found by analyzing online videos is that the videos rarely showed the entire GUIs. Even in some scenes, in which the entire GUIs were visible, there was a limitation in terms of video resolution. In case of low resolution, we decided to not make any assumptions about the blurred parts of the GUIs in order to prevent making incorrect guesses. Therefore, we could not be fully sure whether the GUIs shown in the videos also had these UI elements.

As shown in Table 1, 11 online videos were analyzed in this study. If we look at the numbers within brackets shown in Table 2, multiple camera views (No. 25) is the only UI element that could be found in every video. The reason behind this is because the multiple camera views usually took a significant amount of space of the GUIs, and thus they were easy to recognize even though the GUIs were only visible partially in some of the videos.

5 Reflection

This section presents our reflection after conducting a field study and analyzing online videos for creating the list of UI elements to be made available in the design system.

Table 2. The comparison between the list of relevant UI elements that we collected through field study and analyzing online videos. The numbers inside the brackets indicate the number of videos, in which the UI elements can be clearly seen.

No	Description of the UI elements	Source	
		Field study	Online videos
1	An overview of the storage yard		✓(3)
2	Crane's number	✓	✓(4)
3	Crane's overall status	✓	✓(2)
4	Crane's fault messages	✓	✓(2)
5	Crane's current location in the storage yard	✓	✓(5)
6	Crane's target location in the storage yard	✓	✓(4)
7	Gantry position	✓	✓(3)
8	Gantry speed		✓(2)
9	Trolley position	✓	✓(6)
10	Trolley speed		✓(2)
11	Hoist position	✓	✓(6)
12	Hoist speed		✓(2)
13	Spreader's size		✓(2)
14	Status of the spreader's lock	✓	✓(5)
15	Indicator whether the spreader has landed on the container	✓	✓(4)
16	Spreader's skew	✓	✓(2)
17	Spreader's trim	✓	✓(3)
18	Truck's plate number	✓	✓(2)
19	Indicator whether the truck is parked correctly	✓	✓(2)
20	Container's size	✓	✓(5)
21	Container's number	✓	✓(4)
22	Container's weight	✓	✓(5)
23	Indicator whether the position of the container is stacked correctly on top of another container	✓	✓(1)
24	Wind speed	✓	✓(3)
25	Multiple camera views	✓	✓(11)
26	Five buttons to change which camera views to be shown on the monitor	✓	
27	A number of buttons to change which cranes to be operated remotely	✓	
28	A button to activate automated control	✓	✓(2)
29	A button to activate manual control	✓	✓(2)
30	A button to show the details of the planned lifting job		✓(2)
31	A button to cancel/override the planned lifting job	✓	✓(2)
32	Two buttons to change the spreader's size	✓	
33	A button to call the truck driver in the storage yard	✓	
34	A button to active the crane's horn	✓	

5.1   The Role of Domain Knowledge in Analyzing Online Videos

As mentioned in Subsect. 3.1, one of us had a chance to conduct a field study at a port that used remote RTG cranes before analyzing the online videos. The possibility to visit the port to see an example of GUIs for operating remote RTG cranes from a close distance and talk to the crane operators provided a lot of knowledge about the operation of remote RTG cranes. The materials produced from the field study, for example, the annotated photos, were found really useful for the second author, since they provided her some indications about what kind of UI elements that could possibly exist in the GUIs for remote RTG cranes and how such UI elements could probably look. Having such materials that could be refer to enabled her to perform the video analysis, even though she did not participate in the field study and had no prior experience in this domain. Therefore, having relevant domain knowledge was, without a doubt, valuable when analyzing the online videos.

Although not all the videos fully showed the GUIs, we were able to determine the meaning or the purpose of each UI element, given that the resolution was clear enough. Considering the need for a certain level of domain knowledge, we could imagine that it would be difficult for people who have no domain knowledge to analyze online videos. Although the meaning of some UI elements shown in the videos is quite obvious due to their distinct forms, there were also some UI elements shown in the videos that looked more abstract.

5.2   Using Online Videos Versus Static Marketing Materials

In this study, we analyzed online videos uploaded by crane manufacturers to inspect what kind of UI elements that exist in the GUIs for operating remote RTG cranes. As mentioned in Sect. 4, not all the videos showed the GUIs with clear resolution, which prevented us from specifying every UI element in the GUIs. Therefore, one may argue to consider using static marketing materials, such as brochures or posters, published by crane manufacturers that also show the GUIs for operating remote RTG cranes. See [2,8,9,13,14] for the examples of marketing brochures published by the same crane manufacturers that uploaded the videos in Table 1. Although comparing the results from analyzing online videos and static marketing materials is outside the scope of this paper, we see one major advantage of using online videos over static marketing materials, which is the possibility to briefly see how the GUIs change or animate depending on the ongoing operation. Having such possibility provided not only a more similar experience to observing the GUIs during the field study but also provided more context on the functionality of the UI elements in the GUIs.

5.3   A Complementary or Alternative Method?

Sitompul and Wallmyr [18] outline some possible benefits of analyzing online videos over conducting a traditional field study, such as the possibility of collecting data from different settings, requiring less time to collect the data, and solving the issue of not having access to the object of interest. We also perceived these benefits through the context of this study, since collecting data from different settings would mean visiting multiple ports that use remote RTG cranes from different manufacturers. While time was not a major concern in our case, visiting multiple ports that also employ remote RTG cranes from different manufacturers was not possible, since we had access to one port only.

Considering the benefits mentioned above, should analyzing online videos be considered a complementary or alternative method to conducting a field study? Based on the results presented in Sect. 4, 23 out of 34 UI elements were found by both conducting a field study and analyzing online videos, which suggests a significant overlap between both methods. However, Sect. 4 also shows that there are UI elements that could only be found by either conducting a field study or analyzing online videos. Therefore, in the context of this study, both methods seem to complement each other instead of being an alternative to one another. Regarding the order, we would nonetheless recommend conducting a field study first to obtain the necessary domain knowledge to better understand the content of online videos.

6   Conclusion and Future Work

In this paper, we present a complementary method for creating a list of UI elements for a design system for remote RTG cranes by analyzing online videos uploaded by crane manufacturers. The feasibility of this method was evaluated by comparing the list UI elements elicited from the online videos with the list of UI elements obtained from the field study. The combined results from both methods produced a total of 34 UI elements, of which 23 of them (or 67%) could be found from both methods. This suggests a significant overlap between the two methods.

As mentioned in Sect. 2, the majority of studies that analyze online videos uploaded by individuals or organizations tend to focus on people. The study presented in this paper shows an example of how online videos can be used for inspecting non-living objects. To further validate the feasibility of this method, it would be interesting to analyze online videos to study other non-living objects shown in the videos, which can be used as a source of information for creating a design system or an inspiration for designing anything in general. Finally, as mentioned in Subsect. 5.2 it would also be interesting to compare the analysis of online videos with the analysis of static marketing materials for creating the list of UI elements for the design system.

Acknowledgments. This research received funding from the Department of Design at NTNU, NTNU Discovery, and the SFI AutoShip Centre (the Research Council of Norway under project number 309230). The authors would also like to thank the port management for giving permission to conduct the field study and the crane operators for the information that they provided.

References

1. ABB Marine: www.youtube.com/c/abbmarineandports/videos. Accessed 15 Dec 2022
2. Alho, T., Pettersson, T., Haapa-Aho, M.: The path to automation in an RTG terminal (2018). https://www.kalmarglobal.com/4948ad/globalassets/equipment/rtg-cranes/kalmar-whitepaper-autortg. Accessed 25 Apr 2023
3. Anthony, L., Kim, Y., Findlater, L.: Analyzing user-generated YouTube videos to understand touchscreen use by people with motor impairments. In: Proceedings of the SIGCHI Conference on Human Factors in Computing Systems, CHI '13, pp. 1223-1232. ACM, New York (2013). https://doi.org/10.1145/2470654.2466158
4. Brown, B., Laurier, E.: The trouble with autopilots: Assisted and autonomous driving on the social road. In: Proceedings of the 2017 CHI Conference on Human Factors in Computing Systems, CHI '17, pp. 416-429. ACM, New York (2017). https://doi.org/10.1145/3025453.3025462
5. Edelberg, J., Kilrain, J.: Design systems: consistency, efficiency & collaboration in creating digital products. In: Proceedings of the 38th ACM International Conference on Design of Communication, SIGDOC '20, ACM, New York (2020). https://doi.org/10.1145/3380851.3416743
6. Fusaro, V.A., et al.: The potential of accelerating early detection of autism through content analysis of YouTube videos. PLoS ONE **9**(4), 1–6 (2014). https://doi.org/10.1371/journal.pone.0093533
7. Giglietto, F., Rossi, L., Bennato, D.: The open laboratory: limits and possibilities of using Facebook, Twitter, and YouTube as a research data source. J. Technol. Hum. Serv. **30**(3–4), 145–159 (2012). https://doi.org/10.1080/15228835.2012.743797
8. Johanson, F.: How remote can 'remote' be? (2015). https://new.abb.com/docs/librariesprovider102/default-document-library/how-remote-can-remote-be.pdf?sfvrsn=2. Accessed 25 Apr 2023
9. Kalmar: Be in complete control: the new Kalmar remote console. https://www.kalmarglobal.com/491403/globalassets/media/216100/216100_RC-desk-flyer-web.pdf. Accessed 25 Apr 2023
10. Kalmar Global: www.youtube.com/user/KalmarGlobal/videos. Accessed 15 Dec 2022
11. Karvonen, H., Koskinen, H., Haggrén, J.: Enhancing the user experience of the crane operator: comparing work demands in two operational settings. In: Proceedings of the 30th European Conference on Cognitive Ergonomics, ECCE '12, pp. 37-44. ACM, New York (2012). https://doi.org/10.1145/2448136.2448144
12. Konecranes: https://www.youtube.com/c/konecranes/videos. Accessed 15 Dec 2022
13. Konecranes: The yard revolution: Automated RTG (2013). https://www.konecranes.com/sites/default/files/download/konecranes_artg_brochure_final_0.pdf. Accessed 25 Apr 2023
14. Konecranes: Automated container handling references (2015). https://www.konecranes.com/sites/default/files/download/konecraners_references_automated_systems_global_en_2015_0.pdf. Accessed 25 Apr 2023
15. Nielsen, J.: Coordinating User Interfaces for Consistency. Morgan Kaufmann Publishers, San Francisco (1989)
16. Pace, S.: Citizens on YoutTube: research-method issues. In: Silva, C.N. (ed.) Online Research Methods in Urban and Planning Studies: Design and Outcomes, chap. 15, pp. 249–261. Information Science Reference, Hershey (2012). https://doi.org/10.4018/978-1-4666-0074-4.ch015

17. Sitompul, T.A.: The impacts of different work locations and levels of automation on crane operators' experiences: a study in a container terminal in Indonesia. In: Proceedings of the 34th Australian Conference on Human-Computer Interaction, OzCHI '22, pp. 193-198. ACM, New York (2023). https://doi.org/10.1145/3572921.3572941

18. Sitompul, T.A., Wallmyr, M.: Analyzing online videos: a complement to field studies in remote locations. In: Lamas, D., Loizides, F., Nacke, L., Petrie, H., Winckler, M., Zaphiris, P. (eds.) Human-Computer Interaction - INTERACT 2019. Lecture Notes in Computer Science(), vol. 11748, pp. 371–389. Springer, Cham (2019). https://doi.org/10.1007/978-3-030-29387-1_21

19. Statista: Hours of video uploaded to YouTube every minute as of February 2022 (2022). https://www.statista.com/statistics/259477/hours-of-video-uploaded-to-youtube-every-minute/. Accessed 26 Apr 2023

20. Thomas, S.L., Bestman, A., Pitt, H., Deans, E., Randle, M.J.: The marketing of wagering on social media: an analysis of promotional content on YouTube, Twitter and Facebook. Technical report, Victorian Responsible Gambling Foundation, Melbourne, Australia (2015). https://ro.uow.edu.au/cgi/viewcontent.cgi?article=1694&context=ahsri

21. Vesselov, S., Davis, T.: Building Design Systems: Unify User Experiences through a Shared Design Language. Apress, New York (2019). https://doi.org/10.1007/978-1-4842-4514-9

22. Wallmyr, M.: Exploring heavy vehicle interaction interaction design studies of industrial vehicle operators' information awareness using mixed reality. Ph.D. thesis, Mälardalen University (2020). http://urn.kb.se/resolve?urn=urn%3Anbn%3Ase%3Amdh%3Adiva-52409

23. Wortmeier, A.K., Calepso, A.S., Kropp, C., Sedlmair, M., Weiskopf, D.: Configuring augmented reality users: analysing YouTube commercials to understand industry expectations. Behav. Inf. Technol. 46, 1–16 (2023). https://doi.org/10.1080/0144929X.2022.2163693

Sustainable Human-Work Interaction Designs

Workshop on Sustainable Human-Work Interaction Designs: Introduction and Summary

Morten Hertzum[1]([✉]) [ID], Barbara Rita Barricelli[2] [ID], Elodie Bouzekri[3] [ID],
Torkil Clemmensen[4] [ID], and Masood Masoodian[5] [ID]

[1] Roskilde University, Universitetsvej 1, 4000 Roskilde, Denmark
mhz@ruc.dk
[2] Università degli Studi di Brescia, Via Branze 38, 25123 Brescia, Italy
barbara.barricelli@unibs.it
[3] Department of Electrical and Computer Engineering, McGill University, Montreal, QC,
Canada
elodie.bouzekri@mail.mcgill.ca
[4] Copenhagen Business School, Howitzvej 60, 2000 Frederiksberg, Denmark
tc.digi@cbs.dk
[5] School of Arts, Design and Architecture, Aalto University, 02150 Espoo, Finland
masood.masoodian@aalto.fi

Abstract. Sustainability has become a global concern that requires action at all
levels – from individual households to international politics. The field of human-
computer interaction (HCI) contributes analyses of perceptions and practices relating to sustainability, designs of tools for acting sustainably, and critical discussions of how best to convert green attitudes into green behavior. The workshop
on sustainable human-work interaction designs aimed to support HCI researchers
in making such contributions by providing a forum for sharing (a) methods and
processes for creating sustainable designs and workplaces, (b) case studies of experiences with introducing and learning from sustainability at work, and (c) agenda
items for future research on sustainable HCI. Seven of the nine papers presented at
the workshop were subsequently revised, extended, and included in this workshop
proceedings volume. They investigate sustainability in households, communities,
and workplaces. Individually, they provide illustrative case studies. Collectively,
they contribute valuable insights about the many faces of sustainability. We hope
that the workshop papers will inspire further research.

Keywords: Sustainability · Sustainable HCI · Human work interaction design

1 Introduction

The workshop on sustainable human-work interaction designs was organized jointly by
the IFIP working groups on Human Work Interaction Design (WG13.6) and Human-
Centered Technology for Sustainability (WG13.10). Working Group 13.6 contends that

A. Bramwell-Dicks et al. (Eds.): INTERACT 2023 Workshops, LNCS 14535, pp. 323–331, 2024.
https://doi.org/10.1007/978-3-031-61688-4_31

the integration of work analysis and interaction design is pivotal to the successful development and use of workplace systems [9]. Working Group 13.10 aims to encourage the sustainable use of resources through the design and deployment of technological systems [32]. The collaboration between the two working groups was motivated by the boundary-crossing nature of sustainability.

The aim of the workshop was to investigate ways of creating sustainable designs and workplaces by collecting case studies that analyze experiences – good and bad – with introducing and learning from sustainability at work [4]. This introduction to the workshop provides a framing for the case studies presented at the workshop and summarizes cross-cutting issues. The workshop papers, each a separate chapter in this volume, contain insightful reports on individual case studies with the overarching aim of inspiring and guiding future research on sustainable human work interaction design.

2 Designing for Sustainability at Work

Sustainability has multiple dimensions. The United Nations has formulated these dimensions in terms of goals. Its 17 sustainable development goals have become a shared blueprint for numerous initiatives to promote advances in peace and prosperity for people and the planet [34]. Another widely applied division of sustainability into dimensions is to distinguish between environmental sustainability, economic sustainability, and social sustainability [16]:

- *Environmental sustainability* is about the relationship between humans and nature. Attending to this dimension of sustainability involves that our pursuit of peace and prosperity must not deplete the planet's resources. That is, humans' current needs must be met without compromising future generations' ability to meet their needs.
- *Economic sustainability* is about the relationship between the spendings and earnings of companies (and other economic actors). This dimension of sustainability emphasizes profitability, productivity, and financial performance. Unless companies are economically sustainable, they will not be able to remain in business.
- *Social sustainability* is about relationships among people. This dimension of sustainability is rooted in constitutional human rights and in corporate social responsibility. It involves defending equal opportunities, fighting bias, promoting social justice, and pursuing personal or corporate goals in ways that do not abuse others.

Attending to sustainability involves attending to all three dimensions. In business jargon, this concomitant focus on environmental, economic, and social issues is commonly known as the triple bottom line [14]. It states that rather than focusing solely on their financial performance, businesses should also commit to measuring and following up on their environmental and social impact. To do so, they need tools and processes that support them in being environmentally and socially responsible. That is, they need sustainable human-work interaction designs. The human-computer interaction (HCI) community has taken on the design of such tools and processes [2, 6]. However, the wide scope of the challenges involved has also led to concerns about whether the extensive cross-disciplinarity required to devise effective solutions dilutes the contributions the HCI community can make [6]. In spite of these concerns, research on sustainable HCI has burgeoned and made contributions to reduce workplace energy consumption [27], review the prospects of safely encouraging eco-driving [30], promote repair over replacement [22], explore waste sorting in public spaces [24], quantify the energy consumption of domestic food preparation [8], raise awareness of greenhouse gas emissions [23], mitigate the environmental footprint of digital infrastructures [31], support freshwater conservation [21], share indoor air-quality measurements [28], reflect on unsustainable food practices [7], maintain biodiversity [12], develop a lifecycle assessment tool for carbon accounting [3], understanding the practices of simple living [18], and many more.

The many empirical studies have also been subjected to critical reflection [e.g., 6, 13, 19, 26]. A topic in several of these reflections is the export of unsustainable elements in the product lifecycle from the global North to the global South. A grave example is the dismantling and recycling of aging ocean vessels on beaches in South Asia under unsafe and unhealthy working conditions [11]. Somewhat surprisingly, this topic is absent in the workshop papers in spite of its relevance to social sustainability.

3   Contributed Papers

Of the nine papers presented at the workshop, seven are included in this workshop proceedings volume. All papers have been revised, extended, and reviewed after they were presented and discussed at the workshop. The papers investigate sustainable human-work interaction designs at the levels of the household, community, and workplace.

Two papers research sustainability at *the household level*. The motivation for such research is the substantial resource consumption and waste production at this level, which includes both individual consumers and families. To persuade householders to change their practices, a popular approach in sustainable HCI has been eco-feedback apps. These apps provide householders with information about the greenness of their actions, such as the distribution of their electricity consumption across green-energy and fossil-fuel sources. However, eco-feedback has been criticized for presuming that more information will produce more sustainable practices, thereby overlooking the attitude-behavior gap, and for framing sustainability in an overly individual-centered manner, thereby neglecting systemic causes and collective solutions [e.g., 6, 19]. Thus, the household level is only part of the picture; it must be combined with efforts at other levels. The two workshop papers that target the household level are Goodwin and Woolley [17] and Hertzum [20].

Goodwin and Woolley [17] demonstrate that consumers can extend the functional and useful lifespan of legacy devices by working around the barriers to installing applications on these devices. Vendors such as Apple label devices as "vintage" or "obsolete" when they have not been for sale for five and seven years, respectively. These labels transition devices from a fully compatible state to an unsupported state. However, the study shows that, with some workarounds, a sizeable number of applications can still be downloaded, installed, and run on legacy devices. Thereby, the study questions whether the devices are obsolete and points to ways of reducing e-waste.

Hertzum [20] investigates how sustainability factors into 24 householders' vacuuming practices. While the householders considered sustainability in their decisions about vacuuming, it was a minor consideration compared to other, often conflicting, factors.

The study proposes that vacuuming has similarities to routine work and that household-ers are likely to bring their overall attitude to sustainability with them when they go to work. This way, the household is a microcosm for studying and influencing how people reflect and act on sustainability – with some possibilities for carry-over effects to the workplace, and vice versa.

Another group of two workshop papers addresses sustainability at *the community level*. Both papers in this group investigate educational settings. The focus in sustainabil-ity research at the community level is often on enrolling community members in green thinking, for example by increasing their awareness of environmental issues or providing a forum for taking collaborative action. While sustainability research at the household level has been criticized for being overly individual-centered, sustainability research at the community level often leaves it unclear how and to what extent the initiatives can scale from their local starting point to an activity with wider impact. Scaling is important because "the processes that give rise to the issues indexed by the term sustainability are larger in time, space, organizational scale, ontological diversity, and complexity than the scales and scopes addressed by traditional HCI design, evaluation, and fieldwork methods" [33]. The two workshop papers in this group are Bansal and Lechelt [1] and Garg and Agarwal [15].

Bansal and Lechelt [1] identify the barriers that hinder the student users of a mak-erspace in reducing physical waste throughout their making process. Makerspaces are communal spaces that encourage material exploration and digital fabrication methods but also produce large amounts of scrap materials, leftover encasings, and other waste from the making activities. The study discusses possible strategies for encouraging both student makers and makerspace supervisors to adopt more sustainable practices. Thereby, the study supplements existing makerspace research, which tends to presume and emphasize the positive contributions of makerspaces to repair and repurposing.

Garg and Agarwal [15] present the initiatives of the HaritaDhara Research Develop-ment and Education Foundation (HRDEF) in India to build capacity for climate action among local youth, students, and professionals. The initiatives include workshops on sustainability-related curriculum topics, hands-on activity kits for experiment-based learning, and educational games for advancing the sustainable development goals. By encouraging collaboration, HRDEF aims for its initiatives to reach beyond the atten-dees through peer-to-peer learning in the community. The study illustrates the vast and multifaceted task of educating a large population about sustainable practices.

The third group of workshop papers addresses sustainability at *the workplace level*. To prioritize the sustainability agenda, companies often introduce the triple bottom line. It aims to ensure a consistent focus on how the company balances economic, environ-mental, and social sustainability, thereby aggregating operational sustainability initia-tives into a managerial summary. Research on sustainable HCI focuses mainly on the operational initiatives – their tools, structures, processes, and outcomes. Multiple inter-vention techniques have been developed for such initiatives [35]. While these initiatives are well-intended, critics contend that the required changes to industry will not happen on a voluntary basis: "It will have to be legislated—using the kinds of tough regulations, higher taxes, and steeper royalty rates these sectors have resisted all along" [29]. For such legislation to be passed, strong community-level activities are needed to create a mandate for politicians and legislators to act forcefully. Three of the workshop papers target the workplace level: Bouzekri and Rivière [5], Clemmensen et al. [10], and Joseph et al. [25].

Table 1. The relation of the workshop papers to the 17 UN sustainable development goals

Sustainable development goal	Goodwin and Woolley [17]	Hertzum [20]	Bansal and Lechelt [1]	Garg and Agarwal [15]	Bouzekri and Rivière [5]	Clemmensen et al. [10]	Joseph et al. [25]
No poverty							
Zero hunger							
Good health and well-being							
Quality education				x			
Gender equality							
Clean water and sanitation							
Affordable and clean energy					x		
Decent work and economic growth	x	x	x	x	x	x	x
Industry, innovation, and infrastructure	x		x			x	x
Reduced inequalities							
Sustainable cities and communities							x
Responsible consumption and production	x	x	x		x		
Climate action				x			
Life below water							
Life on land							
Peace, justice, and strong institutions							
Partnerships for the goals				x			

Bouzekri and Rivière [5] propose a design-fiction process for making energy consumption practices at work more sustainable. They specifically target the need for devising provisional practices for the period in between current and future conditions. These provisional practices must be feasible in the current work environment but must also include future practice tasks that, thereby, become relatable and testable today. Rather than focusing exclusively on the future goal, this approach facilitates and keeps track of the practice transformation that is involved in getting from the current situation to a sustainable future one.

Clemmensen et al. [10] devise and test a four-week, peer-tutoring program for training industry workers in job crafting. Job crafting is a bottom-up approach that supports workers in redesigning their own work practices to make them more personally, socially, economically, and/or environmentally sustainable. The study finds that the peer-tutoring program enabled conversations among the workers in the case company about recurrent work problems and their solutions. This way, job crafting promises to deliver sustainability through redesign. By empowering the individual worker, these redesigns are driven by those who know the details of the work processes.

Joseph et al. [25] report from a participatory-design process about the remote operation of unmanned ships for delivering goods in the domain of short-sea shipping. This way of delivering goods is more environmentally sustainable than transport by trucks over the road network. The developed scenarios and user interface focused on the factors most important to the carbon footprint of short-sea shipping – vessel size and scheduling optimization. The study illustrates how user-experience researchers can contribute to sustainability by building a holistic view of the factors involved and designing a user interface that assists the remote ship operators in attending to those factors.

The seven workshop papers span diverse issues, yet they cover only a small part of UN's sustainable development goals [34], see Table 1. There is a strong and urgent need for HCI research to scale up sustainability research in work settings and beyond.

4   Conclusion

HCI research on sustainability targets multiple levels of society, in particular the household, the community, and the workplace. The papers from the workshop on sustainable human-work interaction designs report from case studies at all three of these levels. Thereby, they provide insights specific to the different levels and possibilities for cross-fertilization. We hope that the seven workshop papers included in this workshop proceedings volume will inspire future research.

Acknowledgments. Further information about the two IFIP working groups (WG13.6 and WG13.10) that organized the workshop is available at https://ifip-tc13.org/working-groups.

References

1. Bansal, S., Lechelt, S.: Fostering sustainable making practices in a student makerspace. In: Bramwell-Dicks, A., Evans, A., Winckler, M., Petrie, H., Abdelnour-Nocera, J. (eds.) INTERACT 2023 Workshops. LNCS, vol. 14535, pp. 348–358. Springer, Cham (2024). https://doi.org/10.1007/978-3-031-61688-4_34

2. Blevis, E.: Sustainable interaction design: Invention & disposal, renewal & reuse. In: Proceedings of the CHI2007 Conference on Human Factors in Computing Systems, pp. 503–512. ACM, New York (2007). https://doi.org/10.1145/1240624.1240705
3. Bonanni, L., Hockenberry, M., Zwarg, D., Csikszentmihalyi, C., Ishii, H.: Small business applications of sourcemap: a web tool for sustainable design and suply chain transparency. In: Proceedings of the CHI2010 Conference on Human Factors in Computing Systems, pp. 937–946. ACM, New York (2010). https://doi.org/10.1145/1753326.1753465
4. Bouzekri, E., Barricelli, B.R., Clemmensen, T., Hertzum, M., Masoodian, M.: Sustainable human-work interaction designs. In: Abdelnour Nocera, J., Kristín Lárusdóttir, M., Petrie, H., Piccinno, A., Winckler, M. (eds.) INTERACT2023. LNCS, vol. 14145, pp. 674–679. Springer, Cham (2023). https://doi.org/10.1007/978-3-031-42293-5_92
5. Bouzekri, E., Rivière, G.: Towards an in-between practice to study energy shift at work. In: Bramwell-Dicks, A., Evans, A., Winckler, M., Petrie, H., Abdelnour-Nocera, J. (eds.) INTERACT 2023 Workshops. LNCS, vol. 14535, pp. 367–376. Springer, Cham (2024). https://doi.org/10.1007/978-3-031-61688-4_36
6. Bremer, C., Knowles, B., Friday, A.: Have we taken on too much?: A critical review of the sustainable HCI landscape. In: Proceedings of the CHI2022 Conference on Human Factors in Computing Systems, pp. 1–11. ACM, New York (2022). https://doi.org/10.1145/3491102.3517609
7. Choi, J.H.-J., Comber, R., Linehan, C.: Food for thought: designing for critical reflection on food practices. ACM Interact. **20**(1), 46–47 (2013). https://doi.org/10.1145/2405716.2405727
8. Clear, A.K., Hazas, M., Morley, J., Friday, A., Bates, O.: Domestic food and sustainable design: A study of university student cooking and its impacts. In: Proceedings of the CHI2013 Conference on Human Factors in Computing Systems, pp. 2447–2456. ACM, New York (2013). https://doi.org/10.1145/2470654.2481339
9. Clemmensen, T.: Human work interaction design: A Platform for Theory and Action. Springer, Cham (2021). https://doi.org/10.1007/978-3-030-71796-4
10. Clemmensen, T., Hertzum, M., Nørbjerg, J.: Job crafting to improve low-usability automation: Sustainability through human work interaction designs. In: Bramwell-Dicks, A., Evans, A., Winckler, M., Petrie, H., Abdelnour-Nocera, J. (eds.) INTERACT 2023 Workshops. LNCS, vol. 14535, pp. 377–387. Springer, Cham (2024). https://doi.org/10.1007/978-3-031-61688-4_39
11. Crang, M.: The death of great ships: Photography, politics, and waste in the global imaginary. Environ. Plan. A Econ. Sp. **42**(5), 1084–1102 (2010). https://doi.org/10.1068/a42414
12. Dema, T., Brereton, M., Esteban, M., Soro, A., Sherub, S., Roe, P.: Designing in the network of relations for species conservation: the playful Tingtibi community birdhouse. In: Proceedings of the CHI2020 Conference on Human Factors in Computing Systems, pp. 1–14. ACM, New York (2020). https://doi.org/10.1145/3313831.3376713
13. DiSalvo, C., Sengers, P., Brynjarsdóttir, H.: Mapping the landscape of sustainable HCI. In: Proceedings of the CHI2010 Conference on Human Factors in Computing Systems, pp. 1975–1984. ACM, New York (2010). https://doi.org/10.1145/1753326.1753625
14. Elkington, J.: Accounting for the triple bottom line. Meas. Bus. Excell. **2**(3), 18–22 (1998). https://doi.org/10.1108/eb025539
15. Garg, A.B., Agarwal, M.: Sustainable innovations for lifestyle, SDGs, and greening education. In: Bramwell-Dicks, A., Evans, A., Winckler, M., Petrie, H., Abdelnour-Nocera, J. (eds.) INTERACT 2023 Workshops. LNCS, vol. 14535, pp. 359–366. Springer, Cham (2024). https://doi.org/10.1007/978-3-031-61688-4_35
16. Giovannoni, E., Fabietti, G.: What is sustainability? A review of the concept and its applications. In: Busco, C., Frigo, M.L., Riccaboni, A., Quattrone, P. (eds.) Integrated Reporting, pp. 21–40. Springer, Cham (2013). https://doi.org/10.1007/978-3-319-02168-3_2

17. Goodwin, C., Woolley, S.: "Should I throw away my old iPad?" - Reconsidering usefulness in obsolete devices. In: Bramwell-Dicks, A., Evans, A., Winckler, M., Petrie, H., Abdelnour-Nocera, J. (eds.) INTERACT 2023 Workshops. LNCS, vol. 14535, pp. 332–339. Springer, Cham (2024). https://doi.org/10.1007/978-3-031-61688-4_32

18. Håkansson, M., Sengers, P.: Beyond being green: simple living families and ICT. In: Proceedings of the CHI2013 Conference on Human Factors in Computing Systems, pp. 2725–2734. ACM, New York (2013). https://doi.org/10.1145/2470654.2481378

19. Hansson, L., Pargman, T.C., Pargman, D.: A decade of sustainable HCI: Connecting SHCI to the sustainable development goals. In: Proceedings of the CHI2021 Conference on Human Factors in Computing Systems, pp. 1–19. ACM, New York (2021). https://doi.org/10.1145/3411764.3445069

20. Hertzum, M.: Sustainability and home automation: the case of repairing or replacing vacuum cleaners. In: Bramwell-Dicks, A., Evans, A., Winckler, M., Petrie, H., Abdelnour-Nocera, J. (eds.) INTERACT 2023 Workshops. LNCS, vol. 14535, pp. 340–347. Springer, Cham (2024). https://doi.org/10.1007/978-3-031-61688-4_33

21. Hirsch, T., Anderson, K.: Cross currents: water scarcity and sustainable CHI. In: Extended Abstracts of the CHI2010 Conference on Human Factors in Computing Systems, pp. 2843–2852. ACM, New York (2010). https://doi.org/10.1145/1753846.1753871

22. Jackson, S.J., Ahmed, S.I., Rifat, M.R.: Learning, innovation, and sustainability among mobile phone repairers in Dhaka, Bangladesh. In: Proceedings of the DIS2014 Conference on Designing Interactive Systems, pp. 905–914. ACM, New York (2014). https://doi.org/10.1145/2598510.2598576

23. Jacobs, R., Benford, S., Selby, M., Golembewski, M., Price, D., Giannachi, G.: A conversation between trees: what data feels like in the forest. In: Proceedings of the CHI2013 Conference on Human Factors in Computing Systems, pp. 129–138. ACM, New York (2013). https://doi.org/10.1145/2470654.2470673

24. Jacobsen, R.M., Johansen, P.S., Bysted, L.B.L., Skow, M.B.: Waste wizard: Exploring waste sorting using AI in public spaces. In: NordiCHI2020: Proceedings of the 11th Nordic Conference on Human-Computer Interaction, pp. 1–11. ACM, New York (2020). https://doi.org/10.1145/3419249.3420180

25. Joseph, A.W., Stolt, V., Roto, V.: Participatory design approach to sustainable voyage planning - Case maritime autonomous surface ships. In: Bramwell-Dicks, A., Evans, A., Winckler, M., Petrie, H., Abdelnour-Nocera, J. (eds.) INTERACT 2023 Workshops. LNCS, vol. 14535, pp. 388–393. Springer, Cham (2024). https://doi.org/10.1007/978-3-031-61688-4_38

26. Joshi, S., Pargman, T.C.: In search of fairness: critical design alternatives for sustainability. In: Proceedings of the Fifth Decennial Aarhus Conference on Critical Alternatives, pp. 37–40. ACM, New York (2015). https://doi.org/10.7146/aahcc.v1i1.21301

27. Katzeff, C., Broms, L., Jönsson, L., Westholm, U., Räsänen, M.: Exploring sustainable practices in workplace settings through visualizing electricity consumption. ACM Trans. Comput. Human Interact. 20(5), 1–22 (2013). https://doi.org/10.1145/2501526

28. Kim, S., Paulos, E.: InAir: sharing indoor air quality measurements and visualizations. In: Proceedings of the CHI2010 Conference on Human Factors in Computing Systems, pp. 1861–1870. ACM, New York (2010). https://doi.org/10.1145/1753326.1753605

29. Klein, N.: This changes everything: Capitalism vs. the climate. Simon & Schuster, New York (2014)

30. McIlroy, R.C., Stanton, N.A., Harvey, C., Robertson, D.: Sustainability, transport and design: reviewing the prospects for safely encouraging eco-driving. In: Proceedings of the 5th International Conference on Automotive User Interfaces and Interactive Vehicular Applications, pp. 278–284. ACM, New York (2013). https://doi.org/10.1145/2516540.2516578

31. Preist, C., Schien, D., Blevis, E.: Understanding and mitigating the effects of device and cloud service design decisions on the environmental footprint of digital infrastructure. In: Proceedings of the CHI2016 Conference on Human Factors in Computing Systems, pp. 1324–1337. ACM, New York (2016). https://doi.org/10.1145/2858036.2858378

32. da Hora Rodrigues, K.R., de Almeida Neris, V.P., Piccolo, L., Masoodian, M.: Human-centred technology for sustainable development goals - workshop results. In: Ardito, C., et al. (eds.) INTERACT 2021. LNCS, vol. 13198, pp. 3–9. Springer, Cham (2022). https://doi.org/10.1007/978-3-030-98388-8_1

33. Silberman, M.S., et al.: Next steps for sustainable HCI. ACM Interact. 21(5), 66–69 (2014). https://doi.org/10.1145/2651820

34. United Nations: The 17 goals. https://sdgs.un.org/goals. Accessed 01 Sept 2023

35. Yun, R., Scupelli, P., Aziz, A., Loftness, V.: Sustainability in the workplace: nine intervention techniques for behavior change. In: Berkovsky, S., Freyne, J. (eds.) PERSUASIVE 2013. LNCS, vol. 7822, pp. 253–265. Springer, Heidelberg (2013). https://doi.org/10.1007/978-3-642-37157-8_30

"Should I Throw Away My Old iPad?" - Reconsidering Usefulness in Obsolete Devices

Craig Goodwin(✉) 🆔 and Sandra Woolley 🆔

Keele University, Staffordshire, UK
c.goodwin@keele.ac.uk

Abstract. Device obsolescence contributes to the rising levels of annual e-waste. The research presented in this extended workshop paper summarises the findings of two studies conducted in 2021 and 2022 that highlighted the difficulties faced by consumers in downloading and installing applications on a legacy device classified as 'vintage' and, then subsequently, as 'obsolete'. The results of both studies demonstrated that few applications could be downloaded directly but, with the help of a non-legacy device's purchase history, the majority of applications could be downloaded and, furthermore, were functional. These results raise important questions about legacy devices and whether devices classified as vintage or obsolete could have longer lifespans as functional and useful devices. Informed by discussions at the 'Sustainable Human-Work Interaction Design' workshop at the 2023 INTERACT conference, this paper considers these questions, discusses possible prospects for devices nearing obsolescence and the sustainability implications of continued use of legacy devices.

Keywords: Device Reuse · Usefulness · E-waste · Digital Sustainability · Application Installation

1 Introduction

Apple Inc. classifies devices that are no longer being manufactured as either 'vintage' or 'obsolete', dependent on how long ago they were last distributed for sale [1, 2]. Products are defined as 'vintage' when *"Apple stopped distributing them for sale more than 5 and less than 7 years ago"* and defined as 'obsolete' when *"Apple stopped distributing them for sale more than 7 years ago"* [2]. These classification boundaries are significant landmarks where devices transition away from fully supported, functional app-compatible states into patchier territory where they are less supported, where application support is unclear and where consumers are left with few options to make further use of their devices. In most cases, consumers discard or replace their devices, further contributing to e-waste, or they retain them as dormant unused devices [6, 7].

The lifespan of Apple devices has been estimated to be approximately 4.3 years [9] and Apple have reported that most device users keep their devices for 3 years on average [10]. Alongside functional lifespans, the 'durability' of these devices is also dependent on the emotional attachment of the consumer [11].

© IFIP International Federation for Information Processing 2024
Published by Springer Nature Switzerland AG 2024
A. Bramwell-Dicks et al. (Eds.): INTERACT 2023 Workshops, LNCS 14535, pp. 332–339, 2024.
https://doi.org/10.1007/978-3-031-61688-4_32

Continued use of these devices will help toward reducing levels of e-waste [12]. Methods to improve sustainability are necessary to decrease growing e-waste includes the improvement in techniques to aid device longevity. Sustainability can be defined in several different ways, however in this context, sustainability for legacy devices is heavily focused around the need to reuse [13]. When the device has long surpassed its reuse phase, efforts to sustainably recycle them should be adapted [13].

Previous studies have identified and quantified the carbon footprint of end user computing devices in work and industry [14], with solutions identified for continued usage, but so far, no research has addressed the usefulness of these devices when nearing their 'obsolete' phase. The usefulness of a device in a human-computer interaction (HCI) context can be defined as *"anything that helps you get closer to or meet your goals"* [15]. For example, the usefulness of a legacy iPad Mini (the device used in the studies) would be a subjective judgement of the user based on its ability to achieve their usage goals. For some users, usefulness ends when the device no longer has 100% application support. Other users may deem their device useful if it provides a specific utility or service. Nevertheless, quantifying device usefulness is an area of research which has had little to no exploration.

APPLE RUMBLE Millions of iPhones just became 'obsolete and dangerous' – check your model now

ROTTING APPLE Your old iPhone is about to become obsolete and potentially worthless as the tech giant gets set to stop its support

Fig. 1. Examples of popular press headlines about legacy devices. Image Sources: https://www.thesun.co.uk/news/1993244/old-iphone-obsolete-apple/, https://www.the-sun.com/tech/6380200/millions-iphones-obsolete-dangerous-check-model/

As illustrated in the popular press examples in Fig. 1, older devices are not uncommonly portrayed as "worthless", and their use described as "dangerous". Such reports suggest there is potential misunderstanding that obsolescence equals dangerous. Based on studies conducted in previous papers [3, 16], comparisons are made between two separate studies conducted when an Apple device was 'vintage' and then 'obsolete' to evaluate a) the decrease in device usefulness and b) to attempt to benchmark the quantification of device usefulness by analysing application compatibility [3, 4].

2 Method

Two studies were conducted with a first-generation Apple iPad Mini running iOS version 9.3.5. First produced in 2012, this device was significant as the last 32-bit product manufactured by Apple [8]. At the time of the first study (Sept 2021), the device was in the transitional state between 'vintage' and 'obsolete' classifications. At the time of the second study (May 2022) the device was newly classified as 'vintage'. For both studies, the top-10 free applications across 23 popular categories were selected and attempts were made to download them directly onto the device. If the application failed to download directly, then use was made of a modern, non-legacy device (Apple SE) with a pre-existing purchase history. This workaround is required because there are compatibility barriers in place to directly downloading applications on legacy Apple devices. Applications that could be downloaded directly (DD) or 'downloaded via another device' (DvAD) were then checked for whether they could be installed, if they opened, and finally if they were functional. Table 1 provides a summary of the device materials used in the studies, and Fig. 2 provides a summarised flowchart of the study methodology.

Table 1. Materials Summary for the Study Devices: Direct Download (DD) and Download via Another Device (DvAD)

Device	Classification Study Sept 2021	Classification Sequel Study May 2022
STUDY DD device: Apple iPad Mini tablet, 16GB (Wi-Fi), 1GHz dual core ARM Cortex-A9. Released: 2 Nov 2012. Discontinued: 19 Jun 2015 Last OS update 25 Aug 2016: iOS 9.3.5	Vintage	Obsolete
OTHER DvAD device: Apple iPhone SE. 16GB Released: 31 March 2016. Discontinued 21 March 2017. Last OS update 13 Dec 2022: iOS 15.7.2	Current	Current

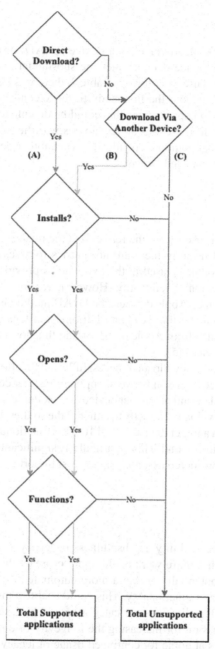

Fig. 2. Flowchart of the experiment application installation process A) Applications that downloaded directly. B) Applications that are downloaded via another device. C) Applications that neither downloaded directly nor via another device.

3 Analysis

The complexity of the download via another device (DvAD) process and the need for an additional non-legacy device demonstrates the substantial hurdles in place to both device reuse and continued use. As shown in Table 2, there was a slight overall decrease in application functionality from the first study to the second study (61.3% vs 57%). There was also a decrease in applications that could be downloaded directly (12.6% vs 8.7%) though an overall decrease was anticipated as was the marginal increase in the number of applications that could be downloaded via another device (given that fewer applications could be downloaded directly).

4 Discussion

The key discussion point taken from the research is the quantification of obsolescence and device usefulness. Currently there are no metrics to assess device usefulness or obsolescence. The methodology used in the two studies provides a means to quantify both in terms of application functionality. However, for individual users looking to install applications on legacy Apple devices, the DvAD method is a difficult and tedious workaround, and it necessitates the use of an additional non-legacy device. Additionally, there is no official guidance from Apple on how to do this nor how to otherwise extend the longevity of these devices [5].

Many of the applications downloaded successfully and functioned. Certain categories were noteworthy in the comparison between applications that could download directly verses those that required the aid of another device. For example, none of the productivity applications could be downloaded directly in either of the studies, however all 10 out of 10 could be downloaded via another device and all 10 were functional in the first study and 9 of 10 were functional in the second. This is particularly significant given that productivity applications might be considered as amongst the most important applications for device utility.

4.1 Future Work

Device longevity and the usability and usefulness of legacy devices are neglected but worthy areas of research. Future work could apply or adapt the methodology to similar Apple devices and potentially enable a more automated assessment of application download, installation, and functionality. This could enable a much faster process such that much more than 10 applications per category could be assessed. Furthermore, the research creates a discussion for increasing the longevity of devices in many different environments. Decisions at home for continued usage of legacy devices lie solely with the consumer. However, in many workplaces, particularly creative environments, Apple products are a necessity. Research on device turnover in different work environments could compare device lifespans and, for example, explore work-based perceptions of obsolescence.

Table 2. Heatmap of the Comparison of App Functionality for Directly and Indirectly Downloadable Apps in the Two Studies

App Category	Functional Apps DD (Sep 2021)	Functional Apps DD (May 2022)	Change	Functional Apps DvAD (Sep 2021)	Functional Apps DvAD (May 2022)	Change
Books	4	0	-4	4	5	1
Business	1	0	-1	7	7	0
Education	3	1	-2	6	6	0
Entertainment	3	0	-3	5	6	1
Finance	1	1	0	6	6	0
Food & Drink	0	1	1	5	5	0
Games	1	4	3	1	3	2
Health & Fitness	0	1	1	6	6	0
Lifestyle	1	1	0	6	6	0
Magazine & Newspapers	5	0	-5	5	6	1
Medical	3	2	-1	3	4	1
Music	0	0	0	9	9	0
Navigation	1	2	1	5	5	0
News	0	1	1	8	8	0
Photo & Video	0	0	0	8	8	0
Productivity	0	0	0	10	9	-1
Reference	1	0	-1	7	7	0
Shopping	0	3	3	7	6	-1
Social Networking	2	1	-1	6	6	0
Sports	0	0	0	6	6	0
Travel	0	1	1	7	6	-1
Utilities	2	1	-1	6	6	0
Weather	1	0	-1	7	7	0
TOTAL	29	20	-9	140	143	3

5 Conclusion

The research discussed in this paper has highlighted the barriers in place to downloading and installing applications on vintage and obsolete Apple devices. The work questions the notion of device obsolescence when legacy devices still have use in terms of substantial and quantifiable application functionality, albeit more limited than that of modern devices. Security must, of course, be a key concern and legacy devices could be susceptible to security issues over time with continued usage. One major question lingers. At what point do consumers give up on efforts to continue making use of their devices?

In more open software ecosystems, methods exist to extend the longevity of devices, whether by use of different distributions of Linux for older PCs or 'Android builds' for older smartphones. Nevertheless, open ecosystems allow for continued use of these devices, which is something not available to Apple users. Attempts have been made to utilise older Apple devices by installing other operating systems on these devices, but without significant time and resources, this is difficult to see in the future. It is recommended that future research pursues the quantification of device usefulness and the understanding of device longevity with the aim of preventing future devices needlessly becoming e-waste sooner than needed.

References

1. Apple Lifecycle Management, Apple(2020). https://www.apple.com/ie/business/docs/resources/Apple_Lifecycle_Management.pdf
2. Apple, Obtaining service for your Apple product after an expired warranty, Apple Support (2023). https://support.apple.com/en-us/HT201624
3. Goodwin, C., Woolley, S.: Barriers to device longevity and reuse: an analysis of application download, installation and functionality on a vintage device. In: Perrouin, G., Moha, N., Seriai, AD. (eds.) Reuse and Software Quality. ICSR 2022. LNCS, vol. 13297, pp. 138–145. Springer, Cham (2022). https://doi.org/10.1007/978-3-031-08129-3_9
4. Usefulness, utility, usability: 3 goals of UX Design. https://www.youtube.com/watch?v=VwgZtqTQzg8
5. Apple Community. https://discussions.apple.com/docs/DOC-13282
6. Jensen, P.B., Laursen, L.N., Haase, L.M.: Barriers to product longevity: a review of business, product development and user perspectives. J. Clean. Prod. 313, 127951 (2021)
7. Bieser, J., Burkhalter, L., Hilty, L., Fuchs, B., Blumer, Y.: Lifetime extension of mobile Internet-enabled devices: Measures, challenges and environmental implications. University of Zurich. University of Limerick Institutional Repository (2021). https://doi.org/10.31880/10344/10165
8. Apple Discussions, Complete List of iPads, release year and current iOS/iPad Os version they can run, Apple Community (2022). https://discussions.apple.com/docs/DOC-250001726
9. Asymco. https://www.asymco.com/2018/03/01/determining-the-average-apple-device-lifespan/
10. Potuck, M.: Here's how long Apple users are holding on to their iPhones. 9to5Mac (2023). https://9to5mac.com/2023/05/10/how-long-people-keep-iphones/
11. Chapman, J.: Design for (emotional) durability. Des. Issues 25(4), 29–35 (2009). https://doi.org/10.1162/desi.2009.25.4.29
12. Heacock, M., et al.: E-waste and harm to vulnerable populations: a growing global problem. Environ. Health Perspect. 124(5), 550–555 (2016). https://doi.org/10.1289/ehp.1509699

13. Forbes.   https://www.forbes.com/sites/charlesradclyffe/2021/08/17/the-four-rs-of-sustai nable-tech/
14. Sutton-Parker, J.: Is sufficient carbon footprint information available to make sustainability focused computer procurement strategies meaningful? Procedia Comput. Sci. **203**, 280–289 (2022). https://doi.org/10.1016/j.procs.2022.07.036
15. The Interaction Design Foundation. https://www.interaction-design.org/literature/topics/use fulness
16. Goodwin, C., Woolley, S., de Quincey, E., Collins, T.: Quantifying device usefulness - how useful is an obsolete device?. In: Abdelnour Nocera, J., Kristín Lárusdóttir, M., Petrie, H., Piccinno, A., Winckler, M. (eds.) Human-Computer Interaction – INTERACT 2023. LCNS, vol 14145, pp. 90–99. Springer, Cham (2023). https://doi.org/10.1007/978-3-031-42293-5_8
17. Blackwood Creative. https://blackwoodcreative.com/why-apple-products-thrive-in-creative-spaces/

Sustainability and Home Automation: The Case of Repairing or Replacing Vacuum Cleaners

Morten Hertzum(✉) [iD]

Roskilde University, Roskilde, Denmark
mhz@ruc.dk

Abstract. Household practices are a microcosm that shows how we think about sustainability on an everyday basis. This study focuses on vacuuming, which is a household chore with similarities to routine activities at work. The 24 participants in the study merely considered sustainability a minor aspect in their decisions about which vacuum cleaner to buy. Brand, price, and suction power were top considerations. With respect to repair/replace decisions, participants tended to favor repair, that is, the more sustainable option. However, decisions to repair a vacuum cleaner that broke down were often on the condition that it could be done cheaply. In contrast, decisions to replace were never conditional. Finally, participants exhibited cross-country differences in the importance they attached to sustainability. These differences suggest that national discourses have the power to influence individual householders' views on sustainability.

Keywords: sustainability · repair · replace · home automation · vacuum cleaner

1 Introduction

Sustainability has become a global concern [2, 17, 18]. It requires action at all levels, including the home. For example, households account for 27% of total energy consumption and 41% of CO_2 emissions in the US [16]. Household practices are a microcosm that shows how we consider – or disregard – sustainability on an everyday basis. Thereby, studies of sustainability at home have value in their own right and can also inform studies of sustainability at work. This study focuses on a single household practice, namely vacuuming.

Vacuuming is a recurring household chore, which is performed using vacuum cleaners at different levels of technical sophistication. Autonomous vacuum-cleaner robots have made it easier to schedule vacuuming for the off-peak periods in energy consumption. At the same time, studies warn that robotic vacuum cleaners may lead to more frequent vacuuming, thereby possibly increasing energy consumption rather than making it greener [13]. Other inventions include bagless vacuum cleaners that reduce waste by collecting the dirt in an emptiable container rather than a disposable bag [23]. However, factors other than environmental sustainability also influence householders' decisions about vacuuming and vacuum cleaners. The omnipresence of such factors is

© IFIP International Federation for Information Processing 2024
Published by Springer Nature Switzerland AG 2024
A. Bramwell-Dicks et al. (Eds.): INTERACT 2023 Workshops, LNCS 14535, pp. 340–347, 2024.
https://doi.org/10.1007/978-3-031-61688-4_33

captured in the recognition that any approach to sustainability must integrate environmental, financial, and social concerns [5]. For vacuum cleaners, the non-environmental concerns for example include hygiene [15], price [4], and anthropomorphic relations to robotic vacuum cleaners [22]. This study investigates householders' thoughts about sustainability in relation to repairing and replacing their vacuum cleaners.

2 Background

A recurring finding in the research on sustainability is the attitude-behavior gap, which reflects that pro-environmental values and intentions often fail to translate into green purchases and ecofriendly practices [11, 16]. This gap shows that efforts to increase consumer knowledge, for example through the provision of information, will likely have little effect on behavior. It also shows that consumer behavior models based on rational choice are deficient because they tend to equate attitudes with behaviors. Instead, much of our environmental impact as consumers comes from activities that are shaped more by habit and convenience than conscious thought. For example, Rabiu and Jaeger-Erben [19] contend that sustainable practices result when "the relevant situational context and the required practice elements in terms of objects, skills, and meanings co-occur and do not contradict the existing socially accepted ways of doing and saying." They also provide a model of ecofriendly consumer practices at three stages in a circular-economy lifecycle [19]:

- At the acquisition stage: second-hand, store (for later use), and refurbish
- At the use stage: replace (with a more ecofriendly option), reuse, repair, and care
- At the disposal stage: resell/donate and recycle

These practices provide welcome contrast to the design-focused lifecycle models that otherwise dominate in human-computer interaction (HCI) and tend to foreground the activities of analysis, design, implementation, and use/maintenance.

Many products are disposed of while they are still functional [12]. This practice may be particularly prominent for lifestyle products such as mobile phones [9], consumer groups such as early adopters [20], and cultural contexts such as Western Europe and North America [8]. Among the occasions for disposal, product breakdowns have attracted particular attention. Breakdowns prompt a decision to repair or replace the product. Sonego et al. [21] review the literature and find that the main motivations to repair are emotional attachment to the product, extended use of the product, high-quality products, preservation of personal data, positive prior experiences with repair services, and environmental reasons. In contrast, the main barriers to repair are cost, time, inconvenience, lack of information, obsolescence of product, expected quality of repair, and negative prior experiences with repair services [21]. The barriers often trump the motivations, including the consumers' positive attitude toward sustainability. The resulting preference for replacement is amplified by the larger over-time increase in the cost of repair compared to that of new products [10].

With specific reference to vacuum cleaners, Visser et al. [23] analyze 950 Western European consumers' purchase of a new vacuum cleaner in 2010 and find that only 27% of them bought an ecofriendly model. Irrespective of whether they bought an ecofriendly model, 94% of the consumers indicated that brand, durability, key features, reliability, and value for money were the main reasons for their purchase decision. Only 6% of the consumers stated that they chose the purchased model for environmental reasons. Multiple factors contribute to the environmental footprint of vacuum cleaners, including materials, production, transport, use, and disposal. However, use is by far the largest contributor, mainly because the use stage is typically years long. Use contributes about 80% of the environmental footprint of a vacuum cleaner [14], thereby making its power consumption during use (the number of watts) almost proportional to its ecofriendliness. The power consumption is, however, also related to the effectiveness of the vacuum cleaner, that is, to its suction power. Thus, consumers who consider purchasing an ecofriendly vacuum cleaner may worry that it is less effective.

3   Method

The study involved 24 participants, each having 1, 2, or 3 vacuum cleaners. In total, the participants had 36 vacuum cleaners distributed across France (8 participants, 11 vacuum cleaners), the Netherlands (8 participants, 12 vacuum cleaners), and Portugal (8 participants, 13 vacuum cleaners). The vacuum cleaners were near evenly distributed among canister-with-bag models (9), canister-without-bag models (10), upright-cordless models (9), and robotic models (8). Each participant took part in a three-week diary study that consisted of sensitizing activities and forms to be filled in. During the sensitizing activities, participants photographed and video-recorded their vacuuming practices. During form fill-in, participants answered questions about their user experience with their vacuum cleaners.

This paper involves six of the questions. Two free-text questions were about why the participants chose their vacuum cleaner and whether they would repair or replace it if it broke down. These questions were analyzed by grouping the content of the 36 answers to each question into reasons for buying and into conditions and causes for repairing or replacing. Three rating-scale questions were about the importance participants attached to sustainability. These questions were analyzed with analyses of variance (ANOVAs) to test for differences across countries. Finally, one rating-scale question about the importance of ease of use was included for comparative purposes.

4   Results

In response to the question "Why did you choose to buy this vacuum cleaner?", the participants provided 65 reasons: brand (9), price (9), practical (8), suction power (8), cordless (5), bagless (4), easy to use (4), efficient (4), automatic (3), size (3), ecofriendly (2), good (2), long cord (2), noise level (1), and aesthetic (1). That is, the environmental dimension of sustainability was merely a minor factor in their decision about which vacuum cleaner to buy. Several participants remarked that good suction power equaled high energy consumption and that they were not prepared to sacrifice suction power for the sake of lower energy consumption. That is, they were not prepared to sacrifice product performance for improved ecofriendliness.

Participants were also asked whether they would have their vacuum cleaner repaired or replaced if it broke down ("Imagine your vacuum cleaner breaks down, do you repair it or buy a new one?"). They would repair 20 of their vacuum cleaners and replace 15 of them. One vacuum cleaner (a robot) would neither be repaired nor replaced because the participant had two vacuum cleaners and did not experience a real need for the robotic vacuum cleaner. Table 1 shows the conditions that qualified the participants' repair/replace decisions and the causes that explained them. Notably, only repair decisions were conditional, mostly on the price of the repair. Apparently, replace decisions did not involve the uncertainty indicated by qualifying conditions. With respect to causes, repairing and replacing were considered the cheaper option about equally often. Low price, ecofriendliness, and satisfaction with the vacuum cleaner were the main causes for repair decisions. In addition, one owner of a robotic vacuum cleaner explained that it would be repaired because it was part of the family and, therefore, not replaceable (it is not uncommon for householders to have anthropomorphic relations to their robotic vacuum cleaners [24]). The main causes for replace decision were dissatisfaction with the current vacuum cleaner, low price, and the opportunity to upgrade to a better model. Overall, repair/replace decisions would be based on competing criteria, of which sustainability was just one.

Table 1. Conditions (*If* column) and causes (*Because* column) for repair/replace decisions.

Decision	If	Because
Repair	Cheap (7), Possible (2), Quick (1)	Cheaper (6), Ecofriendly (3), Happy with it (3), It is not old (2), It is part of the family (1)
Replace	-	Not happy with it (7), Cheaper (5), Upgrade to better model (3), Quicker (1)
Neither	-	No need for it (1)

Note: numbers in parentheses give the number of times a condition or cause was mentioned

The participants considered sustainability issues important but not very important, see Table 2. For example, the first question in the table received a mean rating of 7.43 on a scale from 0 (not important) to 10 (very important). In comparison, the question "Overall, how important is ease of use" received a mean rating of 9.06 ($SD = 1.12$), that is, about one and a half scale point above the sustainability questions. Notably, the importance of sustainability varied across countries for two of the three questions in Table 2. First, the importance of repairability varied across countries, $F(2, 32) = 4.70, p = .016$. Bonferroni-adjusted pairwise comparisons showed that Portuguese participants attached significantly more importance to repairability than Dutch participants did. Second, the importance of recyclability also varied across countries, $F(2, 31) = 8.96, p < .001$. Bonferroni-adjusted pairwise comparisons showed that French and Portuguese participants attached significantly more importance to recyclability than Dutch participants did. For the third question, there was no difference across countries in the importance that participants attached to environmental friendliness in their vacuum cleaner, $F(2, 32) = 3.11, p = .059$.

Table 2. Importance of sustainability across countries (mean and, in parentheses, standard deviation), all questions answered on a scale from 0 (not important) to 10 (very important).

Question	France	Netherlands	Portugal	Total
Overall, how important is repairability for you, $N = 35$ *	7.60 (2.46)	5.83 (3.07)	8.7 (1.48)	7.43 (2.65)
How important is it that your vacuum cleaner can be recycled, $N = 34$ ***	8.60 (1.78)	4.91 (3.11)	8.38 (1.81)	7.32 (2.80)
How important is environmental friendliness for you in a vacuum cleaner, $N = 35$	8.20 (1.62)	6.42 (3.03)	8.54 (1.76)	7.71 (2.38)

Note: * $p < .05$, *** $p < .001$ (analysis of variance)

5 Discussion

While vacuuming is a household chore, it has similarities to routine activities at work. These similarities provide some possibilities for generalizing from home to work – if it is done cautiously. In particular, people will likely bring their overall attitude to sustainability, such as its importance relative to ease of use, with them when they go to work. In this way, the adoption of greener attitudes in relation to household chores will, to some extent, be carried over into the workplace, and vice versa. However, other aspects are specific to the household context. The household context means that the user cannot offload sustainability to other actors, such as management. Either the householder prioritizes sustainability or it is trumped by other considerations. The total set of considerations involves tradeoffs, so sustainability comes at the cost of valuing it over conflicting concerns [1].

Efforts to promote more sustainable practices have been criticized for taking an overly individual-centered approach, thereby not designing with and for communities [7]. An effort beyond the individual level has been the decision by the European Commission to implement legislation that limits the maximum power consumption of household appliances, including vacuum cleaners [23]. Such legislation reduces the burden on the individual consumer at the point of purchase because all models available will meet minimum standards of ecofriendliness. This way, legislation narrows the attitude-behavior gap in a more forceful manner than information and nudging, which aim to stimulate sustainable behavior but leave the choice of whether to act on this stimulus to the consumer. Engaging in work to influence national or international legislation will require that HCI researchers become even more cross-disciplinary in their efforts to promote sustainability. To avoid taking on too much, it has been argued that HCI researchers should instead presume that ambitious climate policies, including legislation, will be passed and, then, make designs to help implement these policies [3].

Effective strategies for inducing sustainable practices will differ across products because their characteristics and contexts of use differ. For vacuum cleaners, strategies to promote repair over replacement must consider that vacuuming tends to be a backstage activity. It is usually not done in front of others but rather in preparation for their arrival – to be able to present a clean and tidy home. As a backstage activity, it is socially visible only through the cleanliness it produces. Any tradeoff between sustainability and effective cleaning will be an element in the more general interaction between private backstage activities and the socially visible frontstage presentation they enable [6]. Householders may feel more strongly about presenting a clean and tidy home to their social relations than about sacrificing sustainability in private. Thus, strategies for facilitating householders in adopting ecofriendly vacuuming practices cannot rely on social norms/control in the same way as for products that are used in social settings. In contrast to vacuum cleaners, mobile phones have become part and parcel of frontstage activities and, therefore, provide more possibilities for interweaving considerations about sustainable phone practices in social interactions. When available, such possibilities should be exploited in designs and strategies to promote repair and other ecofriendly behaviors. When not available, other means must be activated. The cross-country differences in the importance of sustainability suggest that national discourses about environmental issues may be one such means. The identified differences among three Western European countries are also a reminder that even larger differences in sustainability attitudes must be expected in a global sample.

6 Conclusion

The participants in this study considered sustainability in their vacuuming decisions but it was merely a minor consideration compared to factors such as brand, price, and suction power. In terms of frequency of mention, sustainability was a factor in buying decisions on a par with whether the vacuum cleaner had a long cord. On the positive side, participants tended to favor repair over replacement, but decisions to repair were often on the condition that it could be done cheaply. Finally, the cross-country differences in the importance of sustainability suggest that national discourses produce social norms with the power to influence individual householders' views on sustainability.

Acknowledgments. The data analyzed in this study were collected by International Consumer Research and Testing (ICRT), which in this specific case comprised the consumer associations Altroconsumo Edizioni SRL in Italy, Association des Consommateurs Test-Achats SC in Belgium, Consumentenbond in the Netherlands, DECO-Proteste Editores LDA in Portugal, OCU-Ediciones SA in Spain, and UFC - Que Choisir in France. ICRT subsequently made the data available to the author. The author is grateful to Niels Ebbe Jacobsen from ICRT for his support in making the data available for this study.

References

1. Bangsa, A.B., Schlegelmilch, B.B.: Linking sustainable product attributes and consumer decision-making: Insights from a systematic review. J. Clean. Prod. **245**, 118902 (2020). https://doi.org/10.1016/j.jclepro.2019.118902
2. Bouzekri, E., Barricelli, B.R., Clemmensen, T., Hertzum, M., Masoodian, M.: Sustainable human-work interaction designs. In: Abdelnour Nocera, J., Kristín Lárusdóttir, M., Petrie, H., Piccinno, A., Winckler, M. (eds.) INTERACT 2023. LNCS, vol. 14145, pp. 674–679. Springer, Cham (2023). https://doi.org/10.1007/978-3-031-42293-5_92

3. Bremer, C., Knowles, B., Friday, A.: Have we taken on too much?: A critical review of the sustainable HCI landscape. In: Proceedings of the CHI2022 Conference on Human Factors in Computing Systems, pp. 1–11. ACM, New York (2022). https://doi.org/10.1145/3491102.3517609

4. Carames, K., Mui, K., Azad, A., Giang, W.C.W: Studying robot vacuums using online retailer reviews to understand human-automation interaction. In: Proceedings of Human Factors Ergonomics Society Annual Meeting, vol. 65, no. 1, pp. 1029–1033 (2021). https://doi.org/10.1177/1071181321651106

5. Giovannoni, E., Fabietti, G.: What is sustainability? A review of the concept and its applications. In: Busco, C., Frigo, M.L., Riccaboni, A., Quattrone, P. (eds.) Integrated Reporting, pp. 21–40. Springer, Cham (2013). https://doi.org/10.1007/978-3-319-02168-3_2

6. Goffman, E.: The Presentation of Self in Everyday Life. Anchor Books, New York (1959)

7. Hertzum, M., Barricelli, B.R., Bouzekri, E., Clemmensen, T., Masoodian, M.: Workshop on sustainable human-work interaction designs: Introduction and summary. In: INTERACT 2023 Workshops, Selected Papers. Springer, Cham (2024). https://doi.org/10.1007/978-3-031-61688-4_31

8. Jackson, S.J.: Rethinking repair. In: Gillespie, T., Boczkowski, P.J., Foot, K.A. (eds.) Media Technologies: Essays on Communication, Materiality, and Society, pp. 221–239. MIT Press, Cambridge, MA (2014)

9. Jaeger-Erben, M., Frick, V., Hipp, T.: Why do users (not) repair their devices? A study of the predictors of repair practices. J. Clean. Prod. **286**, 125382 (2021). https://doi.org/10.1016/j.jclepro.2020.125382

10. King, A.M., Burgess, S.C., Ijomah, W., McMahon, C.A.: Reducing waste: repair, recondition, remanufacture or recycle? Sustain. Dev. **14**(4), 257–267 (2006). https://doi.org/10.1002/sd.271

11. Kollmuss, A., Agyeman, J.: Mind the gap: Why do people act environmentally and what are the barriers to pro-environmental behavior? Environ. Educ. Res. **8**(3), 239–260 (2002). https://doi.org/10.1080/13504620220145401

12. Magnier, L., Mugge, R.: Replaced too soon? An exploration of Western European consumers' replacement of electronic products. Resour. Conserv. Recycl. **185**, 106448 (2022). https://doi.org/10.1016/j.resconrec.2022.106448

13. Nicholls, L., Strengers, Y.: Robotic vacuum cleaners save energy? Raising cleanliness conventions and energy demand in Australian households with smart home technologies. Energy Res. Soc. Sci. **50**, 73–81 (2019). https://doi.org/10.1016/j.erss.2018.11.019

14. Palma, N.C., Visser, M.: Sustainability creates business and brand value. J. Brand Strateg. **1**(3), 217–222 (2012)

15. Park, J., et al.: Development of a web-based user experience evaluation system for home appliances. Int. J. Ind. Ergon. **67**, 216–228 (2018). https://doi.org/10.1016/j.ergon.2018.05.017

16. Peattie, K.: Green consumption: behavior and norms. Annu. Rev. Environ. Resour. **35**(1), 195–228 (2010). https://doi.org/10.1146/annurev-environ-032609-094328

17. Portney, K.E.: Sustainability. MIT Press, Cambridge, MA (2015)

18. Purvis, B., Mao, Y., Robinson, D.: Three pillars of sustainability: in search of conceptual origins. Sustain. Sci. **14**(3), 681–695 (2019). https://doi.org/10.1007/s11625-018-0627-5

19. Rabiu, M.K., Jaeger-Erben, M.: Appropriation and routinisation of circular consumer practices: a review of current knowledge in the circular economy literature. Clean. Responsible Consum. **7**, 100081 (2022). https://doi.org/10.1016/j.clrc.2022.100081

20. Rogers, E.M.: Diffusion of Innovations, 5th edn. Free Press, New York (2003)

21. Sonego, M., Echeveste, M.E.S., Debarba, H.G.: Repair of electronic products: consumer practices and institutional initiatives. Sustain. Prod. Consum. **30**, 556–565 (2022). https://doi.org/10.1016/j.spc.2021.12.031

22. Sung, J.-Y., Guo, L., Grinter, R.E., Christensen, H.I.: "My roomba is rambo": intimate home appliances. In: Krumm, J., Abowd, G.D., Seneviratne, A., Strang, T. (eds.) UbiComp 2007. LNCS, vol. 4717, pp. 145–162. Springer, Heidelberg (2007). https://doi.org/10.1007/978-3-540-74853-3_9

23. Visser, M., Schoormans, J., Vogtländer, J.: Consumer buying behaviour of sustainable vacuum cleaners - Consequences for design and marketing. J. Clean. Prod. **195**, 664–673 (2018). https://doi.org/10.1016/j.jclepro.2018.05.114

24. Yapici, N.B., Tuglulular, T., Basoglu, N.: Assessment of human-robot interaction between householders and robotic vacuum cleaners. In: TEMSCON2022: Proceedings of the Technology and Engineering Management Conference, pp. 204–209. IEEE, New York (2022). https://doi.org/10.1109/TEMSCONEUROPE54743.2022.9802007

Fostering Sustainable Making Practices
in a Student Makerspace

Shivangi Bansal[✉][ID] and Susan Lechelt[ID]

The University of Edinburgh, Edinburgh EH8 9YL, UK
sbansal2@ed.ac.uk

Abstract. Unsustainable consumption and production practices in the workplace exacerbate the environmental crisis. Student makerspaces are one such workplace that encourages student innovation by offering a supportive environment for experimentation and learning, but also contributes to issues of overconsumption, disposal, and obsolescence. This research explores the question: how can student makerspaces support student makers in making more sustainable choices? We provide empirical insights into the sustainability of student makerspaces, identifying the factors that encourage students in, and the potential barriers that prevent them from, reducing physical waste throughout the making process. Our findings further offer potential strategies for encouraging sustainable behaviour among student makers in a makerspace environment.

Keywords: Sustainable making practice · Student makerspace · attitude-behaviour gap · Design for behaviour change

1 Introduction

Student makerspaces serve as communal workplaces that encourage collaboration, as well as the exchange of knowledge, tools and ideas while learning [2]. Makers can be students, hobbyists, professional designers, researchers, entrepreneurs, or technologists [15,17], engaging in activities that frequently involve a mix of coding, digital fabrication methods like 3D printing, and material exploration [2]. However, makerspace practices often have a high material impact and lead to the production of a large amount of physical waste, such as scrap materials, and unsuccessful or leftover artefacts that are no longer useful after a project is finished. In this study, we focus on how student makers can reflect more deeply on the environmental implications of their projects [see also [4,10]]. To engage in sustainable making, students must examine the consequences of their decisions beyond the design process, actively prevent waste, and manage the waste that they produce [4].

Other research has indicated that makers typically have the right attitude and plan to engage in sustainable making practices, such as using low-impact materials or prototyping ideas early to prevent wasting resources [19]. Yet,

© IFIP International Federation for Information Processing 2024
Published by Springer Nature Switzerland AG 2024
A. Bramwell-Dicks et al. (Eds.): INTERACT 2023 Workshops, LNCS 14535, pp. 348–358, 2024.
https://doi.org/10.1007/978-3-031-61688-4_34

their actions often differ from these objectives, and a lot of waste can be produced as a by-product when making [4,10] revealing a large gap between pro-environmental attitude and actual behaviour [10,24]. This begs the question of why this attitude-behaviour discrepancy arises. Moreover, how can student makerspaces be designed to support students in making more sustainable choices about the materials they utilise, and the waste their projects produce?

We propose that studying the making behaviours and the factors shaping and influencing such choices can lead to the development of design guidelines for interactive systems and interventions supporting more sustainable makerspaces. In line with our aims, we studied how more sustainable making practices could be supported for students from the Design Informatics (DI) Master's programme at the University of Edinburgh who use a dedicated makerspace to work on academic projects. We conducted in-depth interviews with three makerspace supervisors at the University of Edinburgh to gain their insights on: the goals of student makerspaces, the sources of physical waste within makerspaces, the barriers that student makers face that add to physical waste, and possible approaches to reducing and managing waste. Next, we asked student makers to reflect on a previous physical prototype they created, to identify the factors that encourage them to make sustainably as well as the potential barriers that prevent them from engaging in actions to reduce physical waste. Drawing upon the findings we present design considerations and potential behaviour change strategies to help design interactive systems as interventions to help drive sustainable making behaviour.

2   Related Literature

2.1   Waste as a Value Associated with Materials

Waste may often appear unavoidable but is typically the outcome of one's design choices [5]. It is largely attributable to the use of non-recyclable materials, custom-built hardware [11] and the low value (e.g., functional and performative) makers may ascribe to prototyping materials. Additionally, the disposal of "bio-degradable and compostable materials" like PLA in landfills limits their sustainability benefits [20]. This highlights the need for diverse approaches to tackle the challenge of waste as a by-product of making.

Material conservation and repurposing design approaches such as the use of screws or press-fits instead of glue are some of the proposed strategies [9,20] for makers to consider in order to support prolonged material value or circular innovation. Strategies like these can facilitate 'un-making' to disassemble a prototype at the end of its useful life [20]. Furthermore, it is important that makers critically reflect on the things they choose to create in order to support production that is meaningful as opposed to just for the sake of aesthetics [9]. This raises the question: how to encourage critical thinking among student makers towards the value they assign to the materials used and reduce physical waste?

2.2   The Role of Makerspace

A maker's decisions are frequently influenced by the socio-technical affordances of the makerspace environment. While student makerspaces are typically built to facilitate learning [2], the organisational conventions of makerspaces (e.g. time and cost associated with a project, limited access to low-impact materials, restrictions to technical support or waste management practices) can hinder sustainability [6,23].

The makerspace supervisors, as leaders of strategy and operation [14], may not always have the time to address the issue of material waste. However, supervisors sometimes adopt practical strategies and initiatives, like situating storage boxes for scrap materials adjacent to the laser cutters, to encourage makers to use them before utilising fresh material [9]. In this study, we aimed to investigate further how the configuration of a student makerspace, in terms of both community and material factors, can support or obstruct the development of sustainable making cultures.

2.3   Behavioural Antecedents

Individuals change their behaviour when they are well-informed, strongly motivated, and equipped with the necessary skills [1]. An individual is well informed if they possess the necessary knowledge to recognise the opportunity to engage in the target behaviour, for example the need for change [12,22]. Their motivation is influenced by their expectation of a positive outcome (e.g. the expectation that consistent physical exercise shows a visible positive outcome on the body), the values they connect with that outcome (e.g., self-satisfaction or other rewards) and subjective norms like expectations of others from the individual and recognition [22]. Finally, requisite skills (such as availability of materials or techniques with a lower environmental impact) determine an individual's perceived behavioural control i.e., belief in their ability to engage in the behaviour [22]. The question this raises is whether makers need to be informed, motivated or skilled to adopt sustainable behaviour?

Individually these three criteria are necessary but not sufficient to drive behavioural change. While being informed about the impact of one's sustainable actions helps those who are environmentally conscious, however, these advantages may diminish over time [18]. Additionally, informed individuals might not take action because they lack the motivation or the capacity to do so [1]. Establishing information and motivation informs how to consume and the need for change, but it does not always result in goal setting to translate intentions into action [1,18]. Consistent motivation and action require self-efficacy.

2.4   Behaviour Change Strategies

Researchers in design and HCI have proposed numerous strategies for behaviour change over the years. Examples include Oinas-Kukkonen and Harjumaa's 28 persuasive strategies [13], Froehlich et al.'s review of the six most popular motivating techniques [7], and Tang and Bhamra's seven behaviour intervention design strategies [21]. The research identifies Eco-feedback as the commonly used behavioural change strategy [3, 7]. Eco-feedback is information about environmental concerns and potential solutions [3]. Although eco-feedback might assist sustainable behaviour, it often fails to engage users over time. In practice, a combination of such strategies is popularly used in the development of persuasive solutions. Other such strategies include - rewards and penalties: positive and negative reinforcing for sustainable and unsustainable behaviours [3, 13]; options: readily available alternative actions [3]; and comparison: presenting and comparing individual and group behavioural performance, which can potentially be incorporated into design to persuade responsible behaviour change towards by-product waste management in makerspaces [3, 13].

3   Methods

3.1   Semi-structured Interviews with Workshop Supervisors

We carried out semi-structured interviews with 3 student makerspace supervisors at the University of Edinburgh. The goal was to gain their perspectives on of the following topics: the goals of student makerspaces, the causes of physical waste in these makerspaces, the constraints that student makers face that contribute to physical waste, and potential approaches to decreasing and managing waste. The study enabled conversations about their experiences and observations of sustainability challenges within the makerspace.

3.2   Cultural Probes with Student Makers

We also used cultural probes [8] with 8 DI Master's students whose degrees necessitate that they utilise these makerspaces for coursework. Cultural probes typically consist of a collection of artefacts like a diary, a single-use camera, instructions, and prompts to capture participants' thoughts and emotions about a given topic.

The probe kit was designed (see Fig. 1) to elicit reflection on students' making process by recalling a previous physical prototype they created. It aimed to support the participants in reflecting on their motivations for environmental sustainability, their knowledge and experience to consider potential waste management actions within their making process, and the barriers they face within the makerspace that impede the said actions.

The kit was divided into six tasks based on a previous physical prototype they created. It asked the participants to write and reflect on the resources used in their making processes, such as materials, tools, human resources (like makers and supervisors), or other, and the steps they followed along the process onto puzzle-shaped note cards. Following that, it asked them to consider what parts of their prototype and the resources used went to waste and what did not,

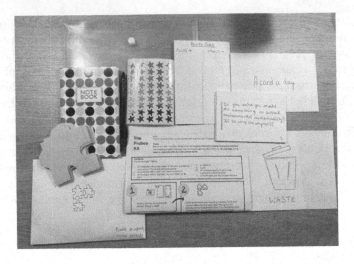

Fig. 1. Probes Kit

and to sort the note cards into two envelopes labelled 'Waste' and 'Not waste,' respectively.

The participants were prompted to consider why the resources were wasted, what an alternative might have been, and why they had not taken the alternative, and to record their responses in a diary. These inquiries aimed to elicit insights on sustainable alternatives based on participants' knowledge and experience of making, as well as to acknowledge the barriers to more sustainable alternatives.

The kit also included a point system for participants to use as a self-evaluation tool. They lost a point for each item they had thrown away, and gained points for having explored sustainable alternatives and acknowledging obstacles to sustainability.

Lastly, the kit included a set of ten daily reflection cards with questions aimed at acquiring insights into the factors influencing the attitudes and behaviours among student makers. The questions centred on the participant's understanding of the sustainable challenges within their makerspace, and the factors that motivate and impede sustainable thinking in both their professional environments and making processes.

3.3 Data Analysis

We audio recorded all the interviews and later transcribed them for analysis. Whereas the probe's data was digitised and sorted based on the tasks and the participants, for interpretation and familiarisation before analysing it. For each of the two studies, we used thematic analysis to detect and analyse recurring patterns of *"sets of experiences, thoughts, or behaviours"* across qualitative data. We coupled thematic analysis with both deductive and inductive coding.

We started with deductively coding the qualitative data using the of target themes in the probes i.e. motivation, barriers and strategies or actions towards sustainable making practices, as an analytical framework (see Fig. 2). Next, the related codes were grouped together within these broad categories. Lastly, we used the *"learn as you go"* approach [16] to inductively code the data and identify common patterns.

4   Findings

In this section, we synthesise across our two studies to demonstrate, from the perspectives of both makerspace supervisors and students, what motivates student makers to engage in sustainable making; what barriers to sustainability student makers face; and potential strategies that might support more sustainable making in makerspaces.

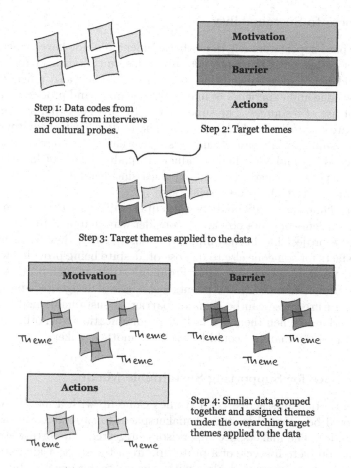

Fig. 2. Framework for Thematic Analysis

4.1   Motivating Factors for Sustainable Making

Motivations are makers' beliefs, which encourage them to carry out a desired action. The students' probes responses showed that they believed that a sustainable makerspace culture where others adopt sustainable making practices would encourage them to make more environmentally conscious decisions. They also expressed that visualising the impacts of their actions such as how much they saved from being polluted, could be motivational. Their responses suggested that making sustainable choices would be more motivating if they were coupled with a tangible benefit, such as a reward or recognition. Another motivation highlighted was the convenience of acting sustainably, for example having easy access to low-impact material options. **For example**, the students reflected that if given the opportunity, they would reuse or recycle scrap material, but the options to do so in their makerspace were currently inadequate or inconvenient.

4.2   Barriers to Sustainability

The makerspace supervisors felt that when students do not have to account for the cost associated with the materials used, this can often lead to ineffective planning and hence overconsumption and wastage. They also reflected that a lack of knowledge and experience of materials, machines and processes can result in inefficient use of resources. The supervisors also observed that students often face a pressure of deadlines which can lead them to de-prioritise environmentally sustainable making, while prioritising ensuring that what they make meets a particular deadline and is of high production quality. Lack of knowledge and instructions, as well as constraints tied to prioritising deadlines, were also barriers that arose in the students' probes reflections.

Another challenge highlighted by the supervisors was that waste is often invisible, as students may not observe or consider what happens to their project's output after a project has been completed. Consequently, they frequently leave unused artefacts for someone else to dispose of, despite being provided with skips for material waste and recycling bins. From the students' perspective, in turn, the cultural probes revealed that students feel a lack of designated space to store material for future reuse can be a major barrier to sustainable material usage. This is exacerbated when there is a lack of communication with other makers to find out if the scrap material could be used by another maker.

4.3   Strategies for Supporting Sustainable Making

Finally, the participants across both studies came up with a number of strategies that could be adopted in student makerspaces to support more sustainable making practice. The makerspace supervisors suggested: supporting students to plan for the complete lifecycle of a prototype from the start; asking students to get involved in the process of "dealing with" the waste, for example by encouraging disassembly and appropriate disposal; encouraging the use of scrap material for low-fidelity testing; and setting project tasks with constraints, like assigning projects necessitating designing with waste. These included supporting better planning to reduce material waste, for example, asking students to use alternate low-impact materials or techniques, making their prototypes easier to dismantle to feed the materials used back into the production cycle or considering what is recyclable before dismantling. Students, on the other hand, felt that analysing and understanding the impact of their design would inform their sustainable decisions and planning. They also brainstormed actions to manage waste produced such as recycling the used materials as well as storing used and leftover materials and prototypes for future reuse to avoid having them go to waste.

5   Discussion

The research findings bring to light the discrepancy in pro-environmental attitudes and behaviours among the makers. Our research demonstrates a number of barriers, motivations and opportunities for strategies that should be considered when exploring how to support sustainability in student makerspaces. As we have demonstrated, student makerspaces are complex environments where a variety of interacting factors influence the extent to which sustainability is prioritised in the making process. For example, students' goals of meeting deadlines, together with a lack of knowledge about the sustainability of particular materials or production methods, and a lack of constraints on using new materials or a lack of a medium to store scrap material for reuse, can all lead to unsustainable making practices.

Our findings of potential strategies for encouraging sustainable making, both from the perspectives of students and makerspace supervisors, also provide a starting point for exploring how interventions might be developed to bridge the attitude-behaviour gap identified in the research [10,24] and to ensure that sustainability is supported. In line with previous research on behaviour change [1,18], we suggest these interventions should combine strategies that inform the student makers of the opportunity and need for change, present motivational incentives to take action and equip them with the necessary skills to translate these intentions into actions. For example, our research suggests that interventions intended to embed sustainability at the core of the making process, might include: rewarding students' sustainable practices, making waste material visible and readily usable for future making, and supporting a learning culture that values material sustainability. These strategies, along with the makerspace supervisors' suggestion of 'designing with waste' and supporting students to plan for the complete prototype lifecycle, concur with Kohtala's and Song & Paulos' suggestion that promoting prolonged material value and circular innovation [9,20] can tackle the challenge of waste as a by-product of making.

However, it is crucial to highlight that, being informed on the consequences of one's design decision alongside readily available low impact materials and techniques, as suggested by the student makers, may not be in itself a sufficient motivation to drive sustainable behaviours. This is because, as noted by both the makers and supervisors in our study, the constrained time is another organisational convention of makerspace that can lead to deprioritising of environmental sustainability [see also [6]].

In our study, the student participants suggested that in addition to accessing information about acting sustainably, and ensuring that doing so in convenient, incentives such as recognition and rewards may support them in engaging in sustainable making behaviour. Recognition and reward have also been suggested by others as a strategy to incentivise sustainable behaviour in other contexts [e.g., [22]]. These constraints and strategies are tangible considerations as the dimensions of an academic makerspace promoting sustainable practices alongside learning, experimentation, and innovation. We invite further research to address what other behaviour change strategies could be incorporated into the design of interventions in student makerspaces to support sustainable making and how to assess their effectiveness.

Currently, the research has only been carried out within one specific makerspace, i.e. a student makerspace as opposed to other industrial or personal digital fabrication spaces. The factors influencing the attitude-behaviour gap and consequently the success of the recommended design considerations may also vary with studies with a more diverse set of makers and varying student makerspaces. Still, the findings provide a strong starting point for design considerations for an intervention aimed to foster sustainable behaviour in other academic digital fabrication spaces beyond the chosen makerspace e.g., in other design-focused programmes at universities.

References

1. Abraham, C., Denford, S.: Design, implementation, and evaluation of behavior change interventions: a ten-task guide. The handbook of behavior change, pp. 269–84 (2020). https://doi.org/10.1017/9781108677318.019
2. Andrews, D., Roberts, D.: Academic makerspaces: contexts for research on interdisciplinary collaborative communication. In: Proceedings of the 35th ACM International Conference on the Design of Communication, pp. 1–7. Association for Computing Machinery, New York, NY, USA (2017). https://doi.org/10.1145/3121113.3121230
3. Coskun, A., Zimmerman, J., Erbug, C.: Promoting sustainability through behavior change: a review. Des. Stud. **41**, 183–204 (2015). https://doi.org/10.1016/j.destud.2015.08.008
4. Dew, K.N., Rosner, D.K.: Designing with Waste: a situated inquiry into the material excess of making. In: Proceedings of the 2019 on Designing Interactive Systems Conference, pp. 1307–1319 ACM, San Diego CA USA (2019). https://doi.org/10.1145/3322276.3322320
5. Ellen MacArthur Foundation: Eliminate waste and pollution. https://ellenmacarthurfoundation.org/eliminate-waste-and-pollution
6. Ford, S., Despeisse, M.: Additive manufacturing and sustainability: an exploratory study of the advantages and challenges. J. Clean. Prod. **137**, 1573–1587 (2016). https://doi.org/10.1016/j.jclepro.2016.04.150

7. Froehlich, J., Findlater, L., Landay, J.: The design of eco-feedback technology. In: Proceedings of the SIGCHI Conference on Human Factors in Computing Systems, pp. 1999–2008. ACM, Atlanta Georgia USA (2010). https://doi.org/10.1145/1753326.1753629

8. Gaver, B., Dunne, T., Pacenti, E.: Design: cultural probes. Interactions **6**(1), 21–29 (1999). https://doi.org/10.1145/291224.291235

9. Kohtala, C.: Making "Making" critical: how sustainability is constituted in fab lab ideology. Des. J. **20**(3), 375–394 (2017). https://doi.org/10.1080/14606925.2016.1261504

10. Kohtala, C., Hyysalo, S.: Anticipated environmental sustainability of personal fabrication. J. Clean. Prod. **99**, 333–344 (2015). https://doi.org/10.1016/j.jclepro.2015.02.093

11. Lechelt, S., Gorkovenko, K., Soares, L.L., Speed, C., Thorp, J.K., Stead, M.: Designing for the end of life of IoT objects. In: Companion Publication of the 2020 ACM Designing Interactive Systems Conference, pp. 417-420 ACM, Eindhoven Netherlands (2020). https://doi.org/10.1145/3393914.3395918

12. Michie, S., Van Stralen, M. M., West, R.: The behaviour change wheel: a new method for characterising and designing behaviour change interventions. Implementation Sci. 6, 1, 42 (2011). https://doi.org/10.1186/1748-5908-6-42

13. Oinas-Kukkonen, H., Harjumaa, M.: Persuasive systems design: key issues, process model, and system features. Commun. Assoc. Inf. Syst. **24**, 28 (2009). https://doi.org/10.17705/1cais.02428

14. Prendeville, S., Hartung, G., Brass, C., Purvis, E., Hall, A.: Circular makerspaces: the founder's view. Int. J. Sustain. Eng. **10**(4–5), 272–288 (2017). https://doi.org/10.1080/19397038.2017.1317876

15. Roedl, D., Bardzell, S., Bardzell, J.: Sustainable Making? Balancing Optimism and Criticism in HCI Discourse. ACM Trans. Comput.-Hum. Interact. 22(3), 1–27 (2015). https://doi.org/10.1145/2699742

16. Saldana, J.: The Coding Manual for Qualitative Researchers, 4th edn. SAGE, Thousand Oaks (2021)

17. Sheridan, K., Halverson, E.R., Litts, B.K., Brahms, L., Jacobs-Priebe, L., Owens, T.: Learning in the making: a comparative case study of three makerspaces. Harvard Educ. Rev. 84(4), 505–531 (2014). https://doi.org/10.17763/haer.84.4.brr34733723j648u

18. Shin, H.D., Bull, R.: Three dimensions of design for sustainable behaviour. Sustainability. **11**(17), 4610 (2019). https://doi.org/10.3390/su11174610

19. Smith, A., Light, A.: Cultivating sustainable developments with makerspaces | Cultivando desenvolvimento sustentável com espaços maker. Liinc em Revista 13(1) (2017). https://doi.org/10.18617/liinc.v13i1.3900

20. Song, K., Paulos, E.: Unmaking: enabling and celebrating the creative material of failure, destruction, decay, and deformation. In: Proceedings of the 2021 CHI Conference on Human Factors in Computing Systems, pp. 1–12 ACM, Yokohama Japan (2021). https://doi.org/10.1145/3411764.3445529

21. Tang, T.K., Bhamra, T.: Putting consumers first in design for sustainable behaviour: a case study of reducing environmental impacts of cold appliance use. Int. J. Sustain. Eng. 5(4), 288–303 (2012). https://doi.org/10.1080/19397038.2012.685900

22. Thieme, A., Comber, R., Miebach, J.T., Weeden, J., Kraemer, N., Lawson, S., Olivier, P.: "We've bin watching you": designing for reflection and social persuasion to promote sustainable lifestyles. In: Proceedings of the SIGCHI Conference on

Human Factors in Computing Systems, pp. 2337–2346. ACM, Austin Texas USA (2012). https://doi.org/10.1145/2207676.2208394

23. Vasquez, L., E.S.L., Wang, H.-C., Vega, K.: Introducing the sustainable proto-typing life cycle for digital fabrication to designers. In: Proceedings of the 2020 ACM Designing Interactive Systems Conference, pp. 1301–1312. ACM, Eindhoven Netherlands (2020). https://doi.org/10.1145/3357236.3395510

24. Wyss, A.M., Knoch, D., Berger, S.: When and how pro-environmental attitudes turn into behavior: the role of costs, benefits, and self-control. J. Environ. Psychol. **79**, 101748 (2022). https://doi.org/10.1016/j.jenvp.2021.101748

Sustainable Innovations for Lifestyle, SDGs, and Greening Education

Anant Bhaskar Garg$^{(\boxtimes)}$ (iD) and Manisha Agarwal (iD)

HaritaDhara Research Development and Education Foundation (HRDEF), Dehradun, India
anantgg@yahoo.com

Abstract. HRDEF is addressing promising developments towards UN Sustainable Development Goals (SDGs) and sustainability of our planet Earth. As per data from various studies, climate education, twenty-first century skills are ignored in mainstream education. To bridge this gap, HRDEF build capacity for citizenship, Climate Action, and SDGs among youth, professionals so that they are able to tackle future challenges. Building an inclusive, effective path for the sustainable future with SHWID require inclusive, quality education. In this regard, learning, engagement with games, hands-on activities are very important, and our work showed that learners understood, took action for climate change, SDGs. HRDEF is developing Educational Games, Hands-on Activities kits for school students, college youth; conducting workshops with them, educators to teach a specific curriculum topic related to sustainability such as climate change, water cycle, energy that increased player's motivation towards science, sustainable work environments. HRDEF presented their work at the UNESCO MGIEP TECH 2017, 2018, UNESCO ESD 2021, and UN HLPF side event 2021, 2022, STI 2022. We discuss the use of games for students and youth in different settings for advancing SDGs, building sustainability concepts for a Healthy Planet. HRDEF inculcate, motivates learners for STEAM, 21st Century Sustainable living. Apps on SDGs, COVID-19, hands-on activities, quiz, model making, projects and other creative forms of expressions increased players motivation towards sustainability. Students, youth of our after-school GOAL program become motivated, equipped with self-confidence to excel in life and creating sustainable future. As systemic changes require continuous working and time for visible performance.

Keywords: Sustainable Lifestyle · SDGs · Greening Education · Climate Action · Education for Sustainable Development · Games · Hands-on · Project Based Learning

1 Introduction

Lifestyle for Environment (LiFE) movement is currently required in our society because of issues of climate change, sustainable development, sustainability of life, its inhabitants, and our planet Earth. twenty-first century skills and pro-environmental behavior are missing in schools, Higher Education Institutions (HEI), and work places. Yale University's research on climate change communications pointed out that 65% of Indian

A. Bramwell-Dicks et al. (Eds.): INTERACT 2023 Workshops, LNCS 14535, pp. 359–366, 2024.
https://doi.org/10.1007/978-3-031-61688-4_35

population is not aware of climate change published in 2016 [15]. Beginning with twenty-first century, the United Nations (UN) started Millennium Development Goals (MDG) and decade of Education for Sustainable Development (ESD) (2005–2014) that highlighted vibrant role of education towards sustainable development for saving our planet as the world witnessed extreme events due to climate change. Further, the UN adopted the 17 Sustainable Development Goals (SDGs) in September 2015 to advocate for SDG 4 that provide inclusive, equitable quality education and promotes lifelong learning opportunities for all to build sustainable, inclusive and resilient societies. Thus, everyone urgently needs to include climate change and ESD in a radical way to address future challenges. Human's impacts are visible in the form of development since industrial age such as burning fossil fuels, deforestation, pollution, and overpopulation which results in soil erosion, poor air quality, health issues, migration, loss of biodiversity, undrinkable water, changes in ecosystem, limitation of natural resources, and food. These human generated activities lead to extreme climatic events, more disasters such as heat waves, rising sea levels, melting glaciers, storms, warming of oceans that directly, or indirectly cause loss of life, livelihoods, biodiversity, infrastructure, and socio-economy in the last couple of decades.

Therefore, we need to think how our lifestyle related to climate change affects such drastic climatic events. Using plastic bags, single use plastic items, wastage of water, energy, fuels, improper waste management, and our modern lifestyle practices or behavior are problem for environment and acts as trigger points for climate change. Five roadblocks identified in a Brookings report needed to resolve in a time of climate change [9]. As per Sandrine Dixson Declève, co-president of the Club of Rome "Behavior change can only do so much without a full turnaround from our pro-growth politics, financial and economic models towards a more holistic well-being economy"[1] and "Without addressing the way the wealthy live, it will not be possible to curb climate change." The research calls for a "rapid and radical" reduction in carbon footprints by the Hot or Cool Institute, based on an analysis of half of the G20 group of countries, to keep the 1.5 °C warming goal within reach [2].

2 Global Partnerships for 'One World'

Through education, we transfer knowledge, values, and skills across generation to facilitate societies to build the foundation for sustainable future. But many barriers to education access, outcomes, and monitoring of progress are main challenges that need to be addressed for achieving SDG 4.7 and interlinkages of SDGs for global partnerships [14]. The global climate education and the concept of ESD are unable to provide radical transformation of education systems needed to guard against climate change. India's Philosophy of 'One World', Global Partnership, and culture of support is known for centuries.

Uniting all the stakeholders for their role in shaping the 2030 Agenda and the SDGs on three pillars of economy, social, environment with culture based on the principles of equality and humanity is very important for the global society.

Children, youth, professionals need to imbibe greener values such as adopting gardening, ReConnect with Nature, sustainable living to maintain the environmental balance, under the action plan of environmental protection, conservation of environment, and to create the awareness among citizens for Greening Education, and ESD are must [7, 8].

Much of the climate change research has been done in USA, Europe, Australia or developed world than in developing countries which have different eco-socio-cultural patterns. Thus, we need to conduct more studies that are universal in nature and merge with balanced factors related to human behavior impact on climate change to unite for 'One World'.

Education ecosystem stakeholders need transformative, cooperative approach, and a roadmap to tackle climate change, SDG, and sustainability for our sustainable future. Thus, possible ways forward are:

Experiential and Embodied Learning: Awareness of Social and Environmental Challenges, their solutions, Sustainable Development Goals (SDGs) to Youth, Educators, and Community. Apply SDGs within education ecosystem especially school, after-school, and community.

Quality Skillful Education: Maker (person who create, produce, or made model, objects as an extension of DIY approach), Hands-on, and Games to foster effective learning habits to change our lifestyle for sustainable living. Maker education derives from the work of Jean Piaget and Seymour Papert multi-disciplinary learning experiences for projects based on real-life knowledge.

Transformation: By what means youth imbibe sustainability concepts, responsibility, accountability, global citizenship, gender equality, and culture diversity.

3 Innovations in Quality Skillful Education: Games for SDGs, Sustainability, and LiFE

The paper describes two case studies conducted during March, 2017 to August, 2018 having students from 4th-10th classes covering sustainability concepts with experiential, embodied learning. Another one was started from Aug, 2019 and focused on Sustainable school, Disaster Risk Reduction (DRR), and climate change capacity building in students, and teachers of government schools.

Games offer experience of adventure, challenge, and hold the attention of players for hours. People acquire new knowledge, complex skills from game play preparing them for sustainable development [11, 13]. This paper is based on case studies for developing sustainable lifestyle, climate change capacity building in students, educators.

Some games are external designed while we designed games keeping in mind Human Work Interaction Design approach through studying work settings and embedding screenplays, rules for better understanding [3, 4]. Youth can be the change agent and driver for ESD through developing skills as given in Fig. 1.

Thus, through our board game on water management, we educate learners and community on related issues. We encourage interactive, embodied learning that help learner to develop creativity, critical thinking, and problem solving that are essential as the 21st Century skills and pro-environmental behavior [10]. We conducted analysis on environment awareness, motivate learners to do good act and they pledged for the same, positive actions for sustainable society. Demographic differences such as household size, family

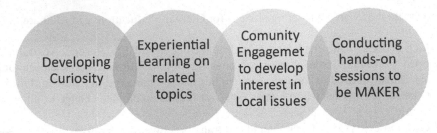

Fig. 1. Young people can be driving force for sustainability and act as change agent

patterns (context, gender, income, minority status, motivation, incentives); psychological factors such as needs, wants, rewards, goals, values, ideologies, beliefs, attitudes, world views; cultural norms, and empathy to nature affect consumption. There is also a need to understand delicate balance between environmentally responsible behaviors, Eco-Consciousness, and happiness based on above factors w.r.t. different economies, and rich-poor divide.

3.1 STEAM, 21st Century Skills, Interactive Learning for ESD

Makers approach, Games-based, and hands-on learning are effective tools for interactive learning, understanding of STEAM and integrating sustainability concepts in curriculum. ESD, Greening Education can contribute to all three dimensions of relevant science education: individual, societal and vocational relevance and Sustainable Development Goals (SDGs) [5, 6, 12].

First case study was conducted during March, 2017 to August, 2018 having students from 4th- 10th classes of government, private schools, and college students, aged from 8–20. This project covered many topics from STEAM, SDGs, Climate Change, computing unplugged (learning computing concepts without using computers generally paper, pen based activities), Solar System, Eclipse, Light, Food chain, Food Web, importance of water, clean water, 3 R, Waste. The students used the HRDEF toolkits and other contents which include multimedia, presentations, board games, and card games for experiential, hands-on learning.

During this study, we witnessed improvement in communication skills, problem solving, imagination, and critical thinking (21st Century skills). Youth showed scientific interest towards current issues of science and climate change. Further, they developed their writing, reading, creativity through participating in various competitions and hands-on activities. The approach of this study was to raise thinking skills through What, Why and how approach that is: What is the problem, identify it, why we need to discuss it, how we can solve it. STEAM approach and usefulness to learn ESD concepts described in Fig. 2. Further, linking elements of STEAM help students to learn wider encompassing knowledge around a project such as water audit, waste reduction, biodiversity audit, and energy conservation.

We conducted a test based on questions from related topics. After that, we conducted sessions and used tools, methods such as videos, digital games, card games, and board games to explain topics and encouraged students to discuss further with what, why and

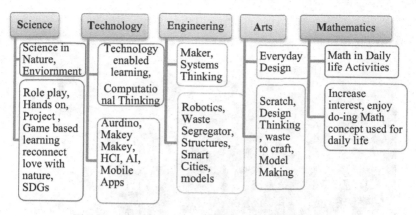

Fig. 2. STEAM concepts for ESD, 21st Century Skills

how. After these sessions, students showed better understanding of curriculum, ESD topics, and able to learn complex concepts of sustainability. All activities are based on school curriculum, age appropriate that improve knowledge and encouraged students to prepare models with waste materials. Parents are also encouraged to attend some sessions to know about E-STEM, and current issues for their understanding.

3.2 Sustainable School Through ESD, Climate Action, and DRR

During second study from 2019 onward, we conducted orientation program for teachers, students for awareness on SDGs, Climate Change and organized sessions on water management, pollution, biodiversity, energy, waste segregation, composting, play games, card game, and climate action. Figure 3 shows students interaction and learning of water concepts in a fun way. We conducted analysis on environment awareness, motivate them to do good act and students pledged for the same, positive actions for sustainable school and society.

Students are encouraged to work on a suitable problem in their neighborhood, or around school to develop plan for sustainable school. Further, students showed improvement in water conservation, single use plastic reduction, and working on environmental project for betterment of school as given in Figs. 4, 5, and 6.

HRDEF provided guidance to students for Environment Sustainability Acts for sustainable campus that result in saving water, biodiversity, energy, and waste. In the above graphs, US denotes urban school, RS rural school and it comprise data from eight schools, four each having classes VI–XII. Almost 60% students carry reusable water bottle thus saving plastic and water waste, thus saving climate.

Fig. 3. Students learning water concepts in fun way

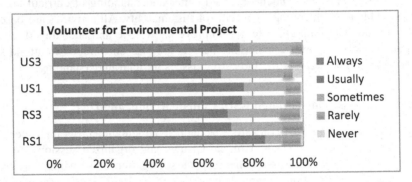

Fig. 4. Students of four rural, urban schools each, willing for Environment Projects

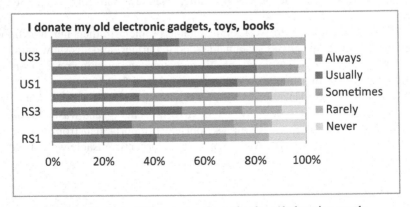

Fig. 5. Students of four rural, urban schools each donation trends

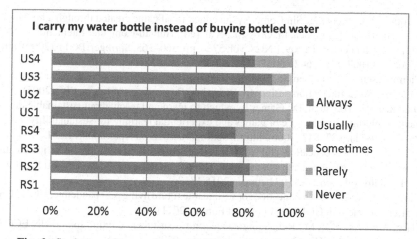

Fig. 6. Students of four rural, urban schools each saving water, reducing plastic

4 Transformation of Education to Create Eco-Consciousness

Education have made important contributions to development but now need more particpatory, community oriented accountability to shape Generation Z's future with sustainability in mind to create Eco-Consciousness. We are motivating individuals, students, youth, and households to reduce their electricity, water consumption, use local resources, carry their own water bottle, bag, segregate waste at source, promote composting, reuse old plastic for crafts, use both sides of paper, reuse it, use cycle or public transport, when possible, donate old items. Developing curiosity through experiential learning on related topics with community engagement and to develop interest in local issues, and conducting hands-on sessions to be MAKER is crucial for transformation of education and eco-consciousness. Learning occurs not just in the game play but other kinds of making activities encourage collaboration among participants, thus provide a context for peer-to-peer teaching and for the emergence of communities of Learners. It will go a long way in nurturing spirit of inquiry, fostering creativity and developing culture of innovation among learners; equipping them with skills and competence to create equitable and sustainable future. We require radical transformation for Climate Action, SDGs, LiFE, and Sustainability Education. We need to adopt sustainable lifestyle, contribute towards climate action, and try to be SDGs change maker.

References

1. Akenji, L., et al.: 1.5–Degree lifestyles: towards a fair consumption space for all. Hot or Cool Institute (2021). https://hotorcool.org/1-5-degree-lifestyles-report/
2. Beh, L.Y.: To fight climate change, we need 'radical' lifestyle changes from the world's wealthiest: study, Thomson Reuters foundation (2021). https://news.trust.org/item/202110 05110948-0t9b6

3. Campos, P., Campos, A.: SimCompany: an educational game created through a human-work interaction design approach. In: Gross, T., et al. (ed.) Human-Computer Interaction – INTERACT 2009. INTERACT 2009, LNCS, vol. 5726, pp. 360–363. Springer, Berlin (2009). https://doi.org/10.1007/978-3-642-03655-2_40

4. Clemmensen, T., Orngreen, R., Pejtersen, A.M.: Describing users in contexts: perspectives on human-work interaction design. In: Workshop Proceedings of Interact'05 (2005)

5. Dieleman, H., Huisingh, D.: Games by which to learn and teach about sustainable development: exploring the relevance of games and experiential learning for sustainability. J. Clean. Prod. **14**(9–11), 837–847 (2006). https://doi.org/10.1016/j.jclepro.2005.11.031

6. Eilks, I.: Science education and education for sustainable development – justifications, models, practices and perspectives. EURASIA J. Math. Sci. Tech. Ed. **11**(1), 149–158 (2015). https://doi.org/10.12973/eurasia.2015.1313a

7. Garg, A.B., Agarwal, M.: Education for sustainable future living post pandemic, UN ECOSOC written statement in High Level Political Forum (2021)

8. Garg, A.B., Agarwal, M.: Reimaging education for sustainable future living, UN ECOSOC written statement in High Level Political Forum (2020)

9. Kwauk, C.: Roadblocks to Quality Education in a Time of Climate Change. Centre for Universal Education, Brookings Institution (2020)

10. Mustaquim, M.M., Nyström, T.: Open sustainability innovation—a pragmatic standpoint of sustainable HCI. In: Johansson, B., Andersson, B., Holmberg, N. (eds.) Perspectives in Business Informatics Research. 014, LNBIP, vol. 194, pp. 101–112. Springer, Cham (2014). https://doi.org/10.1007/978-3-319-11370-8_8

11. Noonoo, S.: Playing games can build 21st-century skills. Research Explains How. (2019) https://www.edsurge.com/news/2019-02-12-playing-games-canbuild-21st-century-skills-research-explains-how

12. Singer, N., Farahaty, E., Mahmoud, E.S.: Motives of the egyptian education future for sustainable development: a comparative analysis between 2020 and 2030, Humanities & Social Sciences Reviews (2020). https://doi.org/10.2139/ssrn.3585908

13. Stommen, S.M., Farley, K.: Games for grownups: the role of gamification in climate change and sustainability, Indicia Consulting LLC, S. Mazur Stommen, & K. Farley, Taxonomy of games, pp. 28–39 (2016)

14. United Nations, SDSN Homepage. https://sustainabledevelopment.un.org/content/documents/23669BN_SDG4.pdf

15. YALE (2016). https://environment.yale.edu/climate-communicationOFF/files/ClimateChange-Indian-Mind.pdf

Towards an *In-Between* Practice to Study Energy Shift at Work

Elodie Bouzekri[✉] and Guillaume Rivière

Univ. Bordeaux, ESTIA - Institute of Technology, EstiaR, 64210 Bidart, France
{elodie.bouzekri,g.riviere}@estia.fr

Abstract. To address the challenges raised by the design of practices for a more sustainable future, we propose to explore a design method based on design fiction. We coupled this approach with interaction-level design methods through task analysis and modelling activities. While design fiction opens up design spaces, we propose to design an *in-between* practice feasible with the support of a system that can be implemented in current context of use. We illustrate this method by designing an *in-between* energy practice at work that enables energy shifting in a current workplace supported by an eco-forecast interface.

Keywords: Sustainability · Energy consumption · Task modelling · Shifting · Practice design

1 Introduction

Sustainability is a multidimensional concept, with intertwined and sometimes conflicting dimensions concerning the relationships between companies economic goals, social equity, and the relationship between humans and the environment [12]. Sustainable HCI (SHCI) field adds environmental issues to the design of interactive systems, whether in their manufacture or use [15]. To make users aware of the impact of their actions on the environment, eco-feedback interfaces sense and feed relative information on these actions [8] such as: resources consumed, waste produced or resource status. However, to tackle systemic change required for dealing with sustainability issues, SHCI actors are now moving towards approaches influencing groups or communities instead of individual-centred approaches [2].

Going beyond interaction level focus, practice-oriented approaches offered a framework to design for groups and communities by embedding know-how, norms, and expectations [4]. Such approaches can be applied to energy use issue. Indeed, energy consumption cannot be narrowed down to individual choices; energy is rather a resource needed to accomplish practices [4] such as brewing coffee or working practices. To make energy consumption more sustainable, current practices need to be modified so that the resources required are in line with the desired goal of sustainability. Because renewable energy availability

A. Bramwell-Dicks et al. (Eds.): INTERACT 2023 Workshops, LNCS 14535, pp. 367–376, 2024.
https://doi.org/10.1007/978-3-031-61688-4_36

is variable and without efficient storage capability, shifting energy demand is a way of maximising the use of renewable rather than non-renewable energy. To support residential users to shift energy use, Brewer et al. [3] identify three challenges related to users' understanding of shifting, the definition of moment when shift must occur, and the unpredictability of renewable energy availability. Considering that similar challenges may be encountered when designing for working environment, we propose to explore a practice design method for energy shift design based on design fiction. We propose to combine this approach with methods to design at the interaction level through task analysis and modelling activities.

Despite being unable to tackle all practices facets (e.g. culture or politics), we show that tasks modelling and analysis through task models can improve practice design process by identifying potential demanding tasks and keeping track of practice transformation from current to future practices tasks. We illustrate this method and process through the example of transforming energy practice at work by enabling energy shifting supported by an eco-forecast interface.

2   Designing Systems to Shift Energy Demand

In order to target sustainable goals, such as energy efficiency, several technology-centred approaches have been developed to optimise energy use of households such as smart home systems [9] or smart grid for communities [22]. On households level, smart home systems make use of various captors to automatically manage heating or light for example. On community level, microgrids supply electricity produced locally to a small amount of consumers. However, user adoption of smart home systems seems to suffer from cost, security and potential usefulness concerns [9].

To enable human-controlled reduction of energy consumption, an explored approach of SHCI is eco-feedback systems [8]. Eco-feedback systems - which deal with reducing or optimising energy consumption - provide information on current energy production [17] or energy storage [6]. Another approach uses eco-forecast [11] to inform users on current and future renewable-energy production [5,11,19]. These interfaces enable users to shift their energy consumption according to production abilities. Daniel et al. [5] investigate a particular shifting strategy in a working environment where laptop batteries can be used as energy storage. Thus, enabling users to shift their consumption without shifting usage.

Going beyond individual-centred approaches, carried by the eco-feedback approaches that suffer from inability to tackle complexity of organisational context [2], approaches capable of influencing groups or communities are of interest to SHCI actors. Such approaches required a deep understanding of contextualised current practices and reasons that shapes them in order to design systems that support more environmental practices [4]. In order to investigate such practices [10] or to influence them [5], tangible systems with a size, location, and aesthetic meant to attract users' attention, curiosity, and encourage discussion with colleagues were proposed. In this paper, we take as an example such kind of interface to support a new practice at the workplace.

3 Designing Practices

Clear and Comber [4] define a practice as a *"socially constituted phenomena that characterises our everyday activities and routines."* To understand practices and to support the design of solutions, several frameworks were proposed such as COWOP [7] or images (i.e. meanings, socially shared idea of what it is), skills (i.e. routines, know-how, expertise, ways of feelings) and stuff (i.e. material elements needed) model [13]. To design new practices, Kuijer et al. [13] propose Generative Improv Performances (GIP) method. GIP method proposes to recreate usage context environment, destabilise normal practices by removing an element, set up a fictional scenario and give users instructions, so they have a baseline to improvise on to be able to perform their practice in this new environment. Clear and Comber [4] develop assertions to consider practice-oriented approaches to design for sustainability comprising understanding of current practices, considering incremental change and going beyond current configurations and resource use. Then, designing new practices requires anticipating possible future environment and usage context.

In order to go beyond current configurations, exploring speculative design and design fiction approaches that relate to anticipation of the future from science-fiction (or other sources of inspiration) to inspire design scenarios has been proposed [4,21]. To describe design fiction, Lindley and Coulton [14] propose a model composed of: a reality layer that represents the world today as users experience it, a story layer that extrapolate reality into a plausible fiction, and a provocation layer describing the system designed into the story. Speculative design and design fiction are mainly used to produce artefacts that are not designed to be implementable but rather to open design spaces for the future of sustainability [20]. However, they enable discussion of "hopeful or optimistic futures", challenge the values and ethics of current practices, encourage public discourse on "climate change, sustainability and the future", and allow "personal narratives about environmental sustainability and the future to emerge" [20]. In the following of this paper we propose to explore design fiction to anticipate future usage context to design an *in-between* practice supported by a system implementable and usable in current usage context.

4 Design Supported by Models of an Energy Practice

To illustrate the proposed method, we explore a light-weighted design fiction based on anticipated future of energy storage. Based on the understanding of current employees practice and context and an anticipated future where renewable energy production and storage is easily disposable and affordable, we design a possible future practice taking place in this fictional future. Then, based both on the current practice and the future practice, an *in-between* practice supported by an eco-forecast system was designed to be feasible in current working environment while anticipating future context. This *in-between* practice includes both current and future practice tasks that can then be tested and anticipated today through user studies. In order to support the design of such practice and the system supporting it in the current usage context, we return to the interaction level and make use of task modelling that enable identification and analysis of current tasks, future tasks, and tasks of the *in-between* practice under design. Figure 1 illustrates the underlying process.

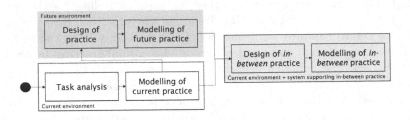

Fig. 1. *In-between* practice design process.

4.1   Illustrative Example: Transforming Energy Practice at Work

We propose to study usages surrounding energy consumption of laptop on the workplace as practice. Using a laptop at work is a routine bodily activity. Every days, workers open their laptop, connect to the power supply, and switch-on the laptop. Typing on the keyboard can be bodily known, with expert users not needing to watch at their keyboard to write text or navigate through pages or menus for example. This practice involves different skills as how to use a laptop, manage battery's autonomy (e.g. frequency of recharges), know appropriate use (e.g. professional use) of laptop at work. It required different kind of materials (i.e. laptop, mouse, electricity, desk, chair, infrastructure, office), and the means of the practice are to work and appear professional.

As an input of our design process, we used previous results [5] on which we iterate. They determine that, currently in offices, most of the employees always or often keep their laptop plugged into the power supply during the day. We describe a typical working day, which consists of settling down at your desk, then working on their laptop. Work can be suspended for a coffee or lunch break. They remain unaware of renewable energy availability through the day. This constitutes our reality layer.

We based our story on a fictional anticipated future where storage is affordable, can store important quantity of renewable energy on a long time, and are accessible to anyone on workplace. In this anticipated future, renewable energy is stored and distributed more efficiently across the grid. To complement this availability in renewable energy at a local level, one can imagine a renewable energy box equipped with plugs displaying percentage of renewable energy stored. This renewable energy box enables users to shift their energy consumption to maximise renewable energy consumption. We model (see Fig. 3) possible employee behaviour working with such renewable energy box. Once settled at their desks, employees see their battery level and plan when they will need to recharge or

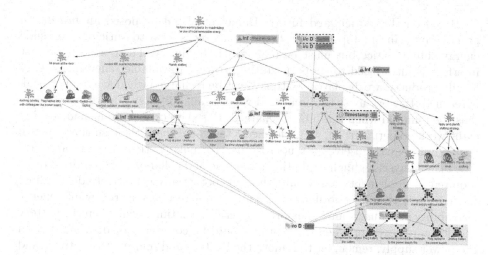

Fig. 2. Task model describing *in-between* practice of employee at work with HAM-STERS [16]. Anticipated future tasks are highlighted in blue, while tasks performed only with the system under design are highlighted in grey. Tasks deleted after the analysis activity are crossed out.

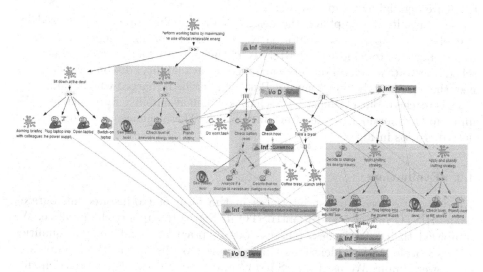

Fig. 3. Task model describing with HAMSTERS [16] anticipated future task of practice of employee at work. Future tasks are highlighted in grey.

unplug their laptop. They may decide to switch energy sources in parallel with their work. Then, working task can be suspended to take or break or to apply shifting: connect to or disconnect from the power supply, check level of renewable energy stored in renewable energy box and laptop battery level to plan next shifting. These anticipated future tasks are highlighted in blue.

Based on this anticipated future, Daniel et al. [5] proposed an *in-between* practice by using laptop battery. Laptop battery is used to anticipate possible energy shift practice but must be managed individually. Then, an eco-forecast interface is introduced to support shifting. Rates of available renewable energy locally produced are displayed. Battery must be recharged when availability peak is reached. Battery must be discharged when availability rates increase. Battery must be removed when it is 50% discharged. Based on observations made during eight-weeks experiment [5], we performed a task analysis of the resulting practice that employees themselves set up together to make it their routine at work. The task analysis highlights additional motoric and collaborative cognitive tasks required to implement energy shift that are potentially cognitively demanding. Indeed, after reading information displayed and recognising renewable energy availability peak, users must memorise or verify peak time, plan when the battery should be removed or when the laptop should be connected or disconnect from the power supply, remember to remove the battery and reinsert the battery, and when to connect the laptop to the power supply. These tasks must be repeated for each peak and for each update. In addition, users declare to be lost after forecast updates. Some users accidentally turn off their laptop by removing the battery when they have previously disconnected their laptop. These *in-between* tasks are highlighted in grey in Fig. 2.

As a result, we simplified the design of energy shift practice proposed by Daniel et al. [5] to propose an alternative *in-between* shifting practice. We decide to no longer ask to remove the battery from the laptop[1]. Thus, users only need to schedule two tasks based on renewable energy availability: disconnect and connect the laptop to the power supply. Battery must be recharged when availability peak is reached. Battery must be discharged when availability rates increase. We limit updates number to one after lunch break. These changes are indicated by dotted crosses in Fig. 2.

4.2   Evaluation

We design two eco-forecast interfaces in the form of bio-inspired histograms (BambHISTO in Fig. 5 and PlantHISTO in Fig. 6) to support the practice. We compared their effectiveness (success rates), pragmatic and hedonic qualities (UEQ-S Scale [18]) to identify when to connect or disconnect the laptop from the power supply. We used LimeSurvey[2] and recruited twenty-five participants (lecturer-researchers and business owners: 12 women, 12 men, 0 non-binary, 1 prefer not to disclose). Illustration of the practice is presented in Fig. 4 and each question is based on a mini-scenario. The interested reader can find more details on this user study in previous work [1].

---

[1] This also enables taking into account that several devices such as laptops, smartphones, and cars use hardly-removable batteries.

[2] https://www.limesurvey.org/fr/.

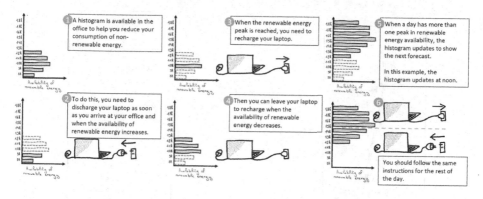

Fig. 4. Instructions describing the energy shift practice given to participants in the online study.

To identify when to recharge battery (T recharge1, T recharge2, and T recharge3) success rate is high (between 84% and 100%) in both conditions. Success rate is lower to identify when to discharge battery (76% and 88% for T discharge1). A Wilcoxon signed-rank test suggests that there is no significant difference between the two conditions (p-*value* = .111) for overall results. A McNemar's test reveals significant differences between the two conditions (p-*value*<.003) for each question. Results are presented in Table 1.

The histograms' embellishments do not significantly impact the pragmatic (BambHISTO: 0.6 ± 0.4, PlantHISTO: 0.5 ± 0.4), hedonic (BambHISTO: 1.0 ± 0.3, PlantHISTO: 1.1 ± 0.2) and global UX (BambHISTO: 0.8 ± 0.3, PlantHISTO: 0.8 ± 0.2) qualities. Overall UX qualities remain low. We assume that these low results are due to the low-fidelity level of the prototypes. In response to open-ended questions, some participants praise the readability of BambHISTO, despite a lower success rate for it, and aesthetic qualities of PlantHISTO.

Table 1. Success rates for BambHISTO (BH) and PlantHISTO (PH), n = 25.

	T recharge1	T recharge2	T discharge1	T recharge3	Overall
BH	92% [77%, 98%]	92% [77%, 98%]	76% [57%, 89%]	88% [71%, 96%]	87% [79%, 92%]
PH	100% [90%, 100%]	100% [90%, 100%]	88% [90%, 100%]	84% [66%, 94%]	93% [87%, 97%]

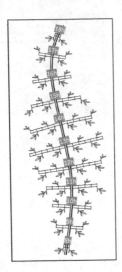

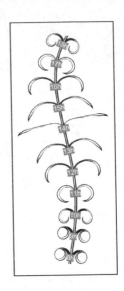

Fig. 5. BambHISTO eco-forecast histogram.

Fig. 6. PlantHISTO eco-forecast histogram.

5   Conclusion

This work is still in progress. Efforts must be made to improve identification of battery discharge times. However, good success rates of this study in identifying battery recharging times are encouraging for a field study of this new practice based on energy shifting with laptop battery and supported by PlantHISTO interface. Finally, if this online study, which was not expensive to develop, allowed us to quickly orient our design process, user studies in a controlled environment are still to be conducted in order to deepen our results with higher fidelity prototypes. Also, realisation of the new practice will be subject to the dynamics, pressures and routines of the user groups in the workplace. These points will be the subject of a future longitudinal study. With the same objective, the presented method and process can be enhanced by conducting co-design or participatory design activities in order to involve bodily performance and better cope with practice complexity.

In this work-in-progress paper, we propose to make use of task modelling and analysis in practice design process to make a step towards new methods and techniques to design and analyse environmental practices for future usage context. This method enables to keep track of the incremental change of practice highlighting already performed task, future task, and tasks of the *in-between* practices under design. Making possible to designers to reason about the gap to fill between current and future desirable practice by identifying layer (current, future, *in-between*) of each task.

References

1. Bouzekri, E., Rivière, G.: Validation des choix de conception pour un histogramme bio-inspiré destiné à accompagner une pratique partagée de propreté énergétique sur le lieu de travail [Validating design choices of a bio-inspired histogram to support a shared practice of clean energy at the workplace]. In: Proceedings of the 34th Conference on l'Interaction Humain-Machine, IHM 2023, ACM, New York, NY, USA (2023). https://doi.org/10.1145/3583961.3583965
2. Bremer, C., Knowles, B., Friday, A.: Have we taken on too much?: A critical review of the Sustainable HCI landscape. In: Proceedings of the 2022 CHI Conference on Human Factors in Computing Systems, CHI 2022, pp. 1–11. ACM, New York, NY, USA, April 2022. https://doi.org/10.1145/3491102.3517609
3. Brewer, R.S., e al.: Challenge: getting residential users to shift their electricity usage patterns. In: Proceedings of the 2015 ACM Sixth International Conference on Future Energy Systems, e-Energy 2015, pp. 83–88. ACM, New York, NY, USA, July 2015. https://doi.org/10.1145/2768510.2770934
4. Clear, A., Comber, R.: Towards a social practice theory perspective on Sustainable HCI research and design. In: Digital Technology and Sustainability, chap. 2, pp. 31–43. Routledge, 1 edn., November 2017. https://doi.org/10.9774/gleaf.9781315465975_6
5. Daniel, M., Rivière, G.: Exploring axisymmetric shape-change's purposes and allure for ambient display: 16 potential use cases and a two-month preliminary study on daily notifications. In: Proceedings of the Fifteenth International Conference on Tangible, Embedded, and Embodied Interaction, TEI 2021, ACM, New York, NY, USA (2021). https://doi.org/10.1145/3430524.3442452
6. Elbanhawy, E.Y., Smith, A.F.G., Moore, J.: Towards an ambient awareness interface for home battery storage system. In: Proceedings of the 2016 ACM International Joint Conference on Pervasive and Ubiquitous Computing: Adjunct, Ubi-Comp 2016, pp. 1608–1613. ACM, New York, NY, USA, September 2016. https://doi.org/10.1145/2968219.2968557
7. Entwistle, J.M., Rasmussen, M.K., Verdezoto, N., Brewer, R.S., Andersen, M.S.: Beyond the individual: The contextual wheel of practice as a research framework for Sustainable HCI. In: Proceedings of the 2015 CHI Conference on Human Factors in Computing Systems, CHI 2015, pp. 1125–1134. ACM, New York, NY, USA, April 2015. https://doi.org/10.1145/2702123.2702232
8. Froehlich, J., Findlater, L., Landay, J.: The design of eco-feedback technology. In: Proceedings of the 2010 CHI Conference on Human Factors in Computing Systems, CHI 2010, pp. 1999–2008. ACM, New York, NY, USA (2010). https://doi.org/10.1145/1753326.1753629
9. Förster, A., Block, J.: User adoption of smart home systems. In: Proceedings of the 2022 ACM Conference on Information Technology for Social Good, GoodIT 2022, pp. 360–365. ACM, New York, NY, USA, September 2022. https://doi.org/10.1145/3524458.3547118
10. Katzeff, C., Broms, L., Jönsson, L., Westholm, U., Räsänen, M.: Exploring sustainable practices in workplace settings through visualizing electricity consumption. ACM Trans. Comput.-Hum. Interact. **20**(5), 31:1–31:22 (2013). https://doi.org/10.1145/2501526
11. Kjeldskov, J., Skov, M.B., Paay, J., Lund, D., Madsen, T., Nielsen, M.: Eco-forecasting for domestic electricity use. In: Proceedings of the 2015 CHI Conference on Human Factors in Computing Systems, CHI 2015, pp. 1985–1988. ACM, New York, NY, USA (2015). https://doi.org/10.1145/2702123.2702318

12. Kuhlman, T., Farrington, J.: What is sustainability? Sustainability **2**(11), 3436–3448 (2010). https://doi.org/10.3390/su2113436
13. Kuijer, L., Jong, A.D., Eijk, D.V.: Practices as a unit of design: an exploration of theoretical guidelines in a study on bathing. ACM Trans. Comput.-Hum. Interact. **20**(4), 21:1–21:22 (2013). https://doi.org/10.1145/2493382
14. Lindley, J., Coulton, P.: Modelling design fiction: what's the story? In: StoryStorm Workshop at ACM DIS 2014 Conference, Vancouver, BC, Canada, 4 p. (2014)
15. Mankoff, J.C., et al.: Environmental sustainability and interaction. In: Proceedings of the 2007 CHI Conference on Human Factors in Computing Systems, CHI EA 2007, pp. 2121–2124. ACM, New York, NY, USA (2007). https://doi.org/10.1145/1240866.1240963
16. Martinie, C., Palanque, P., Winckler, M.: Structuring and composition mechanisms to address scalability issues in task models. In: Campos, P., Graham, N., Jorge, J., Nunes, N., Palanque, P., Winckler, M. (eds.) Human-Computer Interaction - INTERACT 2011, INTERACT 2011, LNCS, vol. 6948, pp. 589–609. Springer, Berlin (2011). https://doi.org/10.1007/978-3-642-23765-2_40
17. Quintal, F., Jorge, C., Nisi, V., Nunes, N.: Watt-I-see: a tangible visualization of energy. In: Proceedings of the International Working Conference on Advanced Visual Interfaces, AVI 2016, pp. 120–127. ACM, New York, NY, USA, June 2016. https://doi.org/10.1145/2909132.2909270
18. Schrepp, M., Hinderks, A., Thomaschewski, J.: Design and evaluation of a short version of the user experience questionnaire (UEQ-S) (2017). https://doi.org/10.9781/ijimai.2017.09.001
19. Simm, W., et al.: Tiree energy pulse: exploring renewable energy forecasts on the edge of the grid. In: Proceedings of the 2015 CHI Conference on Human Factors in Computing Systems, CHI 2015, pp. 1965–1974. ACM, New York, NY, USA, April 2015. https://doi.org/10.1145/2702123.2702285
20. Soden, R., Pathak, P., Doggett, O.: What we speculate about when we speculate about sustainable HCI. In: Proceedings of the 4th ACM SIGCAS Conference on Computing and Sustainable Societies, COMPASS 2021, pp. 188–198. ACM, New York, NY, USA, September 2021. https://doi.org/10.1145/3460112.3471956
21. Wakkary, R., Desjardins, A., Hauser, S., Maestri, L.: A sustainable design fiction: Green practices. ACM Trans. Comput.-Hum. Interact. **20**(4), 23:1–23:34 (2013). https://doi.org/10.1145/2494265
22. Warneryd, M., Håkansson, M., Karltorp, K.: Unpacking the complexity of community microgrids: a review of institutions' roles for development of microgrids. Renew. Sustain. Energy Rev. **121**, 109690 (2020). https://doi.org/10.1016/j.rser.2019.109690

Job Crafting to Improve Low-Usability Automation: Sustainability Through Human Work Interaction Designs

Torkil Clemmensen[1]([✉]) [iD], Morten Hertzum[2] [iD], and Jacob Nørbjerg[1] [iD]

[1] Copenhagen Business School, Frederiksberg, Denmark
tc.digi@cbs.dk
[2] Roskilde University, Roskilde, Denmark

Abstract. In industry 4.0 manufacturing, workers experience a variety of old and new automation and adopt and adapt to this automation to the best of their ability. This paper contributes a design case in which we aimed to support workers' job crafting with a four-week, peer-tutoring training program to create sustainable human work interaction designs. The peer-tutoring program facilitated job crafting by training the workers in identifying problems in their work and proposing solutions to these problems. We find that the peer-tutoring program enabled conversations among the workers about recurrent work problems and their solutions. This finding was achieved despite the low experienced usability of the automation in the case company. In terms of job crafting, the workers focused on their enjoyable tasks and invested in their relationships with their favorite colleagues but did not put a lot of effort into seeing their tasks as important and meaningful. We also encountered a tension between job crafting and management's view of the peer-tutoring program as a means of supporting standardization.

Keywords: Job crafting · Digital peer tutoring · Manufacturing · User experience

1 Introduction

A worker-centric approach to automation is important to the wellbeing of the workforce [1] and hence to socially, economically, and environmentally sustainable work practices [2]. Job crafting promises to deliver *sustainability through design*, that is, to influence workers' (users') decision-making and attitudes to work. Thereby, it will foster more sustainable work-lifestyles [3, 4] and create sustainable human work interaction designs. In the context of this paper, a human work interaction design is an automation situation in manufacturing with a human worker performing work processes using interactive systems. Job crafting supports workers in the bottom-up design of their own work to achieve work engagement [5, 6] and wellbeing [7–9]. By prototyping possible changes in work practices and worker-technology relations, job crafting can be a strategy for empowering the individual worker [10]. In contrast to top-down job design by management, job

A. Bramwell-Dicks et al. (Eds.): INTERACT 2023 Workshops, LNCS 14535, pp. 377–387, 2024.
https://doi.org/10.1007/978-3-031-61688-4_37

crafting is often union-supported [7]. It emphasizes workplace innovation over standardization [7] and has received increasing attention in small and medium-sized enterprises
(SMEs) challenged by robotics and automation [11]. Job crafting shares some resem-
blance with notions like job design, job enrichment, and work customization that all aim
to create wellbeing at work [7]. In this study, we report from a manufacturing company
with low-usability automation (legacy, non-interoperable stamping machines), in which
we aim to foster job crafting with a digital peer-tutoring training program [12]. The low-
usability automation, combined with a high demand for digitally skilled workers [13],
makes job crafting difficult in this situation. However, such a situation is not unusual
because many companies have not designed their automation as a resource that facilitates
job crafting [14]. Instead, many manufacturing SMEs use legacy and non-interoperable
automation in their factories [11]. The usability of these systems may be quite ordinary
[15, 16], though with variations depending on the task, the work shift, the people with
whom the task is done, and other situational factors [15]. We ask the research question:
Is job crafting possible in a situation with low-usability manufacturing automation?
Furthermore, we discuss whether the value produced by job crafting in a low-usability
manufacturing situation led to sustainability improvements such as a sustainable work
life, worker wellbeing, or job engagement.

2 Job Crafting

Job crafting can be about self-initiated changes in one's tasks (task crafting), social
relationships (relational crafting), perception of one's own job (cognitive crafting), and
the time and place of one's work (time-spatial crafting) [7, 8, 17, 18]. A longitudinal
meta-analysis of job crafting found that it is, in general, associated with an increase in
work engagement [19]. Another meta-analysis confirmed this finding and also found
that job crafting had a positive effect on wellbeing [5]. Furthermore, it appears that
job crafting is positively related to work performance [20]. The job-crafting literature
tends to agree that job crafting is, by definition, a bottom-up activity that happens on the
worker's initiative. Thus, job crafting can neither be driven by management, nor can it
be imposed as a job requirement [19]. However, job crafting can be encouraged, and it
can be facilitated with training.

A meta-analysis has shown that interventions are moderately effective at increasing
job crafting, work engagement, and task performance [21]. The interventions tend to
take the form of exercises that involve real-life examples, group discussion, and an
invitation for participants to formulate their own job-crafting plan [22]. As an example,
the Job Crafting Exercise challenges participants to take a step back and think creatively
about their jobs in a visual way supported by a booklet [23]. Relatedly, the Job Crafting
Intervention is a one-day training session followed by a four-week job-crafting period,
during which the job-crafting plans should be put into practice [24]. At the end of the
four-week period, the participants attend a reflection session to discuss the outcomes
and the implications for their work. The literature appears to suggest that job crafting is
related to the workers' personality so that it is mostly proactive workers who engage in
job crafting [19, 25]. This finding indicates that job-crafting interventions will benefit
proactive workers.

3 Case and Approach

This study was part of a regional development project, which aimed to improve the digital capabilities of SMEs in the Capital Region of Denmark through training activities in individual companies. The training activities were tailored to fit the needs and digital capabilities of the individual company and its employees. We were responsible for a digital peer-tutoring training program that aimed to encourage and train workers to share their job-crafting solutions with fellow workers by means of low-fidelity videos recorded with a smartphone or tablet [12]. The videos could describe solutions to operational or collaboration problems, such as how to adjust a collaborative robot, solve an operational problem with a machine, or resolve a coordination issue between two workstations. Digital peer tutoring was designed to support job crafting, but there has also been interest in applying the approach to other types of knowledge sharing, for example instructional videos [12]. The training program was supported by an iPad app with instruction videos, quizzes, and example solution videos. In addition, the iPad was used for recording the videos that were created by the workers during the training program. The training program took four weeks (see Table 1), during which workers studied the material in the app and produced short (1–3 min) videos documenting the identification of work problems and the sketching, prototyping, and evaluation of solutions to the problems. Two project assistants facilitated the workers' discussions and video production.

Table 1. Overview of the digital peer-tutoring training program.

Week	Theme	Topics	Worker-created, how-to videos
1	The problem	Personas Interaction Collaboration with tech	1. A persona 2. An interaction problem 3. A collaboration problem
2	Solution sketch	How to sketch a solution Interaction Collaboration	Three design ideas for 4. Interaction 5. Collaboration
3	Design of prototype	Interaction and collaboration prototypes	6. Elaboration of one design idea into a prototype
4	Evaluation of prototype	How to evaluate prototypes	7. Feedback on the prototype from a colleague

The case company was a Danish SME with around 50 employees. The company produced precision metal components on stamping machines in large series of up to millions of delivered items for a range of sectors, such as pharma, electronics, and automotive. The company's production and quality-assurance processes were ISO certified and, in some cases (pharma), subject to external regulatory requirements. The stamping machines used custom-made tools to cut the products from rolls of metal band that were fed into the machine. Each production worker was responsible for 2–3 machines, including set-up, quality control, and fault correction. The peer-tutoring program targeted the production workers on the day shift, and the tool smiths who built the cutting tools. We met with the company six times over a six-week period. In Week 0, we explained the digital peer-tutoring program and were introduced to the company, employees, and production facilities. Weeks 1–4 were the training program itself. In Week 5, the program was evaluated. Two researchers, a consultant, and two project assistants participated during Weeks 0 and 5, together with management and workers from the company. The project assistants facilitated the training sessions for the workers during Weeks 1–4.

4 Results

There were 16 participants in the peer-tutoring training program. They had completed 3–4 years' education and training (e.g., as automation technicians, production workers, and tool makers) on top of 9 years of basic education. The participants had worked for an average of 12.8 years (range: 0.3–34) in the case company and had an average of 13.5 years (range: 1.9–30) of experience with the stamping machines.

4.1 Job Crafting Data

The participants were asked to fill out a job-crafting scale at the end of the peer-tutoring program (in Week 5). We used the scale proposed by Wrzesniewski and Dutton [17] and further developed and validated by Niessen, Weseler, and Kostova [8] as our job-crafting scale. It measured self-initiated changes in one's tasks (task crafting), social relationships (relational crafting), and job perception (cognitive crafting). We added three new items (questions) about time-place crafting [7, 18]. The items were translated into Danish and subsequently back-translated to validate the Danish wording of the items. All items were preceded with "So that the job I do suits me…" and rated on a five-point rating scale from 1 (not at all) to 5 (absolutely). We named the enhanced scale the self-oriented job-crafting scale (SO-JCS).

From the theory we would expect a four-factor structure in the data corresponding to the four types of crafting (see Table 2). Indeed, an eigen value of 1 in the Scree plot suggested a four-factor structure that explained 79% of the variance in the data. However, the 12 items did not consistently load on the four factors, possibly due to the few data points. Therefore, we proceed by only discussing those items that loaded highly on the factor that they were expected to load on.

First, for task crafting, Item 3 – the time and effort that a worker put into a task – loaded highly on the factor (.928). The ratings on Item 3 indicated that the workers focused on enjoyable tasks (mean 3.85, SD 0.69). Second, for relational crafting all three items loaded positively on the factor. Item 5 with the highest loading (.955) indicated that the workers invested in relationships with their favorite colleagues to a high degree (mean 3.92, SD 0.76). Third, for cognitive crafting, Item 7 that measured the workers' perceptions of their tasks as important loaded highly (.898) on the factor, but the ratings on Item 7 (mean 3.38, SD 0.65) indicated that the workers did not put much effort into seeing their tasks as important and meaningful. Finally, for time-spatial crafting, all three items (10, 11, 12) loaded highly on the factor (.865, .809, and .668). These high loadings were somewhat surprising since this factor was home-made. The ratings indicated however only mediocre efforts from workers to design their work so that they worked at their favorite machine (mean 3.00, SD 0.58) and in their favorite room (mean 2.92, SD 0.64); they did more to choose the hours that they worked (mean 3.68, SD 0.63). Overall, the participants tended to do job crafting (mean 3.53, SD 0.68).

Table 2. Job crafting factor structure and wording of items.

Items	Mean	SD	SO-JCS factor loadings			
			Task	Relational	Cognitive	Temporal-spatial
1. I concentrate on specific tasks	4.08	0.64		.375		.527
2. I undertake or seek for additional tasks	3.69	0.63			.838	
3. I work more intensively on tasks I enjoy	3.85	0.69	.928			
4. I usually limit the amount of time I spend with people I do not get along well with, and only contact them for things that are absolutely necessary	3.00	0.71		.470	-.806	
5. I invest in relationships with people whom I get along with the best	3.92	0.76		.955		
6. I look for opportunities to work together with people whom I get along well with at work	3.85	0.56		.686	.431	

(continued)

Table 2. (*continued*)

Items	Mean	SD	SO-JCS factor loadings			
			Task	Relational	Cognitive	Temporal-spatial
7. I try to look upon the tasks and responsibilities I have at work as having a deeper meaning than is readily apparent	3.38	0.65			.898	
8. I find personal meaning in my tasks and responsibilities at work	3.54	0.88	-.681	.485	.359	
9. I view my tasks and responsibilities as being more than just part of my job	3.46	0.78		.532		-.711
10. I try to be as much as possible at my favorite workplace (machine, workstation)	3.00	0.58				.865
11. I try to be as much as possible at my favorite work location (room, building)	2.92	0.64				.809
12. I actively choose my working hours	3.69	0.63				.668

Note: $N = 13$ participants. The rotated component matrix was constructed to determine what the components represented. The rotation was done with the principal component analysis extraction method, and the rotation method was varimax with Kaiser normalization. The rotation converged in five iterations. The table shows loadings $> .3$

4.2 SUS Scores

To investigate the participants' experience of the stamping machine, we asked them to rate it at the first and last workshop. Among the instruments for measuring how systems are experienced, we chose the System Usability Scale (SUS) because it is widely used and easy to administer [26]. SUS consists of ten items, which are aggregated into a single score. The SUS items were translated into Danish and back-translated to validate the Danish wording. We also wanted to investigate the participants' experience of the peer-tutoring app. For this purpose, we asked them to give their SUS ratings of the app at every workshop.

With mean SUS scores of 63 (Week 1) and 60 (Week 4), there was no significant change in the participants' experience of the stamping machine, $t(11) = 0.03, p = .97$, during the training program. Scores of 60 and 63 are in the lowest quartile of the corpus of SUS scores reported by Bangor et al. [27]. Thus, the participants experienced the stamping machine as a low-usability system. The peer-tutoring app received SUS scores of 59 (Week 1) and 55 (Week 2). SUS scores of this magnitude correspond to a system that is marginally acceptable [27]. In line with this assessment, during the two remaining workshops, the iPad was only used for creating videos; the peer-tutoring concept was instead communicated orally.

4.3 Qualitative Data

We documented all empirical sessions in written notes. This involved the start-up and wrap-up meetings with the participants and management (Weeks 0 and 5) as well as the four peer-tutoring workshops with the participants (Weeks 1 to 4). An additional source of qualitative data was the 76 peer-tutoring videos produced by the participants during Weeks 1 to 4. The qualitative data provided further insights into the effects of the peer-tutoring training program on different aspects of job crafting.

With respect to need identification (Week 1), the participants identified needs specific to concrete persons in other departments as well as needs with more general audiences, such as newcomers to the company. Several of the identified needs involved transferring knowledge from the day shift to the night shift. Currently, some of the machines operated at reduced capacity during night shifts. The CEO learned that the participants had constructive ideas about how to solve many of the identified needs.

With respect to sketching solutions, designing prototypes, and evaluating prototypes (Weeks 2–4), the participants for example sketched how QR codes could solve a production problem by providing ready access to needed information, how 3D images could visualize and simplify a control problem, and how an event-triggered text message from a machine could prevent that it was standing still without anyone noticing. At the same time, the peer-tutoring program made the participants realize how they were important, what special knowledge they held, and how to help each other get their daily work done.

In the wrap-up meeting (Week 5), the workers assessed their production of instructional videos and refresher videos as valuable. The CEO emphasized that the video format helped disseminate knowledge in an approachable and unintimidating manner that reduced the distance among the workers: "*You dethrone them [i.e., the expert workers] when you video their knowledge.*" He particularly appreciated knowledge sharing between day shift workers and the less experienced workers at the night shift. The CEO also expressed interest in using videos instead of written Standard Operating Procedures (SOPs), which were required by certification but difficult to write and read for workers.

According to a development manager, several participants wanted to continue making peer-tutoring videos, but others were not accustomed to making videos and found it awkward to disseminate their knowledge in this medium.

5 Discussion

Our data support that job crafting can be achieved in a manufacturing SME with low-usability automation. With a mean overall job-crafting score of 3.53, the workers in our study were job crafting at about the same level as participants in other studies. For example, Niessen et al. [8] found a mean score of 3.28 in a 466-participant study that did not include time-spatial job crafting and Lazauskaite-Zabielske et al. [28] found a mean time-spatial job-crafting score of 3.4 in a sample of 176 employees in an IT company. Contrary to Niessen et al. [8], the workers in our study did not put a lot of effort into seeing their tasks as important and meaningful. Instead, they focused on their enjoyable tasks and invested in their relationships with their favorite colleagues. Our qualitative data showed that the workers identified needs specific to concrete persons and had constructive ideas about how to solve many of the identified needs. Furthermore, the peer-tutoring program enabled conversations among the workers about the problems and their solutions. In this way, the peer-tutoring program was more like a co-design activity [29] than the training activities provided to support job crafting in other studies [19]. In addition to facilitating the workers' individual job crafting, the peer tutoring also shaped it by encouraging information sharing, such as in the instructional and refresher videos. We contend that the format of the peer-tutoring program helped the workers appreciate that they were producing something of value to themselves, their peers, and the company. These are important elements in achieving sustainability through design [3].

Sustainability through design can be studied at individual, group, and societal levels [3]. A major aim with this study was to evaluate whether the value produced by job crafting in a low-usability manufacturing situation included sustainability improvements such as a more sustainable work life, worker wellbeing, or job engagement. The study outcomes can be interpreted as the result of sustainability through design at the level of the individual worker and at the level of the peer group. First, individual workers co-designed more sustainable ways of working. In addition, the finding that the digital peer-tutoring tool made the workers appreciate that they created something of value could be interpreted as increased job engagement [19]. However, designing a more usable app will be key to the possibilities for easily transferring the peer-tutoring program to other companies. Furthermore, the relation between job crafting and the usability of the automation in the companies is currently not clear. Low-usability automation may increase the need for job crafting, reduce the possibilities for it, or both. Second, at the group/organization level, our findings indicate that manufacturing companies can be supported in further developing sustainable ways of production. There is, however, a caveat to this positive result. While the digital peer-tutoring training program aimed to support shopfloor workers' bottom-up job crafting, it was the CEO's expressed wish to strengthen standardization – including standardization across shifts – by replacing written SOPs with worker-created videos. These opposing aims united to push the outcome of the peer-tutoring training program from sharing creative ideas about changes or improvements toward knowledge sharing about existing jobs, and from worker initiatives toward management plans and strategies. The resulting tension raises questions about how the organizational context influences job crafting interventions such as the digital peer-tutoring program. If job crafting interventions are interpreted by management as their initiative or as a standardization activity, then the defining feature of job crafting as self-initiated and the related benefits in the form of long-term improvements in worker engagement and well-being [22] may fail to materialize. Designing a digital tool for job crafting interventions should therefore be considered a sociotechnical HCI design that mediates *sustainability through design* by balancing the interests of workers and managers.

6 Conclusion

Overall, this study finds that job crafting is possible in a situation with low-usability manufacturing automation, as evidenced by our quantitative and qualitative data. We contend that the value produced by the job crafting exemplifies how sustainability improvements can be achieved through human work interaction design. The improvements have conceptual, practical, and methodical implications.

Conceptually, the participants' job crafting in the peer-tutoring program focused on improved information sharing and other ways of making work more efficient. This focus aligned well with management interests but also begs the question of how increased efficiency relates to work engagement and wellbeing. Initiatives such as the digital peer-tutoring program may need to address this relation more explicitly to maintain a focus on job crafting. It is for future work to resolve this issue.

Practically, the peer-tutoring program enabled conversations among the staff in the case company about identifying and solving recurrent problems in their work. Other companies may apply the program, provided that the supporting iPad app is revised. Future work should investigate the long-term impact of the program and its integration into organizational processes: Are the prototypes turned into changes in work practices? Does the creation of videos continue? Do the videos engender collaborative discussion among staff? How is a focus on work engagement and wellbeing maintained?

Methodologically, we find that time-spatial crafting is an additional dimension of job crafting, as suggested by [18]. Our three items for gauging time-spatial crafting were well intercorrelated and did not cross-load on the other factors. We consider time-spatial crafting important in manufacturing, where time and place are often to a large extent dictated by machinery, as well as in digital workplaces, where time and place are often more flexible because the work can be distributed and remote.

Acknowledgments. This study was conducted in the context of the regional development project KomDigital, which facilitated the contact to the case company. Special thanks are due to the management and employees of the case company. The four-week, peer-tutoring training program was run by project assistants Latife Jawhar and Magnus Stidsholt Buus.

References

1. Kaasinen, E., et al.: Empowering and engaging industrial workers with operator 4.0 solutions. Comput. Ind. Eng. **139**, 105678 (2020). https://doi.org/10.1016/j.cie.2019.01.052
2. Giovannoni, E., Fabietti, G.: What is sustainability? A review of the concept and its applications. In: Busco, C., Frigo, M.L., Riccaboni, A., Quattrone, P. (eds.) Integrated Reporting, pp. 21–40. Springer, Cham (2013). https://doi.org/10.1007/978-3-319-02168-3_2
3. Mankoff, J.C., et al.: Environmental sustainability and interaction. In: Proceedings of the CHI2007 Conference on Human Factors in Computing Systems, pp. 2121–2124. ACM (2007). https://doi.org/10.1145/1240866.1240963
4. Zhan, X., Walker, S.: Craft as leverage for sustainable design transformation: a theoretical foundation. Des. J. **22**, 483–503 (2019). https://doi.org/10.1080/14606925.2019.1613040
5. Lichtenthaler, P.W., Fischbach, A.: A meta-analysis on promotion-and prevention-focused job crafting. Eur. J. Work Organ. Psy. **28**, 30–50 (2019). https://doi.org/10.1080/1359432X.2018.1527767
6. Roto, V., Clemmensen, T., Häätäjä, H., Law, E.L.-C.: Guest editors' introduction: designing interactive systems for work engagement. Hum. Technol. **14**, 135–139 (2018). https://doi.org/10.17011/ht/urn.201808103814
7. Scoppetta, A., Davern, E., Geyer, L.: Job carving and job crafting - a review of practices (EU report). European Commission (2019). KE-01-19-557-EN-N
8. Niessen, C., Weseler, D., Kostova, P.: When and why do individuals craft their jobs? The role of individual motivation and work characteristics for job crafting. Hum. Relat. **69**, 1287–1313 (2016). https://doi.org/10.1177/0018726715610642
9. Geldenhuys, M., Bakker, A.B., Demerouti, E.: How task, relational and cognitive crafting relate to job performance: a weekly diary study on the role of meaningfulness. Eur. J. Work Organ. Psy. **30**, 83–94 (2021). https://doi.org/10.1080/1359432X.2020.1825378
10. Woods, D.D.: Commentary designs are hypotheses about how artifacts shape cognition and collaboration. Ergonomics **41**, 168–173 (1998). https://doi.org/10.1080/001401398187215
11. Ludwig, T., Kotthaus, C., Stein, M., Pipek, V., Wulf, V.: Revive old discussions! socio-technical challenges for small and medium enterprises within industry 4.0. In: Proceedings of 16th European Conference on Computer-Supported Cooperative Work (2018). https://doi.org/10.18420/ecscw2018_15
12. Clemmensen, T., Nørbjerg, J.: Digital peer-tutoring: early results from a field evaluation of a UX at work learning format in SMEs. In: Abdelnour Nocera, J., et al. (eds.) INTERACT 2019. LNCS, vol. 11930, pp. 52–58. Springer, Cham (2020). https://doi.org/10.1007/978-3-030-46540-7_6
13. Buonocore, F., Agrifoglio, R., de Gennaro, D.: The role of digital competencies and creativity for job crafting in public administration. In: Metallo, C., Ferrara, M., Lazazzara, A., Za, S. (eds.) Digital Transformation and Human Behavior. LNISO, vol. 37, pp. 87–97. Springer, Cham (2021). https://doi.org/10.1007/978-3-030-47539-0_7
14. Demerouti, E.: Turn digitalization and automation to a job resource. Appl. Psychol. **71**, 1205–1209 (2022). https://doi.org/10.1111/apps.12270
15. Clemmensen, T., Hertzum, M., Abdelnour-Nocera, J.: Ordinary user experiences at work: a study of greenhouse growers. ACM Trans. Comput. Hum. Interact. **27**, 1–31 (2020). https://doi.org/10.1145/3386089
16. Meneweger, T., Wurhofer, D., Fuchsberger, V., Tscheligi, M.: Factory workers' ordinary user experiences: an overlooked perspective. Hum. Technol. **14**, 209–232 (2018). https://doi.org/10.17011/ht/urn.201808103817
17. Wrzesniewski, A., Dutton, J.E.: Crafting a job: Revisioning employees as active crafters of their work. Acad. Manag. Rev. **26**, 179–201 (2001). https://doi.org/10.5465/AMR.2001.4378011

18. Wessels, C., Schippers, M.C., Stegmann, S., Bakker, A.B., van Baalen, P.J., Proper, K.I.: Fostering flexibility in the new world of work: a model of time-spatial job crafting. Front Psychol. **10**, 505 (2019). https://doi.org/10.3389/fpsyg.2019.00505
19. Frederick, D.E., VanderWeele, T.J.: Longitudinal meta-analysis of job crafting shows positive association with work engagement. In: Cogent Psychology. p. Article 1746733. Cogent OA (2020). https://doi.org/10.1080/23311908.2020.1746733
20. Rofcanin, Y., Bakker, A.B., Berber, A., Gölgeci, I., Las Heras, M.: Relational job crafting: exploring the role of employee motives with a weekly diary study. Hum. Relat. **72**, 859–886 (2019). https://doi.org/10.1177/0018726718779121
21. Oprea, B.T., Barzin, L., Vîrgă, D., Iliescu, D., Rusu, A.: Effectiveness of job crafting interventions: a meta-analysis and utility analysis. Eur. J. Work Organ. Psy. **28**, 723–741 (2019). https://doi.org/10.1080/1359432X.2019.1646728
22. Laenen, J.J.: Continuous and autonomous Job Crafting support in the home-work environment. Unpublished working paper (2020)
23. Berg, J.M., Dutton, J.E., Wrzesniewski, A., Baker, W.E.: Job Crafting Exercise. University of Michigan (2013). https://positiveorgs.bus.umich.edu/wp-content/uploads/Job-Crafting-Exercise-Teaching-Note-Aug-101.pdf
24. Van den Heuvel, M., Demerouti, E., Peeters, M.C.W.: The job crafting intervention: effects on job resources, self-efficacy, and affective well-being. J. Occup. Organ. Psychol. **88**, 511–532 (2015). https://doi.org/10.1111/joop.12128
25. Bakker, A.B., Tims, M., Derks, D.: Proactive personality and job performance: the role of job crafting and work engagement. Hum. Relat. **65**, 1359–1378 (2012). https://doi.org/10.1177/0018726712453471
26. Brooke, J.: SUS: A "quick and dirty" usability scale. In: Jordan, P.W., Thomas, B., Weerdmeester, B.A., and McClelland, A.L. (eds.) Usability Evaluation in Industry, pp. 189–194. Taylor & Francis (1996). https://doi.org/10.1201/9781498710411
27. Bangor, A., Kortum, P.T., Miller, J.T.: An empirical evaluation of the system usability scale. Int. J. Hum. Comput. Interact. **24**, 574–594 (2008). https://doi.org/10.1080/10447310802205776
28. Lazauskaite-Zabielske, J., Ziedelis, A., Urbanaviciute, I.: Who benefits from time-spatial job crafting? The role of boundary characteristics in the relationship between time-spatial job crafting, engagement and performance. Balt. J. Manag. **16**, 1–19 (2020). https://doi.org/10.1108/BJM-07-2020-0236
29. Sanders, E.B.-N., Stappers, P.J.: Co-creation and the new landscapes of design. CoDesign **4**, 5–18 (2008). https://doi.org/10.1080/15710880701875068

Participatory Design Approach to Sustainable Voyage Planning – Case Maritime Autonomous Surface Ships

Antony William Joseph[✉] ⓘ, Vivian Stolt, and Virpi Roto ⓘ

Department of Design, Aalto University, Helsinki, Finland
antony.joseph@aalto.fi

Abstract. Research in the design and development of sustainable operations in the maritime industry has received a great deal of attention in the recent past. Increased demand of sustainability, growth, skilled workforce, and competitiveness of maritime industry paved the way for unmanned vessels. This paper reports a participatory design process on sustainable voyage planning for maritime autonomous surface ships. The participatory approach in this study included a Futures Wheel workshop, semi-structured interviews, scenario design, and a scenario workshop. These helped us to identify opportunities to improve voyage sustainability by optimizing the vessel size and efficient scheduling, and to include them in the use scenarios that guide the next steps of the solution design.

Keywords: Sustainability · Participatory Design · Unmanned Vessels · Voyage Planning · Futures Workshop · Scenarios

1 Introduction

The maritime industry has recently paid a great deal of attention to the factors that enable the sustainable remote and autonomous shipping operations. The Maritime Autonomous Surface Ship (MASS) is currently focusing on vessels that utilize automated control system with advanced sensor technology to improve safety, increase efficiency and reduce fuel usage [1]. Rolls Royce [11] predicted that MASS or fully autonomous marine fleets are expected to increase in 10 or 15 years time. Advancement in the port infrastructure, logistics, and energy-efficient vessels will increase the demand for marine trading [6]. At the same time, the industry is progressively moving towards digitalization to find solution to modern challenges [12].

The global marine trading is very essential part of the global logistical chain and is crucial to world economy [4]. Ships carry more than 90% of the world's cargo transports because of its cost-effectiveness. Shipping produces 2.2% of the world's total greenhouse gas emissions and it has a much lower carbon footprint per ton-mile than trucks and airplanes. Still, there is a need for a drastic reduction of the carbon footprint of shipping, and it is seen this can be achieved, e.g., by reducing the speed of ships to just about 10

A. Bramwell-Dicks et al. (Eds.): INTERACT 2023 Workshops, LNCS 14535, pp. 388–393, 2024.
https://doi.org/10.1007/978-3-031-61688-4_38

knots. This would mean drastically slower transport times and would require many more and bigger ships with more personnel. At the same time, marine industry suffers from shortage of employees. Porathe [9] estimates that unmanned ships will be necessary to reach the sustainability goals. Clean fuels in marine transport is estimated to bring remarkable changes in the maritime policy, focusing on reducing carbon emissions [12].

Vessel electrification is also an important development towards more sustainable marine operations. In recent times, a good number of efforts being put into electrification as a key factor for sustainable and environmentally friendly marine operations [8]. The fast growing marine electric technologies established a strong base for adapting new ships buildings to either hybrid or full electric propulsion [3]. A recent research study shows that nearly two-thirds of the electrified marine vessels function in hybrid mode and the rest are pure electric [2]. Additionally, the study indicates that Norway, Denmark and Scotland are the dominant countries that advocate green energy and design minimum one ferry per year in the last five years. The author Koumentakos [7] in his study observed that variation in electric vessel sizes with different capabilities and needs may bring down emissions significantly and reduced the environmental impact on the maritime sector. Currently, electrification is considered as the most favorable environmentally friendly energy resource for the maritime sector [10].

This paper reports a participatory design study of how a pre-voyage mission planning can influence sustainable operation of Maritime Autonomous Surface Ships. Mission planning is a process that begins months before the actual voyage, and it includes a variety of activities. This paper focuses on those activities that have the biggest impact on sustainability, which turned out to be part of the voyage planning. The participatory design included a Futures Wheel workshop, semi-structured interviews, designing scenarios with rough user interface ideas, and evaluation of those scenarios.

2 Case Study: Voyage Planning of Autonomous Ships

The authors of this paper study remote operation of unmanned ships that deliver goods to Norwegian food markets over a fjord. In this case, shipping the goods over the fjord is more sustainable than transporting them by trucks via the roads along the fjord. The main research goal is to design human-centred remote operation, since sustainability issues are important to the client companies and they come up in our studies.

Our research proceeded through participatory design studies (Fig. 1). The first study, a workshop utilizing a Futures Wheel [5], was conducted to establish foundational understanding of sustainable future mission planning. The workshop was conducted remotely with participants communicating and collaborating via Microsoft Teams, and the workshop materials were shared and collaboratively edited in Miro, an online collaborative whiteboard. As the key material, the authors of this paper prepared the core for a Futures Wheel that guided the discussion in the workshop (Fig. 2). Sustainability was one of the six themes, each of which was planned to gain the same amount of time and attention in the discussions. In addition to the two first authors, 10 experts from two organizations took part in the workshop. The workshop lasted for 2,5 h, and included introduction, two rounds of small group discussion on all six Futures Wheel themes, and conclusions. The participants worked in three teams of 3–4 individuals, themes, and conclusions. The participants worked in three teams of 3–4 individuals, expanding the Futures Wheel by notes from their discussions.

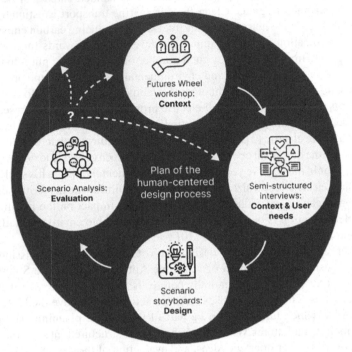

Fig. 1. Participatory design process in this project.

The workshop with the Futures Wheel helped us to understand the different aspects influencing the future of remote operation of the vessels. In the workshop, the company participants raised the need for sustainable operations through two ways to reduce emissions in the voyage planning phase, which was the focus of this project. First, it is important to optimize the vessel size to match the amount of cargo to reduce emissions of the voyage. In an early phase of voyage planning, the system can help the mission planner to book both a ship of an optimal size for the estimated cargo and a crew capable of operating that ship model at a given time. Second, the system can help the voyage planner to optimize the use of energy by scheduling the voyage to a time when the wind and waves are favorable, and the other traffic allows the vessel to forward in a steady speed and directly to the destination. These decisions need to be made much later than the vessel and crew booking, since the weather and traffic cannot be accurately estimated weeks before.

The Futures Wheel workshop offered a framework for the second phase, the goal of which was to gather feedback from employees who operate in a non-fully automated workplace but are aware of the development of automated operations. Six in-person semi-structured interviews were conducted with a Ship Operator's employees to investigate deeper levels of information collected from the Futures Wheel workshop. In this study,

Fig. 2. Futures Wheel used in the workshop to guide discussions.

it was harder to collect information on the sustainability aspects, but participants did raise the need for frequent route calculations when new information about the weather and traffic conditions is available.

The Design phase of the process built on the data collected from the Futures Wheel workshop and semi-structured interviews. The data on the essential aspects, not only sustainability, was used to build storyboards addressing the key tasks of a mission planner. The rough user interfaces addressing sustainability were integrated in storyboards as parts of the mission planning processes (Fig. 3).

The fourth phase of the participatory design process was a scenario analysis workshop, which was conducted with 6 professionals from two client companies to collect feedback on the scenarios. The scenarios were analyzed in three phases: 1) Starting a mission plan, 2) Assigning captains, and 3) Voyage plan. Each phase was presented to the participants with storyboards. The workshop focused on navigation, waypoints, ship capabilities, external factors, anticipated contingencies, and advanced technologies. Each participant was instructed to go through each scenario and discuss with other participants in the workshop. The participants were asked to add notes about potential impacts, risks and opportunities, important plot points that align with their vision, likings, scenes from other fields and other ideas that emerges from the stories.

The participants pointed out that a more automated system could help the mission planner in choosing an optimized vessel size to reduce energy, emissions, as well as save the planner's time and resources. Automation would help scheduling the voyage

Fig. 3. Excepts of storyboard visualizations: weather and vessel size as sustainable considerations in voyage planning scenarios.

based on the weather and traffic. In relation to the vessel electrification consequences, there was discussion about vessel charging activities at the port and planning the time for charging the vessel batteries.

3   Conclusion

Research in the maritime industry is growing rapidly and unmanned vessels have the potential to reduce the environmental impact in the maritime sector. Researchers with the background in user experience design can contribute to the sustainability goals by gaining a holistic view of the factors influencing the carbon footprint and designing a user interface that help the operator to address those aspects. In the reported case, it was the vessel size and scheduling optimization that were found important in reducing energy, emissions, and resources of operators, so the user scenarios were designed to include these aspects.

Due to the complex and often unique combinations of parameters affecting sustainability (the amount of cargo, availability of vessels, trucks and trains and their crews, weather, and traffic) in the two activities, the mission planner and the intelligent system should work as a team. For example, when there is little room for delaying the voyage due to difficult weather or traffic conditions, the system should calculate and compare the greenhouse gas emissions between the vessel and other forms of transport (trucks or train) to help the mission planner schedule the delivery with least emissions.

Based on this case study, the Futures Wheel provided a balanced way to consider sustainability as one of the top-level considerations with a multi-disciplinary set of workshop participants. Such a set of participants might not have participated if the workshop would have concentrated on sustainability only. Throughout the described studies, sustainability considerations were an integrated part of the process. Since sustainability is an important part of developing the future of maritime operations, the participants even without dedicated expertise in sustainability knew the requirements and effective opportunities to reduce greenhouse gas emissions. We hope these considerations through participatory design will contribute to a more sustainable maritime transportation and inspire other user experience researchers to consider sustainability aspects in their participatory design projects.

References

1. Alsos, O.A., Hodne, P., Skåden, O.K., Porathe, T.: Maritime autonomous surface ships: automation transparency for nearby vessels. In: Journal of Physics on Conference Series, vol. 2311, no. 1, p. 012027. IOP Publishing (2022)
2. Anwar, S., Zia, M.Y.I., Rashid, M., Rubens, G.Z.D., Enevoldsen, P.: Towards ferry electrification in the maritime sector. Energies 13(24), 6506 (2020)
3. Bosich, D., et al.: Early-stage design of integrated power and energy systems for naval vessels electrification: advanced modeling using CSI. In: 2017 IEEE Transportation Electrification Conference and Expo, pp. 387–392. IEEE (2017)
4. Boviatsis, M., Vlachos, G.: Sustainable operation of unmanned ships under current international maritime law. Sustainability 14(12), 7369 (2022)
5. Glenn, J.C., Gordon, T.J.: Futures research methodology-version 3-0. Editorial desconocida (2009)
6. Hesse, M., McDonough, E.: 27. Ports, cities and the global maritime infrastructure. In: Handbook on the Geographies of Globalization, vol. 354 (2018)
7. Koumentakos, A.G.: Developments in electric and green marine ships. Appl. Syst. Innov. 2(4), 34 (2019)
8. Lind, M., et al.: The future of shipping: Collaboration through digital data sharing. In: Lind, M., Michaelides, M., Ward, R., Watson, R.T. (eds.) Maritime informatics. PI, pp. 137–149. Springer, Cham (2021). https://doi.org/10.1007/978-3-030-50892-0_9
9. Porathe, T.: A navigating navigator onboard or a monitoring operator ashore? Towards safe, effective, and sustainable maritime transportation: findings from five recent EU projects. Transp. Res. Procedia 14, 233–242 (2016)
10. Prousalidis, J., D'Agostino, F.: Looking toward the energy-sustainable smart port: a resilient energy hub in the electric grids. IEEE Electrification Mag. 11(1), 90–92 (2023)
11. Rolls Royce. Oceangoing fully autonomous ships in next 15 years. Market Business News (2017). https://marketbusinessnews.com/oceangoing-fully-autonomous-ships-next-15-years-says-rolls-royce/153587/
12. Zhou, Y., Soh, Y.S., Loh, H.S., Yuen, K.F.: The key challenges and critical success factors of blockchain implementation: policy implications for Singapore's maritime industry. Mar. Policy 122, 104265 (2020)

Author Index

Printed in the United States
by Baker & Taylor Publisher Services